OXFORD WORLD'S CLASSICS

SAYINGS OF THE BUDDHA

[illegible] HE SUTT[illegible]
Nikāyas [illegible]
from perhaps the fourth or third [illegible] BCE, they present the
teachings of the Buddha as remembered and passed down by the first generations of his disciples and in them we come as close to the words of the Buddha as we can get. Within the Nikāyas we find the Buddha addressing Buddhist monks and laity, kings, ordinary householders, members of different religious groups, and gods; we find the story of the Buddha's own quest for knowledge, advice on ethical conduct, philosophical discourse, instruction in meditation, tales of the distant past; we find short sayings as well as extended narratives. The selection of sayings of the Buddha contained in the present volume covers the full variety of texts found in the Nikāyas.

RUPERT GETHIN is Reader in Buddhist Studies at the University of Bristol, where he is also co-director of the Centre for Buddhist Studies. His publications include books and articles on the early theory of Buddhist meditation and on aspects of Buddhist systematic thought (*abhidhamma*), as well as an introductory textbook, *The Foundations of Buddhism* (Oxford, 1998). Since 2003 he has been President of the Pali Text Society.

OXFORD WORLD'S CLASSICS

For over 100 years Oxford World's Classics have brought readers closer to the world's great literature. Now with over 700 titles—from the 4,000-year-old myths of Mesopotamia to the twentieth century's greatest novels—the series makes available lesser-known as well as celebrated writing.

The pocket-sized hardbacks of the early years contained introductions by Virginia Woolf, T. S. Eliot, Graham Greene, and other literary figures which enriched the experience of reading. Today the series is recognized for its fine scholarship and reliability in texts that span world literature, drama and poetry, religion, philosophy, and politics. Each edition includes perceptive commentary and essential background information to meet the changing needs of readers.

OXFORD WORLD'S CLASSICS

Sayings of the Buddha

A selection of suttas from the Pali Nikāyas

Translated with an Introduction and Notes by
RUPERT GETHIN

OXFORD
UNIVERSITY PRESS

OXFORD
UNIVERSITY PRESS

Great Clarendon Street, Oxford OX2 6DP

Oxford University Press is a department of the University of Oxford.
It furthers the University's objective of excellence in research, scholarship,
and education by publishing worldwide in

Oxford New York

Auckland Cape Town Dar es Salaam Hong Kong Karachi
Kuala Lumpur Madrid Melbourne Mexico City Nairobi
New Delhi Shanghai Taipei Toronto

With offices in

Argentina Austria Brazil Chile Czech Republic France Greece
Guatemala Hungary Italy Japan Poland Portugal Singapore
South Korea Switzerland Thailand Turkey Ukraine Vietnam

Oxford is a registered trade mark of Oxford University Press
in the UK and in certain other countries

Published in the United States
by Oxford University Press Inc., New York

First published as an Oxford World's Classics paperback 2008

British Library Cataloguing in Publication Data
Data available

Library of Congress Cataloging-in-Publication Data
Data available

Typeset by Cepha Imaging Private Ltd., Bangalore, India
Printed in Great Britain
on acid-free paper by
Clays Ltd., St Ives plc

ISBN 978-0-19-283925-1

4

For Hugh Gethin

1918–1999

PREFACE

DESPITE their being some of the oldest and most important Buddhist literary works, the suttas of the Pali Nikāyas are not widely known nor generally read (either in translation or the original) beyond Buddhist circles, except perhaps in the context of university courses in Indian or religious studies. I hope that the present volume might go some way to making these striking texts more accessible and familiar to a general readership.

In translating this selection of suttas, I should like to acknowledge the debt I owe to previous scholars and translators generally, but in particular my understanding of Pali texts owes much to conversations with and the published works of Steven Collins, Margaret Cone, L. S. Cousins, Oskar von Hinüber, and K. R. Norman; I am grateful to Mr Norman for answering my queries on several passages, while the first part (a–kh) of Margaret Cone's *Dictionary of Pali* has been invaluable, and like all scholars of Pali I look forward to the publication of the rest of this dictionary. Over the course of working on these translations I have had many conversations on questions relating to Pali literature with my wife, Rita Langer, and these, as well as her own work on Buddhist funeral rituals, have also fed into my understanding of Pali texts generally and of particular passages. I am also grateful to Ken Robinson, who read through the whole typescript meticulously, pointing out numerous mistakes and making valuable suggestions. Any mistakes that remain, however, are entirely my responsibility. Finally, I would like to thank Judith Luna, the editor of the Oxford World's Classics series, for waiting and also for her quick and judicious advice.

siddhir astu
śubham astu

CONTENTS

ABBREVIATIONS

Editions of Pali texts (except for Vism) are those now published by the Pali Text Society; dates given are of the first publication of the editions, which are all kept in print by the PTS. Translations (where they exist) are listed in the Select Bibliography.

A	*Aṅguttara-nikāya*, 5 vols., ed. R. Morris, A. K. Warder, and E. Hardy (1885–1900; 2nd edn. of I, 1961)
BHSD	William Franklin Edgerton, *Buddhist Hybrid Sanskrit Grammar and Dictionary*, 2 vols. (New Haven and London, 1953)
CPD	V. Trenckner and others, *A Critical Pāli Dictionary* (Copenhagen, 1924–)
D	*Dīgha-nikāya*, 3 vols., ed. T. W. Rhys Davids and J. E. Carpenter (1889–1911)
Dhp-a	*Dhammapada-aṭṭhakathā*, ed. H. C. Norman (1906–14)
DOP	Margaret Cone, *A Dictionary of Pali*, Part I, a–kh (Oxford, 2001)
DPPN	G. P. Malalasekera, *Dictionary of Pali Proper Names*, 2 vols. (London, 1937; repr. 1974)
Ja	*The Jātaka together with its commentary*, ed. V. Fausbøll (1877–96)
M	*Majjhima-nikāya*, 3 vols., ed. V. Trenckner and R. Chalmers (1888–1902)
Mil	*Milindapañho*, ed. V. Trenckner (1880; repr. with *ṭīkā* 1961)
Mhv	*Mahāvaṃsa*, ed. W. Geiger (1908)
Mp	*Manorathapūraṇī*, 5 vols., ed. M. Walleser and H. Kopp (1924–57) = commentary to A
MW	M. Monier-Williams, *A Sanskrit–English Dictionary* (Oxford, 1899; repr. 1979)
PED	T. W. Rhys Davids and William Stede, *Pali–English Dictionary* (Chipstead, 1921–5; repr. Oxford, 1999)

Ps	*Papañcasūdanī*, 5 vols., ed. J. H. Woods, D. Kosambi, and I. B. Horner (1922, 1928, 1933, 1937, 1938) = commentary to M
PTS	Pali Text Society
S	*Saṃyutta-nikāya*, 5 vols., ed. L. Feer (1884, 1888–98)
SBV	*The Gilgit Manuscript of the Saṅghabhedavastu*, ed. R. Gnoli (Rome, 1977)
Skt	Sanskrit
Sp	*Samantapāsādikā*, 7 vols., ed. J. Takakusu and M. Nagai (1924–47) = commentary to Vin
Spk	*Sāratthappakāsinī*, 3 vols., ed. F. L. Woodward (1929–37) = commentary to S
Sv	*Sumaṅgalavilāsinī*, 3 vols., ed. T. W. Rhys Davids and J. E. Carpenter (1929–32) = commentary to D
Thī	*Therīgāthā*, ed. R. Pischel (1883); 2nd edn., ed. K. R. Norman and L. Alsdorf (1966).
Vin	*Vinaya-piṭaka*, 5 vols., ed. H. Oldenberg (1879–83)
Vism	*Visuddhimagga*, ed. H. C. Warren and D. Kosambi (Cambridge, Mass., 1950)

INTRODUCTION

THE present volume, entitled *Sayings of the Buddha*, contains an anthology of ancient Buddhist texts translated from an ancient Indian language known today as Pali. These texts are referred to in Pali as *suttas* or 'well spoken utterances'.[1] They have been selected from the Pali Nikāyas, ancient collections of the Buddha's sayings. The Pali Nikāyas thus represent examples of Buddhist scriptures, and it might be tempting simply to characterize them as the Buddhist equivalent of the Bible or the Qur'an. And yet unlike, for example, Christianity, Judaism, or Islam, neither Hinduism nor Buddhism has a similarly strictly defined, closed 'canon' of scriptures universally accepted as uniquely authoritative by all those we would wish to call (or who would wish to be called) 'Hindu' or 'Buddhist'. Certainly Hinduism has the Vedas, but as a body of literature these have never been defined as strictly as the Bible or Qur'an.[2] Moreover, for different groups of Hindus other collections of scriptures assume a greater significance than the Vedas.[3]

As for Buddhism, we are faced with the existence of at least three canonical collections of Buddhist scriptures containing 'the word of the Buddha' (*buddha-vacana*): the Pali canon of 'Three Baskets' (*Tipiṭaka*); the Chinese 'Three Baskets' (*Sān zàng*) or 'Great Treasury of Sūtras' (*Dàzàng jīng*); the Tibetan *Kanjur* or 'Translated word of the Buddha' (*bKa' 'gyur*). Each of these canons is authoritative for different traditions of Buddhism: the Pali canon for the Theravāda Buddhists of South and South-East Asia (the Buddhists of present-day Sri Lanka, Burma, Thailand, Cambodia, and Laos); the Chinese *Sān zàng* for East Asian Buddhists of China, Korea, and Japan; the Tibetan *Kanjur* for the Buddhists of Tibet and Mongolia.[4] While there

[1] The precise meaning of Pali *sutta* is problematic. Buddhist tradition eventually took it as equivalent to Sanskrit *sūtra*, a word that came to be used to designate concise aphoristic texts, as in *Kāma-sūtra*. But it seems more likely that it derives from Sanskrit *sūkta* or 'well said', a term which was used of the ancient verses of the Veda. See K. R. Norman, *A Philological Approach to Buddhism*, 2nd edn. (Lancaster, 2006), 135.

[2] J. Gonda, *Vedic Literature* (Wiesbaden, 1975).

[3] So, for example, in the case of a follower of Śaiva Siddhānta, it is the twenty-eight Śaiva Āgamas that constitute the crucial divine revelation of Lord Śiva.

[4] Possibly we should include a fourth Buddhist canon, the Sanskrit *Nava Grantha* or *Nava Dharma* of Newar Buddhism: *Prajñāpārāmitā*, *Saddharmapuṇḍarīka*,

is some overlap insofar as one canon might contain versions of certain scriptures contained in another canon, these versions are not straightforward translations into different languages, and it is not possible to identify a universally accepted common core. Moreover, while the Pali canon can be regarded as more or less fixed and closed by the fifth century CE, the Chinese and Tibetan canons have never been formally closed and there is no definitive final list of the works they contain. Certainly the Pali, Chinese, and Tibetan Buddhist canons are all considerably greater in extent than the Christian Bible. The Pali canon comprises twenty-eight works, and printed editions usually fill in the region of forty-five volumes. The older catalogues of the Chinese canon list some 1,500 works, while the modern Taishō edition (1924–32) fills fifty-five volumes, each containing 1,000 pages of Chinese characters, with 2,184 separate works.[5] Editions of the Tibetan canon comprise some 700–800 works in just over 100 volumes.[6] In the case of the Chinese Buddhist canon especially, what we have is not so much a strictly defined canon of scriptures as a library containing all the Chinese translations of Indian Buddhist texts made over the centuries, as well as a variety of indigenous Chinese treatises relating to Buddhism.

What this means in sum is that the defining text or texts of Buddhism are not identifiable in the same way as they are for Christianity, Judaism, and Islam: it is not entirely clear just what is the Buddhist equivalent to the Bible. The texts translated in the present volume are taken from the Pali canon of Buddhist scriptures. Does that mean they are Buddhist 'classics' only for the Theravāda Buddhist tradition? Strictly the answer has to be 'yes', but in important and significant ways the texts translated here are classics of Buddhism as a whole. These texts, or versions of texts very like them

Lalitavistara, *Suvarṇaprabhāsa*, *Laṅkāvatāra*, *Daśabhūmika*, *Gaṇḍhavyūha*, *Samādhirājā*, *Guhyasamāja-tantra*, although as Lewis points out, other texts also have authority for Newar Buddhism; see Todd T. Lewis, 'A Modern Guide for Mahāyāna Buddhist Life-Cycle Rites: The *Nepāl Jana Jīvan Kriyā Paddhati*', *Indo-Iranian Journal*, 37 (1994), 1–46 (8).

[5] For a detailed analysis of the Taishō edition, see Louis Renou and Jean Filliozat, *L'Inde classique*, 2 vols. (Paris, 1947–57), ii. 431–61.

[6] Kenneth Ch'en, 'The Tibetan Tripiṭaka', *Harvard Journal of Asian Studies*, 9 (1945–7), 53–62; Renou and Filliozat, *L'Inde classique*, ii. 388–97; Tadeusz Skorupski, *A Catalogue of the sTog Palace Kanjur* (Tokyo, 1985); Paul Harrison, 'A Brief History of the Tibetan bKa' 'gyur', in José Ignacio Cabezón and Roger R. Jackson (eds.), *Tibetan Literature: Studies in Genre* (Ithaca, NY, 1996), 70–94.

written in different ancient Indian dialects and which survive today either only in Chinese translation or in fragments recovered from the sands and caves of Central Asia and modern-day Afghanistan, represent extracts from a body of literature that was authoritative for ancient Indian Buddhism more generally and is part of the common heritage of Buddhism today. To understand more clearly just how this is so, we must turn to the story of Buddhism's beginnings in ancient India.

The historical Buddha

The diverse traditions of Buddhism that exist in the world today all refer back in one way or another to the Buddha or 'Awakened One'. Who, and indeed what, was the Buddha? Buddhist tradition as a whole is agreed that he was Siddhattha Gotama (Skt: Siddhārtha Gautama),[7] Sakyamuni (Skt: Śākyamuni), the 'sage of the Sakya people' who lived in the distant past in India.

While almost inevitably some early western scholars doubted that such a person ever existed, a more reasonable judgement is that of the great Belgian scholar of Buddhism, Étienne Lamotte. Lamotte observed that unless we accept that Buddhism has its origins in the strong personality of its founder, Buddhism would remain inexplicable.[8] While the dating of this historical Buddha is not without its problems, there is today a more or less established consensus in modern scholarship that the man early Buddhist sources refer to as Gotama the Buddha lived and flourished during the fifth century BCE in eastern India and died some time around 400 BCE.[9] Thus, a critical evaluation of Buddhist textual sources as well as the earliest material Buddhist remains indicate that we can trace the origins of Buddhism to eastern India on the Gangetic plains during the second half of the first millennium BCE.

[7] As this book is primarily concerned with Pali literature, precedence is generally given to the Pali forms of names and technical terms, followed by the Sanskrit equivalents. However, in the Introduction, when referring to Buddhism more generally Sanskrit forms are used.

[8] Étienne Lamotte, *History of Indian Buddhism* (Louvain, 1988), 639.

[9] Heinz Bechert (ed.), *The Dating of the Historical Buddha*, 3 vols. (Göttingen, 1991–7); L. S. Cousins, 'The Dating of the Historical Buddha: A Review Article', *Journal of the Royal Asiatic Society*, 6 (1996), 57–63.

If we consider Buddhist sources alongside other ancient Indian sources, we can confirm that Gotama was a *samaṇa* (Skt: *śramaṇa*). This term means literally 'one who strives', and belongs to the technical vocabulary of Indian religion, referring as it does to 'one who strives' religiously or spiritually. The word *samaṇa* can be conveniently rendered into English as 'ascetic', but the word points towards a particular tradition that in one way or another has been of great significance in Indian religious history, be it Buddhist, Jain, or Hindu. This tradition is sometimes called the 'renouncer (*saṃnyāsin*) tradition'. What we are concerned with here is the phenomenon of individuals renouncing their normal role in society as a member of an extended 'household' in order to devote themselves to some form of religious or spiritual life. The 'renouncer' abandons conventional means of livelihood, such as farming or trade, and adopts instead the religious life: he becomes a religious mendicant dependent on alms.

The principal events that constitute the life of Gotama the Buddha for the most part simply follow from the bare fact of his existence as a wandering ascetic or *samaṇa* in the fifth century BCE who succeeded in attracting a considerable following. It appears he was born into relatively wealthy and privileged circumstances and enjoyed a comfortable upbringing. At some point he became disillusioned and was attracted to the life of a wandering ascetic. If the tradition did not tell us, we might have assumed anyway that he at first pursued this vocation as part of a group of like-minded ascetics under the guidance of one or more teachers. Not satisfied with their teachings, he eventually went his own way. Subsequently it appears that he came to regard himself as having achieved 'awakening' (*bodhi*), an understanding of the nature of reality that for him represented a solution to the problems posed by the suffering and pain he experienced in his own life and that he saw in others. He spent the rest of his life attempting to communicate this understanding to others and to teach a method for its realization. To this end he founded a community (*saṅgha*) of mendicant monks (*bhikkhu/bhikṣu*) and nuns (*bhikkhunī/bhikṣuṇī*). This community was defined by formal ordination procedures and a comprehensive monastic rule. Gotama died an old man, revered as a great teacher, an 'awakened one' (*buddha*), the Lord or 'Blessed One' (*bhagavat*), by a relatively established group of ascetics and their supporters. Such, in short, was the life of Gotama the Buddha, and thus we have 'the three jewels' (*ti-ratana/tri-ratna*) revered by all Buddhists: the Buddha or awakened Teacher, the Dhamma (Skt: *dharma*) or profound Truth he taught, and the Saṅgha or community of realized disciples.

The development of Buddhist literature in India

Our canons of Buddhist scriptures all contain texts which relate the events of the first 'communal recitation' (*saṃgīti*) of the Buddha's teaching. Soon after his death 500 mendicant followers of the Buddha, all *arahats* (Skt: *arhat*)—Buddhist saints who had, like the Buddha, achieved awakening—gathered in Rājagaha (Skt: Rājagṛha) to agree upon and recite the Buddha's teachings.[10] As far as we know, neither the Buddha nor any of his immediate disciples ever wrote any of the teachings down. At this period in India texts were composed and communicated entirely orally. A sense that knowledge is not properly communicated by the written word colours the traditional Indian attitude to learning in general: knowledge should be passed from teacher to pupil directly. The oral origins of traditional Indian learning continued to inform its structure long after texts had begun to be committed to writing.[11]

Whether or not this first communal recitation, or Buddhist Council as it is often styled, is precisely an historical event cannot be known for certain. But that some early communal recitation took place at some point after the Buddha's death seems almost certain. What texts were recited? Since recitation at this first council would lend a text authority, later Indian Buddhist schools tended to suggest that the texts just as their school preserved them were recited. Thus we are told that the master of ceremonies, the senior monk Mahākassapa (Skt: Mahākaśyapa), questioned Upāli as to the circumstances for the establishment of the

[10] Not all sources agree on the place and number of participants; see Lamotte, *History of Indian Buddhism*, 128.

[11] William Graham, *Beyond the Written Word: Oral Aspects of Scripture in the History of Religion* (Cambridge, 1987), 56–77. On the development of writing in India see Richard Salomon, 'On the Origin of the Early Indian Scripts: A Review Article', *Journal of the American Oriental Society*, 115 (1995), 271–9. On the oral nature of specifically Buddhist literature, see L. S. Cousins, 'Pāli Oral Literature', in P. Denwood and A. Piatigorsky (eds.), *Buddhist Studies: Ancient and Modern* (London, 1983), 1–11; S. Collins, 'Notes on Some Oral Aspects of Pali Literature', *Indo-Iranian Journal*, 35 (1992), 121–35; M. Allon, 'The Oral Composition and Transmission of Early Buddhist Texts' in P. Connolly and S. Hamilton (eds.), *Indian Insights: Buddhism, Brahmanism and Bhakti* (London, 1997), 39–61; Norman, *A Philological Approach to Buddhism*, 53–74.

vinaya or monastic discipline, and the Buddha's attendant, Ānanda, as to where and when the texts that comprise the *dhamma* more generally were expounded. This latter category is taken to refer in the present context to a type of relatively short text relating a dialogue of the Buddha and subsequently known as a *sutta* (Skt: *sūtra*)—the type of text anthologized in the present volume. Buddhist *suttas* all begin with a stock phrase: '*This is what I have heard. Once the Blessed One was staying at* . . .' They then proceed to relate the dialogue of the Buddha on a particular occasion with monks, lay people, kings, gods, or some other interlocutor. The 'I' of the initial phrase is traditionally understood to be Ānanda, recalling at the first Buddhist Council what he had heard the Buddha teach. Yet from what we understand of the development of Indian Buddhist literature, it is hardly possible that any Buddhist text survives today just as it was recited at this first council. Nonetheless, it is extremely likely that at least some of these *suttas* that come down to us are among the oldest surviving Buddhist texts and contain material that goes back directly to the Buddha.

The modern Buddhist canons also contain texts that tell something of the story of the subsequent history and development of Buddhism in India, how from its beginnings in eastern India in the fifth century BCE it spread across the whole of the Indian subcontinent, until by the beginning of the first century CE it had become a pan-Indian phenomenon. The ancient sources for the history of Indian Buddhism are not always consistent, but their critical evaluation allows us to sketch a general outline.[12] Perhaps one hundred years after the death of the Buddha (i.e. *c.*300 BCE) there was a second major communal recitation of the Buddha's teaching in the city of Vesālī (Skt: Vaiśālī), prompted by certain disputes relating to the interpretation of the monastic rule. Matters seem to have been resolved, but not long afterwards the Saṅgha or community of monks and nuns seems to have formally split into two parties: the Theras (Skt: Sthavira) or 'elders' on the one hand, and the Mahāsaṃghikas (Skt: Mahāsāṃghika) or majority party on the other. Tradition records

[12] The standard scholarly works on the early Buddhist councils and the evolution of the Indian Buddhist schools remain André Bareau's *Les Premiers Conciles bouddhiques* (Paris, 1955) and *Les Sectes bouddhiques du petit véhicule* (Paris, 1955). On the Buddhist councils and early Buddhist literature more generally see also Lamotte, *History of Indian Buddhism*, 124–91, 517–40. For a more introductory sketch and further references see R. Gethin, *The Foundations of Buddhism* (Oxford, 1998), 35–58, 307–9.

how, over the next century or so, further subdivisions occurred within the Saṅgha on both sides of this initial divide.

It is important to register that we are dealing here with divisions in the monastic Saṅgha and not splits in the Buddhist community as a whole. The divisions are matters of monastic affiliation, of how Buddhists monks and nuns trace back their line of ordination and relate to the monastic rule. How such monastic divisions would have affected and involved the wider Buddhist community in ancient India is unclear. The factors driving these divisions seem to have been varied and complex; they include the simple fact of the Saṅgha's dispersal across a vast subcontinent, groupings around particular monastic teachers, disagreement over approach to the monastic rule, and association with a particular understanding of points of Buddhist systematic thought or *abhidhamma* (Skt: *abhidharma*). We should also be extremely wary of the temptation to think of the evolution of these Buddhist monastic divisions by way of models derived from the history of early Christianity, and to imagine some sort of Buddhist equivalents of the early Church Councils of Nicea and Chalcedon ruling on issues of 'heresy' and 'orthodoxy'. It is also worth noting that all three presently existing orders of Buddhist monks and nuns—the South and South-East Asian Theravādins, the East Asian Dharmaguptakas, and the Tibetan Mūlasarvāstivādins—derive their monastic lineage from the Sthavira side of the initial division.

According to Buddhist tradition there were eventually eighteen different schools of Buddhism resulting from these divisions. The number eighteen appears to be ideal, and how many effective divisions there were in practice remains unclear; a number closer to ten is probably nearer the mark. In principle, it seems that all these ancient Indian schools of Buddhism would have preserved their own particular recensions of Buddhist texts: their own particular versions of the Tipiṭaka (Skt: Tripiṭaka) or 'three baskets', consisting of the Vinaya-piṭaka (containing the monastic rule), the Sutta-piṭaka (containing collections of the dialogues of the Buddha), and thirdly, by this stage in the development of Indian Buddhism, the Abhidhamma-piṭaka, a third basket of texts concerned with systematic Buddhist thought.

If all the ancient schools did have their own distinctive versions of the Tripiṭaka, then they have been largely lost. To give a rough indication, what has come down to us are six versions of the complete Vinaya (but only one in full in an ancient Indian language, the others in Chinese and Tibetan translation), one complete sūtra collection, and two complete Abhidharma collections (again only one in full in an ancient Indian language, the other in Chinese translation). Substantial portions of two other sūtra collections survive in ancient Indian languages and in Chinese translation. In short, there is only one ancient Tripiṭaka that survives complete in an ancient Indian language, and that is the Pali Tipiṭaka of the Theravādin school of Buddhism that flourishes today in Sri Lanka, Burma, Thailand, Cambodia, and Laos. This makes the Pali canon as a whole a uniquely important source for the study of ancient Buddhism, although it does not, of course, mean that the traditions it contains are necessarily older and closer to the Buddha than those of other schools whose texts happen to survive only in fragments or in Chinese translation.

When were these ancient Buddhist canons fixed and closed? It is not easy to give a definite answer to this question. Certainly they remained open for some time. Thus, for example, the Vinaya-piṭakas contain accounts of the events of the second communal recitation at Vaiśālī which clearly could not have been included in the first communal recitation a hundred years earlier at Rājagṛha. The Sūtra-piṭakas also contain discourses delivered by monks that are explicitly placed some time after the Buddha's death. And the divergent contents of the two Abhidharma-piṭakas that survive suggest that they especially are the product of a period when Buddhism had already divided into schools. Equally, the substantial and broad correspondence in content in the case of the surviving Vinaya- and Sūtra-piṭakas suggests a relatively early date for these collections. Early on, it seems, the sayings of the Sūtra-piṭaka were arranged in four principal collections termed *nikāya* or *āgama*: the long (*dīgha/dīrgha*) sayings, the middle-length (*majjhima/madhyama*) sayings, the grouped (*saṃyutta/saṃyukta*) sayings, and the numbered (*aṅguttara/ekottarika*) sayings. While it is apparent that different Buddhist schools did not always distribute their versions of the dialogues across these collections in precisely the same way, and there are variations in the mode of expression and the arrangement of topics, there remains a significant agreement; Étienne Lamotte pointed out fifty years ago that, as far as we can judge, the doctrinal basis common to the collections of sūtras surviving in Pali and Chinese translation, for example, is remarkably uniform.[13] Far from representing sectarian Buddhism, these sūtras above all constitute the common ancient heritage of Buddhism.

Against this background, Buddhist sūtras continued to emerge in ancient India. Some of these sūtras were criticized as developing new and unwarranted ideas on the basis of the older ideas found in the more generally accepted sūtras. Their advocates, however, claimed that these sūtras contained the profoundest teachings of the Buddha, teachings that had hitherto been kept hidden. These were the sūtras of the Mahāyāna or 'great vehicle'. In India these sūtras, which began to emerge around the beginning of the first century CE, were for several centuries accepted only by a small minority and were never universally accepted. Even among the advocates of the Mahāyāna, the sūtras contained in the Nikāyas or Āgamas remained authoritative. Thus, when Buddhist texts began to be translated into Chinese in the second century CE, both Mahāyāna and pre-Mahāyāna materials were translated. Over time, in certain circles the older pre-Mahāyāna sūtras, although not rejected, became neglected, even though the teachings they contained continued to be referred to. Thus, among those Buddhists who took Buddhist thought and practice into Tibet from the seventh century, the teachings contained in the older sūtras had in effect been subsumed in subsequent texts, with the result that only a handful of the older sūtras were ever translated into Tibetan.

The Pali Canon

The sūtras, or rather suttas, contained in the present volume are, then, taken from the Pali canon, the only canon of ancient Indian Buddhist scriptures to survive complete in an ancient Indian language. The ancient Pali commentaries and chronicles, texts that come down to us in a form that was fixed in Ceylon[14] (modern-day Sri Lanka) in the fourth or fifth century CE, relate how this particular canon of Buddhist texts was brought to Ceylon during the reign of the great Mauryan emperor Aśoka, who ruled from his capital in Pāṭaliputra

[13] Lamotte, *History of Indian Buddhism*, 156.

[14] I use the name 'Ceylon' to refer to the island, rather than 'Sri Lanka', which is the name of a modern state, just as India refers generally to the lands of the Indian subcontinent, which correspond generally to the modern states of India, Pakistan, Bangladesh, and parts of Nepal.

(modern Patna) in the middle of the third century BCE. Following a third communal recitation in Pāṭaliputra, an elder monk named Moggaliputtatissa is said to have organized Buddhist missions to various border regions. One group of five monks, headed by the emperor's own son, Mahinda, journeyed to Ceylon and is said to have brought the Pali canon with it. Whatever the value of this tradition, from the third and second centuries BCE we have material evidence of the presence of Buddhism in Ceylon in the form of monuments and donative inscriptions over caves that were adapted for use as Buddhist monastic dwellings. And if Buddhist monks were there, it seems likely that Buddhist texts were also there.

At this stage in the history of Buddhist texts we are still dealing with an oral literature. Thus, we find in the ancient sources mention of schools of reciters (*bhāṇaka*) who specialized in preserving and reciting the principal collections of suttas. According to the Pali sources, these schools traced their lineage back to the first communal recitation when the 500 arahats entrusted these collections to the Buddha's direct disciples: thus the Dīgha-bhāṇakas or 'reciters of the long sayings' represented the lineage of Ānanda, the Majjhima-bhāṇakas or 'reciters of the middle-length sayings' that of Sāriputta's pupils (since Sāriputta himself had died before the first communal recitation), the Saṃyutta-bhāṇakas or 'reciters of the grouped sayings' that of Anuruddha, the Aṅguttara-bhāṇakas or 'reciters of the numbered sayings' that of Mahākassapa.[15] Pali tradition records that the texts of the Tipiṭaka were in fact first written down during the first century BCE.[16] It also records that the commentary (*aṭṭhakathā*) on these texts was written down at the same time. To what extent the text of the Pali canon as we have it today can be traced back to the canon as it existed and was written down in the first century BCE once more remains unclear. We have no manuscripts that date back to anything like this period. Manuscripts do not survive well in a humid tropical climate, and probably the majority of the manuscripts of the Pali canon date from the eighteenth and nineteenth centuries; and in general, the very oldest manuscripts do not date from before the fifteenth century.[17] The oldest Pali manuscript that has so far

[15] Sv I 15.

[16] Dīp XX 20–1; Mhv XXXIII 100–1; cf. K. R. Norman, *Pāli Literature* (Wiesbaden, 1983), 10–11.

[17] Oskar von Hinüber, 'Chips from Buddhist Workshops: Scribes and Manuscripts from Northern Thailand', *Journal of the Pali Text Society*, 22 (1996), 35–57.

come to light is a portion of the Vinaya found far away from Ceylon in Nepal, which can be dated to the eighth or ninth century.[18] The oldest Buddhist manuscripts in general are the Gāndhārī fragments that have been found in Afghanistan and can be dated to the first or second century CE, and seem to belong to the Dharmaguptaka school.[19]

Despite the absence of manuscripts, we know that by the end of the fourth century CE the text of the Pali canon must have been fixed substantially as we have it now. This is established by the existence of the Pali commentaries, which comment in detail on the text and can be dated to the fifth century CE. The Pali commentaries were fixed in their present form by a number of scholar monks, the most famous of whom was Buddhaghosa, who all belonged to the Mahāvihāra or Great Monastery, one of three principal monasteries in the ancient capital of Ceylon, Anurādhapura. These were the monks probably responsible for the final closing of the Pali canon.[20] According to their own account of their work, their commentaries were based on earlier commentaries (now lost) which seem to have been composed and, up until this point, handed down in various Middle Indian dialects or Prakrits. The language of the commentaries was now standardized in conformity with 'the language of the canon' or *pāli-bhāsā*. (This expression eventually came to be interpreted as 'the Pali language', hence the modern usage of 'Pali' as the name of a language.)[21] At the same time, the list of works that constituted the Pali canon and were considered to be the 'word of the Buddha' (*buddha-vacana*) by the Mahāvihāra was finalized. While the final form of the Pali commentaries dates from the fifth century CE, the fact that they make no mention of people who lived after the first century CE suggests that in terms of their contents they are in substance works that belong to a period three or four centuries earlier.[22] And given that they comment on the text of the Pali canon, the works of the canon as we have it must date at least to a period a century or so before that.

[18] Oskar von Hinüber, *The Oldest Pāli Manuscript: Four Folios of the Vinaya-Piṭaka from the National Archives, Kathmandu* (Mainz, 1991).

[19] Richard Salomon, *Ancient Buddhist Scrolls from Gandhāra* (London, 1999).

[20] S. Collins, 'On the Very Idea of the Pali Canon', *Journal of the Pali Text Society*, 15 (1990), 89–126.

[21] See Oskar von Hinüber, 'On the History of the Name of the Pali Language', *Selected Papers*, 2nd edn. (Oxford, 2005), 76–90.

[22] E. W. Adikaram, *Early History of Buddhism in Ceylon* (Migoda, Ceylon, 1946), 87.

We can say a little more about the early history of the texts that have come down to us in the Pali canon. The broad correspondence in terms of structure and contents between the surviving recensions of the four principal collections (*nikāya/āgama*) that make up the Sūtra-piṭaka (the long, middle-length, grouped, and numbered sayings) is in itself indicative of a relatively early date, prior to the division of the Buddhist Saṅgha into separate schools, for the basic contents of these collections. It seems likely, then, that these collections took on their current form during the third and second centuries BCE. The language of the Pali canon also tells a tale. According to the traditions of the commentaries, the language of the Pali canon is Māgadhī, on the assumption, one presumes, that the canon contains the words of the Buddha and the Buddha lived in Magadha and therefore spoke its language. All the evidence suggests, however, that Pali is not in fact Māgadhī. The inscriptions which Aśoka commissioned in local dialects across the Indian subcontinent allow us to establish a general language map of India a century or so after the death of the Buddha.[23] This suggests that Pali—the language of the Pali canon—has more in common with a western dialect than an eastern dialect, of which Māgadhī would be an example. Nonetheless, Pali does seem to exhibit some eastern features—sometimes referred to as 'Māgadhisms'. The detailed study of the language of the canon in fact suggests that various dialects through which the texts have been filtered in the course of their evolution have left their traces.[24] Finally, we see in Pali the beginnings of 'sanskritization', the process by which Buddhist texts which had been preserved in different dialects were rendered closer to the norms of Sanskrit. This linguistic story *perhaps* reflects the early history and evolution of the texts that have come down to us in the Pali canon. This history possibly begins with the Buddha teaching in some form of Māgadhī as opposed to Sanskrit, a language which at that time was too closely associated with the brahmanical tradition, to which the Buddha represented a challenge; subsequently his teachings are transposed into different local dialects as Buddhist monks spread out from Magadha; finally, as Sanskrit begins to lose its exclusively brahmanical association and to take on the role of the language in which to communicate learning and culture right across India, certain terms, such as *brāhmaṇa*, signifying

[23] Richard Salomon, *Indian Epigraphy* (New York, 1998), 72–6.

[24] Norman, *A Philological Approach to Buddhism*, 75–97.

a 'brahman' or member of the priestly class, are transposed into their Sanskritic forms. Thus, the language of the Pali canon does appear to have become frozen at a relatively early date, resisting both the more thoroughgoing sanskritization that is a feature of some other early Buddhist texts and also any influence from Sinhalese Prakrit during its long transmission in Ceylon.[25]

In sum, although we cannot date the texts translated in this volume with any final certainty, we can say that they are likely to date in something close to their present form to the third or second century BCE. We cannot claim that the Pali version of the suttas translated here represent the oldest version or are closer than other surviving versions to some ideal original. Yet this is equally true of these other surviving versions. Certainly there have been some attempts to compare versions and date them relatively, and also attempts to distinguish earlier from later strata within the collections of Pali suttas themselves, yet the exercise is fraught with uncertainties, and the results of such attempts have proved inconclusive and not been universally accepted by scholars.[26] The Pali suttas are, then, among the oldest Buddhist texts we have—certainly no texts can claim to be older. In their words we are presented with an understanding of what the Buddha taught that is likely to go back directly to his earliest disciples; here we are as close to the presence of the Buddha as we are likely to get.

The texts of the Pali canon are arranged by way of three basic divisions or 'baskets' (*piṭaka*): the Vinaya-piṭaka or 'basket of discipline'; the Sutta-piṭaka or 'basket of sayings'; the Abhidhamma-piṭaka or 'basket of further teaching'.

The Vinaya-piṭaka consists of three works: (1) the Sutta-vibhaṅga sets out and explains in detail the 227 and 311 'training rules' (*sikkhāpada*) to be followed by Buddhist monks (*bhikkhu*) and nuns (*bhikkhunī*) respectively; (2) the Khandhaka sets out in twenty-two sections (*khandhaka*) the procedures for conducting the various formal communal acts of the Saṅgha; (3) the Parivāra is an appendix that contains various kinds of material aimed at assisting the study and understanding of the Vinaya.

The Sutta-piṭaka consists of five 'collections' (*nikāya*): (1) the Dīgha-nikāya or 'collection of long sayings' comprises thirty-four

[25] K. R. Norman, *Collected Papers*, 8 vols. (Oxford, 1990–2007), i. 238–46; ii. 30–51.

[26] As an example of a sustained attempt to distinguish between early and late in the Pali Nikāyas, see G. C. Pande, *Studies in the Origins of Buddhism*, 2nd edn. (Delhi, 1974).

suttas arranged in three divisions (*vagga*) of thirteen, ten, and eleven suttas respectively; (2) the Majjhima-nikāya or 'collection of middle-length sayings' comprises 152 suttas arranged in three divisions of fifty, fifty and fifty-two suttas respectively; (3) the Saṃyutta-nikāya or 'collection of grouped sayings' arranges its suttas into fifty-six groups (*saṃyutta*) according to topic, further arranged into five main divisions; (4) the Aṅguttara-nikāya or 'collection of numbered sayings' arranges its suttas into eleven sections (*nipāta*)—the section on 'ones' through to the section on 'elevens'—according to the number of items that form the main subject-matter of a sutta; (5) finally, the Khuddaka-nikāya or 'collection of minor works' contains fifteen miscellaneous works of varying length, including such well-known writings as the *Dhammapada* and *Jātaka* (stories of the former lives of the being destined to become the Buddha).

Finally, the Abhidhamma-piṭaka consists of seven separate works that set out the details of Buddhist metaphysics and psychology in general terms that are in principle elaborated on the basis of the teachings contained in the suttas.

The present volume contains a selection of suttas from the four primary Nikāyas of the Pali canon.[27] The selection is intended to reflect something of the structure of the Pali canon and—as far as we can tell—of other ancient Indian Buddhist canons. Thus we have five suttas from the Dīgha-nikāya; six from the Majjhima-nikāya; a selection of suttas representing the fivefold structure of the Saṃyutta-nikāya and the eleven most important *saṃyuttas* or 'groups' that underlie the arrangement of that collection; and finally a selection of eleven suttas reflecting the numerical arrangement of the Aṅguttara-nikāya. The suttas are presented in the order in which they appear in the Nikāyas. Introductions to the individual suttas describe their contents in more detail.

The selection is also intended to represent the principal teachings found in the Nikāyas—teachings on the Buddhist path and different types of meditation (*Sāmaññaphala-sutta*, *Satipaṭṭhāna-sutta*, *Vitakkasaṇṭhāna-sutta*, and the suttas from the Mahāvagga of the Saṃyutta-nikāya), teachings on the theories of the five 'aggregates' and 'not self' (the *Alagaddūpama-sutta*, and the suttas from the *khandha-saṃyutta* and *saḷāyatana-saṃyutta*), teachings on 'dependent

[27] The selection is perhaps in the order of 5% of the four Nikāyas.

arising' (the suttas from the *nidāna-saṃyutta*), teachings on everyday conduct (the *Sigālovāda-sutta*), teachings on the evolution of the world and society (the *Aggañña-sutta*), teachings on actions and their consequences for rebirth (the *Mahā-Kammavibhaṅga-sutta*).

Three suttas focus on important episodes in the Buddha's life: the *Bodhirājakumāra-sutta* provides an account in the first person of the Buddha's struggle for awakening and his ultimate success; the *Dhammacakkappavattana-sutta* (of the *Mahā-vagga* of the Saṃyutta-nikāya) gives an account of the 'turning of the wheel of the Teaching', the first sermon of the Buddha; the *Mahāparinibbāna-sutta* relates the story of the Buddha's final journey and of his death and funeral.

The anthology also represents something of the different literary styles of the suttas, ranging from the more philosophical and technical analysis of, say, the *Alagaddūpama-sutta* to the mythic narrative and visual imagery of the *Mahāsudassana-sutta*. Finally, there are here suttas addressed to a variety of different audiences: to monks, brahmans, laymen, kings, and gods.[28]

Anyone reading Buddhist suttas for the first time is likely to be struck by a certain repetitiveness that manifests itself in various ways: the repetition of passages when events that have just been narrated are related to another person, and the use of stock formulas to describe events, people, ideas, to give but two examples. This repetitiveness is in part a reflection of the fact that suttas were composed orally and transmitted orally for several centuries before being

[28] For full translations of the Pali Nikāyas, see the following works. T. W. and C. A. F. Rhys Davids, *Dialogues of the Buddha*, 3 vols. (London, 1899–1921; repr. 1995) is a pioneering translation of the Dīgha-nikāya that, despite its age and its Victorian biblical English style, is a work of considerable scholarship whose notes and discussions remain very useful; Maurice Walshe, *The Long Discourses of the Buddha* (Boston: Wisdom Publications, 1995), is a more recent readable translation into modern English. For the Majjhima-nikāya there are two complete English translations: I. B. Horner, *The Collection of Middle-Length Sayings*, 3 vols. (London, 1954–9), and Bhikkhu Ñāṇamoli and Bhikkhu Bodhi, *The Middle-Length Discourses of the Buddha* (Boston, 1995). In the case of the Saṃyutta-nikāya, the earlier C. A. F. Rhys Davids and F. L. Woodward, *The Book of the Kindred Sayings*, 5 vols. (London, 1917–1930; repr. 1990–5), has been largely superseded by Bhikkhu Bodhi, *The Connected Discourses of the Buddha* (Boston, 2000). E. M. Hare and F. L. Woodward, *The Book of the Gradual Sayings*, 5 vols. (London, 1923–6; repr. 1994–5), remains the only complete translation of the Aṅguttara-nikāya, although a substantial selection is found in Nyanaponika Thera and Bhikkhu Bodhi, *Numerical Discourses of the Buddha: An Anthology of Suttas from the Aṅguttara Nikāya* (Walnut Creek, Calif., 1999).

written down: repetition is a useful mnemonic device in an oral culture. But repetition is also used by the suttas to affect both the reciter and listener, and is integral to the suttas as literary works that are in some sense to be performed.

The use of repetition thus gives the suttas a particular literary rhythm: there is no hurry to get information across; ideas and similes that are repeated have a meditative and poetic effect; they evoke images in our minds and stir our emotions as slowly we contemplate them again and again. When the suttas were written down (and perhaps even when they were being recited in some contexts) they were abbreviated, usually with the word *peyyāla* (itself abbreviated to *pe*) meaning something like 'repetition', the Pali equivalent of '. . .' to indicate omission.

India at the time of the Buddha

It is generally thought—though it is also a matter of some controversy—that some time after the beginning of the second millennium BCE groups of a nomadic tribal people began to move south from ancient Iran, through the passes of the Hindu Kush and down into the plains of the Indus valley.[29] These people spoke dialects of Old Indo-Aryan, that is, of Sanskrit, and they are known as the Āryas. The Āryas who moved into India were descendants of nomadic pastoralists who had occupied the grasslands of central Asia, and some of whom similarly moved west into Europe.

Once in India, the Āryas' cultural influence gradually spread southwards and eastwards across the plains of northern India. By the time the Buddha was born, probably early in the fifth century BCE, the Āryas had been in India for perhaps a thousand years, and their cultural influence extended down the Ganges valley as far as modern Bengal. Our sources indicate that the northern half of the Indian subcontinent then comprised sixteen 'countries' (*mahājanapada*). Of these, four constituted significant kingdoms: farthest to the east down the Ganges valley was Magadha, with its capital at Rājagaha (Skt: Rājagṛha), further to the west up the Ganges valley was the kingdom of Vaṃsa (Skt: Vatsa), centred on the city of Kosambī

[29] On the sometimes heated debate provoked by the issue of the original homeland of the Āryas see Edwin F. Bryant and Laurie L. Patton (eds.), *The Indo-Aryan Controversy: Evidence and Inference in Indian History* (London, 2005).

(Skt: Kauśambī); to the north was the kingdom of Kosala (Skt: Kośala), centred on the city of Sāvatthī (Skt: Śrāvastī); some way to the south and west of these three kingdoms was Avanti, centred on the city of Ujjenī (Skt: Ujjayanī). Apart from these kingdoms there were a number of smaller republics (*gaṇa*), the most important of which was that of the Vajjis (Skt: Vṛji), lying to the north of Magadha and centring on the city of Vesālī. Further to the west, bordering on the kingdom of Kosala, were the smaller republics of the Mallas, centring on Pāpā, and of the Sākiyas, centring on Kapilavatthu (Skt: Kapilavastu) and the country of the Buddha's birth.[30]

Early Buddhist texts depict the Buddha leaving his homeland and journeying south-east into Magadha, where he finally achieved his awakening. From there he wandered west into Kāsī (Skt: Kāśī) to begin his teaching career in a deer park outside Bārāṇasī (modern Benares). The Buddha's subsequent career is spent wandering and teaching in a region more or less defined by the kingdoms of Magadha, Vaṃsa, and Kosala, and the republic of the Vajjis.

The coming of the Āryas did not bring political unity to northern India, but it did bring a certain cultural vision and ideology that constitutes one of the principal components of Indian culture. This vision of society was principally developed and articulated by a hereditary group within the society of the Āryas known as *brāhmaṇas* or, in the Anglo-Indian spelling, brahmans. The original literature of the brahmans is known as the *Vedas*, the oldest portions of which, found in the *Ṛg Veda*, date from about 1500 BCE. By the time of the Buddha, Vedic literature probably already comprised several different classes: the four collections (*saṃhitā*) of verses attributed to the ancient seers (*ṛṣi*), the ritual manuals (also known as *brāhmaṇas*) giving instruction in the carrying out of the elaborate Vedic sacrificial ritual, and 'the forest books' (*āraṇyaka*) explaining the esoteric meaning of this sacrificial ritual. The final class of Vedic literature, the Upaniṣads, containing further esoteric explanations of the sacrificial ritual, was still in the process of formation.

Two aspects of the brahmanical vision are of particular importance, namely an understanding of society as reflecting a hierarchy of ritual 'purity', and a complex system of ritual and sacrifice. From the brahmanical perspective society comprises two groups: the Āryas

[30] On the early Indian kingdoms and republics, see A. L. Basham, *The Wonder that was India*, 3rd edn. (London, 1967), 44–136.

and the non-Āryas. The former consists of the three hereditary classes (*varṇa*) in descending order of purity: *brāhmaṇas* (whose prerogative and duty it is to teach and maintain the Vedic tradition), *kṣatriyas* or rulers (whose prerogative and duty is to maintain order and where necessary inflict appropriate punishment), and the *vaiśyas* (whose prerogative and duty is to generate wealth through farming and trade). These three classes are termed 'twice born' (*dvija*) by virtue of the fact that traditionally male members undergo an initiation (*upanayana*) into a period of study of the Vedic tradition under the supervision of a brahman teacher; at the end of this period of study it is their duty to maintain the household sacrificial fires and, with the help of brahmans, carry out various sacrificial rituals—offerings into the sacrificial fire—in accordance with the prescriptions of Vedic tradition. The non-Āryas make up the fourth class, the *śūdras* or servants, whose basic duty it is to serve the three other classes. While it is important not to confuse these four classes (*varṇa*) and the countless castes (*jāti*) of later Indian society, it is nonetheless the ideology of the relative ritual purity of the classes that underpins the medieval and modern Indian 'caste system'.[31]

The brahmans' hereditary ritual status empowered them to carry out certain ritual functions that members of other classes were excluded from, but at the time of the Buddha not all brahmans were full-time 'priests'. Precisely how brahmans related to the various groups of wandering ascetics is not clear. In part we must see the brahmanical vision of society and that of the wandering ascetics as opposed to each other, in part we must see the two as influencing each other. To accept the brahmanical view of the world was to accept brahmanical authority as an aspect of the eternal structure of the universe and, as such, unassailable. Yet alongside the brahmans were the various groups of wandering ascetics or 'renouncers'. At least some of these threatened brahmanical supremacy by offering rival visions of the world and society.[32] On the other hand, within brahmanical circles we find the development of certain esoteric theories of the nature of the sacrificial ritual and philosophical views about the ultimate nature of man and his relationship to the universe at

[31] On the early Vedic and brahmanical tradition generally see Thomas J. Hopkins, *The Hindu Religious Tradition* (Belmont, Calif., 1971), 3–51.

[32] See Padmanabh S. Jaini, 'Śrāmaṇas: Their Conflict with Brāhmaṇical Society', in J. W. Elder (ed.), *Chapters in Indian Civilization*, vol. 1 (Dubuque, 1970), 39–81.

large. These theories may to some extent have drawn on ideas developing amongst the groups of wandering ascetics; at the same time they may have substantially contributed to the theories of the wanderers themselves, since it is clear that brahman circles were an important recruiting-ground for the various groups of wandering ascetics. Yet it seems clear that in certain respects the Buddha's teachings were formulated as a response to certain Brahmanical teachings.[33]

The origins of the 'renouncer' tradition are not clear. Whether it is best understood as evolving within the context of specifically brahmanical religion or outside it is a matter of scholarly debate.[34] Nevertheless, by the fifth century BCE the tradition was well established. Yet, while 'renouncers' had in common the fact that they had 'gone forth from the household life into homelessness' (to use a phrase common in Buddhist sources), the kinds of lifestyle they then adopted varied considerably. This is suggested by some of the terms that we find in the texts: in addition to 'one who strives' (*śramaṇa/samaṇa*) and 'renouncer' (*saṃnyāsin*), we find 'wanderer' (*parivrājaka/paribbājaka*), 'one who begs his share (of alms)' (*bhikṣu/bhikkhu*), 'naked ascetic' (*acelaka*), 'matted-hair ascetic' (*jaṭila*), as well as a number of other terms. Some of these wanderers and ascetics seem to have been loners, while others seem to have organized themselves into groups and lived under a teacher. Early renouncers seem to have been for the most part male, although with the growth of Buddhism and Jainism it is certainly the case that women too began to be numbered among their ranks.

Three kinds of activity seem to have preoccupied these wanderers and ascetics. First, there is the practice of austerities, such as going naked in all weather, enduring all physical discomforts, fasting, or undertaking the vow to live like a cow or even a dog.[35] Secondly, there is the cultivation of meditative and contemplative techniques aimed at producing what might, for the lack of a suitable technical term in English, be referred to as 'altered states of consciousness'. In the technical vocabulary of Indian religious texts such states

[33] See Richard Gombrich, *Theravāda Buddhism: A Social History from Ancient Benares to Modern Colombo* (London, 1988), and 'Recovering the Buddha's Message', in Tadeusz Skorupski (ed.), *The Buddhist Forum*, vol. 1 (London, 1990), 5–20.

[34] See Gavin Flood, *An Introduction to Hinduism* (Cambridge, 1996), 87–90.

[35] D I 161–77; M I 387–92.

come to be termed 'absorptions' (*dhyāna/jhāna*) or 'concentrations' (*samādhi*); the attainment of such states of consciousness was generally regarded as bringing the practitioner to some deeper knowledge and experience of the nature of the world. Lastly there is the development of various philosophical views providing the intellectual justification for particular practices and the theoretical expression of the 'knowledge' to which they led. While some groups and individuals seem to have combined all three activities, others favoured one at the expense of the others, and the line between the practice of austerities and the practice of meditation may not always be clear: the practice of extreme austerity will certainly alter one's state of mind.

The existence of some of these different groups of ancient Indian wanderers and ascetics with their various practices and theories finds expression in Buddhist texts in a stock description of 'six teachers of other schools', who are each represented as expounding a particular teaching and practice. Another list, with no details of the associated teachings and practices, gives ten types of renouncer. In fact, two other ancient Indian traditions that were subsequently of some importance in the religious life of India (the Ājīvikas and the Jains) find a place in both these ancient Buddhist lists; the Jain tradition, of course, survives to this day.[36]

A sketch of early Buddhist thought and practice[37]

The word *buddha* means literally 'one who has woken up'.[38] In early Buddhist sources that word is used to characterize a particular type of person: a *buddha* is someone who has woken up from a particular kind of sleep: the sleep of ignorance.

Buddhas are, from the perspective of ordinary humanity, extremely rare and quite extraordinary. In contrast to these buddhas or 'awakened ones', the mass of humanity is asleep—asleep in the sense that people pass through their lives never knowing and seeing the world 'as it is' (*yathā-bhūtaṃ*). As a consequence, they suffer. A buddha, on the

[36] For the list of six teachers see e.g. D I 51–9 (below, pp. 10–16); for the list of ten see A III 276; cf. A. L. Basham, *History and Doctrines of the Ājīvikas* (London, 1951).

[37] For a fuller picture and further reading see Gethin, *Foundations of Buddhism*.

[38] Not 'enlightened'; the Buddha attains 'awakening' (*bodhi*) rather than 'enlightenment', as it is often translated.

other hand, awakens to the knowledge of the world as it truly is, and in so doing finds release from suffering. Moreover—and this is perhaps the greatest significance of a buddha for the rest of humanity, and indeed for all the beings who make up the universe—a buddha teaches. He teaches out of sympathy and compassion for the suffering of beings, for the benefit and welfare of all beings; he teaches in order that others might awaken, like him, to the understanding that brings final relief from suffering. An ancient formula, part of which is still used in Buddhist devotions today, puts it as follows:

For the following reasons is he the Blessed One—he is an arahat, a perfect buddha, accomplished in knowledge and conduct, happy, one who understands the world, an unsurpassed charioteer of men to be tamed, the teacher of gods and men, a blessed buddha . . . He gains for himself a direct knowledge of this world with its gods, its Māra and Brahmā, of this generation with its ascetics and brahmans, its princes and peoples, and having experienced this directly he makes it known. He teaches the Truth that is beautiful in the beginning, beautiful in the middle, beautiful in the end, both in its spirit and in its letter. He makes clear the pure spiritual life in all its perfection.[39]

The formula describes a buddha as, amongst other things, one who gains 'knowledge of this world with its gods, its Māra and Brahmā'. Buddhas appear in a world or universe made up of countless world spheres or systems, that consist of various levels and realms of beings ranging from the hellish to the divine. All beings in the universe—whether hellish, animal, human, or divine—are born, live, die, and are reborn again in accordance with their actions, their 'karma' (or, in Pali, *kamma*). This perpetual round of birth, death, and rebirth is called *saṃsāra*, and has no known beginning and no known end. On a larger scale clusters of world systems go through great cycles of expansion and contraction across vast aeons of time. Again, this process has no known beginning and no known end. There is thus no definite limit that can be put on the universe, either temporally or spatially. This universe is inhabited by a great variety of beings, both seen and unseen, and including various gods, both minor and major. And yet the universe was not created by, nor is it controlled by, any one omnipotent God. Certain gods, such as the great Brahmā, may, however, have a certain limited jurisdiction over certain parts of the universe and may even get the idea that they created it; some human

[39] D I 49, 62; *Sāmaññaphala-sutta*, translated in full below.

beings may also worship Brahmā as the creator. Other gods, such as Māra, 'the Bad One', and his retinue actively try to mislead and delude beings. But although these gods' life-spans may be of incalculable length, none is immortal. All will eventually die, to be reborn in some other part of the universe, though, in the case of Brahmā and Māra, another being will be reborn in their place to take over their roles. It is in this universe that buddhas appear; and it is this universe that buddhas get to know.[40]

As we have seen, our earliest Buddhist sources present themselves as a record of the life and teachings of one particular buddha—Gotama or Sakyamuni, 'the sage of the Sakya people'—as remembered and passed down by his pupils. While the principal events that constitute the life of Gotama the Buddha for the most part simply follow from the bare fact of his existence as a wandering ascetic or *samaṇa* in the fifth century BCE, the later Buddhist tradition elaborates the Buddha's life-story into a kind of parable of his teachings.[41] Thus, while the very earliest sources seem to indicate no more than that the Buddha was relatively wealthy and privileged, later versions of the story tell how the Buddha was born into fabulous luxury as a prince whose father did the utmost to shield and protect his son from all life's unpleasantness, providing him with attendants who saw to his every need. Yet one day, while out enjoying the countryside, this privileged prince is confronted for the first time in his life by various sights that are shocking to him: first an old man, decrepit, leaning on a stick, his youth long vanished; secondly a sick man, in severe pain, lying in his own excrement and urine; and thirdly a funeral procession carrying a corpse to the cremation ground. Deeply affected by what he has seen, the young Gotama returns home to brood on the fact that his life of luxury and pleasure is lived overshadowed by old-age, sickness, and death. The moral of the story is a simple one: even if you have everything you could possibly want, you cannot escape the realities of old-age, sickness, and death. The story thus vividly illustrates what is the starting-point of Buddhist teaching: suffering is a fact, a reality that we cannot avoid. Even if we try to lose ourselves in life's undoubted pleasures, sooner

[40] On Buddhist cosmology more generally see Gethin, *Foundations of Buddhism*, 112–32.

[41] For an account and discussion of the Buddha as presented in a variety of ancient sources see John S. Strong, *The Buddha: A Short Biography* (Oxford, 2001).

or later we are going to have to face the fact that we, and those around us, will age, become sick, and die.

Buddhist teaching thus seeks to speak to that in us which is troubled by life. The Buddhist term for this is *dukkha*. The term *dukkha* is perhaps most literally rendered into English as 'pain'. Life's pains come in various shapes and sizes. There is the obvious pain and associated mental anguish of physical injury and sickness. There is also the pain of having that which we want to keep taken away from us, or that which we would prefer not to have at all thrust upon us. There is also the deeper pain of simply finding that even when we manage to get and hold on to the things we want, somehow, strangely, they do not bring us the happiness and contentment we thought they would. There is thus suffering that is simply pain, suffering that consists of change, and suffering that consists in the conditioned nature of things.

To return to the story of the Buddha's life: there is one other thing we are told that the young Gotama saw: a wandering ascetic with shaven head, wearing ochre robes. To the troubled prince who had lost his appetite for his life of luxury, the sight of an ascetic is an inspiration. Gotama resolves that he will leave home and pursue the religious life, the life of a wandering, homeless ascetic.

The life of the homeless wandering ascetic is often presented by the subsequent Buddhist tradition as the ideal way to pursue an answer to the questions posed by the problems of suffering. One early Buddhist source puts it like this: there are two kinds of quest—first the quest of ordinary life, when someone who is himself subject to old-age, sickness, and death dedicates his life to the pursuit of that which is also subject to old-age, sickness, and death; secondly the quest of the religious life, when someone who is subject to old-age, sickness, and death dedicates his life to seeking release from that which is subject to old-age, sickness, and death.

In theory and ideally, the life of the Buddhist monk (*bhikkhu*) or nun (*bhikkhunī*) is conceived as the life of the wandering homeless ascetic who has dedicated his or her life to the religious or spiritual quest. The life of the Buddhist monk or nun involves in the first place a turning away from and letting go of the pursuit of worldly pleasure in order to focus efforts in a different direction. The monk or nun's commitment to the religious quest is manifest in his or her appearance and simple lifestyle. Monks and nuns shave their heads and wear simple robes; for a dwelling, they should be content with the root of a tree; for food, with whatever is offered to them in alms. Their life-style is further defined by a monastic rule aimed at restraining certain kinds of behaviour: they are prohibited from all sexual activity, from killing living creatures, from taking what is not given, from lying and deception, from handling gold and silver, from overeating. Whether or not all Buddhist monks and nuns have at all times and in all places lived up to this ideal, the values embodied in this lifestyle have been and remain an inspiration for both Buddhist monks and nuns and also their supporters. Mention of the supporters of Buddhist monks and nuns brings us to the point that not all those who have found comfort in and been followers of the Buddha's teachings over the last two-and-a-half thousand years have been moved to leave behind entirely the quest for fulfilment in the pursuit of worldly aims.

It is sometimes implied that the ideal of the Buddhist monk or nun who turns his or her back on society in order to pursue a personal religious quest betrays an antisocial spirit, even a certain selfishness at the heart of Buddhism. Yet we should note that, even as Buddhist monks and nuns turn away from the values and aims that motivate much of ordinary secular society, their monastic rule forces them back into a relationship with society. Ideally a Buddhist monk or nun should eat only what has been offered to him or her by another; he or she should not store food or dig the ground. Thus the Buddhist monastic rule, far from encouraging isolation, independence, and self-sufficiency, forces the Buddhist monastic community into a position of dependence on society as a whole. Where there is no support for the monastic community, it cannot survive. Why might members of society who choose not to become monks and nuns give their support to those who do? Ultimately, because of a common set of shared values. Even though Buddhist laity remain to some degree committed to the pursuit of worldly secular aims, they recognize in the lifestyle of monks and nuns something that they themselves aspire to. The monks and nuns are a reminder of a set of values other than those of profit, fame and gain, and so on. They are a pointer to something beyond the endless routine, the cycle of day-to-day life. In return for the gift of material support, the monks and nuns give the gift of the Buddha's teaching.

The Buddhist quest for release from the pain of birth, old-age, sickness, and death has as its basis, then, a particular lifestyle and discipline that is exemplified by the Buddhist monk or nun. Yet something of that lifestyle can be incorporated into both a lay and monastic life: a monk and a layperson can undertake to live by the five precepts or rules of training: to refrain from killing living creatures, to refrain from taking what is not given, to refrain from sexual misconduct, to refrain from untrue speech, to refrain from intoxicants that bring about heedlessness. While these precepts are the basis of the Buddhist path, Buddhist teaching is more than merely a system of moral training. In order to bring the quest for release from suffering to its conclusion something more is required. This is, of course, once more illustrated by the story of the Buddha himself. After adopting the lifestyle of a wandering ascetic, he sought out various teachers and eventually followed a particular path of practice that brought him to awakening. And in order to understand this path we must first attempt to understand something of Buddhist theory.

As we have seen, prior to embarking on his religious quest Gotama the Buddha was confronted by the reality of life's pain and suffering. The reality of life's pain and suffering is sometimes likened to a disease from which we all suffer. The Buddha is then likened to a physician who diagnoses the disease, identifies its cause, assesses the possibility of cure, and then prescribes the appropriate medicine. So if suffering is the disease, what is its cause? The answer, in a word, is *taṇhā*— 'thirst' or 'craving'.

The suggestion is that deep in the minds of beings there is a greed or desire that manifests as an unquenchable thirst which is the principal condition for the arising of suffering. This thirst or craving takes different forms: I may crave objects, things, and possessions. Or I may crave to be some particular kind of person; I may crave fame and even immortality. Alternatively, I may bitterly and resentfully turn my back on ambition, craving to be a nobody; I may become depressed and long not to exist, wishing that I had never been born; in this state I may even take my own life. I may passionately believe that I possess an immortal soul and that I will exist after death; or I may be absolutely certain in my conviction that death will be the final end, and that I shall die and there will be no more of me. From the perspective of Buddhist thought, all these feelings, desires, and beliefs are the products of the workings of craving, and our attachment to them can in the long run only cause us suffering.

Of course, to crave in the way we do is perfectly natural: we think that when our craving is fulfilled we will find happiness. At this point it begins to become apparent just how and why, in the Buddhist view, craving leads to suffering. There is a discrepancy between our craving and the world we live in, between our expectations and the way things are. We want the world to be other than it is. Our craving is based on a fundamental misjudgement of the situation: a judgement that assumes that when our craving gets what it wants we will be happy, that when our craving possesses the objects of its desire we will be satisfied. But such a judgement assumes a world in which things are permanent, unchanging, stable, and reliable. But the world is simply not like that. In short, in craving we fail to see how things truly are, and in failing to see how things truly are we crave. Craving and ignorance become bound in a vicious circle: the more we crave, the more confused and muddled we become; and the more confused and muddled we become, the more we crave.

It follows from this that if only we could suspend our craving for a while, and still and calm our minds, we might begin to see things more clearly; and in seeing things more clearly we might find that our craving, our thirst, is quenched. This brings us to the topic of Buddhist meditation. The methods and techniques of Buddhist meditation are many and diverse, but one common way of presenting these techniques and methods is in terms of calm meditation and insight meditation.

Inasmuch as our minds are habitually restless with craving—chasing after objects, thoughts and ideas yet never finding contentment—it follows that in order to calm the mind we need to try to stop this restless flitting from object to object and anchor the mind to one simple object or idea. This is the primary task of calm meditation: to take a suitable object or idea and focus on that to the exclusion of other objects or ideas. The Buddhist tradition suggests a variety of meditation objects. One example is the breath. One early Buddhist text puts it like this: 'Just mindful, he breathes in. Just mindful, he breathes out. As he breathes in a long breath, he knows he is breathing in a long breath; as he breathes out a long breath, he knows he is breathing out a long breath. As he breathes in a short breath, he knows he is breathing in a short breath; as he breathes out a short breath, he knows he is breathing out a short breath.'[42] Anyone who

[42] M I 56; *Satipaṭṭhāna-sutta*, translated in full below.

tries such an exercise for more than a few seconds will find that it is not as easy as it may sound. Soon our minds are wandering and we are not thinking of the breath at all. According to the theory of calm meditation, there are in our minds particular mental obstacles to stilling and calming the mind. In the earliest Buddhist sources these are often identified as five in number: desire for the objects of the senses, hostility, dullness and lethargy, agitation and worry, and finally doubt.[43] As long as we have not succeeded in overcoming these, our minds will not find even temporary stillness and peace. Of course, such mental obstacles are not exclusively the obstacles to meditation practice.

Anyone who has sat down to apply his or her mind to some task—understanding a difficult intellectual concept, learning a musical instrument, learning another language—has grappled with the obstacles I have just mentioned. First there is the problem that we would rather be doing something else—watching a film, reading a novel, going out with friends. This is desire for the objects of the senses. Then there is the problem that everything seems to be conspiring to make it difficult for us to get on with our task—the neighbours or children are making too much noise, the room is too cold or hot, the task has not been explained to us properly. We find ourselves getting irritable—the second obstacle in the form of hostility. Then, as we contemplate the task our eyelids begin to feel heavy and a little rest seems just what we need: dullness and lethargy. Strangely though, if someone were to knock on our door at that very moment and suggest some other, more interesting activity, our sleepiness and tiredness would vanish in a moment. Yet suppose we persevere with our original task and begin to make some progress. Suddenly we become overexcited at our success; and then when the task throws up further difficulties and complexities this excitement seems premature; we become dispirited and anxious about it. We experience the ups and downs of agitation and worry. Finally we begin to doubt the point of the whole enterprise. Such are the five obstacles that the practitioner of calm meditation must confront.

But what happens when the meditator perseveres and succeeds in overcoming these obstacles and hindrances? According to the ancient accounts, as the meditator's mind becomes increasingly absorbed in

[43] On the five hindrances, see the full translation of the *Sāmaññaphala-sutta* below (D I 71–3).

the object of contemplation, the meditator experiences deeper and deeper contentment and happiness. The suggestion seems to be that, far from needing a great variety of objects and ideas to make our minds happy, if we simplify our minds, if we bring our minds to rest on one simple object, we begin to discover that our minds were in fact content and happy all along. To quote just one of the ancient similes for the attainment of this kind of meditation: 'It is as if there were a pool where water sprang up, but which had no water flowing into it from the east, the west, the north, or the south . . . Now when the cool waters sprang up in that pool they would suffuse, fill, soak, and drench that same pool with cool water so that no part of that pool would be untouched by the cool water.'[44]

The happiness and contentment the mind finds in this kind of mental absorption is associated with a clarity of mind. The mind can be compared to a bowl of water. Now the mind possessed and overcome by desire for the objects of the senses, by ill-will, by dullness and lethargy, by agitation and worry, by doubt is like a bowl of water that is mixed with colouring; that has been heated on a fire and is steaming and boiling; that is covered with moss and leaves; that is ruffled by the wind, disturbed, stirred round, and rippling; that is dirty, unclear, muddy, and placed in the dark. A person with good eyesight looking down into such a bowl of water for the reflection of his own face would not know and see it as it is. On the other hand, if a person with good eyesight should look down into a bowl of water that is unmixed with colouring; that has not been heated on a fire, is not steaming and boiling; that is not covered with moss and leaves; that is not ruffled by the wind, but is undisturbed, not stirred round, not rippling; that is clear, bright, clean, and placed in the light; then he would know and see the reflection of his face just as it is. The state of meditation achieved by calm meditation thus allows the possibility of seeing things more clearly. This brings us to what the later Buddhist tradition often refers to as insight meditation.

If, according to Buddhist teaching, we are ordinarily befuddled by the sleep of ignorance, which means that we do not see things as they truly are, then what is it that we are supposed to see when we awake from this sleep to knowledge and understanding? How are things truly? Again, none of the various traditions of Buddhism would give

[44] D I 74–5 (*Sāmaññaphala-sutta*).

precisely the same answer to this question, but there are some common themes. Because of craving and ignorance we tend to be taken in by superficial appearances. We are, as it were, immature and emotionally naive and fail to look beneath the surface. We see and experience, therefore, a world that consists of substantial objects and beings. But, so it is said, under closer scrutiny the substantial nature of things proves elusive; this world of substantial objects and beings begins to evaporate. Just as modern physics tells us that what we experience as a table is in reality a pattern of subatomic particles, and that these 'particles' are not so much little bits but rather forces of some sort, so too the Buddha tells us that what we think of as 'me', 'you', 'others' are rather patterns of mental and physical events. In ultimate reality there is no 'I' or 'you'. Words such as 'I' or 'self' or 'person' are mere conventional labels for patterns of thoughts, feelings, desires, and emotions. There is no separate 'I' or 'self' apart from the thoughts, feelings, desires, and emotions; there is no separate 'I' or 'self' having the thoughts, feelings, desires, and emotions. In truth, the world, the universe, consists not of substantial beings or entities, but of evanescent fleeting mental and physical events. And this, it is claimed, is what the Buddha came to see directly in the stillness of his meditation one full-moon night some two-and-a-half thousand years ago. This is what the meditator who follows in the path of the Buddha hopes to come to see directly too.

According to the ancient accounts, as the meditator contemplates and investigates the things that constitute the world, he finds not a world consisting of enduring and solid objects, but rather things that vanish almost as soon as they appear—like dewdrops at sunrise, like a bubble on water, like a line drawn on water, like a mustard-seed placed on the point of an awl, like a flash of lightning. Moreover, these things lack substance and always elude one's grasp—like a mirage, a conjuring trick, a dream, the circle formed by a whirling fire brand, a fairy city, foam, or like the trunk of a banana tree (which lacks any heartwood). There is nothing to grasp or hold on to. And so the meditator, like the Buddha, does the only thing he or she can do—and lets go. The meditator stops craving and lets go of everything—even what is perhaps the ultimate possession, his or her own 'self'. For, on the Buddhist view, as long as we cling to 'self' we are staking our own individual claim to some bit of reality, to some part of the universe as 'mine'. We are, as it were, saying: 'This is mine, not yours. Keep off!' So where does this leave the meditator? Lost in some dark nothingness, some meaningless void? On the contrary, says the Buddhist tradition; in this ultimate and final letting go of everything, the meditator finds an even profounder peace and happiness. In fact this is the only true peace and happiness there is. This is the peace and happiness of *nibbāna* (Skt: *nirvāṇa*)—the peace and happiness of the unconditioned, where there is no birth, old-age, sickness, and death.

Paradoxically, in letting go of the 'self', of the conceit 'I am', in ceasing to strive to make our-*selves* happy, we find what we have been craving all along: true and lasting happiness. But not only is this good for us, it is good for others. In letting go of our-*selves*, of the conceit 'I am', we can at last truly act *self*-lessly, for the benefit of others. And, of course, this is precisely how the Buddhist tradition sees the Buddha acting. For forty-five years after he attained awakening he wandered the plains of eastern India teaching others and gathering a following. In his eightieth year it is said that he died in a small town called Kusinārā. So what became of the Buddha when he died? Certainly, it is said that he is not reborn in the normal way. One who has gained awakening like the Buddha escapes finally the perpetual round of birth, death, and rebirth known as *saṃsāra*. But does he somehow even now exist in the peace and happiness of nirvana? The early Buddhist tradition says that this question cannot be answered in categorical terms. The Buddha and all those who have reached awakening and died are strictly 'untraceable'. One cannot say that they exist; one cannot say that they do not exist; one cannot say that they both exist and do not exist; one cannot say that they neither exist nor do not exist.

Whatever the precise metaphysical status of the Buddha, it is clear that one thing remains, and that is what the Buddhist tradition calls the *dhamma* (or, in Sanskrit, *dharma*). The term *dhamma* refers in the first place to the Buddha's teachings. But *dhamma* is not understood merely as a set of doctrines and theories contained in written texts. The *dhamma* is also the practices—the Buddha's prescriptions for how we should behave and what needs to be done in order to bring about a true understanding of the way things are. And this brings us to a third sense of *dhamma*. The *dhamma* is the profound truth about the world that the Buddha himself realized on the night of his awakening, and to which his teachings show the way. *Dhamma* is thus at once the Buddha's teachings, practices, and realization. According to the Buddhist understanding, the Buddha's teachings and practices will eventually, with the passing of time, disappear from the world. But the *dhamma*, in the sense of the ultimate truth about the world, remains whether or not there is any Buddha in the world who sees it and teaches it. And although the Buddha Gotama's teachings will disappear and be lost, sooner or later the next Buddha will come and once more discover that truth and again teach it to the world. Indeed, according to Buddhist tradition Metteyya (Skt: Maitreya), a being far advanced on the path to awakening is even now waiting in one of the realms of the gods until the teachings of the present Buddha have disappeared. Then it will be time for Metteyya to be reborn in the human realm and become the next Buddha.

NOTE ON THE TEXT AND TRANSLATION

In presenting a selection from the Pali canon I have made the decision to present complete suttas. Over the last hundred years or so a number of anthologies of Buddhist scriptures including Pali suttas have been published. Quite often editors and translators have resorted to giving short extracts. While there is nothing wrong with this practice as a means of providing in a convenient single volume a comprehensive survey of Buddhist teachings as presented in the suttas themselves, it does obscure the literary quality of the suttas.[1] The suttas of the Pali canon have been composed as relatively short literary pieces that are complete works in their own right; characteristically, a particular Buddhist teaching is framed in a particular narrative that draws out and adds depth to the meaning of the ideas presented.

Any modern translator of Pali texts is thus faced with the problem of how to present in the form of a modern book texts that were originally composed and performed orally. We are used today to reading silently in private, but things were not always so, even in cultures where the book has been predominant. Reading aloud was probably common even until quite recently, at least until the advent of radio and television.[2] So in dealing with repetition I have had in mind the possibility of reading aloud, and would suggest that this is necessary to appreciate the particular literary quality of the suttas. As I indicated above, the MSS and editions themselves frequently resort to abbreviation, although they are not always consistent in this respect; modern western editors and translators have tended to be the most radical, such that on occasion they have provoked protest from traditionalists.[3] While I too have in places introduced abbreviations not found in the PTS editions of the texts, I have avoided the

[1] On the tendency of modern scholars to treat Pali suttas as pieced together rather than redacted wholes, see S. Collins, *Nirvana and Other Buddhist Felicities* (Cambridge, 1998), 480–1.

[2] On these questions generally, see William A. Graham, *Beyond the Written Word: Oral Aspects of Scripture in the History of Religion* (Cambridge, 1987); see pp. 32–3 specifically on the question of silent reading.

[3] See Norman, *A Philological Approach to Buddhism*, 113.

kinds of device that have sometimes been used by translators (ellipsis that interrupts the grammar of sentences, the use of phrases such as 'the paragraph above is here repeated in full'); even in silent reading such devices tend to interrupt the flow of reading, and hence understanding and appreciation, as we struggle to work out exactly what is repeated.

All the suttas presented in this volume have been translated into English before, some (such as the *Satipaṭṭhāna-sutta*) many times, others (such as the *Mahāsudassana-sutta*) perhaps only two or three times, but in comparison with translators of Homer or Virgil or the Jewish and Christian biblical texts, the translator of Pali texts is exploring relatively uncharted territory with the aid of the limited materials bequeathed by a small band of pioneers. Of course, given where they set out from little more than 150 years ago, what they achieved in less than a century remains truly impressive, and sometimes it seems that most of us at least simply follow in their footsteps, hardly venturing into new territory. I would thus hesitate to claim any great advances in understanding for the present set of translations. Nevertheless, in certain places I do believe I have—either on the basis of my own understanding or perhaps more often on the basis of what has been pointed out by others in the scholarly literature—been able to correct some mistakes made by earlier translators. No doubt there are other mistakes that have gone unnoticed and been repeated. I should like to think that I have not introduced new mistakes, but probably this is a vain hope.

More generally, my aim has been to produce a readable and accessible English rendering. But the ideas and concepts of early Buddhism are sometimes technical and often unfamiliar to western readers. At the same time, certain English words have acquired the status of standard renderings of particular Buddhist technical terms, and have thereby become familiar as Buddhist terms for those in the know. This has led to a situation where some complain of a tendency among translators of Pali and Sanskrit Buddhist texts to produce incomprehensible translations in 'Buddhist hybrid English' (after an expression used to characterize the way Buddhist Hybrid Sanskrit fails to conform to the norms of classical Sanskrit). I have done my best to avoid over-literalness and lapsing into Buddhist hybrid English by asking myself, as Margaret Cone recommends: 'What would an Indian hearer have understood from this passage? . . . what is he saying?'[4] But inevitably there is a question of balance between preserving something of the idiom in which ancient Buddhists chose to express themselves, and achieving patterns of expression familiar to the native speaker of English. Some may think I have gone too far, others not far enough.

I have though aimed at full translation, and for the most part kept my translation free of technical Pali terms. Of course, some of the technical vocabulary of Indian culture and religion has found its way into the English language and into the *Oxford English Dictionary* (*OED*). Where this is the case I have sometimes, but not always, used the Pali or Sanskrit term in one of its accepted English spellings, even where the definitions offered in English dictionaries may leave something to be desired from the perspective of strict Buddhist understanding. Thus we have 'brahman' (*brāhmaṇa*) rather than 'a member of the priestly class'; the awakened disciples of the Buddha, the Buddhist 'worthy ones' or 'saints', remain simply 'arahats'; the final goal of the Buddhist path, the escape from the round of rebirth, is left as 'nibbana' (since this Pali spelling is recognized by the *OED* alongside the more familiar Sanskrit 'nirvana'). Another word now found in the *OED*, and which I have for the most part left untranslated, is 'Tathāgata', an epithet of the Buddha, and the term commonly used by the Buddha apparently to refer to himself. The precise significance of the term is not clear, but in certain contexts it seems to be used more generally to refer to anyone who has achieved awakening, and in a sense close to its literal meaning of 'one like this' or 'one who has reached this state'. Another, less frequent epithet of the Buddha, namely *sugata* or 'one who has reached a happy or good state', I have rendered as 'the Happy One'.

Another important epithet of the Buddha is *bhagavat*. This is the term normally used in Buddhist writings to refer to the Buddha. It means literally 'possessing good fortune', but early in Indian literature came to be used as an honorific title for gods and holy men. In later literature it comes especially to be used as a term for 'the Lord' in the sense of the divine or God, as in *Bhagavad-gītā* or 'song of the

[4] Margaret Cone, '*caveat lector*', *Journal of the Pali Text Society*, 29 (2007), 95–106. See also P. J. Griffiths, 'Buddhist Hybrid English: Some Notes on Philology and Hermeneutics for Buddhologists', *Journal of the International Association of Buddhist Studies*, 4 (1981), 17–32; K. R. Norman, 'On Translating from Pāli', *Collected Papers*, III (Oxford, 1992), 60–81.

Lord', that is, Kṛṣṇa as an incarnation of God, the supreme Viṣṇu. For some, the English 'Blessed One' might suggest the blessing of God or a priest, yet a glance in the *OED* reminds us that the word 'blessed' in English has a long history of being used in such senses as 'adorable', 'happy', and 'fortunate', and enough of this usage survives in modern English to make it an appropriate translation.

Sometimes even where the word is acceptable in English, I have chosen to translate; thus *buddha* appears quite frequently (though not always) as 'awakened'. One term that is given in the *OED* in both its Sanskritic and Pali spelling is *dharma* or *dhamma*. This is, of course, a term of some complexity and depth. It is, I would argue, used in the Pali texts in a number of distinct senses which at the same time refer to and assume each other.[5] In the first place, *dhamma* is the fundamental basis or nature of things generally, the Truth about the way things are. Secondly, it is the behaviour, the practice, prescribed by the Buddha in order to achieve a direct realization of the Truth about the way things are; *dhamma* is the Teaching of the Buddha. And thirdly, *dhammas* are the good qualities that should be developed in order to progress along the Buddhist path. Fourthly, a *dhamma* is the fundamental basis or nature of things taken individually; *dhammas* are the particular qualities that together are reality. Buddhist writings are at pains, however, to point out that the fundamental basis or nature of things is not some underlying, immanent absolute, but rather the ultimate quality of things is simply that they rise and fall in dependence on each other. Nonetheless, realization of this quality is the ultimate freedom from suffering. These meanings of *dhamma* are not always mutually exclusive in a given context, but having made the decision to translate *dhamma* in all contexts, I have nonetheless opted for one of 'Truth', 'teaching', 'practice', or 'quality'. To some my choice will no doubt appear arbitrary, and sometimes even wrong. Certainly, in some cases I might have chosen otherwise.

Some Indian terms, while found in the *OED*, remain relatively unfamiliar. Thus, for example, despite the occurrence of both 'bhikku' and 'bhikshu' in the dictionary, I have rendered *bhikkhu* as 'monk'. Some might complain that this is misleading, since a *bhikkhu*

[5] See R. Gethin, 'He who sees *dhamma* sees *dhammas*: Dhamma in Early Buddhism', *Journal of Indian Philosophy*, 32 (2004), 513–42.

is not precisely the same as a Christian monk. True, but I have judged that to talk of Buddhist 'monks' is the norm among English speakers, and that 'monk' conveys a sufficiently meaningful sense of what a *bhikkhu* is.

Another problem facing translators of Pali texts is the treatment of honorifics and forms of address. The tendency in the modern cultures where English is the first language is increasingly to do away with titles and surnames ('Mrs Smith', 'Dr Jones') as tied to an outmoded and even 'politically incorrect' social hierarchy. All exchanges, whatever the context, become reduced to first-name—or even nickname—familiarity ('Sue' and 'Bob'), often from the outset. The Pali suttas were composed in a culture where this was not so, where forms of respectful address indicated social status and standing relative to the person addressed. Thus, kings are addressed by some as *deva* or 'god', which I have rendered as 'lord', by others, such as the Buddha, as *mahārāja* which I have rendered as 'your majesty', though it might have been retained as sufficiently familiar in English. The term *āvuso* is a polite form of address that nevertheless indicates that the speaker claims a rank that is at least equal to the person addressed; thus it is commonly used in the Pali texts when those who are not followers of the Buddha address the Buddha. Among Buddhist monks it is only to be used by a senior monk addressing a more junior monk. Brahmans, on the other hand, always address the Buddha as '*bho* Gotama', using the honorific *bho* and his clan name; one might render this as 'Mr Gotama', except that its effect would be comical. Followers of the Buddha address monks as *bhante* without the addition of any name. Such forms of address cannot be translated literally; like the English 'Mr', they have in Pali lost any meaning apart from their use as honorifics. I have chosen to render *āvuso* as 'friend', and both *bho* and *bhante* as 'sir'.

Pali tends to repeat titles in full every time a person is mentioned. Thus, in the first sutta translated in this volume the king is always 'King Ajātasattu of Magadha, son of the princess of Videha'. Such repetition seems unnatural and excessive in English, so I have reduced it to 'King Ajātasattu of Magadha'. Similarly, Pali tends to repeat vocative forms of address and the names of those addressed in a way that again seems unnatural and excessive in English, so these are sometimes omitted.

There are no standard critical editions of the texts of the Pali canon. Like other ancient Indian languages, Pali is also not associated with one particular system of writing and has for many centuries been written in a variety of scripts. These all ultimately derive from the Brahmī script used by the emperor Aśoka for his inscriptions in the third century BCE. Most surviving Pali manuscripts are written in Sinhala, Burmese, or Mūl (Cambodian) script. The first printed editions of Pali texts were produced in the nineteenth century, and from 1882 the Pali Text Society (PTS), founded by T. W. Rhys Davids (1843–1922) in 1881, began publishing European editions of the works of the Pali canon and its commentaries transliterated into a Roman alphabet expanded by the use of diacritical marks to reflect Indian scripts. By the end of the first decade of the twentieth century the PTS had published editions of most of the works of the canon. These were pioneering editions, often based on one or two manuscripts that happened to be available. While some have since been revised and corrected, most have not. Important Asian editions of the Pali canon have been published in Siam in Thai script (King Chulalongkorn's edition of 1893–4 and the Syāmaraṭṭhassa Tepiṭakaṃ of 1925–8), in Burma in Burmese script (the Chaṭṭhasaṃgīti or Sixth Council edition of 1956–62), and in Ceylon in Sinhala script (the Buddha Jayanti Tripiṭaka of 1957–89).[6] The last three of these editions have also recently been digitized. Nevertheless, since the PTS editions have remained widely available and are kept in print to this day by the Society, it is these, despite their imperfections, that have become the scholarly basis for study of the Pali canon. The present translation is thus based in the first place on the edition of the Pali text as published by the PTS. I have, however, also referred to Asian editions, and where I have preferred a reading from these that significantly affects the translation I have drawn attention to this in the notes. To allow cross-referencing with the original Pali text and other translations, the pagination of the PTS edition of the Pali text is given in the margins. An asterisk in the text refers to the Explanatory Notes at the back of the book.

[6] On editions of Pali texts see Günter Grönbold, Karl Dachs, and Renate Stephan, *Die Worte des Buddha in den Sprachen der Welt* (Munich, 2005), 31–59.

SELECT BIBLIOGRAPHY

Adikaram, E. W., *Early History of Buddhism in Ceylon* (Migoda, Ceylon, 1946).

Allon, M., 'The Oral Composition and Transmission of Early Buddhist Texts', in P. Connolly and S. Hamilton (eds.), *Indian Insights: Buddhism, Brahmanism and Bhakti* (London, 1997), 39–61.

Bailey, Greg, and Ian Mabbett, *The Sociology of Early Buddhism* (Cambridge, 2003).

Basham, A. L., *History and Doctrines of the Ājīvikas* (London, 1951).

—— *The Wonder That Was India: A Survey of the History and Culture of the Indian Subcontinent before the Coming of the Muslims*, 3rd edn. (London, 1967; repr. 1982).

Bechert, Heinz (ed.), *The Dating of the Historical Buddha*, 3 vols. (Göttingen, 1991–7).

Bodhi, Bhikkhu (trans.), *The Connected Discourses of the Buddha: A New Translation of the Saṃyutta Nikāya* (Boston, 2000).

Bryant, F., and Laurie L. Patton (eds.), *The Indo-Aryan Controversy: Evidence and Inference in Indian History* (London, 2005).

Burlingame, Eugene Watson (trans.), *Buddhist Legends, Translated from the Original Pali Text of the Dhammapada Commentary*, 3 vols. (London, 1921; repr. 1995).

Collins, S., *Selfless Persons: Imagery and Thought in Theravāda Buddhism* (Cambridge, 1982).

—— 'On the Very Idea of the Pāli Canon', *Journal of the Pāli Text Society*, 15 (1990), 89–126.

—— 'Notes on Some Oral Aspects of Pali Literature', *Indo-Iranian Journal*, 35 (1992), 121–35.

—— *Nirvana and Other Buddhist Felicities: Utopias of the Pali Imaginaire* (Cambridge, 1998).

Cone, Margaret, '*caveat lector*', *Journal of the Pali Text Society*, 29 (2007), 95–106.

Conningham, Robin, 'The Archaeology of Buddhism', in Timothy Insoll (ed.), *Archaeology and World Religion* (London, 2001), 61–95.

Cousins, L. S., 'Pāli Oral Literature', in P. Denwood and A. Piatigorsky (eds.), *Buddhist Studies: Ancient and Modern* (London, 1983), 1–11.

—— 'The Dating of the Historical Buddha: A Review Article', *Journal of the Royal Asiatic Society*, 6 (1996), 57–63.

Cowell, E. B., *et al.* (trans.), *The Jātaka, or Stories of the Buddha's Former Births* (London, 1895–1907; repr. 1990).

Dundas, Paul, *The Jains*, 2nd edn. (London, 2000).
Flood, Gavin, *An Introduction to Hinduism* (Cambridge, 1996).
Geiger, Wilhelm (trans.), *Mahāvaṃsa or the Great Chronicle of Ceylon* (London, 1912; repr. 1980).
Gethin, Rupert, *The Buddhist Path to Awakening: A Study of the Bodhi-Pakkhiyā Dhammā* (Leiden, 1992; repr. Oxford, 2001).
—— *The Foundations of Buddhism* (Oxford, 1998).
Gombrich, R. F., *Theravāda Buddhism: A Social History from Ancient Benares to Modern Colombo* (London, 1988).
Graham, William A., *Beyond the Written Word: Oral Aspects of Scripture in the History of Religion* (Cambridge, 1987).
Griffiths, P. J., 'Buddhist Hybrid English: Some Notes on Philology and Hermeneutics for Buddhologists', *Journal of the International Association of Buddhist Studies*, 4 (1981), 17–32.
Grönbold, Günter, Karl Dachs, and Renate Stephan, *Die Worte des Buddha in den Sprachen der Welt: The Words of the Buddha in the Languages of the World: Tipiṭaka, Tripiṭaka, Dazangjing, Kanjur* (Munich, 2005).
Hare, E. M., and F. L. Woodward, *The Book of the Gradual Sayings (Aṅguttara-Nikāya) or Numbered Suttas*, 5 vols. (London, 1923–6; repr. 1994–5).
Harrison, Paul, 'A Brief History of the Tibetan bKa' 'gyur', in José Ignacio Cabezón and Roger R. Jackson (eds.), *Tibetan Literature: Studies in Genre* (Ithaca, NY, 1996), 70–94.
von Hinüber, Oskar, *A Handbook of Pāli Literature* (Berlin, 1996).
—— 'Chips from Buddhist Workshops: Scribes and Manuscripts from Northern Thailand', *Journal of the Pali Text Society*, 22 (1996), 35–57.
—— 'On the History of the Name of the Pali Language', *Selected Papers*, 2nd edn. (Oxford, 2005), 76–90.
Horner, I. B. (trans.), *The Collection of Middle-Length Sayings (Majjhima-Nikāya)*, 3 vols. (London, 1954–9).
—— (trans.), *Milinda's Questions*, 2 vols. (London, 1963–4).
Lamotte, Étienne, *History of Indian Buddhism, from the Origins to the Śaka Era*, trans. Sara Webb-Boin (Louvain, 1988).
Ñāṇamoli, Bhikkhu (trans.), *The Path of Purification (Visuddhimagga)*, 2nd edn. (Colombo, 1964; repr. Kandy, 1975).
—— and Bhikkhu Bodhi (trans.), *The Middle-Length Discourses of the Buddha: A New Translation of the Majjhima Nikāya* (Boston, 1995).
Norman, K. R., *Pāli Literature: Including the Canonical Literature in Prakrit and Sanskrit of all the Hīnayāna Schools of Buddhism* (Wiesbaden, 1983).
—— *A Philological Approach to Buddhism*, 2nd edn. (Lancaster, 2006).
—— *Collected Papers*, 8 vols. (Oxford, 1990–2007).

Norman, K.R. (trans.), *The Group of Discourses (Suttanipāta)*, 2nd edn. (Oxford, 2001).

—— (trans.), *Elders' Verses (Theragāthā and Therīgāthā)*, 2 vols., 2nd edn. (Lancaster, 2007).

Nyanaponika Thera and Bhikkhu Bodhi (trans.), *Numerical Discourses of the Buddha: An Anthology of Suttas from the Aṅguttara Nikāya* (Walnut Creek, Calif., 1999).

Olivelle, Patrick (trans.), *Upaniṣads* (Oxford, 1996).

Pande, G. C., *Studies in the Origins of Buddhism*, 2nd edn. (Delhi, 1974).

Rahula, Walpola, *History of Buddhism in Ceylon: The Anurādhapura Period, 3rd century BC–10th century AD*, 2nd edn. (Colombo, 1966; repr. Dehiwala, 1993).

Renou, Louis, and Jean Filliozat, *L'Inde classique*, 2 vols. (Paris, 1947–57).

Rhys Davids, C. A. F., and F. L. Woodward (trans.), *The Book of the Kindred Sayings (Saṃyutta-Nikāya) or Grouped Suttas*, 5 vols. (London, 1917–30; repr. 1990–5).

Rhys Davids, T. W. and C. A. F. (trans.), *Dialogues of the Buddha*, 3 vols. (London, 1899–1921; repr. 1995).

Salomon, Richard, *Ancient Buddhist Scrolls from Gandhāra* (London, 1999).

Schopen, Gregory, *Bones, Stones, and Buddhist Monks: Collected Papers on the Archaeology, Epigraphy, and Texts of Monastic Buddhism in India* (Honolulu, 1997).

Strong, John S., *The Buddha: A Short Biography* (Oxford, 2001).

Walshe, Maurice (trans.), *The Long Discourses of the Buddha: A Translation of the Dīgha Nikāya* (Boston, 1995).

Wijayaratna, Mohan, *Buddhist Monastic Life: According to the Texts of the Theravāda Tradition* (Cambridge, 1990).

Further Reading in Oxford World's Classics

The Dhammapada, trans. John Ross Carter and Mahinda Palihawadana.

Śāntideva, *The Bodhicaryāvatāra*, trans. Kate Crosby and Andrew Skilton.

NOTE ON THE PRONUNCIATION OF PALI AND SANSKRIT

Pali and Sanskrit are written in a variety of scripts which are in principle phonetic, assigning one character in the script to each distinctive sound. Since both languages use more than twenty-six sounds, in order to transliterate Pali and Sanskrit into the Roman script the number of letters must be extended by the addition of diacritical marks. The following is intended only as an approximate guide; for a more detailed account of Sanskrit phonology (which is essentially similar to that of Pali) see, for example, Michael Coulson, *Sanskrit: An Introduction to the Classical Language*, 2nd edn. (London, 1992; repr. 2006), 4–16.

Pali/Sanskrit	**as in English**
a	h*u*t
ā	f*a*r
i	s*i*t
ī	s*ee*t
u	p*u*t
ū	fl*u*te
r̥	*ri*sk
e	s*a*y
ai	s*i*gh
o	h*o*pe
au	s*ou*nd
ṃ	nasalizes preceding vowel, as in French *bon*
g	*g*ive (never as in '*g*iant')
ṅ	a*n*ger
c	*ch*urch (never as in '*c*at' or 'pa*c*e')
ñ	pu*n*ch, ca*ny*on
s	*s*it (never as in 'dog*s*')

Consonants have an unaspirated and aspirated form; the latter is indicated in the Roman alphabet by the addition of an 'h'; thus, for example, *kh* is pronounced as in 'bac*kh*and', *gh* as in 'eg*gh*ead', *th* as in 'righ*th*and' (never as in 'wi*th*'), *ph* as in 'to*p h*eavy' (never as in *ph*oto), etc.

The retroflex sounds *ṭ*, *ṭh*, *ḍ*, *ḍh*, *ṇ* should properly be distinguished from the dental *t*, *th*, *d*, *dh*, *n*: the latter are pronounced with the tip of the tongue placed against the back of the upper front teeth, while the former are pronounced with the tip of the tongue striking the roof the mouth further back; in practice this distinction is rather difficult for speakers of European languages to maintain as are the distinctions between *l* and *ḷ* (both can be pronounced as in '*l*ord') and the palatal and retroflex sibilants *ś* and *ṣ* (which can both be pronounced as in '*sh*ip').

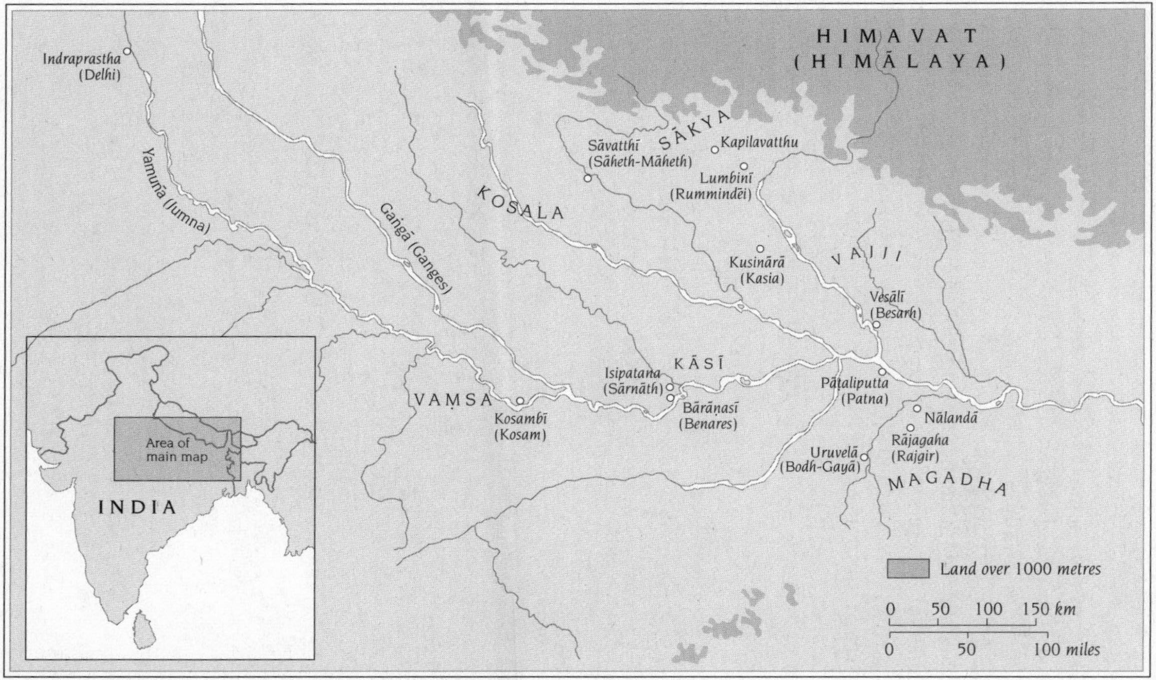

The Ganges basin at the time of the Buddha

SAYINGS OF THE BUDDHA

FROM THE COLLECTION OF LONG SAYINGS

(Dīgha-nikāya)

THE FRUITS OF THE ASCETIC LIFE

SĀMAÑÑAPHALA-SUTTA (D I 47–86)

Introduction

This, the second discourse of the 'collection of long sayings' of the Buddha, is placed by tradition towards the end of the Buddha's life. The bulk of the sutta takes the form of a dialogue between King Ajātasattu of Magadha and the Buddha. Ajātasattu is known also from Jain and Hindu sources. Considerable narrative tension at the beginning of the sutta derives from the fact that the listeners know that King Ajātasattu has been an associate of the monk Devadatta who, as an early Buddhist tradition tells us, sought to challenge the Buddha for authority over the Saṅgha and indeed on several occasions even attempted to kill him.[1] Encouraged by Devadatta, Ajātasattu took the throne of Magadha and killed his father, King Bimbisāra. He is thus a deeply troubled man, tormented in his sleep by disturbing dreams;[2] he is in desperate need of some means of salving his guilty conscience. At the opening of this sutta we find this king seated outside on a beautiful, still, moonlit night which, it seems, only has the effect of heightening his own sense of inner torment. His ministers, eager perhaps to please a potentially dangerous master, nervously suggest the names of various religious teachers he might visit, not daring, in view of the king's past, to suggest the Buddha.[3] But, as we presently find out, Ajātasattu has heard what these other well-known religious teachers of his day have to say, and he has not been impressed. In fact it is precisely a meeting with the Buddha that he desires; but, given his past conduct, he feels in need of some help in approaching the Buddha. Finally Jīvaka Komārabhacca, the royal physician and one of the great lay supporters (*upāsaka*) of the Buddha and his monks, comes to his rescue.

The six religious teachers whom it is suggested King Ajātasattu might visit are usually referred to in early Buddhist texts as a group; each is represented as making a claim to 'direct knowledge' (*abhiññā*) (D II 150–1; M I 198). Collectively they come to be referred to by the Buddhist tradition as the six *titthiyas* (Skt: *tīrthika*), a term which is often rendered 'heretic', but which seems to be short for *añña-titthiya*, meaning strictly only 'belonging to a religious sect or school other than one's own'. Three

[1] Vin II 184–203.

[2] Sv 140.

[3] The ancient commentary records a slightly different motivation on the part of the king's ministers: each is eager to promote his own religious teacher (Sv 142).

of the teachers (Pūraṇa Kassapa, Makkhali Gosāla, and Pakudha Kaccāyana) are to be associated with the ancient Indian religion of Ājīvikism, which taught a doctrine of strict determinism (*niyati*), and flourished at least down to the fourteenth century.[4] Ajita Kesakambalin is associated with the materialist doctrine of the Lokāyata or Cārvāka system, known from other Indian sources; Nigaṇṭha Nātaputta is none other than Mahāvīra, the historical founder of Jainism; finally Sañjaya Belaṭṭhiputta expounds a kind of scepticism that refuses to commit to any proposition.

At the heart of the discourse is an exposition of the progressive stages of the Buddha's path: the cultivation of good conduct, the four stages of absorption (*jhāna*), the various direct knowledges (*abhiññā*) culminating in the knowledge of suffering, its arising, its cessation, and the path leading to its cessation (i.e. the four *ariya-sacca* or 'noble truths') which constitutes 'awakening' (*bodhi*). This is the classic early account of the Buddhist path, repeated in full in ten of the thirteen suttas of the first volume of the Dīgha-nikāya and, with some variation, in a number of suttas of the Majjhima-nikāya.[5]

The sutta sets this account of the path in a framework which presents it as an answer to a basic question (here posed by Ajātasattu): why embark on the difficult and demanding life of an ascetic? The answer the sutta seeks to give is, in short, not because it promises rewards after death, but because, more surely than any other way of life, it brings with it a secure happiness here and now: the freedom of the life of a religious wanderer or ascetic (*samaṇa*); the happiness of a guilt-free conscience (*anavajja-sukha*) that comes with a life lived in accordance with moral precepts; the happiness of the composed mind (*avyāseka-sukha*) of one who is mindful in all he does; the joy, happiness, and peace of the *jhānas*; such extraordinary abilities (*iddhi*) that come with mastery of the *jhānas* as multiplying one's body, making oneself invisible, passing through walls, walking on water, flying through the air; and finally, the direct knowledge that one is freed from the endless cycle of rebirth.

This is what I have heard.* Once the Blessed One was staying in Rājagaha in the mango grove of Jīvaka Komārabhacca* with a great

[4] See A. L. Basham, *History and Doctrine of the Ājīvikas* (London, 1951).

[5] In the Dīgha-nikāya see the *Ambaṭṭha-*, *Soṇadaṇḍa-*, *Kūṭadanta-*, *Mahāli-*, *Jaliya-*, *Kevaddha-*, and *Lohicca-suttas*; the *Poṭṭhapāda-* and *Tevijja-suttas* also in the main follow this scheme, departing from it only after the account of the fourth *jhāna*, where they insert descriptions of the four formless attainments and 'sublime ways of living' (*brahma-vihāra*) respectively. In the Majjhima-nikāya see the *Cūḷahatthipadopama-*, *Mahātaṇhāsaṅkhāya-*, *Kandaraka-*, *Chabbisodhana-*, and *Dantabhūmi-suttas*.

company of monks—twelve hundred and fifty monks.* It was the occasion of the observance day known as White Lotus,* the fifteenth day at the end of the fourth month; and on that full-moon night King Ajātasattu of Magadha, son of the princess of Videha,* was seated up on the roof of his fine palace surrounded by his ministers. Now on that observance day King Ajātasattu of Magadha breathed a sigh: 'Delightful indeed is this moonlit night! Beautiful indeed is this moonlit night! Lovely indeed is this moonlit night! Peaceful indeed is this moonlit night! Auspicious indeed is this moonlit night! What ascetic or brahman might we visit tonight so that our heart might be set at rest?'

At these words one of the ministers said to King Ajātasattu of Magadha: 'There is, lord, Pūraṇa Kassapa. He has a company and a following and is the teacher of that following; he is well known, of some repute, one who has found a way across;* he is thought holy by many, and possesses the pearls of wisdom;* he went forth into the religious life long ago and is experienced and of great age. My lord could visit Pūraṇa Kassapa. If my lord were to visit Pūraṇa Kassapa his heart would certainly be set at rest.' At these words King Ajātasattu of Magadha remained silent.

Another of the ministers said to king Ajātasattu of Magadha:
'There is, lord, Makkhali Gosāla. He has a company and a following 48
and is the teacher of that following; he is well known, of some repute, one who has found a way across; he is thought holy by many, and possesses the pearls of wisdom; he went forth into the religious life long ago and is experienced and of great age. My lord could visit Makkhali Gosāla. If my lord were to visit Makkhali Gosāla his heart would certainly be set at rest.' At these words King Ajātasattu of Magadha remained silent.

Yet another of the ministers said to King Ajātasattu of Magadha: 'There is, lord, Ajita of the Blanket of Hair. He has a company and a following and is the teacher of that following; he is well known, of some repute, one who has found a way across; he is thought holy by many, and possesses the pearls of wisdom; he went forth into the religious life long ago and is experienced and of great age. My lord could visit Ajita of the Blanket of Hair. If my lord were to visit Ajita of the Blanket of Hair his heart would certainly be set at rest.' At these words King Ajātasattu of Magadha remained silent.

Yet another of the ministers said to King Ajātasattu of Magadha: 'There is, lord, Pakudha Kaccāyana. He has a company and a following and is the teacher of that following; he is well known, of some repute, one who has found a way across; he is thought holy by many, and possesses the pearls of wisdom; he went forth into the religious life long ago and is experienced and of great age. My lord could visit Pakudha Kaccāyana. If my lord were to visit Pakudha Kaccāyana his heart would certainly be set at rest.' At these words King Ajātasattu of Magadha remained silent.

Yet another of the ministers said to King Ajātasattu of Magadha:
49 'There is, lord, Nigaṇṭha Nātaputta. He has a company and a following and is the teacher of that following; he is well known, of some repute, one who has found a way across; he is thought holy by many, and possesses the pearls of wisdom; he went forth into the religious life long ago and is experienced and of great age. My lord could visit Nigaṇṭha Nātaputta. If my lord were to visit Nigaṇṭha Nātaputta his heart would certainly be set at rest.' At these words King Ajātasattu of Magadha remained silent.

Yet another of the ministers said to King Ajātasattu of Magadha: 'There is, lord, Sañjaya Belaṭṭhiputta. He has a company and a following and is the teacher of that following; he is well known, of some repute, one who has found a way across; he is thought holy by many, and possesses the pearls of wisdom; he went forth into the religious life long ago and is experienced and of great age. My lord could visit Sañjaya Belaṭṭhiputta. If my lord were to visit Sañjaya Belaṭṭhiputta his heart would certainly be set at rest.' At these words King Ajātasattu of Magadha remained silent.

Now at that time Jīvaka Komārabhacca was seated keeping his silence not far from King Ajātasattu of Magadha. Then the king said to Jīvaka Komārabhacca.

'But why, good Jīvaka, do you remain silent?'

'There is, lord, the Blessed One, an arahat and perfect buddha,* who is staying in my mango grove with a great company of monks—twelve hundred and fifty monks. Moreover this lovely report has been spread abroad concerning the Blessed Gotama: For the following reasons is he the Blessed One—he is an arahat, a perfect buddha, accomplished in knowledge and conduct, happy, one who understands the world, an unsurpassed charioteer of men to be tamed, teacher of gods and men, a blessed buddha. My lord could visit the Blessed One. If my lord were to visit the Blessed One his heart would certainly be set at rest.'

'Then have the elephants made ready for the journey, good Jīvaka!'

'So be it, lord,' replied Jīvaka Komārabhacca to King Ajātasattu of Magadha.

He had five hundred she-elephants made ready, and a riding tusker for the king. Then he announced to King Ajātasattu of Magadha: 'The elephants have been made ready for your journey, lord. It is now time for you to do as you think fit.'

Then King Ajātasattu of Magadha had one of his wives mounted on each of the five hundred she-elephants, while he himself mounted the riding tusker, and then accompanied by torch-bearers he went out from Rājagaha in great royal splendour, and set off towards Jīvaka Komārabhacca's mango grove. Now not far from the mango grove King Ajātasattu of Magadha was gripped by fear; he was para-
lysed and the hairs of his body stood on end. Frightened and agitated, 50
with his hair standing on end, King Ajātasattu of Magadha said to Jīvaka Komārabhacca: 'Are you perhaps deceiving me, good Jīvaka? Are you perhaps tricking me, good Jīvaka? Are you perhaps going to hand me over to my enemies, good Jīvaka? For how can it be that from a great company of twelve hundred and fifty monks there is not a sneeze, not a cough, not a murmur?'

'Do not be afraid, your majesty. I am not deceiving you. I am not tricking you. I am not going to hand you over to your enemies. Go on, your majesty! Go on! There are the lamps burning in the centre of the pavilion.'

Then when he had gone by elephant as far as the ground would allow, King Ajātasattu of Magadha dismounted and approached the entrance of the assembly hall on foot. As he was approaching, he said to Jīvaka Komārabhacca: 'But where is the Blessed One, good Jīvaka?'

'There is the Blessed One, your majesty. There is the Blessed One, your majesty, seated in front of the company of monks, resting his back on the central pole, facing east.'

Then King Ajātasattu of Magadha approached the Blessed One and stood to one side. As he stood there surveying the company of monks which remained completely silent like a still pool, King Ajātasattu of Magadha breathed a sigh: 'May my son the prince Udāyibhadda* come to possess such calm as is now possessed by the company of monks!'

'Your thoughts have turned to one you love.'

'The prince Udāyibhadda is dear to me, sir. May my son the prince Udāyibhadda come to possess such calm as is now possessed by the company of monks!'

Then having saluted the Blessed One respectfully and bowed to
51 the company of monks with cupped hands,* King Ajātasattu of
Magadha sat down to one side.

Once seated, King Ajātasattu of Magadha said to the Blessed One: 'Sir, I have something I would like to ask the Blessed One about—that is, if the Blessed One will agree to answer a question for me on this occasion.'

'Ask what you like, your majesty.'

'There are various professions, sir. There are elephant riders, cavalrymen, charioteers, archers, standard-bearers, spies, quartermasters, high-ranking royal officers, front-line soldiers, great fighters, warriors, leather-clad soldiers, household slaves, cooks, barbers, bath attendants, sweet-makers, garland-makers, washermen, weavers, basket makers, potters, those skilled in accounts and calculation, and various other professions of a similar sort. These people enjoy the evident fruits of their labour here and now: by their work they bring happiness and joy to themselves, they bring happiness and joy to their mothers and fathers, to their wives and children, and to their friends and acquaintances; and they provide ascetics and brahmans with excellent offerings, for the sake of the world to come, bringing happy results and making for a heavenly rebirth. Is it possible to point out a fruit of the ascetic life that is similarly evident here and now?'

'Do you recall having asked this question of other ascetics and brahmans, your majesty?'

'I do recall having asked this question of other ascetics and brahmans, sir.'

'Your majesty, if it is not too much trouble for you, please tell me how they answered you.'

'It is no trouble where the Blessed One or one like the Blessed One
52 is concerned.'

'Then please speak, your majesty.'

'Once, sir, I approached Pūraṇa Kassapa. Having approached, I saluted him respectfully and exchanged pleasing and polite words with him, before sitting down to one side. Once seated, I said to Pūraṇa Kassapa: "Kassapa sir, there are various professions—elephant riders, cavalrymen, charioteers, archers, standard-bearers, spies, quartermasters, high-ranking royal officers, front-line soldiers, great fighters, warriors, leather-clad soldiers, household slaves, cooks, barbers, bath attendants, sweet-makers, garland-makers, washermen, weavers, basket-makers, potters, those skilled in accounts and calculation, and various other professions of a similar sort. These people enjoy the evident fruits of their labour here and now: by their work they bring happiness and joy to themselves, they bring happiness and joy to their mothers and fathers, to their wives and children, and to their friends and acquaintances; and they provide ascetics and brahmans with excellent offerings, for the sake of the world to come, bringing happy results and making for a heavenly rebirth. Is it possible to point out a fruit of the ascetic life that is similarly evident here and now?"

'When I had asked this, Pūraṇa Kassapa answered me as follows: "When one injures or gets another to injure, wounds or gets another to wound, tortures or gets another to torture, causes grief or distress, intimidates or gets others to intimidate; when one harms living creatures, takes what is not given, breaks into houses, plunders, commits burglary, waits in ambush on the road, goes with others' wives, tells lies—when one acts then no wrong is done. If someone were to take a razor-edged discus and make of the creatures of this earth one single mass of flesh, one single heap of flesh, there would be nothing bad in that, nothing bad would come of it. Again, if someone were to go along the southern bank of the Ganges killing and getting others to kill, wounding and getting others to wound, torturing and getting others to torture, there would be nothing bad in that, nothing bad would come of it. Again, if someone were to go along the northern bank of the Ganges making gifts and getting others to make gifts, performing sacrifices and getting others to perform sacrifices, there
would be nothing good in that, nothing good would come of it. In 53
giving, discipline, restraint and speaking the truth, there is nothing good, nothing good comes of them."

'In this way, sir, when he was asked about an evident fruit of the ascetic life, Pūraṇa Kassapa gave an explanation of the non-existence of action.* It is as if someone who was asked about a mango gave an explanation of a breadfruit, or someone who was asked about a breadfruit gave an explanation of a mango.

'Then, sir, I thought, "But how is a person like me to judge whether an ascetic or brahman living in my realm should be reproached?"* So I neither agreed nor disagreed with Pūraṇa Kassapa's words. And although my heart was not gladdened, I did not voice my dissatisfaction, but got up from my seat and went away, neither accepting his words nor countering them.

'And once, sir, I approached Makkhali Gosāla. Having approached, I saluted him respectfully and exchanged pleasing and polite words with him, before sitting down to one side. Once seated, I said to Makkhali Gosāla: "Gosāla sir, there are various professions . . . These people enjoy the evident fruits of their labour here and now . . . Is it possible to point out a fruit of the ascetic life that is similarly evident here and now?"

'When I had asked this Makkhali Gosāla answered me as follows: "There is no reason nor cause for the defilement of beings: beings become defiled without any reason and without any cause. There is no reason nor cause for the purification of beings: beings become purified without any reason and without any cause. There is nothing one can do, nothing anyone else can do. No human action, no force, no effort, no human striving, no human endeavour has any effect. All beings, all breathing things, all living things, all organisms are impotent, without any power or strength: they are developed by fate, chance, and nature, experiencing happiness and unhappiness in
54 the six types of existence.* There are 1,400,000 principal kinds of birth, plus 6,000 and 600; there are 500 actions, plus 5 actions, 3 actions, 1 action, and half an action; there are 62 ways, 62 lesser aeons, 6 types, 8 human stages; there are 4,900 births as an ascetic, 4,900 as a wanderer, 4,900 among the Nāgas,* 2,000 as companions of the chief of gods,* 36 in dusty places, 7 sentient births, 7 insentient births, 7 births without bonds, 7 divine, 7 human, 7 demonic; there are 7 lakes, 7 transferences of the soul plus 700,* 7 falls plus 700, 7 dreams plus 700—for 8,400,000 great aeons the fool and the wise man alike will roam and wander before bringing suffering to an end. So it is no use thinking that by means of virtuous behaviour, by some vow, penance, or spiritual practice, one can bring unripe karma to fruition, or deliberately exhaust ripe karma. This cannot be done. Happiness and unhappiness come in fixed measures, and the round of rebirth has a definite limit. There is no way to make it longer or shorter, no way to make it better or worse. It is just like a ball of string that has been let go so that it rolls out until it has unravelled—in exactly the same way the fool and wise man alike will roam and wander before bringing suffering to an end."

'In this way, sir, when he was asked about an evident fruit of the ascetic life, Makkhali Gosāla gave an explanation of purification through the round of birth. It is as if someone who was asked about a mango gave an explanation of a breadfruit, or someone who was asked about a breadfruit gave an explanation of a mango.

'Then, sir, I thought, "But how is a person like me to judge whether an ascetic or brahman living in my realm should be reproached?" So I neither agreed nor disagreed with Makkhali 55
Gosāla's words. And although my heart was not gladdened, I did not voice my dissatisfaction, but got up from my seat and went away, neither accepting his words nor countering them.

'And once, sir, I approached Ajita of the Blanket of Hair. Having approached, I saluted him respectfully and exchanged pleasing and polite words with him, before sitting down to one side. Once seated, I said to Ajita of the Blanket of Hair: "Ajita sir, there are various professions . . . These people enjoy the evident fruits of their labour here and now . . . Is it possible to point out a fruit of the ascetic life that is similarly evident here and now?"

'When I had asked this Ajita of the Blanket of Hair answered me as follows: "Giving is nothing, sacrifice and offerings are nothing; good and bad deeds have no fruit or result; there is no this world and the next; one's mother and father are nothing; there are no beings born in heaven, no ascetics or brahmans who have reached perfection and live the perfect life, who gain for themselves a direct knowledge of this world and the next, and, having experienced it directly, make it known. A person is formed of the four elements, and when he dies the earth returns to and merges with the general mass of earth, the water with the general mass of water, the fire with the general mass of fire, the air with the general mass of air; the sense faculties pass into the ether. Four men put the dead body on a bier and go. They talk about him as far as the cremation ground, and there his bones turn grey, and his offerings end in ashes. The idea of giving is stupid—the empty and lying prattle of those who declare there is some point to life. After the breaking up of the body the fool and the wise man alike are cut off and perish. They do not survive after death."

'In this way, sir, when he was asked about an evident fruit of the ascetic life, Ajita of the Blanket of Hair gave an explanation of the doctrine of nihilism. It is as if someone who was asked about a mango
gave an explanation of a breadfruit, or someone who was asked about 56
a breadfruit gave an explanation of a mango.

'Then, sir, I thought, "But how is a person like me to judge whether an ascetic or brahman living in my realm should be reproached?" So I neither agreed nor disagreed with Ajita of the Blanket of Hair's words. And although my heart was not gladdened, I did not voice my dissatisfaction, but got up from my seat and went away, neither accepting his words nor countering them.

'And once, sir, I approached Pakudha Kaccāyana. Having approached, I saluted him respectfully and exchanged pleasing and polite words with him, before sitting down to one side. Once seated, I said to Pakudha Kaccāyana: "Kaccāyana sir, there are various professions . . . These people enjoy the evident fruits of their labour here and now . . . Is it possible to point out a fruit of the ascetic life that is similarly evident here and now?"

'When I had asked this Pakudha Kaccāyana answered me as follows: "There are seven primary constituents that are not made nor constructed, not created nor produced; they cannot be damaged, and stand erect and firm as pillars. They do not move or alter; they cannot bring harm to one another, nor can one affect the happiness, unhappiness, or happiness and unhappiness of the others. What are these seven? The constituent of earth, the constituent of water, the constituent of fire, the constituent of wind, happiness, unhappiness, and the soul the seventh. These are the seven primary constituents . . . So there is no one who kills or causes one to kill, no one who hears or causes one to hear, no one who perceives or causes one to perceive. If someone cuts off someone's head with a sharp sword, he doesn't take anyone's life: the sword just passes through the space between
57 these seven constituents."

'In this way, sir, when he was asked about an evident fruit of the ascetic life, Pakudha Kaccāyana gave an explanation of one thing in terms of another. It is as if someone who was asked about a mango gave an explanation of a breadfruit, or someone who was asked about a breadfruit gave an explanation of a mango.

'Then, sir, I thought, "But how is a person like me to judge whether an ascetic or brahman living in my realm should be reproached?" So I neither agreed nor disagreed with Pakudha Kaccāyana's words. And although my heart was not gladdened, I did not voice my dissatisfaction, but got up from my seat and went away, neither accepting his words nor countering them.

'And once, sir, I approached the Nigaṇṭha Nātaputta.* Having approached, I saluted him respectfully and exchanged pleasing and polite words with him, before sitting down to one side. Once seated,

I said to the Nigaṇṭha Nātaputta: "Aggivessana* sir, there are various professions . . . These people enjoy the evident fruits of their labour here and now . . . Is it possible to point out a fruit of the ascetic life that is similarly evident here and now?"

'When I had asked this the Nigaṇṭha Nātaputta answered me as follows: "A Nigaṇṭha is controlled by the discipline of the four restraints:* he is disciplined in his use of water, he is committed to avoiding evil, he is cleansed by avoiding evil, he is filled with the sense of avoiding evil . . . And when, your majesty, a Nigaṇṭha is controlled by the discipline of the four restraints in this way, he is called one who is accomplished in himself, one who is controlled in himself, one who is firm in himself." 58

'In this way, sir, when he was asked about an evident fruit of the ascetic life, the Nigaṇṭha Nātaputta gave an explanation of the discipline of the four restraints. It is as if someone who was asked about a mango gave an explanation of a breadfruit, or someone who was asked about a breadfruit gave an explanation of a mango.

'Then, sir, I thought, "But how is a person like me to judge whether an ascetic or brahman living in my realm should be reproached?" So I neither agreed nor disagreed with Nigaṇṭha Nātaputta's words. And although my heart was not gladdened, I did not voice my dissatisfaction, but got up from my seat and went away, neither accepting his words nor countering them.

'And once, sir, I approached Sañjaya Belaṭṭhiputta. Having approached, I saluted him respectfully and exchanged pleasing and polite words with him, before sitting down to one side. Once seated, I said to Sañjaya Belaṭṭhiputta: "Sañjaya sir, there are various professions . . . These people enjoy the evident fruits of their labour here and now . . . Is it possible to point out a fruit of the ascetic life that is similarly evident here and now?"

'When I had asked this, Sañjaya Belaṭṭhiputta answered me as follows: "Is there another world? If you asked me this, then if what I thought was that there was another world, then 'There is another world' is the answer I would give you. But that is not what I think. I do not say it is so, I do not say it is otherwise, I do not say it is not so, and I do not say that it is not not so. Is there no other world? . . . Is it that there both is and is not another world? . . . Is it that there neither is nor is not another world? . . . Are there beings born in heaven? . . . Are there no beings born in heaven? . . . Is it that there

both are and are not beings born in heaven? . . . Is it that there neither
are nor are not beings born in heaven? . . . Do good and bad deeds
have any fruit or result? . . . Do good and bad deeds have no fruit or
result? . . . Do good and bad deeds both have and not have any fruit
or result? . . . Do good and bad deeds neither have nor not have any
59 fruit or result? . . . Does the Tathāgata exist after death? . . . Does
the Tathāgata not exist after death? . . . Does the Tathāgata both
exist and not exist after death? . . . Does the Tathāgata neither exist
nor not exist after death? If you asked me this, then if what I thought
was that the Tathāgata neither existed not did not exist after death,
then 'The Tathāgata neither exists nor does not exist after death' is
the answer I would give you. But that is not what I think. I do not
say it is so, I do not say it is otherwise, I do not say it is not so, and I do
not say that it is not not so."

'In this way, sir, when he was asked about an evident fruit of the ascetic life, Sañjaya Belaṭṭhiputta gave an explanation by way of prevaricating. It is as if someone who was asked about a mango gave an explanation of a breadfruit, or someone who was asked about a breadfruit gave an explanation of a mango.

'Then, sir, I thought, "Of all these ascetics and brahmans, he is the biggest fool and the most confused.* But how is a person like me to judge whether an ascetic or brahman living in my realm should be reproached?" So I neither agreed nor disagreed with Sañjaya Belaṭṭhiputta's words. And although my heart was not gladdened, I did not voice my dissatisfaction, but got up from my seat and went away, neither accepting his words nor countering them.

'So now, sir, I put my question to the Blessed One too. There are
various professions . . . These people enjoy the evident fruits of their
60 labour here and now . . . Is it possible, sir, to point out to me a fruit
of the ascetic life that is similarly evident here and now?'

'It is possible, your majesty. Now, I shall ask you a question in return, and you should answer it as you like. What do you think, your majesty? There might be one of your men, a slave and servant, who gets up before you and goes to bed after you, who waits for your instructions, who is pleasing in his conduct and gracious in his speech, hanging on your words. He might think: "How remarkable, how extraordinary the outcome and result of good deeds! There is King Ajātasattu of Magadha, son of the princess of Videha, a man, and I too am a man. There is King Ajātasattu of Magadha, son of the princess of Videha provided and furnished with the pleasures of the five senses, amusing himself like some god, while I am his slave and servant, getting up before him and going to bed after him, waiting for his instructions, pleasing in my conduct and gracious in my speech, hanging on his words. Surely if I were to perform some good deeds I would be like him. Why don't I shave off my hair and beard, put on ochre robes, and go forth from home into homelessness?" And after some time he might shave off his hair and beard, put on ochre robes, and go forth from home into homelessness. Once he had gone forth like this, he might live keeping check on his body, speech, and mind, content with the minimum of food and clothing, taking pleasure in seclusion. Now if your men should tell you, "Lord, you really ought to know that one of your men who is a slave and servant, who gets up before you and goes to bed after you, who waits for your instructions, who is pleasing in his conduct and gracious in his speech, hanging on your words, has shaved off his hair and beard, put on ochre robes, and gone forth from home into homelessness; and now that he has gone forth like this, he lives keeping check on his body, speech, and mind, content with the minimum of food and clothing, taking pleasure in seclusion," would you really say, "Gentlemen, that man should return to me and once again be a slave and servant, getting up before me and going to bed after me, waiting for my instructions, pleasing in his conduct and gracious in his speech, hanging on my words"?'

'Not this, sir. In fact we would salute him respectfully, and get up 61
and invite him to sit down, offering the requisites of robes, alms, lodging, medicine in case of illness, and provide him with proper care and protection.'*

'What do you think, your majesty? If that is the case, is there an evident fruit of the ascetic life, or not?'

'Certainly, sir, if that is the case, there is an evident fruit of the ascetic life.'

'Your majesty, this is the first fruit of the ascetic life evident here and now that I have indicated to you.'

'But is it possible, sir, to point out to me a further fruit of the ascetic life that is similarly evident here and now?'

'It is possible, your majesty. Now, I shall ask you a question in return, and you should answer it as you like. What do you think, your majesty? There might be one of your men, a farmer and householder

in your service who increases your store of wealth. He might think: "How remarkable, how extraordinary the outcome and result of good deeds! There is King Ajātasattu of Magadha, son of the princess of Videha, a man, and I too am a man. There is King Ajātasattu of Magadha, son of the princess of Videha, provided and furnished with the pleasures of the five senses, amusing himself like some god, while I am a farmer and householder in his service increasing his store of wealth. Surely if I were to perform some good deeds I would be like him. Why don't I shave off my hair and beard, put on ochre robes, and go forth from home into homelessness?" And after some time he might give up his possessions, whether many or few, and leave behind his circle of relatives, whether small or large. Then he might shave off his hair and beard, put on ochre robes, and go forth from home into homelessness. Once he had gone forth like
62 this, he might live keeping check on his body, speech, and mind, content with the minimum of food and clothing, taking pleasure in seclusion. Now if your men should tell you, "Lord, you really ought to know that one of your men, a farmer and householder in your service who increases your store of wealth, has shaved off his hair and beard, put on ochre robes, and gone forth from home into homelessness; and now he has gone forth like this, he lives keeping check on his body, speech, and mind, content with the minimum of food and clothing, taking pleasure in seclusion," would you really say, "Gentlemen, that man should return to me and once again be a farmer and householder in my service who increases my store of wealth"?'

'Not this, sir. In fact we would salute him respectfully, and get up and invite him to sit down, offering the requisites of robes, alms, lodging, medicine in case of illness, and provide him with proper care and protection.'

'What do you think, your majesty? If that is the case, is there an evident fruit of the ascetic life, or not?'

'Certainly, sir, if that is the case, there is an evident fruit of the ascetic life.'

'Your majesty, this is the second fruit of the ascetic life evident here and now that I have indicated to you.'

'But is it possible, sir, to point out to me a further fruit of the ascetic life that is similarly evident here and now—one that is superior and more refined?'

'It is possible, your majesty. Listen. Pay careful attention to what I shall say.'

'Yes, sir,' King Ajātasattu of Magadha, son of the princess of Videha, replied.

'Now, your majesty, a Tathāgata appears in the world, an arahat, a perfect buddha, accomplished in knowledge and conduct, happy, one who understands the world, unsurpassed charioteer of men to be tamed, teacher of gods and men, a blessed buddha. He gains for himself a direct knowledge of this world with its gods, its Māra and Brahmā, of this generation with its ascetics and brahmans, its princes and peoples, and having experienced this directly he makes it known. He teaches the Truth that is beautiful in the beginning, beautiful in the middle, beautiful in the end, both in its spirit and in its letter. He makes clear the pure spiritual life in all its perfection. A householder, his son, or someone born of some family hears this Truth, and when he hears it he gains faith in the Tathāgata. Having acquired 63
such faith, he reflects as follows: "Living in a house is restricted and cluttered, going forth is a life wide open. It is not easy to practise the spiritual life in all its fullness and purity, like a polished shell, while living in a house. Why don't I shave off my hair and beard, put on ochre robes, and go forth from home into homelessness?" And after some time he might give up his possessions, whether many or few, and leave behind his circle of relatives, whether small or large. Then he might shave off his hair and beard, put on ochre robes, and go forth from home into homelessness. Once he has gone forth like this, he lives according to the restraints of the monastic rule.* He is accomplished in his conduct and dealings with people; seeing danger in the smallest of faults, he undertakes and trains in the precepts, his acts of body and speech are wholesome, he follows a completely pure way of life, is accomplished in his moral behaviour, guards the doors of the senses, possesses mindfulness and full awareness, and is content.

'And how, your majesty, is he accomplished in his moral behaviour?* In this, a monk refrains from killing living creatures. He discards sticks and swords, and is gentle and full of concern, remaining sympathetic and well disposed towards all creatures and beings. This is one aspect of his moral behaviour.

'Letting go of what has not been given to him, he refrains from taking what is not given. Accepting and wanting only what is given, he lives honestly, without stealing. This is a further aspect of his moral behaviour.

'Giving up the non-celibate life, he follows a life of celibacy. He lives detached, refraining from the vulgar practice of copulation. This is a further aspect of his moral behaviour.

'Giving up untrue speech, he refrains from untrue speech. He speaks the truth, is committed to the truth; he is reliable, trustworthy, and does not deceive people. This is a further aspect of his moral behaviour.

'Giving up malicious speech, he refrains from malicious speech. When he hears something from people here, he does not tell others
64 in order to create a rift with the people here, nor, when he hears something from others does he tell the people here in order to create a rift with those others. Thus he brings together those who are divided and encourages* those who are united. As one who takes pleasure in and is pleased with harmony, as one who is delighted with harmony, he speaks words that will bring about harmony. This is a further aspect of his moral behaviour.

'Giving up unkind speech, he refrains from unkind speech. He speaks the kind of words that are not hurtful, but pleasing to the ear, warm, touching the heart, courteous, that people find pleasing and charming. This is a further aspect of his moral behaviour.

'Giving up idle chatter, he refrains from idle chatter. He speaks at the right time, in accordance with the facts, with words that are helpful, and concern the teaching and the discipline. He speaks words that should be treasured, that are appropriate to the occasion, to the point and helpful. This is a further aspect of his moral behaviour.

'He refrains from harming seeds and plants.* He takes one meal a day, not eating at night, refraining from food at the wrong time.* He refrains from attending shows of dancing, singing, and music. He refrains from wearing, adorning, and beautifying himself with garlands, perfumes, and ointments. He refrains from using high and luxurious beds. He refrains from accepting silver or gold. He refrains from accepting uncooked grain . . . raw meat . . . women or girls . . . male and female slaves . . . sheep and goats . . . chickens and pigs . . . elephants, cattle, horses, and mares . . . fields and land. He refrains from acting as a go-between or messenger. He refrains from buying and selling. He refrains from cheating with false weights, metals and measures. He refrains from the crooked practices of bribery, cheating, and fraud. He abstains from maiming, murder, imprisoning, robbery, pillage, and violence. This is a further aspect of his moral behaviour.

[Here ends the shorter section on conduct]

'Whereas some ascetics and brahmans consume the food offered by the faithful while still habitually harming seeds and plants—roots, stems or shoots or buds or seeds—he refrains from harming such seeds and plants. This is a further aspect of his moral 65
behaviour.

'Whereas some ascetics and brahmans consume the food offered by the faithful while still habitually keeping stored-up goods—of foods, drinks, clothing, carriages, bedding, perfumes, and foodstuffs—he refrains from keeping such stored-up goods. This is a further aspect of his moral behaviour.

'Whereas some ascetics and brahmans consume the food offered by the faithful while still habitually visiting shows—dances, singing, music, fairs, recitations, hand-clapping, the chanting of bards, drumming, fairy scenes, acrobatics, fights of elephants, horses, buffaloes, bulls, goats, rams, cocks, and quails, bouts at quarterstaff, boxing, wrestling, sham fights, roll-calls, battle manoeuvres, reviews—he refrains from visiting such shows. This is a further aspect of his moral behaviour.

'Whereas some ascetics and brahmans consume the food offered by the faithful while still indulging in games and recreations—games on boards with eight or ten rows, visualized board games, hopscotch, spillikin, dice, sticks, painting shapes with the hand, ball games, blowing through toy pipes, playing with toy ploughs, turning somersaults, playing with toy windmills made of leaves; playing with toy measures, toy carts, or toy bows; guessing at letters, guessing thoughts, mimicking deformities—he refrains from such games. This is a further aspect of his moral behaviour.

'Whereas some ascetics and brahmans consume the food offered by the faithful while still habitually using high and luxurious beds—settees, divans, goats' hair coverlets, patchwork coverlets, white blankets, woollen coverlets embroidered with flowers, quilts stuffed with cotton wool, coverlets embroidered with figures of lions and tigers, rugs with fur on both sides, rugs with fur on one side, coverlets embroidered with gems, silk coverlets, giant rugs, elephant,

horse, and chariot rugs, rugs of antelope skins, rugs of deerskins, rugs with awnings above, couches with red pillows for the head and
66 feet—he refrains from using such high and luxurious beds. This is a further aspect of his moral behaviour.

'Whereas some ascetics and brahmans consume the food offered by the faithful while still habitually adorning and beautifying themselves—rubbing in scented powders, shampooing, bathing, massaging, using mirrors, ointments, garlands, powders, cosmetics, bracelets, necklaces, walking-sticks, boxes, rapiers, sunshades, embroidered slippers, turbans, diadems, whisks of the yak's tail, and long-fringed white robes—he refrains from such adorning and beautifying of himself. This is a further aspect of his moral behaviour.

'Whereas some ascetics and brahmans consume the food offered by the faithful while still addicted to childish conversation—talk of kings, thieves, ministers, armies, horrors, battles, food, drink, clothes, beds, garlands, perfumes, relations, carriages, villages, towns, cities, and countries, women, heroes; gossip on the streets or at wells; talk about the departed, talk of this and that, speculations about the world and the ocean, talk of what is and isn't—he refrains from such childish conversation. This is a further aspect of his moral behaviour.

'Whereas some ascetics and brahmans consume the food offered by the faithful while still addicted to quarrelsome talk—"You don't understand this teaching and discipline, I do." "How could you understand this teaching and discipline ?" "Your practice is quite wrong—mine is right!" "What I say can be backed up, what you say can't." "You are stating last what ought to be said first, and first what ought to be said last." "What you have thought out, has been overturned." "Your point has been bettered—you're refuted." "Go and work out how to save your argument, or disentangle yourself if you can."—he refrains from such quarrelsome talk. This is a further aspect of his moral behaviour.

'Whereas some ascetics and brahmans consume the food offered by the faithful while still acting as messengers and go-betweens—for
67 kings, their ministers, members of the Ruler class, brahmans, householders, young men, who say, "Go there, come here, take this, bring that here"—he refrains from acting as a messenger and go-between in this way. This is a further aspect of his moral behaviour.

'Whereas some ascetics and brahmans consume the food offered by the faithful while still scheming, talking, hinting, belittling others, pursuing gain with gain*—he refrains from such scheming and talking. This is a further aspect of his moral behaviour.

[Here ends the middle section on conduct]

'Whereas some ascetics and brahmans consume the food offered by the faithful while pursuing a wrong means of livelihood and making their living by means of childish arts—such as palm reading, reading omens and signs, interpreting celestial portents, interpreting dreams, fortune-telling from marks on the body, reading omens from the marks on cloth gnawed by mice, offering fire oblations, offering oblations from a ladle, offering to the gods husks, red rice-powder, ghee, and oil, making offerings from the mouth into the fire, offering oblations of blood, reading the knuckles, determining the site of a house as lucky or not, making predictions for ministers of state, laying demons in a cemetery, laying ghosts, knowing the charms for living in an earthen house, snake-charming, poison craft, scorpion craft, mouse craft, bird craft, crow craft, telling the number of years a man has to live, reciting charms to protect against arrows, knowing the language of animals—he refrains from pursuing a wrong means of livelihood and making his living by means of such childish arts. This is a further aspect of his moral behaviour.

'Whereas some ascetics and brahmans consume the food offered by the faithful while pursuing a wrong means of livelihood and making their living by means of childish arts—such as reading the good-luck signs in gems, staffs, garments, swords, arrows, bows, weapons, women, men, boys, girls, slaves, slave-girls, elephants, horses, buffaloes, bulls, oxen, goats, sheep, chickens, quails, monitor lizards, ear-rings, tortoises, and other animals—he refrains from pursuing a wrong means of livelihood and making his living by means of such childish arts. This is a further aspect of his moral behaviour.

'Whereas some ascetics and brahmans consume the food offered by the faithful while pursuing a wrong means of livelihood and
making their living by means of childish arts—such as making pre- 68
dictions: the princes will march out, they will march back; our princes will attack, the enemy's will retreat; the enemy's princes will attack, and ours will retreat; our princes will gain the victory, and the enemy's suffer defeat; the enemy's princes will gain the victory, and

ours suffer defeat; thus victory will be theirs, and defeat theirs—he refrains from pursuing a wrong means of livelihood and making his living by means of such childish arts. This is a further aspect of his moral behaviour.

'Whereas some ascetics and brahmans consume the food offered by the faithful while pursuing a wrong means of livelihood and making their living by means of childish arts—such as predicting there will be an eclipse of the moon, an eclipse of the sun, an eclipse of a star; the sun or the moon will follow their normal course, the sun or the moon will depart from their normal course; the stars will follow their normal course, the stars will depart from their normal course; there will be a fall of meteors, a glow in the skies,* an earthquake, thundering of the gods; there will be a rising or setting, a darkening or brightening of the sun, moon, stars; by predicting such and such a result from an eclipse of the moon . . . of the sun . . . their departure from their normal course . . . a fall of meteors . . . the brightening of the sun, moon, or stars—he refrains from pursuing a wrong means of livelihood and making his living by means of such childish arts. This is a further aspect of his moral behaviour.

'Whereas some ascetics and brahmans consume the food offered by the faithful while pursuing a wrong means of livelihood and mak-
69 ing their living by means of childish arts—such as predicting abundant rainfall, a drought, a good harvest, a famine, peace, danger, disease, health; making calculations on the fingers, or in the head, estimating amounts, composing verse, studying the nature of the world*—he refrains from pursuing a wrong means of livelihood and making his living by means of such childish arts. This is a further aspect of his moral behaviour.

'Whereas some ascetics and brahmans consume the food offered by the faithful while pursuing a wrong means of livelihood and making their living by means of childish arts—such as fixing a lucky day for bringing home or sending out a bride or groom to be married; fixing a lucky time for making or breaking contracts, for saving or spending money, using charms to make people lucky or unlucky, giving medicine to stop a woman miscarrying, making charms to paralyse the tongue or lock the jaw, reciting spells to control a man's hands or to cause deafness; obtaining oracular answers from a mirror, a girl, or a god; worshipping of the Sun, the Great One,* breathing fire, invoking Sirī*—he refrains from pursuing a wrong means of livelihood and making his living by means of such childish arts. This is a further aspect of his moral behaviour.

'Whereas some ascetics and brahmans consume the food offered by the faithful while pursuing a wrong means of livelihood and making their living by means of childish arts—such as vowing gifts to a god in return for favour, paying such vows, repeating the charms for living in an earthen house, causing virility, causing impotence, determining lucky sites for building, consecrating such sites, ritually rinsing the mouth, giving ritual baths, making offering into the sacrificial fire; administering emetics and purgatives, expectorants, ear-drops, eye-drops, nose-drops, collyrium and ointment for the eyes; practising as an eye-doctor, a surgeon, a children's doctor, administering medicines from roots, administering and expelling herbal medicines*—he refrains from pursuing a wrong means of livelihood and making his living by means of such childish arts. This is a further aspect of his moral behaviour.

[Here ends the long section on conduct]

'Your majesty, a monk who is accomplished in moral behaviour in this way sees no danger anywhere on account of his restraint in moral behaviour. Just as an anointed ruler who has defeated his enemies sees no danger anywhere on account of his enemies, in exactly the 70
same way, a monk who is accomplished in moral behaviour in this way sees no danger anywhere on account of his restraint in moral behaviour. Possessed of this whole range of noble moral behaviour, he experiences the happiness of being without guilt. It is in this way, your majesty, that he is accomplished in moral behaviour.

'And how, your majesty, does a monk guard the doors of the senses? In this, when he looks at a visible object with his eyes he does not hold on to the general experience nor particular aspects. Since someone who lives with the sense of sight unchecked might be affected by longing and discontent, by bad, unwholesome mental qualities, he tries to practise checking the sense of sight; he guards it, and achieves restraint. When he hears a sound with his ears . . . When he smells a smell with his nose . . . When he tastes a taste with his tongue . . . When he touches an object of touch with his body . . . When he is conscious of a thought in his mind he does not grasp at the general experience nor at particular aspects. Since someone who lives with the mind faculty unchecked might be affected by longing and discontent, by bad, unwholesome mental qualities, he tries to practise checking the mind faculty; he guards it, and achieves restraint. Possessed of this noble restraint of the senses, he experiences a natural happiness in himself. It is in this way, your majesty, that he guards the doors of the senses.

'And how, your majesty, does a monk possess mindfulness and full awareness? In moving forward and turning back, a monk acts in full awareness; in looking ahead and looking around, he acts with full awareness; in bending and straightening his limbs, he acts with full awareness; in wearing his inner and outer robes and carrying his alms bowl, he acts with full awareness; in eating, drinking, chewing, and swallowing, he acts with full awareness; in defecating and urinating, he acts with full awareness; in walking, standing, sitting, falling asleep, waking up, speaking, and keeping silent, he acts with full
71 awareness. It is in this way, your majesty, that a monk possesses mindfulness and full awareness.

'And how, your majesty, is a monk content? In this, a monk is content with the robe to cover the body, and with alms food to fill his stomach. Wherever he needs to go, he can just go taking these. Just as a winged bird flies wherever it needs to fly with its wings* as its only burden, in exactly the same way, wherever he needs to go, a monk can just go taking these. It is in this way, your majesty, that a monk is content.

'Possessed of this whole range of noble moral behaviour, this noble restraint of the senses, this noble mindfulness and full awareness, and this noble contentment, he chooses a secluded dwelling—the forest, the root of a tree, a mountain, a rocky ravine, a cave, cremation ground, forest grove, the open air,* a pile of straw. When he has returned from collecting alms food and eaten his meal, he sits down crossing his legs, straightens his body, and establishes mindfulness in front of him.

'Giving up longing for the world, he lives with a mind that is free of longing; he purifies his mind of longing. Giving up hostility and hatred, he lives with a mind that is without hostility; sympathetic and well disposed towards all creatures and beings, he purifies his mind of hostility and hatred. Giving up dullness and lethargy, he lives with a mind that is free of dullness and lethargy; with his consciousness bright, he is mindful and fully aware, and purifies his mind of dullness and lethargy. Giving up agitation and worry, he lives unagitated; with his mind calmed, he purifies his mind of agitation and worry. Giving up doubt, he lives as one who has overcome his doubt; free of uncertainty about wholesome qualities, he purifies his mind of doubt.

'It is as if, your majesty, a person were to take out a loan in order to undertake some business, and that business were to succeed so that he could pay off the original loan and the interest and have something left over for jewellery for his wife.* He would then think, "Previously I took out a loan in order to undertake some business,
and that business has succeeded so that I have paid off the original 72
loan and the interest and have something left over for jewellery for my wife." And as a result that person would be glad, and would take pleasure in that.

'It is as if, your majesty, a person were sick, and being in pain and seriously ill he might go off his food, and his body would lose all its strength. After a time he might recover from that sickness and regain his appetite so that his body would get strong. He would then think, "Previously I was sick, and being in pain and seriously ill I went off my food, and my body lost all its strength. But now I have recovered from that sickness and regained my appetite, and my body is strong." And as a result that person would be glad, and would take pleasure in that.

'It is as if, your majesty, a person were locked up in prison. After a time he might be released from that imprisonment, safe and sound, and without any loss of his property. He would then think, "Previously I was locked up in prison. But now I have been released from that imprisonment, safe and sound, and without any loss of my property." And as a result that person would be glad, and would take pleasure in that.

'It is as if, your majesty, a person were a slave, not his own master but subject to someone else and unable to go where he pleased. After a time he might be freed from that slavery, and become his own master, not subject to someone else and, as a free man, able to go where he pleased. He would then think, "Previously I was a slave, not my own master but subject to someone else and unable to go where I pleased. But now I have been freed from that slavery, and become my own master, not subject to someone else and, as a free
man, able to go where I please." And as a result that person would be 73
glad, and would take pleasure in that.

'It is as if, your majesty, a rich and wealthy man were to set out on a long journey through a wilderness where food was scarce and the dangers many. After a time he might get across that wilderness and reach the edge of a town unharmed, somewhere safe, without dangers. He would then think, "Previously I set out on a long journey through a wilderness where food was scarce and the dangers many. But now I have got across that wilderness and reached the edge of a town unharmed, somewhere safe, without dangers." And as a result that person would be glad, and would take pleasure in that.

'Your majesty, as long as a monk sees that these five hindrances have not been given up in himself, a monk views them in exactly that way: as a debt, an illness, a prison, slavery, and a long journey through a wilderness. Similarly, when a monk sees that the five hindrances have been given up in himself, he views that precisely as being free of debt, free of illness, release from imprisonment, being a freedman, and reaching a safe place.

'When he sees that the five hindrances have been given up in himself, gladness arises, and when one is glad, joy arises. When the mind is joyful, the body becomes tranquil, and when the body is tranquil one experiences happiness; the mind of someone who is happy becomes concentrated. Completely secluded from sense desires and unwholesome qualities, he lives having attained the joy and happiness of the first absorption,* which is accompanied by thinking and examining, and born of seclusion. He suffuses, fills, soaks, and drenches this very body with the joy and happiness that come from seclusion, so that there is no part of his body that is untouched by
74 that joy and happiness.

'It is as if a skilled bath attendant or his pupil were to sprinkle bath powder into a bronze dish, and then knead it together adding the water drop by drop so that the ball of soap absorbed and soaked up the moisture until it was saturated with moisture, yet not quite dripping. In exactly the same way the monk suffuses, fills, soaks, and drenches this very body with the joy and happiness that come from seclusion, so that there is no part of his body that is untouched by that joy and happiness.

'Your majesty, this is a fruit of the ascetic life evident here and now that is superior and more refined than the previous ones.

'Furthermore, your majesty, by stilling thinking and examining, a monk lives having attained the joy and happiness of the second absorption, a state of inner clarity and mental unification that is without thinking and examining, and is born of concentration. He suffuses, fills, soaks, and drenches this very body with the joy and happiness that come from concentration, so that there is no part of his body that is untouched by that joy and happiness.

'It is as if there were a pool where water sprang up, but which had no water flowing into it from the east, the west, the north, or the south, and which the god did not fill* with rain from time to time. Now when the cool waters sprang up in that pool they would suffuse, fill, soak, and drench that same pool with cool water, so that no part of that pool would be untouched by the cool water. In exactly the same way the monk suffuses, fills, soaks, and drenches this very body with the joy and happiness that come from concentration, so that there is no part of 75
his body that is untouched by that joy and happiness.

'Your majesty, this is a fruit of the ascetic life evident here and now that is superior and more refined than the previous ones.

'Furthermore, your majesty, by having no desire for joy a monk lives equanimously, mindful and fully aware; he experiences the bodily happiness of which the noble ones speak saying "equanimous and mindful, one lives happily", and so lives having attained the third absorption. He suffuses, fills, soaks, and drenches this very body with a happiness distinct from joy, so that there is no part of his body that is untouched by that happiness.

'It is as if, your majesty, in a pond of blue, red, or white lotuses, there were some lotuses that had come into bud and grown in the water, never rising out of the water, but flourishing beneath its surface. Those lotuses would be suffused, filled, soaked, and drenched from root to tip with cool water, so that no part of those blue, red, or white lotuses would be untouched by the cool water. In exactly the same way the monk suffuses, fills, soaks and drenches this very body with a happiness distinct from joy, so that there is no part of his body that is untouched by that happiness.

'Your majesty, this is a fruit of the ascetic life evident here and now that is superior and more refined than the previous ones.

'Furthermore, your majesty, by letting go of happiness and unhappiness, as a result of the earlier disappearance of pleasure and pain, a monk lives having attained the pure equanimity and mindfulness of the fourth absorption, which is free of happiness and unhappiness. He sits suffusing this very body with a mind that is thoroughly purified and cleansed, so that there is no part of his body that is 76
untouched by that thoroughly purified and cleansed mind.

'It is as if, your majesty, a person were to sit down having wrapped himself from head to foot in a freshly washed cloth, so that there was no part of his body that was untouched by that freshly washed cloth. In exactly the same way the monk sits suffusing this very body with a mind that is thoroughly purified and cleansed, so that there is no part of his body that is untouched by that thoroughly purified and cleansed mind.

'Your majesty, this is a fruit of the ascetic life evident here and now that is superior and more refined than the previous ones.

'Once his mind is concentrated in this way,* once it is thoroughly purified and cleansed—stainless, without defilements, having become sensitive, workable, and steady, reaching a state that is unshakeable—he applies and directs his mind towards knowledge and vision. He understands that this body of his has a physical form consisting of the four primary elements, that it is produced from a mother and father and sustained by rice and gruel, that it is impermanent, gets scraped and bumped, breaks up and falls apart, and yet this is what his consciousness depends on, what it is bound up with.

'It is as if, your majesty, there were a gem, a beautiful cat's eye, pure, expertly cut with eight facets, bright, clear, without flaw, perfect in every respect. And enclosed within that gem there might be a blue, yellow, red, white, or pale thread. A man with good eyes might take that gem in his hand and examine it, thinking, "This is a beautiful cat's eye gem, pure, expertly cut with eight facets, bright, clear, without flaw, perfect in every respect. And enclosed within it there is a blue, yellow, red, white, or pale thread." In exactly the same way, once his mind is concentrated in this way . . . the monk applies and directs his mind towards knowledge and vision. He understands that
77 this body of his has a physical form . . . yet this is what his consciousness depends on, what it is bound up with.

'Your majesty, this is a fruit of the ascetic life evident here and now that is superior and more refined than the previous ones.

'Once his mind is concentrated in this way, once it is thoroughly purified and cleansed—stainless, without defilements, having become sensitive, workable, and steady, reaching a state that is unshakeable—he applies and directs his mind towards creating a body made of mind. From his own body he creates another body, that has a physical form made of mind; it possesses all limbs and bodily parts, and lacks none of the senses.

'It is as if, your majesty, a man were to draw out a reed from reed grass. He would think, "This is the reed grass and this the reed; the reed grass is one thing, the reed another; yet the reed has been drawn out from this reed grass." Or again, as if a man were to draw out a knife from its sheath. He would think, "This is the sheath and this the knife; the sheath is one thing, the knife another; yet the knife has been drawn out from this sheath." Or again, as if a man were to pull out a snake from its slough. He would think, "This is the slough and this the snake; the slough is one thing, the snake another; yet the snake has been drawn out from this slough." In exactly the same way, once his mind is concentrated in this way . . . the monk applies and directs his mind towards creating a body made of mind . . .

'Your majesty, this is a fruit of the ascetic life evident here and now that is superior and more refined than the previous ones.

'Once his mind is concentrated in this way, once it is thoroughly purified and cleansed—stainless, without defilements, having become sensitive, workable, and steady, reaching a state that is unshakeable—he applies and directs his mind towards the various accomplishments in meditation.* He enjoys the different accom- 78
plishments in meditation: being one, he becomes many, being many he becomes one; he appears then vanishes; he passes unhindered through house walls, through city walls, and through mountains as if through air; he rises up out of the earth and sinks down into it as if it were water; he walks on water as if it were solid like earth; he travels through the sky cross-legged as if he were a bird with wings; he touches and strokes with his hand things of such power and energy as the sun and moon; he has mastery with his body as far as the world of Brahmā.

'It is as if, your majesty, a skilled potter or his apprentice were to make or produce out of properly prepared clay any kind of vessel that he liked; or a skilled ivory-worker or his apprentice were to make or produce out of properly prepared ivory any kind of ivory-work that he liked; or a skilled goldsmith or his apprentice were to make or produce out of properly prepared gold any kind of gold item that he liked. In exactly the same way, once his mind is concentrated in this way . . . the monk applies and directs his mind towards the various accomplishments in meditation . . . 79

'Your majesty, this is a fruit of the ascetic life evident here and now that is superior and more refined than the previous ones.

'Once his mind is concentrated in this way, once it is thoroughly purified and cleansed—stainless, without defilements, having become sensitive, workable, and steady, reaching a state that is unshakeable—he applies and directs his mind towards the sense of hearing that is godlike. With the godlike sense of hearing, which is purified and surpasses that of men, he hears sounds which are both divine and human, far and near.

'It is as if, your majesty, a man who had set out on a long journey were to hear the sound of a kettle-drum, the sound of a tabor, the sound of a conch, cymbals, or big drum, and were to think, "This is the sound of a kettle-drum, this the sound of a tabor, this the sound of a conch, cymbals, or big drum." In exactly the same way, once his mind is concentrated in this way . . . the monk applies and directs his mind towards the sense of hearing that is godlike . . .

'Your majesty, this is a fruit of the ascetic life evident here and now that is superior and more refined than the previous ones.

'Once his mind is concentrated in this way, once it is thoroughly purified and cleansed—stainless, without defilements, having become sensitive, workable, and steady, reaching a state that is unshakeable—he applies and directs his mind towards the knowledge of states of mind. Using his mind he knows the state of mind of other beings and people. He knows a mind affected with desire as a mind affected with desire; he knows a mind unaffected with desire as
80 a mind unaffected with desire. He knows a mind affected with hate as a mind affected with hate; he knows a mind unaffected with hate as a mind unaffected with hate. He knows a mind affected with delusion as a mind affected with delusion; he knows a mind unaffected with delusion as a mind unaffected with delusion. He knows a dull mind as a dull mind; he knows a distracted mind as a distracted mind. He knows a higher mind as a higher mind; he knows a lower mind as a lower mind. He knows an inferior mind as an inferior mind; he knows a superior mind as a superior mind. He knows a concentrated mind as a concentrated mind; he knows an unconcentrated mind as an unconcentrated mind. He knows a freed mind as a freed mind; he knows an unfreed mind as an unfreed mind.

'It is as if, your majesty, a woman, man, or young boy fond of their appearance, while examining the reflections of their faces in a clear, clean mirror or on the surface of a bowl of water, were to know a face with blemishes as a face with blemishes, and to know a face with no

blemishes as a face with no blemishes. In exactly the same way, once his mind is concentrated in this way . . . the monk applies and directs
his mind towards the knowledge of states of mind . . . 81

'Your majesty, this is a fruit of the ascetic life evident here and now that is superior and more refined than the previous ones.

'Once his mind is concentrated in this way, once it is thoroughly purified and cleansed—stainless, without defilements, having become sensitive, workable, and steady, reaching a state that is unshakeable—he applies and directs his mind towards the knowledge of recollection of previous lives. He remembers his numerous previous lives: one birth, two births, three, four, five births; ten, twenty, thirty, forty, fifty births; a hundred, a thousand, a hundred thousand births; over many periods of expansion of the universe, over many periods of contraction, over many periods of expansion and contraction. He remembers, "In that life I had that name, belonged to that family, that class, had that food, experienced that unhappiness, that happiness, and met my end in that way. When I died there I was born in that place. There I had that name, belonged to that family, that class, had that food, experienced that unhappiness, that happiness, and met my end in that way. When I died there I was born here." In this way he remembers the various circumstances and details of his many previous lives.

'It is as if, your majesty, a person were to go from his own village to another village, and then from that village to another village, and then from that village back again to his own village. He might think, "I went from my own village to that village. There I stood in that way, sat down in that way, spoke in that way, remained silent in that way. From that village I went to that village. There I stood in that way, sat
down in that way, spoke in that way, remained silent in that way. 82
From that village I came back again to my own village." In exactly the same way, once his mind is concentrated in this way . . . the monk applies and directs his mind towards the knowledge of recollection of previous lives.

'Your majesty, this is a fruit of the ascetic life evident here and now that is superior and more refined than the previous ones.

'Once his mind is concentrated in this way, once it is thoroughly purified and cleansed—stainless, without defilements, having become sensitive, workable, and steady, reaching a state that is unshakeable—he applies and directs his mind towards the knowledge

of the death and birth of beings. With the godlike vision that is purified, surpassing that of men, he sees beings dying and being born. He understands how beings are inferior or superior, fair or ugly, fortunate or unfortunate according to their actions:* "These beings behaved badly in body, badly in speech, badly in thought; disparaging the noble ones, they held wrong views and performed the sorts of action that follow from wrong view. At the breaking up of the body after death they were born in hell, a realm of loss, misfortune, and torment. These beings, on the other hand, behaved well in body, well in speech, well in thought; not disparaging the noble ones, they held right views and performed the sorts of action that follow from right view. At the breaking up of the body after death they were born in a happy heaven world." In this way, with the
83 godlike vision that is purified, surpassing that of men, he sees beings dying and being born. He understands how beings are inferior or superior, fair or ugly, fortunate or unfortunate according to their actions.

'It is as if, your majesty, there were a building with an upper terrace at the crossroads in the middle of a town. A person with good eyes standing up there would see the people entering houses and leaving houses, walking along the streets or sitting at the crossroads. He would think, "These people are entering houses, these are leaving, these are walking along the streets, these are sitting at the crossroads." In exactly the same way, once his mind is concentrated in this way . . . the monk applies and directs his mind towards the knowledge of the death and birth of beings.

'Your majesty, this is a fruit of the ascetic life evident here and now that is superior and more refined than the previous ones.

'Once his mind is concentrated in this way, once it is thoroughly purified and cleansed—stainless, without defilements, having become sensitive, workable, and steady, reaching a state that is unshakeable—he applies and directs his mind towards the knowledge of the destruction of the taints.* He truly understands what
84 suffering is, he truly understands what the arising of suffering is, he truly understands what the cessation of suffering is, he truly understands what the practice leading to the cessation of suffering is. He truly understands what taints are, he truly understands what the arising of taints is, he truly understands what the cessation of taints is, he truly understands what the practice leading to the cessation of

taints is. In the course of knowing this and seeing this, his mind is freed from the taint of sense desire, his mind is freed from the taint of being, his mind is freed from the taint of ignorance. And when it is freed, there is knowledge that it is freed: he knows: "Birth is destroyed, the spiritual life lived, done is what was to be done—there is nothing further required to this end."'*

'It is as if, your majesty, there were a pool of water in a mountain valley—bright, clear, and still. A person standing on the bank would see, either moving about in it or remaining still, shellfish, sand and pebbles, and shoals of fish. He would think, "This is a pool of water—bright, clear, and still. Moving about in it or remaining still are shellfish, sand and pebbles, and shoals of fish." In exactly the same way, once his mind is concentrated in this way . . . the monk applies and directs his mind towards the knowledge of the destruction of the taints . . . 85

'Your majesty, this is a fruit of the ascetic life evident here and now that is superior and more refined than the previous ones. Your majesty, there is no fruit of the ascetic life evident here and now that is superior and more refined than this.'

When these words had been spoken, King Ajātasattu of Magadha said to the Blessed One, 'Excellent, sir! Excellent! As if someone were to set upright what had been knocked down, or reveal what had been hidden, or point out the way to someone who was lost, or hold a lamp up in the dark so that those with eyes could see—just so the Blessed One has made the Truth* clear in various ways. Sir, I go to the Blessed One for refuge, and to the Teaching and the Community of monks. Let the Blessed One accept me as a lay follower who has taken refuge from this day for as long as I live. Sir, foolish, deluded, and weak man that I am, I have done something wrong. In pursuit of power, I have taken the life of my father, the righteous and lawful king. Let the Blessed One accept this confession of my wrongdoing and in the future there will be restraint.'*

'Indeed, foolish, deluded, and weak man that you are, you have done something wrong. In pursuit of power, you have taken the life of your father, the righteous and lawful king. But since you have seen your wrongdoing as wrongdoing and properly repented of it, I accept your confession. For when one sees a wrong doing as wrong doing and properly repents of it, achieving restraint in the future, this is progress in the discipline of a noble one.'

At these words King Ajātasattu of Magadha said to the Blessed One, 'And now I must go. I have many duties and much to do.'

'It is now time for you to do as you think fit.'

Then King Ajātasattu of Magadha, son of the princess of Videha, delighting and rejoicing in what the Blessed One had said, got up from his seat, saluted the Blessed One respectfully, and left, keeping his right side towards him.

86 Not long after King Ajātasattu of Magadha had left, the Blessed One addressed the monks: 'Monks, this king is ruined, he is destroyed. If he had not taken the life of his father,* a righteous and lawful king, then the spotless and stainless vision of the Truth* would have arisen as he sat right here.'

This is what the Blessed One said. Gladdened, those monks felt joy at the Blessed One's words.

THE BUDDHA'S FINAL NIBBANA

MAHĀPARINIBBĀNA-SUTTA (D II 72–168)

Introduction

The *Mahāparinibbāna-sutta* is the longest sutta in the Pali canon, consisting of six recitation sections. From one point of view, it is a narrative stitched together by incorporating various shorter accounts, many of which are found elsewhere in the canon. Rhys Davids estimated that *in toto* only about one-third of the sutta is original. Nevertheless, as Steven Collins points out, the sutta is also a carefully crafted whole.[1]

Beginning on Vultures' Peak outside the Magadhan capital of Rājagaha, it tells the story of the Buddha's final journey, death, and funeral. Two themes run throughout: the welfare of the Buddhist community after the death of the Buddha, and the devotions due the Buddha. But the sutta is also a majestic and poignant meditation on a more general Buddhist theme, that of impermanence and loss. We are reminded throughout the sutta that 'we must lose and be deprived of and separated from everything pleasant and dear', that it cannot happen 'that something that is born, come into being, conditioned, and of a nature to decay should not decay'. At the same time, against the background of the Buddha's attainment of final nibbana, the sutta reiterates that the Buddha has done what buddhas must do; he has established the monastic community and taught the way for others to also reach nibbana.

At the beginning of the sutta the Buddha is visited by King Ajātasattu's minister Vassakāra to seek advice on the wisdom of waging war on the republican state of the Vajjis. This becomes the prompt for the Buddha to set out at length the principles to be followed by the Buddhist Saṅgha if it is to avoid decline. From Rājagaha the Buddha journeys north to Nālandā where he meets, apparently for the last time, his disciple who was said to be chief in wisdom, Sāriputta. From Nālandā he continues north-west to the village of Pāṭali where he once more encounters Vassakāra, this time engaged in building defences against the Vajjis in a village that will become capital of the Mauryan empire and the most important city in India: Pāṭaliputra (modern Patna).

The Buddha then crosses the Ganges and continues in stages to Vesālī, the principal city of the Vajjis. He spends the three months of the rainy season (July to October) at Beluva, a village outside Vesālī, where he falls ill.

[1] Collins, *Nirvana and Other Buddhist Felicities* (Cambridge, 1998), 437–45.

Although he recovers from this illness, he soon afterwards renounces the possibility of living longer, even until the end of the aeon; having informed Māra that he will die in three months' time, he makes his announcement to the assembled monks of Vesālī. Continuing his journey northwestwards he reaches Pāvā, where he eats a meal offered to him by Cunda the smith which is the cause of his final sickness. On the way from Pāvā to Kusināra he meets Pukkusa and accepts him as his last lay disciple. Outside Kusinārā he asks Ānanda to prepare a bed for him between two sāl trees.

In one of the most poignant episodes of the sutta, after a conversation with the Buddha about how his body should be treated after his death, the reality of his teacher's imminent death is brought home to Ānanda, the Buddha's faithful attendant, who has yet to reach the final goal of arahatship. Ānanda withdraws and breaks down in tears. He is summoned again by the Buddha, who encourages him to make the effort to achieve the final goal. Ānanda then urges the Buddha not to die in the tiny, insignificant town of Kusinārā, at which the Buddha recounts how in ages long past Kusinārā was a fabulous royal capital. This tale itself becomes a mythic meditation on impermanence that, when expanded, forms a sutta in itself, the *Mahāsudassana-sutta*, which follows the *Mahāparinibbāna-sutta* and is also included in the present volume.

Having ordained his last monk, Subhadda, a wanderer from another school, the Buddha addresses the monks for the last time and attains final nibbana. There then follow accounts of the arrival of a group of monks headed by Mahākassapa (destined to become the master of ceremonies at the communal recitation at Rājagaha), and of the Buddha's funeral and the distribution of his relics.

The sutta and its various parallels in Sanskrit, Chinese, and Tibetan have been the subject of considerable scholarly discussion; see, for example, D. Snellgrove, 'Śākyamuni's final Nirvāṇa', *Bulletin of the School of Oriental and African Studies*, 36 (1973), 399–411; for further references and discussion of the Buddha's funeral and his relics, see John Strong, *Relics of the Buddha* (Princeton: 2004), 98–123, and Rita Langer, *Buddhist Rituals of Death and Rebirth* (London, 2007), 99–115.

---

72 [*First section for recitation*]

This is what I have heard. Once the Blessed One was staying at Rājagaha, on the mountain called Vultures' Peak.

Now at that time King Ajātasattu of Magadha, son of the princess of Videha, wishing to wage war on the Vajjis, declared: 'I will attack those powerful and mighty Vajjis,* I will cut them down, I will destroy them, I will bring about their ruin and devastation!'

So King Ajātasattu of Magadha spoke to the brahman Vassakāra, his chief minister: 'Brahman, go to the Blessed One, and having approached him bow down at his feet with your head in my name and ask if he is free of sickness and disease, if he is in good health and strong, if he lives at ease, saying, "Sir, King Ajātasattu of Magadha bows down at your feet with his head and asks if you are free of sickness and disease, if you are in good health and strong, if you live at ease." And then say, "Sir, King Ajātasattu of Magadha wishes to wage war on the Vajjis. He has declared that he will attack the powerful and mighty Vajjis, that he will cut them down, that he will destroy them, that he will bring about their ruin and devastation!" Then you should 73
note carefully what the Blessed One says in response and come and tell me, for the Tathāgatas do not speak what is untrue.'

'Yes, my lord,' replied the brahman Vassakāra, the chief minister of Magadha.

And then he had the best carriages harnessed, and mounting one he drove out of Rājagaha in a cortege of carriages and set off for Vultures' Peak. When he had gone by carriage as far as the ground would allow, he dismounted and approached the Blessed One on foot. Having approached, he saluted the Blessed One respectfully and exchanged pleasing and polite words with him, before sitting down to one side.

Once seated, he said to the Blessed One: 'Gotama sir, King Ajātasattu of Magadha bows down at your feet with his head and asks if you are free of sickness and disease, if you are in good health and strong, if you live at ease. Gotama sir, King Ajātasattu of Magadha wishes to wage war on the Vajjis. He has declared that he will attack the powerful and mighty Vajjis, that he will cut them down, that he will destroy them, that he will bring about their ruin and devastation!'

Now at that time the venerable Ānanda was standing behind the Blessed One fanning him, and the Blessed One spoke to him:* 'Ānanda, have you heard that the Vajjis meet together frequently and regularly?'

'I have heard this, sir.'

'Ānanda, as long as the Vajjis continue to meet together frequently and regularly, then they can be expected to prosper, not to decline. Ānanda, have you heard that the Vajjis sit down together in 74 concord, get up together in concord, and conduct their business in concord?'

'I have heard this, sir.'

'Ānanda, as long as the Vajjis continue to sit down together in concord, to get up together in concord, and to conduct their business in concord, then they can be expected to prosper, not to decline. Ānanda, have you heard that the Vajjis do not make pronouncements that have not been agreed, do not revoke pronouncements that have been agreed, but proceed in accordance with the ancient laws of the Vajjis that are agreed pronouncements?'

'I have heard this, sir.'

'Ānanda, as long as the Vajjis continue not to make pronouncements that have not been agreed, not to revoke pronouncements that have been agreed, but to proceed in accordance with the ancient laws of the Vajjis that are agreed pronouncements, then they can be expected to prosper, not to decline. Ānanda, have you heard that the Vajjis respect, honour, revere, and worship those among them who are their elders, and that they listen to what they say?'

'I have heard this, sir.'

'Ānanda, as long as the Vajjis continue to respect, honour, revere, and worship those among them who are their elders, and to listen to what they say, then they can be expected to prosper, not to decline. Ānanda, have you heard that the Vajjis do not abduct and force women and girls of good family into sexual relations?'

'I have heard this, sir.'

'Ānanda, as long as the Vajjis continue not to abduct and force women and girls of good family into sexual relations, then they can be expected to prosper, not to decline. Ānanda, have you heard that the Vajjis respect, honour, revere, and worship their ancestral shrines, both those that are central and those that are outlying, and do not neglect the appropriate offerings that were given and made in
75 the past?'

'I have heard this, sir.'

'Ānanda, as long as the Vajjis continue to respect, honour, revere, and worship their ancestral shrines, both those that are central and those that are outlying, and not to neglect the appropriate offerings that were given and made in the past, then they can be expected to prosper, not to decline. Ānanda, have you heard that the Vajjis provide holy men with proper care, protection, and guard, such that those who have not come to their realm are encouraged to come, and those that have come live easily?'

'I have heard this, sir.'

'Ānanda, as long as the Vajjis continue to provide holy men with proper care, protection, and guard, such that those who have not come to their realm are encouraged to come, and those that have come live easily, then they can be expected to prosper, not to decline.'

Then the Blessed One spoke to the brahman Vassakāra, the chief minister of Magadha: 'Once, brahman, when I was staying in Vesālī at the Shrine of Sārandada, I taught the Vajjis these seven principles for avoiding decline, and as long as these seven principles remain established among the Vajjis, as long as they abide by them, then they can be expected to prosper, not to decline.'

At this the brahman Vassakāra, the chief minister of Magadha, said to the Blessed One, 'Gotama sir, if the Vajjis keep to any one of these seven principles for avoiding decline, then they can be expected
to prosper, not to decline—never mind seven principles for avoiding 76
decline! Clearly King Ajātasattu of Magadha, son of the princess of Videha, will not overcome the Vajjis in war without some intrigue, without creating dissension among them.* And now, Gotama sir, I should be going. I have much to do and many duties.'

'It is now time for you to do as you think fit.'

Then the brahman Vassakāra, the chief minister of Magadha, having enjoyed and expressed his appreciation of what the Blessed One had said, got up from his seat and went away.

Not long after the brahman Vassakāra had left, the Blessed One spoke to Ānanda: 'Ānanda, go and assemble in the attendance house all the monks who are living in dependence on Rājagaha for alms.'

'Yes, sir,' replied the venerable Ānanda to the Blessed One.

And when he had assembled in the attendance house all the monks who were living in dependence on Rājagaha for alms, he approached the Blessed One, saluted him respectfully, and stood to one side.

Standing there he said to the Blessed One: 'Sir, the community of monks have assembled. It is now time for you to do as you think fit.'

Then the Blessed One got up from his seat and went to the attendance house and sat down on the prepared seat.

When he was seated he addressed the monks: 'Monks, I shall teach you seven principles for avoiding decline. Listen. Pay careful attention to what I shall say.'

'Yes, sir,' replied those monks to the Blessed One.

This is what the Blessed One said: 'Monks, as long as monks continue to meet together frequently and regularly, then they can be expected to prosper, not to decline. As long as monks continue to sit down together in concord, to get up together in concord, and to
77 conduct the business of the community in concord, then they can be expected to prosper, not to decline. As long as monks continue not to make pronouncements that have not been agreed, not to revoke pronouncements that have been agreed, but to proceed in accordance with the precepts that are agreed pronouncements, then they can be expected to prosper, not to decline. As long as monks continue to respect, honour, revere, and worship those monks who are elders, possess the pearls of wisdom, went forth into the religious life long ago, are the fathers and leaders of the community, and to listen to what they say, then they can be expected to prosper, not to decline. As long as monks are not overcome by the kind of craving that leads to rebirth when that arises, then they can be expected to prosper, not to decline. As long as monks continue to have regard for living in the forest, then they can be expected to prosper, not to decline. As long as monks individually continue to establish mindfulness, such that well-behaved companions in the spiritual life who have not come are encouraged to come, and those that have come live easily, then they can be expected to prosper, not to decline. Monks, as long as these seven principles remain established among monks, as long as they abide by them, then they can be expected to prosper, not to decline.

'Monks, I shall teach you seven further principles for avoiding decline. Listen. Pay careful attention to what I shall say.'

'Yes, sir,' replied those monks to the Blessed One.

This is what the Blessed One said: 'Monks, as long as monks do
78 not become attracted to doing things, enamoured of doing things, preoccupied with the pleasure of doing things, then they can be expected to prosper, not to decline. As long as monks do not become attracted to conversation, enamoured of conversation, preoccupied with the pleasure of conversation, then they can be expected to prosper, not to decline. As long as monks do not become attracted to sleep, enamoured of sleep, preoccupied with the pleasure of sleep, then they can be expected to prosper, not to decline. As long as monks do not become attracted to company, enamoured of company,

preoccupied with the pleasure of company, then they can be expected to prosper, not to decline. As long as monks do not have harmful desires, are not overcome by harmful desires, then they can be expected to prosper, not to decline. As long as monks do not have bad friends, bad companions, bad associates, then they can be expected to prosper, not to decline. As long as monks do not give up halfway with some inferior achievement, then they can be expected to prosper, not to decline. Monks, as long as these seven principles remain established among monks, as long as they abide by them, then they can be expected to prosper, not to decline.

'Monks, I shall teach you seven further principles for avoiding decline. Listen. Pay careful attention to what I shall say.'

'Yes, sir,' replied those monks to the Blessed One.

This is what the Blessed One said: 'Monks, as long as monks continue to have faith, self-respect, and conscience, to be learned, to put 79
forth energy, to maintain mindfulness, to be wise, then they can be expected to prosper, not to decline. Monks, as long as these seven principles remain established among monks, as long as they abide by them, then they can be expected to prosper, not to decline.

'Monks, I shall teach you seven further principles for avoiding decline. Listen. Pay careful attention to what I shall say.'

'Yes, sir,' replied those monks to the Blessed One.

This is what the Blessed One said: 'Monks, as long as monks continue to cultivate the constituent of awakening that is mindfulness, the constituent of awakening that is investigation of qualities, the constituent of awakening that is energy, the constituent of awakening that is joy, the constituent of awakening that is tranquillity, the constituent of awakening that is concentration, the constituent of awakening that is equanimity, then they can be expected to prosper, not to decline. Monks, as long as these seven principles remain established among monks, as long as they abide by them, then they can be expected to prosper, not to decline.

'Monks, I shall teach you seven further principles for avoiding decline. Listen. Pay careful attention to what I shall say.'

'Yes, sir,' replied those monks to the Blessed One.

This is what the Blessed One said: 'Monks, as long as monks continue to cultivate the notion of impermanence, the notion of not-self, the notion of ugliness, the notion of danger, the notion of abandoning, the notion of dispassion, the notion of cessation, then they can

80 be expected to prosper, not to decline. Monks, as long as these seven principles remain established among monks, as long as they abide by them, then they can be expected to prosper, not to decline.

'Monks, I shall teach you six further principles for avoiding decline. Listen. Pay careful attention to what I shall say.'

'Yes, sir,' replied those monks to the Blessed One.

This is what the Blessed One said. 'Monks, as long as monks continue to show friendliness to their companions in the spiritual life in their acts of body, both in their presence and in private, then they can be expected to prosper, not to decline. As long as monks continue to show friendliness to their companions in the spiritual life in their acts of speech, both in their presence and in private, then they can be expected to prosper, not to decline. As long as monks continue to show friendliness to their companions in the spiritual life in their acts of thought, both in their presence and in private, then they can be expected to prosper, not to decline. As long as monks continue to use their rightful possessions, rightfully obtained, impartially, right down to the portion of food contained in an alms bowl, and to share those in common with their virtuous companions in the spiritual life, then they can be expected to prosper, not to decline. As long as monks continue to live, both in the presence of their companions in the spiritual life and in private, committed to the same ways of good conduct—ways of conduct of the kind that are unbroken, without defect, unblemished, without flaw, clear, praised by the discerning, untarnished, conducive to concentration—then they can be expected to prosper, not to decline. As long as monks continue to live, both in the presence of their companions in the spiritual life and in private, committed to the same vision—the kind of vision that is noble, to do with release, which brings with it the release of the complete destruction of suffering—then they can be expected to pros-
81 per, not to decline. Monks, as long as these six principles remain established among monks, as long as they abide by them, then they can be expected to prosper, not to decline.'

Now while he was staying in Rājagaha on Vultures' Peak, the Blessed One talked to the monks a lot about the teaching in these terms: he explained how it is with good conduct, how it is with concentration, how it is with wisdom—how concentration that is invested with good conduct is of great fruit and of great benefit, how wisdom that is invested with concentration is of great fruit and of great benefit, and how the mind that is invested with wisdom is fully released from the taints, namely the taint of sense desire, the taint of being, the taint of view, the taint of ignorance.*

Now when the Blessed One had stayed at Rājagaha as long as he wanted, he spoke to the venerable Ānanda: 'Come, Ānanda, we shall move on to Ambalaṭṭhikā.'

'Yes, sir,' replied the venerable Ānanda to the Blessed One.

Then the Blessed One made his way with a large community of monks to Ambalaṭṭhikā, where he stayed in the royal rest-house. Now while he was staying in Ambalaṭṭhikā in the royal house, the Blessed One talked to the monks a lot about the teaching in these terms: he explained how it is with good conduct, how it is with concentration, how it is with wisdom—how concentration that is invested with good conduct is of great fruit and of great benefit, how wisdom that is invested with concentration is of great fruit and of great benefit, and how the mind that is invested with wisdom is fully released from the taints, namely the taint of sense desire, the taint of being, the taint of view, the taint of ignorance.

Now when the Blessed One had stayed at Ambalaṭṭhikā as long as he wanted, he spoke to the venerable Ānanda: 'Come, Ānanda, we shall move on to Nālandā.'

'Yes, sir,' replied the venerable Ānanda to the Blessed One.

Then the Blessed One made his way with a large community of monks to Nālandā, where he stayed in Pāvārika's mango grove. Then the venerable Sāriputta* approached the Blessed One, and having
saluted him respectfully sat down to one side. 82

Once seated, the venerable Sāriputta said to the Blessed One: 'Such is my confidence in the Blessed One: there has not been, there will not be nor is there now another ascetic or brahman any greater in knowledge than the Blessed One when it comes to perfect awakening.'

'Fine and courageous are the words you have spoken, Sāriputta. You have made a claim, you have roared the lion's roar when you say, "Such is my confidence in the Blessed One: there has not been, there will not be nor is there now another ascetic or brahman greater in knowledge than the Blessed One when it comes to perfect awakening." Sāriputta, the perfectly awakened arahats that existed in the past—do you know all these Blessed Ones, encompassing their minds with yours, such that you can say, "Their conduct was like this, their practice like this, their wisdom like this, the way they lived like this, their freedom like this"?'

'Not this, sir.'

'Then, Sāriputta, the perfectly awakened arahats that will exist in the future—do you know all these Blessed Ones, encompassing their minds with yours, such that you can say, "Their conduct will be like this, their practice like this, their wisdom like this, the way they will live like this, their freedom like this"?'

'Not this, sir.'

'But, Sāriputta, I am now a perfectly awakened arahat—do you know me, encompassing my mind with yours, such that you can say, "His conduct is like this, his practice like this, his wisdom like this, the way he lives like this, his freedom like this"?'

'Not this, sir.'

'Sāriputta, in these matters you do not have knowledge that encompasses the minds of the perfectly awakened arahats of the past, present and future. Then why have you spoken these fine and coura-
83 geous words, Sāriputta? Why have you made a claim? Why have you roared the lion's roar . . . ?'

'Sir, I do not have knowledge that encompasses the minds of the perfectly awakened arahats of the past, present, and future. Nevertheless, the way of Truth is known. It is as if, sir, a king had a town on his borders with strong foundations, walls, and towers, and with a single gate; and at that gate there were a gate-keeper, experienced, clever, and astute, who kept out those unknown to him and let in those he knew. And in following the path going right round the town he might not see a crack in the walls, an opening in the walls, big enough for even a cat to squeeze through. And it might occur to him that all creatures of any size which came into or left the town did so only by the gate. Exactly so, sir, is the way of Truth that I know. Whoever were perfectly awakened arahats in the past, all those Blessed Ones awakened to the highest perfect awakening by abandoning the five hindrances, which are defilements that weaken wisdom, and then, with their minds well established in the four ways of establishing mindfulness, by duly cultivating the seven constituents of awakening.* Whoever will be perfectly awakened arahats in the future, all those Blessed Ones will awaken to the highest perfect awakening by abandoning the five hindrances, which are defilements that weaken wisdom, and then, with their minds well established in the four ways of establishing mindfulness, by duly cultivating the seven constituents of awakening. And, sir, the Blessed One, who is a perfectly awakened arahat now, awakened to the highest perfect awakening by abandoning the five hindrances, which are defilements that weaken wisdom, and then, with his mind well established in the four ways of establishing mindfulness, by duly cultivating the seven constituents of awakening.'

Now while he was staying at Nālandā in Pāvārika's mango grove, 84
the Blessed One talked to the monks a lot about the teaching in these terms: he explained how it is with good conduct, how it is with concentration, how it is with wisdom—how concentration that is invested with good conduct is of great fruit and of great benefit, how wisdom that is invested with concentration is of great fruit and of great benefit, and how the mind that is invested with wisdom is fully released from the taints, namely the taint of sense desire, the taint of being, the taint of view, the taint of ignorance.

Now when the Blessed One had stayed at Nālandā as long as he wanted, he spoke to the venerable Ānanda: 'Come, Ānanda, we shall move on to the village of Pāṭali.'

'Yes, sir,' replied the venerable Ānanda to the Blessed One.

Then the Blessed One made his way with a large community of monks to the village of Pāṭali. When the lay followers in Pāṭali heard the news that the Blessed One had reached Pāṭali, they approached the Blessed One, saluted him respectfully, and sat down to one side.

Once seated, those lay followers said to the Blessed One: 'May the Blessed One accept our invitation to stay in the rest-house.'

By his silence the Blessed One accepted. Understanding that he had accepted their invitation, the lay followers of Pāṭali got up from their seats, respectfully saluted the Blessed One, and, keeping him on their right, went to the rest-house. There they spread the rest-house floor fully with a covering, prepared seats, brought a water pot, and raised an oil lamp. Then they approached the Blessed One, saluted him respectfully, and sat down to one side.

Once seated, those lay followers said to the Blessed One: 'The rest-house floor is fully spread with a covering, the seats are prepared, a water pot has been brought, and an oil lamp raised. It is now time for you to do as you think fit.' 85

Then the Blessed One put on his outer robes and, taking his bowl, went to the rest-house together with the community of monks.

When he had had his feet washed on arrival, he entered the rest-house and sat down facing east with his back to the central post. When the community of monks had had their feet washed they too entered the rest-house, where they sat down just behind the Blessed One, facing east with their backs to the western wall. When the lay followers of Pāṭali had had their feet washed they too entered the rest-house, where they sat down in front of the Blessed One, facing west with their backs to the eastern wall.

Then the Blessed One addressed the lay followers of Pāṭali: 'Householders, for someone who is without virtue there are these five dangers in his failure in conduct. What five? When someone is without virtue and fails in his conduct he suffers great loss of wealth on account of his negligence. This is the first danger. Again, when someone is without virtue and fails in his conduct his bad reputation spreads around. This is the second danger. Again, when someone is without virtue and fails in his conduct, whenever he enters an assembly, whether of rulers, brahmans, householders, or ascetics, he does so lacking confidence and nervously. This is the third danger. Again, when someone is without virtue and fails in his conduct, he dies troubled. This is the fourth danger. Again, when someone is without virtue and fails in his conduct, at the breaking up of the body, after death, he is reborn in a state of misfortune, an unhappy destiny, a state of affliction, hell. This is the fifth danger. These are the five dangers
86 in his failure in conduct for someone who is without virtue.

'For someone who is virtuous there are these five benefits of his success in conduct. What five? When someone is virtuous and succeeds in his conduct he accumulates great wealth on account of his lack of negligence. This is the first benefit. Again, when someone is virtuous and succeeds in his conduct his good reputation spreads around. This is the second benefit. Again, when someone is virtuous and succeeds in his conduct, whenever he enters an assembly, whether of rulers, brahmans, householders, or ascetics, he does so with confidence and not nervously. This is the third benefit. Again, when someone is virtuous and succeeds in his conduct, he dies untroubled. This is the fourth benefit. Again, when someone is virtuous and succeeds in his conduct, at the breaking up of the body, after death, he is reborn in a happy destiny, a heavenly world. This is the fifth benefit. These are the five benefits of his success in conduct for someone who is virtuous.'

And the Blessed One instructed the lay followers of Pāṭali with talk about the teaching long into the night, encouraging, enthusing, and inspiring them. Then he let them go, saying, 'It is well into the night. It is now time for you to do as you think fit.'

'Yes, sir,' replied those lay followers to the Blessed One. Then, getting up from their seats, they respectfully saluted the Blessed One and, keeping him on their right, went away. Not long after they had left, the Blessed One retired to a deserted house.

Now at that time Sunīdha and Vassakāra, chief ministers of Magadha, were building a city at the village of Pāṭali as a defence against the Vajjis, and deities were occupying the sites of Pāṭali 87
in their thousands. In those places where high-ranking deities occupied the sites, the high-ranking princes and ministers of the realm were inclined to build their houses; in those places where middle-ranking deities occupied the sites, the middle-ranking princes and ministers of the realm were inclined to build their houses; in those places where low-ranking deities occupied the sites, the low-ranking princes and ministers of the realm were inclined to build their houses.

With his godlike vision that is purified, surpassing that of men, the Blessed One saw those deities occupying the sites of the village in their thousands, and when he had risen after the night at dawn, he asked Ānanda who was it that was building a city at Pāṭali.

'Sir, Sunīdha and Vassakāra, chief ministers of Magadha, are building a city at the village of Pāṭali as a defence against the Vajjis.'

'Ānanda, it is as though they had taken the advice of the Gods of the Heaven of the Thirty-Three in building the city: with my godlike vision that is purified, surpassing that of men, I have seen deities occupying the sites of the village in their thousands . . . As far as the Ariyan sphere extends, as far as merchants travel, this will be the chief city: Pāṭaliputta—where "the seed sacks are split open".* But 88
Pāṭaliputta will suffer from three hazards—fire, water, and dissension among its people.'

Then Sunīdha and Vassakāra, the chief ministers of Magadha, came to the Blessed One and saluted him respectfully, exchanging pleasing and polite words with him.

Then, standing there, they said to him: 'May Gotama along with the community of monks accept our invitation for today's meal.'

By his silence the Blessed One accepted. Understanding that he had accepted their invitation, Sunīdha and Vassakāra went to their own residence, where they had fine foods of different sorts prepared. Then they had the Blessed One informed: 'It is time. The meal is ready.'

Then, early in the morning, the Blessed One put on his outer robes and, taking his bowl, went together with the community of monks to the residence of Sunīdha and Vassakāra, where he sat down on the prepared seat. Then Sunīdha and Vassakāra waited on the Blessed One and the community of monks, serving them with fine foods with their own hands. And when the Blessed One had finished eating and washed his hands and bowl,* they brought a low seat and sat down to one side. When they had sat down, the Blessed One expressed his appreciation to them with these verses:

'Having offered food to the virtuous and restrained practitioners
 of the spiritual life
In the place where he builds his home, the one who is wise
Should make an offering* to the gods who may be there:
When worshipped they worship him, when revered they revere
89 him,
And so they show concern for him, as a mother for her own son,
And with the concern of the gods a man always sees good things.'

When the Blessed One had expressed his appreciation* to Sunīdha and Vassakāra with these verses, he got up from his seat and left.

At that time Sunīdha and Vassakāra followed closely behind the Blessed One, thinking, 'The gate by which the ascetic Gotama leaves today we shall call "Gotama Gate", and the crossing by which he crosses the River Ganges we shall call "Gotama Crossing".' And the gate by which the Blessed One left they called 'Gotama Gate'.*

Then the Blessed One came to the River Ganges. At that time the Ganges was full, right up to the banks, so that crows could drink from it. And people who wanted to cross back and forth were looking for boats or dinghies, or were binding rafts. Then, just as a strong man might straighten his bent arm or bend his straightened arm, the Blessed One disappeared from the near shore of the Ganges and reappeared on the further shore, together with the community of monks. And the Blessed One saw the people who wanted to cross back and forth looking for boats or dinghies, or binding rafts.

And the Blessed One, understanding the significance of this, immediately breathed a sigh:

'Those who cross the ocean's seas by making a bridge and
avoiding the pools,
Are the wise who have already crossed while people bind their
rafts.' 90

[*Second section for recitation*]

Then the Blessed One spoke to the venerable Ānanda: 'Come, Ānanda, we shall move on to the village of Koṭi.'

'Yes, sir,' replied the venerable Ānanda to the Blessed One.

Then the Blessed One made his way with a large community of monks to the village of Koṭi.

While he was staying there he addressed the monks: 'Monks, it is because of not understanding, not penetrating the four noble truths that both you and I have run and wandered the round of rebirth in this way for such a long time. Which four? It is because of not understanding, not penetrating the noble truth of suffering . . . of the arising of suffering . . . of the cessation of suffering . . . of the practice leading to the cessation of suffering, that both you and I have run and wandered the round of rebirth for such a long time. But once the noble truth that this is suffering is understood and penetrated, once the noble truth of the arising of suffering is understood and penetrated, once the noble truth of the cessation of suffering is understood and penetrated, once the noble truth of the practice leading to the cessation of suffering is understood and penetrated, then craving for existence is cut off, the conductor of existence is destroyed, and no longer is there rebirth.'

This is what the Blessed One said. And when the Happy One had
said this, the Teacher spoke again: 91

'Through not truly seeing four realities as do the noble ones,
One journeys a long time through various births.
But when they are seen, the conductor of existence is removed,
The root of suffering is cut, and no longer is there
rebirth.'

Now while he was staying at the village of Koṭi the Blessed One talked to the monks a lot about the teaching in these terms: he explained how it is with good conduct, how it is with concentration, how it is with wisdom—how concentration that is invested with good conduct is of great fruit and of great benefit, how wisdom that is invested with concentration is of great fruit and of great benefit, and how the mind that is invested with wisdom is fully released from the taints, namely the taint of sense desire, the taint of being, the taint of view, the taint of ignorance.

Now when the Blessed One had stayed at the village of Koṭi as long as he wanted, he spoke to the venerable Ānanda: 'Come, Ānanda, we shall move on to Nādika.'

'Yes, sir,' replied the venerable Ānanda to the Blessed One.

Then the Blessed One made his way with a large community of monks to Nādika, where he stayed in the brick house. Then Ānanda approached him, and having saluted him respectfully sat down to one side.

Once seated, he said to the Blessed One: 'Sir, the monk Sāḷha has
died in Nādika. What is his destiny, what is his fate? The nun Nandā
92 has died in Nādika. What is her destiny, what is her fate? The layman
Sudatta has died in Nādika. What is his destiny, what is his fate? The laywoman Sujātā has died in Nādika. What is her destiny, what is her fate? The laymen Kakudha, Kāliṅga, Nikaṭa, Kaṭissabha, Tuṭṭha, Santuṭṭha, Bhadda, Subhassa have died in Nādika. What is their destiny, what is their fate?'*

'Ānanda, the monk Sāḷha, by destroying the taints, lived here in this world, having experienced and attained for himself through direct knowledge the freedom of mind and wisdom that is without taints. The nun Nandā, by completely destroying the five lower fetters, is someone who is reborn purely* who will attain final nibbana in that world and will not return from there. The layman Sudatta, by completely destroying three fetters and by weakening greed, hatred, and delusion, is someone who returns once; having returned once to this world he will make an end of suffering. The laywoman Sujātā, by completely destroying three fetters, is someone who has entered the stream and is beyond affliction, destined to full awakening for sure. The laymen Kakudha, Kāliṅga, Nikaṭa, Kaṭissabha, Tuṭṭha, Santuṭṭha, Bhadda, Subhassa, by completely destroying the five
lower fetters, are those who are reborn purely who will attain final
93 nibbana in that world and will not return from [93] there.

'Ānanda, a further fifty lay followers who have died in Nādika have, by completely destroying the five lower fetters, become those who are reborn purely who will attain final nibbana there and will not return from that world. Over ninety lay followers who have died in Nādika have, by completely destroying three fetters and by weakening greed, hatred, and delusion, become those who return once; having returned once to this world they will make an end of suffering. More than five hundred lay followers who have died in Nādika have, by completely destroying three fetters, become those who have entered the stream and are beyond affliction, destined to full awakening for sure.

'Now, that human beings should die is not out of the ordinary, Ānanda. But if you are going to come to the Tathāgata and ask him this question every time someone should die, that will be a nuisance to him. So I shall teach you a way of Truth called "the mirror of Truth". With this the noble disciple who wishes could by himself describe himself as having finished with birth in hell, as an animal, or a ghost, as having finished with misfortune, unhappy destinies, and affliction, as someone who has entered the stream and is beyond affliction, destined to full awakening for sure.

'What, Ānanda, is the mirror of Truth, the way of Truth with which the noble disciple who wishes could by himself describe himself . . . ? In this connection a noble disciple has confidence in the Buddha because he knows that he is the Blessed One in that he is an arahat, a perfect buddha, accomplished in knowledge and conduct, happy, one who understands the world, the unsurpassed charioteer of men to be tamed, the teacher of gods and men, a blessed buddha. He has confidence in the Truth because he knows that the Truth that is clear, immediate, accessible, practical, and that one who is discerning can come to know for himself, has been well explained by the Blessed One.* He has confidence in the Community because he knows that the Community of the Blessed One consisting of the eight persons in four pairs* conducts itself well, honestly, skilfully, and properly, that 94
it is a Community deserving of offerings, hospitality, presents, and respect, an unsurpassed field of merit for the world. He possesses ways of conduct that are dear to the noble ones, of the kind that are unbroken, without defect, unblemished, without flaw, clear, praised by the discerning, untarnished, and conducive to concentration. This, Ānanda, is the mirror of Truth, the way of Truth with which the noble disciple who wishes could by himself describe himself . . . '

Now while he was staying at Nādika, the Blessed One talked to the monks a lot about the teaching in these terms: he explained how it is with good conduct, how it is with concentration, how it is with wisdom—how concentration that is invested with good conduct is of great fruit and of great benefit, how wisdom that is invested with concentration is of great fruit and of great benefit, and how the mind that is invested with wisdom is fully released from the taints, namely the taint of sense desire, the taint of being, the taint of view, the taint of ignorance.

Now when the Blessed One had stayed at Nādika as long as he wanted, he spoke to the venerable Ānanda: 'Come, Ānanda, we shall move on to Vesālī.'

'Yes, sir,' replied the venerable Ānanda to the Blessed One.

Then the Blessed One made his way with a large community of monks to Vesālī, where he stayed in Ambapālī's grove.

There the Blessed One addressed the monks: 'A monk should live mindfully, with full awareness. This is my instruction to you. How does a monk live mindfully? In this case a monk lives watching the
95 body as body; he is determined, fully aware, mindful, overcoming his longing for and discontent with the world. He lives watching feelings as feelings; he is determined, fully aware, mindful, overcoming his longing for and discontent with the world. He lives watching mind as mind; he is determined, fully aware, mindful, overcoming his longing for and discontent with the world. He lives watching qualities as qualities; he is determined, fully aware, mindful, overcoming his longing for and discontent with the world. It is in this way that a monk lives mindfully.

'How does a monk live with full awareness? In moving forward and turning back, a monk acts with full awareness; in looking ahead and looking around, he acts with full awareness; in bending and straightening his limbs, he acts with full awareness; in wearing his inner and outer robes and carrying his alms bowl, he acts with full awareness; in eating, drinking, chewing and swallowing, he acts with full awareness; in defecating and urinating, he acts with full awareness; in walking, standing, sitting, falling asleep, waking up, speaking, and keeping silent, he acts with full awareness. It is in this way that a monk lives with full awareness. A monk should live mindfully, with full awareness. This is my instruction to you.'

Now when the courtesan Ambapālī* heard people say that the Blessed One had reached Vesālī and was staying in her mango grove, she had the best carriages harnessed, and mounting one, she drove out of Vesālī in a cortege of carriages and set off for the park. When she had gone by carriage as far as the ground would allow, she dismounted and approached the Blessed One on foot. Having approached, she saluted the Blessed One respectfully and exchanged pleasing and polite words with him, before sitting down to one side. Once Ambapālī was seated, the Blessed One instructed her with talk about the teaching, encouraging, enthusing, and inspiring her.

Instructed, encouraged, enthused, and inspired by his talk, she said to the Blessed One: 'May the Blessed One along with the community of monks accept my invitation for tomorrow's meal.'

By his silence the Blessed One accepted. Understanding that he had accepted her invitation, Ambapālī got up from her seat, respectfully saluted the Blessed One, and left, keeping him on her right. Now when the Licchavis* of Vesālī heard people say that the Blessed One [96] had reached Vesālī and was staying in Ambapālī's grove, they had the best carriages harnessed, and mounting them, they drove out of Vesālī in a cortege of carriages. Some of these Licchavis were in blue—made up in blue, dressed in blue, and adorned with 96
blue. Some were in yellow—made up in yellow, dressed in yellow, and adorned with yellow. Some were in red—made up in red, dressed in red, and adorned with red. Some were in white—made up in white, dressed in white, and adorned with white.

And when the courtesan Ambapālī came past, scraping the young Licchavis' axles, wheels, and yokes with hers, the Licchavis asked her: 'Ambapālī, how come you are scraping past the young Licchavis like this?'

'Because, young men, I have just invited the Blessed One and the community of monks for tomorrow's meal.'

'Ambapālī, give up this meal for a hundred thousand pieces!'

'Young men, even if you were to give me Vesālī and its countryside, I would not give up a meal of this importance.'

Then the Licchavis snapped their fingers. 'We've been outdone by the mango girl! We've been cheated by the mango girl!'*

Then the Licchavis went on to Ambapālī's grove. When the Blessed One saw the Licchavis coming in the distance, he said to the monks: 'Any monks who have never seen the Gods of the Thirty-Three should just look at this group of Licchavis—gaze on it and focus on it as though it were the assembly of the Thirty- 97
Three.'*

When the Licchavis had gone by carriage as far as the ground would allow, they dismounted and approached the Blessed One on foot. Having approached, they saluted the Blessed One respectfully and exchanged pleasing and polite words with him, before sitting down to one side. When they were seated, the Blessed One instructed the Licchavis with talk about the teaching, encouraging, enthusing, and inspiring them. Instructed, encouraged, enthused, and inspired by his talk, they said to the Blessed One: 'May the Blessed One along with the community of monks accept our invitation for tomorrow's meal.'

'Licchavis, I have accepted the courtesan Ambapālī's invitation for tomorrow's meal.'

Then the Licchavis snapped their fingers: 'We've been outdone by the mango girl! We've been cheated by the mango girl!'

When the Licchavis had enjoyed and expressed their appreciation of what the Blessed One said, they got up from their seats, respectfully saluted the Blessed One, and left, keeping him on their right.

When the night was over, Ambapālī had fine foods of different sorts prepared in her own park. Then she had the Blessed One informed: 'It is time, sir. The meal is ready.'

Then, early in the morning, the Blessed One put on his outer robes and, taking his bowl, went together with the community of monks to where the meal was being served and sat down on the prepared seat. Then Ambapālī the courtesan waited on the Blessed One and the community of monks, serving them with the fine foods with her own hands. And when the Blessed One had finished eating and
98 washed his hands and bowl, she brought a low seat and sat down to one side.

Once seated, she said to the Blessed One: 'Sir, I am giving this park to the Buddha and his community of monks.'

The Blessed One accepted the park, and then after he had instructed Ambapālī with talk about the teaching, encouraging, enthusing, and inspiring her, he left.

Now while he was staying at Vesālī in Ambapālī's grove, the Blessed One talked to the monks a lot about the teaching in these terms: he explained how it is with good conduct, how it is with concentration, how it is with wisdom—how concentration that is invested with good conduct is of great fruit and of great benefit, how wisdom that is invested with concentration is of great fruit and of great benefit, and how the mind that is invested with wisdom is fully released from the taints, namely the taint of sense desire, the taint of being, the taint of view, the taint of ignorance.

Now when the Blessed One had stayed in Ambapālī's grove as long as he wanted, he spoke to the venerable Ānanda: 'Come, Ānanda, we shall move on to the village of Beluva.'

'Yes, sir,' replied the venerable Ānanda to the Blessed One. Then the Blessed One made his way with a large community of monks to the village of Beluva.

While he was staying there he addressed the monks: 'Monks, go anywhere around Vesālī—where you have friends, where you are known, where you have supporters—and enter upon the rainy season* there. I will enter upon it here in the village of Beluva.'

'Yes, sir,' replied those monks.

And so they entered upon the rainy season around Vesālī . . . and 99
the Blessed One entered upon it in Beluva. When the Blessed One had entered upon the rainy season he fell seriously ill, suffering severe pains as though he were close to death. Without complaining, the Blessed One accepted the pains mindfully and with full awareness. Then it occurred to the Blessed One: 'It would not be right for me to reach final nibbana without my having addressed those attending on me and having taken my leave of the community of monks. Suppose I should suppress this illness by force and live by controlling the vital energy.'

So the Blessed One suppressed his illness by force and lived by controlling his vital energy. And so he recovered from his illness. Soon after he had recovered he came out from his dwelling and sat down on the prepared seat in the shade of the building. Then the venerable Ānanda came to him and sat down to one side.

Once seated, he spoke to the Blessed One: 'I can see that the Blessed One is comfortable. I can see that the Blessed One is bearing up. And although when the Blessed One was ill my body seemed to be drugged and I did not know where to turn and things were not clear to me, nevertheless I had just enough confidence to feel that the Blessed One would not reach final nibbana without saying something about the Community of monks.' 100

'But what does the Community of monks want from me, Ānanda? I have taught the Truth without considering who is an insider and who an outsider. The Tathāgata is not the kind of teacher who is tight-fisted with matters of Truth. Surely if there is someone who thinks that it is he who should be in charge of the Community of monks or that the Community of monks is his particular concern, then it is he who should say something about the Community of monks. But the Tathāgata does not think that it is he who should be in charge of the Community of monks or that the Community of monks is his particular concern, so why should he say something about the Community of monks?

'I am an old and aged man, Ānanda, an elder who has done his time and reached old age. I have turned eighty, and just as a worn-out cart is kept going with the help of repairs,* so it seems is the Tathāgata's body kept going with repairs. The only time that the Tathāgata can make his body comfortable is when he lives having attained a state of mental concentration without sensation, and specific feelings cease through not paying attention to any sensations.

'So, Ānanda, you should live with yourselves as your island of refuge and not someone else, with the Truth as your island of refuge* and not something else. And how does one live with oneself as one's island of refuge, with the Truth as one's island of refuge? A monk should live mindfully, with full awareness. This is my instruction to you. How does a monk live mindfully? In this case a monk lives watching the body as body; he is determined, fully aware, mindful, overcoming his longing for and discontent with the world. He lives watching feelings as feelings . . . mind as mind . . . qualities as qualities; he is determined, fully aware, mindful, overcoming his longing for and discontent with the world. It is in this way that a monk lives mindfully. This is how one lives with oneself as one's island of refuge, with the Truth as one's island of refuge.

'Whoever of my monks, either now or after I have gone, live
with themselves as their island of refuge and not someone else,
with the Truth as their island of refuge and not something else,
they will be guides in the darkness,* whoever are desirous of
102 training.'

[*Third section for recitation*]

Then, early in the morning, the Blessed One put on his outer robes and, taking his bowl, went into Vesālī for alms. Having collected alms, he returned from the alms round and after the meal he spoke to Ānanda: 'Bring something to sit on, Ānanda. Let us go and spend the day at the shrine of Cāpāla.'

'Yes, sir,' replied the venerable Ānanda. And taking something to sit on, he followed close behind the Blessed One. When the Blessed One reached the shrine of Cāpāla he sat down on the prepared seat, and having saluted him, the venerable Ānanda sat down to one side.

Once the venerable Ānanda was seated, the Blessed One said to him: 'How delightful is Vesālī! How delightful are the shrines of Udena, Gotamaka, Sattambaka, Bahuputta, and Sārandada! And how delightful is the shrine of Cāpāla! 103

'Ānanda, anyone who has cultivated and made much of the four bases of accomplishment, who has worked with them and is grounded in them, who has attended to and familiarized himself with them, who has undertaken their practice fully, could, if he so wished, live on for an aeon or what remains of it.* The Tathāgata has cultivated and made much of the four bases of accomplishment, he has worked with them and is grounded in them, he has attended to and familiarized himself with them, he has undertaken their practice fully. He could, if he so wished, live on for an aeon or what remains of it.'

And so the venerable Ānanda, even when the Blessed One gave such an obvious sign, such an obvious hint, was unable to understand and did not say to the Blessed One: 'Let the Blessed One live on for an aeon! Let the Happy One live on for an aeon, for the good and happiness of the many, out of sympathy for the world, for the benefit, good, and happiness of gods and men.' For Māra had possessed his mind.

A second time . . . And a third time the Blessed One said to Ānanda: 'How delightful is Vesālī! . . . Anyone who has cultivated and made much of the four bases of accomplishment . . . could, if he so wished, live on for an aeon . . .'

And so the venerable Ānanda, even when the Blessed One gave such an obvious sign . . . did not say to him: 'Let the Blessed One live on for an aeon! . . .' For Māra had possessed his mind. 104

Then the Blessed One spoke to Ānanda: 'Go, Ānanda. It is now time for you to do as you think fit.'

'Yes, sir,' replied the venerable Ānanda.

And getting up from his seat, he saluted the Blessed One respectfully, and keeping him to the right, he went and sat down at the root of a nearby tree. Not long after the venerable Ānanda had gone, Māra the Bad approached the Blessed One and stood to one side.

Standing there, Māra the Bad said to the Blessed One: 'Let the Blessed One attain final nibbana now! Let the Happy One attain final nibbana now! Now is the time for the Blessed One to attain final nibbana! The Blessed One has said this to me: that he would not attain final nibbana as long as his monks were not realized disciples, accomplished, experienced, learned; were not bearers of the Truth, practised in the teaching and its subtleties, conducting themselves properly and living in accordance with the Truth; were not learning what their teachers say and proclaiming it, teaching it, making it known, substantiating it, demonstrating it, explaining it, making it clear; were not refuting the contrary teachings that have arisen which are easily refuted by Truth, and teaching the Truth and its wonders. The
105 Blessed One's monks are now realized disciples . . . teaching the Truth and its wonders. Let the Blessed One attain final nibbana now! Let the Happy One attain final nibbana now! Now is the time for the Blessed One to attain final nibbana!

'The Blessed One has said this to me: that he would not attain final nibbana as long as his nuns . . . his laymen . . . his laywomen were not realized disciples . . . teaching the Truth and its wonders. The
106 Blessed One's laywomen are now realized disciples . . . teaching the Truth and its wonders. Let the Blessed One attain final nibbana now! Let the Happy One attain final nibbana now! Now is the time for the Blessed One to attain final nibbana!

'The Blessed One has said this to me: that he would not attain final nibbana until this spiritual practice of his had become successful and prosperous, spreading far, popular and widespread, until it was renowned among men. The Blessed One's spiritual practice has now become successful and prosperous . . . renowned among men. Let the Blessed One attain final nibbana now! Let the Happy One attain final nibbana now! Now is the time for the Blessed One to attain final nibbana!'

At this the Blessed One said to Māra the Bad: 'Do not worry, Bad One. The Tathāgata's final nibbana will not be long: three months from now he will attain final nibbana.'

Then, at the shrine of Cāpāla the Blessed One mindfully and with full awareness gave up the force of life. And when he gave up the force of life the earth quaked, frightening, making the hairs stand on

end, and claps of thunder rent the sky. And the Blessed One, under- 107
standing the significance of this, immediately breathed a sigh:

> 'Balancing* the incomparable against existence, the sage gave up the force of becoming:
> Concentrated deep within, he rent his own existence like a coat of mail.'

And Ānanda thought, 'This is remarkable, this is extraordinary—the earth quaked, the earth quaked violently, frightening, making my hairs stand on end, and claps of thunder rent the sky! What is the cause, what is the reason for the occurrence of this earthquake?'

Then the venerable Ānanda went to the Blessed One, saluted him, and then sat down to one side.

Once seated, he spoke to the Blessed One: 'This is remarkable, this is extraordinary—the earth quaked, the earth quaked violently, frightening, making my hairs stand on end, and claps of thunder rent the sky! What is the cause, what is the reason for the occurrence of this earthquake?'

'There are these eight causes of and reasons for the occurrence of earthquakes. Which eight? This great earth rests on water, the water on wind, and the wind on space. At times the great winds blow; when they disturb the water, the disturbed water disturbs the earth. This
is the first reason and cause. Again, when an ascetic or brahman 108
who has abilities and has gained the mastery of the mind, or when a god of great accomplishment and power has cultivated the notion of earth as insignificant and of water as immeasurable, then he disturbs the earth, shaking it, causing it to shudder, and quake. This is the second reason and cause. Again, when one who is intent on awakening falls from the company of the Contented Gods and mindfully and fully aware descends into his mother's womb, then the earth is disturbed, it shakes, shudders, and quakes. This is the third reason and cause. Again, when one who is intent on awakening mindfully and with full awareness leaves his mother's womb, then the earth is disturbed, it shakes, shudders, and quakes. This is the fourth reason and cause. Again, when the Tathāgata awakens to the unsurpassed complete awakening, then the earth is disturbed, it shakes, shudders, and quakes. This is the fifth reason and cause. Again, when the Tathāgata turns the unsurpassed wheel of Truth, then the earth is disturbed, it shakes, shudders, and quakes. This is

the sixth reason and cause. Again, when the Tathāgata mindfully and with full awareness gives up the force of life, then the earth is disturbed, it shakes, shudders, and quakes. This is the seventh reason
109 and cause. Again, when the Tathāgata attains nibbana by means of the nibbana that is without any remnant of attachment,* then the earth is disturbed, it shakes, shudders, and quakes. This is the eighth reason and cause.

'Ānanda, there are these eight assemblies. Which eight? The assembly of rulers, the assembly of brahmans, the assembly of householders, the assembly of ascetics, the assembly of the Gods of the Four Kings, the assembly of the Gods of the Thirty-Three, the assembly of Māras, the assembly of Brahmās.

'Ānanda, I recall in the past approaching an assembly of several hundred rulers where I sat down, had conversation, and engaged in discussion. In that assembly I matched my appearance to their appearance, I matched the sound of my voice to the sound of theirs, and I instructed them with talk about the teaching, encouraging, enthusing, and inspiring them. And while I was speaking they did not know who I was and thought: "Who is this who speaks, a god or a man?" And when I had instructed them with talk about the teaching, encouraging, enthusing, and inspiring them, I disappeared. And when I had disappeared they did not know who I was, and thought: "Who was it that disappeared, a god or a man?" I recall in the past approaching an assembly of several hundred brahmans . . . householders . . . ascetics . . . Gods of the Four Kings . . . Gods of the Thirty-Three . . . Māras . . . Brahmās, where I sat down, had conversation, and engaged in discussion. In that assembly I matched my appearance to their appearance, I matched the sound of my voice to the sound of theirs, and I instructed them with talk about the teaching, encouraging, enthusing, and inspiring them. And while I was speaking they did not know who I was and thought: "Who is this who
110 speaks, a god or a man?" And when I had instructed them with talk about the teaching, encouraging, enthusing, and inspiring them, I disappeared. And when I had disappeared they did not know who I was, and thought: "Who was it that disappeared, a god or a man?"

'There are these eight spheres of mastery. Which eight? Conceiving of visible forms within, someone sees small external visible forms that are pleasant or unpleasant in appearance; he is conscious of those forms with the thought that he knows and sees them, having mastered them. This is the first sphere of mastery.

'Conceiving of visible forms within, someone sees immeasurably large external visible forms that are pleasant or unpleasant in appearance; he is conscious of those forms with the thought that he knows and sees them, having mastered them. This is the second.

'Without conceiving of visible forms within, someone sees small external visible forms that are pleasant or unpleasant in appearance; he is conscious of those forms with the thought that he knows and sees them, having mastered them. This is the third.

'Without conceiving of visible forms within, someone sees immeasurably large external visible forms that are pleasant or unpleasant in appearance; he is conscious of those forms with the thought that he knows and sees them, having mastered them. This is the fourth.

'Without conceiving of visible forms within, someone sees external visible forms that are blue—blue in colour, blue in appearance, bright blue—like the flax flower, or a piece of Benares cloth that has been finished on both sides, which are blue—blue in colour, blue in appearance, bright blue. In exactly the same way . . . he sees blue visible forms . . . he is conscious of those forms with the thought that he knows and sees them, having mastered them. This is the fifth. 111

'Without conceiving of visible forms within, someone sees external visible forms that are yellow—yellow in colour, yellow in appearance, bright yellow—like the kaṇikāra flower, or a piece of Benares cloth that has been finished on both sides, which are yellow—yellow in colour, yellow in appearance, bright yellow. In exactly the same way . . . he sees yellow visible forms . . . he is conscious of those forms with the thought that he knows and sees them, having mastered them. This is the sixth.

'Without conceiving of visible forms within, someone sees external visible forms that are red—red in colour, red in appearance, bright red—like the bandhujīvaka flower, or a piece of Benares cloth that has been finished on both sides, which are red—red in colour, red in appearance, bright red. In exactly the same way . . . he sees red visible forms . . . he is conscious of those forms with the thought that he knows and sees them, having mastered them. This is the seventh.

'Without conceiving of visible forms within, someone sees external visible forms that are white—white in colour, white in appearance, bright white—like the Bright Star,* or a piece of Benares cloth that has been finished on both sides, which are white—white in colour, white in appearance, bright white. In exactly the same way . . . he sees white visible forms . . . he is conscious of those forms with the thought that he knows and sees them, having mastered them. This is the eighth. These are the eight spheres of mastery.

'There are these eight liberations. Which eight? Having visible
112 form, someone sees visible forms. This is the first liberation. Conceiving of visible forms within, someone sees external visible forms. This is the second. Someone becomes focused on just the idea of the beautiful. This is the third. By passing entirely beyond notions of visible form, by stopping notions of the resistant, and by not paying attention to notions of differentiation, someone takes the idea of space as infinite and lives attaining the sphere of infinity of space. This is the fourth. By passing entirely beyond the sphere of infinity of space, someone takes the idea of consciousness as infinite and lives attaining the sphere of infinity of consciousness. This is the fifth. By passing entirely beyond the sphere of infinity of consciousness, someone takes the idea of there being nothing and lives attaining the sphere of nothingness. This is the sixth. By passing entirely beyond the sphere of nothingness, someone lives attaining the sphere of neither consciousness nor unconsciousness. This is the seventh. By passing entirely beyond the sphere of neither consciousness nor unconsciousness, someone lives attaining the cessation of conception and feeling. This is the eighth liberation. These are the eight liberations.

'Once, Ānanda, just after I had become awakened I was staying at Uruvelā on the banks of the River Nerañjarā by the goatherd's banyan tree, and Māra the Bad came to me and stood to one side. Standing there, he said to me: "Let the Blessed One attain final nibbana now! Let the Happy One attain final nibbana now! Now is the time for the Blessed One to attain final nibbana!"

'When Māra the Bad said this I replied: "I will not attain final nibbana as long as my monks are not realized disciples, accomplished, experienced, learned; are not bearers of the Truth, practised in the teaching and its subtleties, conducting themselves properly and living in accordance with the Truth; are not learning what their
113 teachers say and proclaiming it, teaching it, making it known, substantiating it, demonstrating it, explaining it, making it clear; are not refuting the contrary teachings that have arisen which are easily

refuted by Truth, and teaching the Truth and its wonders. I will not attain final nibbana as long as my nuns . . . my laymen . . . my laywomen are not realized disciples . . . teaching the Truth and its wonders. I will not attain final nibbana until this spiritual practice of mine has become successful and prosperous, spreading far, popular and widespread, until it is renowned among men."

'Today, Ānanda, just now, Māra the Bad approached me and stood to one side. Standing there, Māra the Bad said to me: "Let the Blessed One attain final nibbana now! Let the Happy One attain final nibbana now! Now is the time for the Blessed One to attain final
nibbana! The Blessed One has said this to me: that he would not 114
attain final nibbana as long as his monks were not realized disciples . . . The Blessed One's monks are now realized disciples . . . The Blessed One has said this to me: that he would not attain final nibbana as long as his nuns . . . his laymen . . . his laywomen were not realized disciples . . . The Blessed One's laywomen are now realized disciples . . . The Blessed One has said this to me: that he would not attain final nibbana until this spiritual practice of his had become successful and prosperous . . . The Blessed One's spiritual practice has now become successful and prosperous . . . renowned among men. Let the Blessed One attain final nibbana now! Let the Happy One attain final nibbana now! Now is the time for the Blessed One to attain final nibbana!"

'When Māra the Bad said this, Ānanda, I replied: "Do not worry, Bad One. The Tathāgata's final nibbana will not be long: three months from now he will attain final nibbana."

'Today, Ānanda, just now, at the shrine of Cāpāla the Tathāgata
mindfully and with full awareness gave up the force of life.' 115

When the Blessed One said this the venerable Ānanda said: 'Let the Blessed One live on for an aeon! Let the Happy One live on for an aeon, for the good and happiness of many, out of sympathy for the world, for the benefit, good, and happiness of gods and men.'

'Enough, Ānanda, do not ask the Blessed One now! Now is not the time to ask!'

A second time . . . and a third time the venerable Ānanda said: 'Let the Blessed One live on for an aeon! Let the Happy One live on for an aeon, for the good and happiness of many, out of sympathy for the world, for the benefit, good, and happiness of gods and men.'

'Ānanda, do you have faith in the Tathāgata's awakening?'

'Yes, sir.'

'Then why do you press the Tathāgata as many as three times?'

'I have heard directly from the Blessed One, I have learnt directly from him that anyone who has cultivated and made much of the four bases of accomplishment, who has worked with them and is grounded in them, who has attended to and familiarized himself with them, who has undertaken their practice fully, could, if he so wished, live on for an aeon or what remains of it. I have learnt directly from him that the Tathāgata has cultivated and made much of the four bases of accomplishment . . . that he could, if he so wished, live on for an aeon or what remains of it.'

'Do you believe this, Ānanda?'

'Yes, sir.'

'Then it is you who are at fault, Ānanda, you who have failed: even when the Blessed One gave such an obvious sign, such an obvious hint, you were unable to understand and you did not say to the Tathāgata: "Let the Blessed One live on for an aeon . . . for the good and happiness of many . . . " If you had asked, the Blessed One would have twice refused your request, but the third time he would have agreed. So it is you who are at fault, Ānanda, you who have failed.

'Once, Ānanda, I was staying at Rājagaha on Vultures' Peak, and
116 while there I told you: "How delightful is Rājagaha, Ānanda, how
delightful Vultures' Peak. Anyone who has cultivated and made much of the four bases of accomplishment, who has worked with them and is grounded in them, who has attended to and familiarized himself with them, who has undertaken their practice fully, could, if he so wished, live on for an aeon or what remains of it. The Tathāgata has cultivated and made much of the four bases of accomplishment . . . he could, if he so wished, live on for an aeon or what remains of it." Even when the Tathāgata gave such an obvious sign, such an obvious hint, you were unable to understand and you did not say to the Tathāgata: "Let the Blessed One live on for an aeon . . . for the good and happiness of many . . . " If you had asked, the Blessed One would have twice refused your request, but the third time he would have agreed. So it is you who are at fault, Ānanda, you who have failed.

'Once I was staying there in Rājagaha in Gotama's banyan park . . . at Robbers' Cliff . . . in the Sattapaṇṇi cave on the slope of Vebhāra . . . at Black Rock on the slope of Isigili . . . in the Sīta grove in the Sappasoṇḍika ravine . . . in the Tapodā park . . . in the bamboo grove

at the Squirrels' Feeding Ground . . . in Jīvaka's mango grove . . . in the Maddakucchi deer park . . . Once I was staying right here in 117
Vesālī at the shrine of Udena . . . of Gotamaka . . . of Sattambaka . . . 118
of Bahuputta . . . of Sārandada . . . And today, just now, Ānanda, at the shrine of Cāpāla I told you: "How delightful is Vesālī, Ānanda, how delightful the shrine of Cāpāla. Anyone who has cultivated and made much of the four bases of accomplishment, who has worked with them and is grounded in them, who has attended to and familiarized himself with them, who has undertaken their practice fully, could, if he so wished, live on for an aeon or what remains of it. The Tathāgata has cultivated and made much of the four bases of accomplishment . . . he could, if he so wished, live on for an aeon or what remains of it." Even when the Tathāgata gave such an obvious sign, such an obvious hint, you were unable to understand and you did not say to the Tathāgata: "Let the Blessed One live on for an aeon . . . for the good and happiness of many . . . " If you had asked, the Blessed One would have twice refused your request, but the third time he would have agreed. So it is you who are at fault, Ānanda, you who have failed.*

'Ānanda, have I not warned about this before: we must lose and be deprived of and separated from everything pleasant and dear? So how else could it be? That something that is born, come into being, conditioned and of a nature to decay should not decay—this cannot happen. This is what the Tathāgata has renounced, cast off, let go, abandoned, relinquished: he has given up the force of life. The Tathāgata has said unequivocally that his final nibbana will not be long: three months 119
from now he will attain final nibbana. That, in order to live, the Tathāgata should take back what he has said, this cannot happen. Come, Ānanda, we shall go to the Great Grove and the gabled hall.'

'Yes, sir,' replied the venerable Ānanda to the Blessed One.

Then the Blessed One went with the venerable Ānanda to the Great Grove and the gabled hall.

When they arrived he spoke to him: 'Ānanda, go and assemble in the attendance house all the monks who are living in dependence on Vesālī for alms.'

'Yes, sir,' replied the venerable Ānanda to the Blessed One.

And when he had assembled in the attendance house all the monks who were living in dependence on Vesālī for alms, he approached the Blessed One, saluted him respectfully, and stood to one side.

Standing there, he said to the Blessed One: 'Sir, the community of monks have assembled. It is now time for you to do as you think fit.'

Then the Blessed One went to the attendance house and sat down on the prepared seat.

When he was seated he addressed the monks: 'So, monks, those practices that I have taught to you for the purpose of direct knowledge—having properly grasped them, you should pursue them, cultivate them, make much of them so that the spiritual life might continue and endure long; this will be for the good and the happiness of the many, out of sympathy for the world, for the benefit, good, and
120 happiness of gods and men. And what are those practices . . . ? Just these—the four ways of establishing mindfulness, the four ways of right application, the four bases of accomplishment, the five faculties, the five powers, the seven constituents of awakening, the noble eightfold path.* These are the practices that I have taught to you for the purpose of direct knowledge. Having properly grasped them, you should pursue them, cultivate them, make much of them so that the spiritual life might continue and endure long; this will be for the good and the happiness of the many, out of sympathy for the world, for the benefit, good and happiness of gods and men.'

Then the Blessed One said to the monks: 'Well, monks, now I take my leave of you:* it is of the nature of things to decay, but if you are attentive you will succeed! The Tathāgata's final nibbana will not be long: three months from now he will attain final nibbana.'

This is what the Blessed One said. And when the Happy One had said this, the Teacher spoke again:

'I am mature in age, my life is over;
I must leave you behind and go, acting as my own refuge.
Be attentive, monks! Be mindful and of good conduct.
121 With your thoughts well focused, keep your minds protected.
He who lives without neglecting this practice and discipline
Will give up wandering from birth to birth and bring suffering
122 to an end.

[*Fourth section for recitation: the Āḷāra dialogue*]

Then early in the morning the Blessed One put on his outer robes and, taking his bowl, went into Vesālī for alms. Having collected alms, he returned from the alms round. After the meal he turned to look back at Vesālī as an elephant does,* and spoke to Ānanda.

'This is the last time the Tathāgata will see Vesālī. Come, we shall move on to the village of Bhaṇḍa.'

'Yes, sir,' replied the venerable Ānanda to the Blessed One.

Then the Blessed One made his way with a large community of monks to the village of Bhaṇḍa.

While he was staying there he addressed the monks: 'It is because of not understanding, not penetrating four qualities that you and I have run and wandered the round of rebirth in this way for such a long time. Which four? It is because of not understanding, not penetrating noble conduct . . . noble concentration . . . noble wisdom . . . noble freedom that you and I have run and wandered the round of rebirth in this way for such a long time. But once noble conduct is
understood and penetrated, once noble concentration is understood 123
and penetrated, once noble wisdom is understood and penetrated, once noble freedom is understood and penetrated, then craving for existence is cut off, the conductor of existence is destroyed, and no longer is there rebirth.'

This is what the Blessed One said. And when the Happy One had said this, the Teacher spoke again:

'Conduct, concentration, wisdom and freedom unsurpassed—
These are the qualities that famed Gotama has understood.
Knowing these directly, he has proclaimed the Truth to monks.
The Teacher with vision has brought suffering to an end and is completely satisfied.'

Now while he was staying at the village of Bhaṇḍa, the Blessed One talked to the monks a lot about the teaching in these terms: he explained how it is with good conduct, how it is with concentration, how it is with wisdom—how concentration that is invested with good conduct is of great fruit and of great benefit, how wisdom that is invested with concentration is of great fruit and of great benefit, and how the mind that is invested with wisdom is fully released from the taints, namely the taint of sense desire, the taint of being, the taint of view, the taint of ignorance.

Now when the Blessed One had stayed at Bhaṇḍa as long as he wanted, he spoke to the venerable Ānanda: 'Come, Ānanda, we shall move on to the village of Hatthi . . . Amba . . . Jambu . . . the town of Bhoga.'

'Yes, sir,' replied the venerable Ānanda to the Blessed One.

Then the Blessed One made his way with a large community of monks to the town of Bhoga, where he stayed at the shrine of Ānanda.

There he addressed the monks: 'Monks, I shall teach you the four great authorities. Listen. Pay careful attention to what I shall
124 say.'

'Yes, sir,' replied those monks to the Blessed One.

This is what the Blessed One said: 'Now if a monk should say that he has heard directly from the Blessed One, that he has learnt directly from him that such is the practice, such the discipline, such the Teacher's instruction, then what this monk says should neither be accepted nor rejected. Without being accepted or rejected, his words and expressions should be learnt and then compared against the Teaching and examined against the Discipline. If, when they are compared against the Teaching and examined against the Discipline, they do not in fact compare with the Teaching and do not bear examination with the Discipline, then the conclusion must be drawn that this is certainly not the word of the Blessed One but something the monk has mistakenly learnt, in which case you should discard it. If, when they are compared against the Teaching and examined against the Discipline, they do in fact compare with the Teaching and do bear examination with the Discipline, then the conclusion must be drawn that this is certainly the word of the Blessed One and something the monk has correctly learnt. This is the first great authority you should hold to.

'Now if a monk should say that there is a community of elders and eminent monks staying in a monastery of some particular name, and that he has heard directly from that community, that he has learnt directly from that community that such is the practice, such the discipline, such the Teacher's instruction, then what this monk says should neither be accepted nor rejected . . . his words and expressions should be learnt and then compared against the Teaching and examined against the Discipline. If . . . they do in fact compare with the Teaching and do bear examination with the Discipline, then the
125 conclusion must be drawn that this is certainly the word of the Blessed One and something the monk has correctly learnt. This is the second great authority you should hold to.

'Now if a monk should say that there are many elder monks staying in a monastery of some particular name who are learned, have mastered the tradition, and know the teachings, the discipline, and the summary lists,* and that he has heard directly from those monks, that he has learnt directly from them that such is the practice, such the discipline, such the Teacher's instruction, then what this monk says should neither be accepted nor rejected . . . his words and expressions should be learnt and then compared against the Teaching and examined against the Discipline. If . . . they do in fact compare with the Teaching and do bear examination with the Discipline, then the conclusion must be drawn that this is certainly the word of the Blessed One and something the monk has correctly learnt. This is the third great authority you should hold to.

'Now if a monk should say that there is an individual elder monk staying in a monastery of some particular name who is learned, has mastered the tradition, and knows the teachings, the discipline, and the summary lists, and that he has heard directly from that monk, that he has learnt directly from him that such is the practice, such the discipline, such the Teacher's instruction, then what this monk says should neither be accepted nor rejected. Without being accepted or rejected his words and expressions should be learnt and then compared against the Teaching and examined against the Discipline. If, when they are compared against the Teaching and examined against the Discipline, they do not in fact compare with the Teaching and do not bear examination with the Discipline, then the conclusion must be drawn that this is certainly not the word of the Blessed One but something the monk has mistakenly learnt, in which case you should discard it. If, when they are compared against the Teaching and examined against the Discipline, they do in fact compare with the Teaching and do bear examination with the Discipline, then the conclusion must be drawn that this is certainly the word of 126
the Blessed One and something the monk has correctly learnt. This is the fourth great authority you should hold to. Monks, hold to these four great authorities.'

Now while he was staying in Bhoga at the shrine of Ānanda, the Blessed One talked to the monks a lot about the teaching in these terms: he explained how it is with good conduct, how it is with concentration, how it is with wisdom—how concentration that is invested with good conduct is of great fruit and of great benefit, how wisdom that is invested with concentration is of great fruit and of great benefit, and how the mind that is invested with wisdom is fully released from the taints, namely the taint of sense desire, the taint of being, the taint of view, the taint of ignorance.

Now when the Blessed One had stayed in the town of Bhoga as long as he wanted, he spoke to the venerable Ānanda: 'Come, Ānanda, we shall move on to Pāvā.'

'Yes, sir,' replied the venerable Ānanda to the Blessed One. Then the Blessed One made his way with a large community of monks to Pāvā, where he stayed in the mango grove of Cunda the smith. Now when Cunda heard people say that the Blessed One had reached Pāvā and was staying in his mango grove, he went to the Blessed One and on arrival saluted him respectfully before sitting down to one side. Once Cunda the smith was seated, the Blessed One instructed him with talk about the teaching, encouraging, enthusing, and inspiring him. Instructed, encouraged, enthused, and inspired by his talk, he said to the Blessed One: 'May the Blessed One along with the community of monks accept my invitation for tomorrow's meal.'

By his silence the Blessed One accepted. Understanding that
127 he had accepted his invitation, Cunda got up from his seat, respectfully saluted the Blessed One, and left, keeping him on his right. When the night was over, Cunda had fine foods of different sorts, including a large quantity of tender boar,* prepared in his own home. Then he had the Blessed One informed: 'It is time, sir. The meal is ready.'

Then early in the morning the Blessed One put on his outer robes and, taking his bowl, went together with the community of monks to Cunda the smith's home and sat down on the prepared seat.

When he had sat down he said to Cunda: 'Cunda, serve me with the tender boar you have had prepared, serve the community of monks with the other sorts of food you have had prepared.'

'Yes, sir,' replied Cunda the smith, and he served the Blessed One with the tender boar he had had prepared, and the community of monks with the other sorts of food he had had prepared.

Then the Blessed One said to Cunda: 'Whatever tender boar you have left, bury it in a hole. I do not see anyone in this world with its gods, its Māra and Brahmā, anyone of this generation with its ascetics and brahmans, its princes and peoples who could properly digest it once eaten, except the Tathāgata.'

'Yes, sir,' replied Cunda the smith, and whatever tender boar was left he buried in a hole.

Then he went to the Blessed One and, having respectfully saluted him, sat down to one side. Once Cunda was seated the Blessed One instructed him with talk about the teaching, encouraging, enthusing, and inspiring him. Then the Blessed One got up from his seat and left. After the Blessed One had eaten Cunda the smith's meal he fell seriously ill, passing blood in his stools and suffering severe pains as
though he were close to death. Without complaining, the Blessed 128
One accepted the pains mindfully and with full awareness.

Then the Blessed One spoke to the venerable Ānanda: 'Come, Ānanda, we shall move on to Kusinārā.'

'Yes, sir,' replied the venerable Ānanda to the Blessed One.

What I have heard is that after eating Cunda the smith's meal,
The sage suffered a serious illness bringing him close to death.
When he had eaten tender boar
The Teacher became seriously sick.
The Blessed One, continually having to relieve himself, said:
I am going to the town of Kusinārā.

Then the Blessed One left the path and went over to the root of a tree. There he spoke to the venerable Ānanda: 'Could you fold my outermost robe in four for me, Ānanda? I am tired and must sit down.'

'Yes, sir,' replied the venerable Ānanda, and he folded the outermost robe in four.

The Blessed One sat down on the prepared seat, and when he was seated he spoke to the venerable Ānanda: 'Could you bring me some water, Ānanda? I am thirsty and must drink.'

At this the venerable Ānanda said to the Blessed One: 'Sir, just now five hundred carts passed by and the water has been cut through by their wheels—it flows feebly, and is stirred up and muddy. The River Kakutthā is close by—clean and with easy banks, it is delightful and its water is clear, good, and cool. There the Blessed One can 129
drink water and cool his limbs.'

A second time the Blessed One said to the venerable Ānanda: 'Could you bring me some water, Ānanda? I am thirsty and must drink.'

A second time the venerable Ānanda said to the Blessed One: 'Sir, just now five hundred carts passed by and the water has been cut through by their wheels—it flows feebly, and is stirred up and muddy.

The River Kakutthā is close by—clean and with easy banks, it is delightful and its water is clear, good, and cool. There the Blessed One can drink water and cool his limbs.'

A third time the Blessed One said to the venerable Ānanda: 'Could you bring me some water, Ānanda? I am thirsty and must drink.'

'Yes, sir,' replied the venerable Ānanda and taking his bowl he went to the stream. And as he approached, the stream, which, cut through by wheels, had been flowing feebly, stirred up and muddy, appeared clear, bright, and free of mud.

And the venerable Ānanda thought, 'This is remarkable, this is extraordinary—the great accomplishment and great power of the Tathāgata! For this stream, which, cut through by wheels, was flowing feebly, stirred up and muddy, when I approach flows clear, bright, and free of mud.'

Taking water in his bowl, the venerable Ānanda went to the Blessed One and said: 'This is remarkable, this is extraordinary, sir—the great accomplishment and great power of the Tathāgata! The stream, which, cut through by wheels, had been flowing feebly, stirred up and muddy, when I approached just now appeared clear, bright, and free of mud. Let the Blessed One drink the water, let the Happy One drink the water.'

130 Then the Blessed One drank the water. At that time Pukkusa, a young man of Malla and a disciple of Āḷāra the Kālāma,* was travelling on the main road from Kusinārā to Pāvā. He saw the Blessed One seated at the root of the tree and approached him. Having saluted him respectfully, he sat down to one side.

Once seated, he spoke to the Blessed One: 'This is remarkable, this is extraordinary, sir—how those who have gone forth live life in such peace. Once in the past, when Āḷāra the Kālāma was travelling on the main road, he left the path and sat down at the root of a tree to spend the day there. Now five hundred carts passed right by Āḷāra the Kālāma. A man who was coming along behind the caravan of carts went over to Āḷāra and spoke to him: "Sir, did you see those five hundred carts pass by?" "I did not see them." "Then did you hear the noise, sir?" "I did not hear the noise." "Then were you asleep, sir?" "I was not asleep." "Then were you conscious, sir?" "I was." "So, while conscious and awake you neither saw the five hundred carts pass right by nor did you hear the noise—yet your outer robe is all covered in dust." "That is so." And then that man thought how

remarkable, how extraordinary that those who have gone forth live
life in such peace that while conscious and awake they will neither 131
see nor hear the sound of five hundred carts passing right by. So,
expressing his deep faith in Āḷāra the Kālāma, he went.'

'What do you think, Pukkusa? Which is harder to accomplish and master: that one should be conscious and awake and neither see nor hear the sound of five hundred carts passing right by, or that one should be conscious and awake and neither see anything nor hear a sound when the god rains down, the skies rumble, lightning flashes, and thunderbolts rend the air?'

'Whether it is five, six, seven, eight, nine, or ten hundred carts, whether a hundred or a thousand—what difference can it make? That one should be conscious and awake and neither see anything nor hear a sound when the god rains down, the skies rumble, lightning flashes, and thunderbolts rend the air—certainly this is harder to accomplish and master.'

'Once I was staying at Ātumā in a threshing barn when the god rained down, the skies rumbled, lightning flashed and thunderbolts rent the air, and two ploughmen who were brothers and four oxen were killed. Now a great crowd of people came out from Ātumā and went to where the ploughmen and oxen had been killed. By that time I had come out of the threshing barn and was walking up and down in the open air by the entrance. A man from the crowd came up to me and, having approached, he saluted me respectfully and stood to one side. As he stood there I asked him why that great crowd had
gathered: "Sir, just now," he said, "the god rained down, the skies 132
rumbled, lightning flashed and thunderbolts rent the air, and two ploughmen who were brothers and four oxen were killed. So this great crowd has gathered. But, sir, where were you?" "I was right here, friend." "But didn't you see anything?" "I did not." "Then did you hear the noise, sir?" "I did not." "Then were you asleep, sir?" "I was not asleep." "Then were you conscious, sir?" "I was, friend." "So, while conscious and awake you neither saw anything nor heard a sound when the god rained down, the skies rumbled, lightning flashed, and thunderbolts rent the air?" "That is so, friend." And then, Pukkusa, that man thought how remarkable, how extraordinary that those who have gone forth live life in such peace that, while conscious and awake, they will neither see anything nor hear a sound when the god rains down, the skies rumble, lightning

flashes, and thunderbolts rend the air. So expressing his deep faith in me he saluted me respectfully, and keeping me to his right he went away.'

At this Pukkusa said to the Blessed One: 'What faith I had in Āḷāra the Kālāma I let the wind blow away as chaff, or a swift-flowing river wash away. Excellent, sir! Excellent! As if someone were to set upright what had been knocked down, or reveal what had been hidden, or point out the way to someone who was lost, or hold a lamp up in the dark so that those with eyes could see—just so the Blessed One has made the Truth clear in various ways. Sir, I go to the
133 Blessed One for refuge, and to the Teaching and the Community of monks. Let the Blessed One accept me as a lay follower who has taken refuge from this day for as long as I live.'

Then Pukkusa spoke to one of his men: 'Please, bring me a pair of garments of finished cloth, the colour of gold.'

'Yes, sir,' he replied and brought a pair of garments of finished cloth, the colour of gold.

And Pukkusa offered that pair of garments to the Blessed One, saying: 'Sir, out of sympathy may the Blessed One accept this pair of garments of finished cloth, the colour of gold.'

'Then clothe me in one, Pukkusa, and Ānanda in the other.'

'Yes, sir,' he replied and clothed the Blessed One in one and Ānanda in the other.

Then the Blessed One instructed Pukkusa with talk about the teaching, encouraging, enthusing, and inspiring him. Instructed, encouraged, enthused, and inspired by his talk, Pukkusa got up from his seat and respectfully saluted the Blessed One and, keeping him on his right, went away. Not long after he had left, the venerable Ānanda offered both the garments to the Blessed One to cover his body,* but once on his body they faded and seemed to lose their lustre.

Then the venerable Ānanda said to the Blessed One: 'This is remarkable, sir, this is extraordinary—the colour of the Tathāgata's skin is so pure and clear! I have offered the Blessed One both gar-
134 ments of finished cloth the colour of gold to cover his body, but once on his body they fade and seem to lose their lustre.'

'That is so, Ānanda. There are two occasions when the colour of the Tathāgata's skin is very pure and clear. Which are they? The night the Tathāgata awakens to the highest perfect awakening, and the night he attains final nibbana by the element of nibbana that is without any remnant of attachment. These are the two occasions when the colour of the Tathāgata's skin is very pure and clear. So tonight, in the last watch, at Upavattana, the sāl grove of the Mallas at Kusinārā, between two sāl trees,* the final nibbana of the Tathāgata will happen. Come, Ānanda, we shall move on to the River Kakutthā.'

With two pieces of finished cloth, the colour of gold, Pukkusa came:
Clothed in them the Teacher's complexion shone like gold.

Then the Blessed One went with a large community of monks to the River Kakutthā, where he went down into the water to bathe and drink. On coming back out, he went to the mango grove and spoke to the venerable Cundaka: 'Could you fold my outermost robe in four for me, Cundaka? I am tired and must lie down.'

'Yes, sir,' replied the venerable Cundaka and he folded the outermost robe in four. Then the Blessed One lay down on his right side as a lion does, covering one foot with the other, mindful and fully
aware, bringing to mind when he would get up, while the venerable 135
Cundaka sat down there in front of him.

The Buddha went to the River Kakutthā,
Bright with water clear and good;
His body exhausted, the Teacher plunged in—
The Tathāgata, without equal in the world.
And when the Teacher had bathed and drunk, he emerged,
Revered among the company of monks.
The Blessed Teacher who sets the Truth in motion here,
The great sage, went to the mango grove.
He addressed the monk called Cundaka:
'Spread the fourfold robe for me: I must lie down.'
Directed* by the one realized in himself, Cunda
Quickly spread the fourfold robe.
His body exhausted, the Teacher lay down
And Cunda sat down there in front of him.

Then the Blessed One said to the venerable Ānanda: 'It is possible that someone might make Cunda regretful by suggesting to him that for the Tathāgata to have reached final peace after eating a last meal

offered by him is something that counts against him, something disadvantageous to him. Any such regret of Cunda's should be dispelled by telling him: "For the Tathāgata to have reached final peace after eating a last meal offered by you, Cunda, is something that counts for you, something very advantageous to you. I have heard directly from the Blessed One, I have learnt directly from him that there are two
136 meals whose offering is exactly the same in result and effect but much greater in result and benefit than the offering of other meals: the offering of the meal after eating which the Tathāgata awakens to the unsurpassed complete awakening, and the offering of the meal after eating which the Tathāgata attains final nibbana with the element of nibbana that is without any remnant of attachment. These are the two meals whose offering is exactly the same in result and effect but much greater in result and benefit than the offering of other meals. The good Cunda has done a deed to his credit that will conduce to long life, to good looks, to fame, to happiness, to heaven, and to authority." This is how any regret of Cunda the smith's should be dispelled.'

And the Blessed One, understanding the significance of this, immediately breathed a sigh:

'When one gives, merit increases; when one is in control of
oneself, hostility is not stored up;
The skilful man gives up what is bad; with the destruction of
137 greed, hatred and delusion he is at peace.'

[*Fifth section for recitation: Hiraññavatī*]

Then the Blessed One said to the venerable Ānanda, 'Come, Ānanda, we shall move on to the further bank of the River Hiraññavatī, to Upavattana, the sāl grove of the Mallas at Kusinārā.'

'Yes, sir,' replied the venerable Ānanda to the Blessed One.

Then the Blessed One made his way with a large community of monks across the Hiraññavatī to the sāl grove at Kusinārā in the land of the Mallas.

There he spoke to the venerable Ānanda: 'Ānanda, could you prepare a bed for me between two sāl trees with the head to the north? I am tired and must lie down.'

'Yes, sir,' replied the venerable Ānanda to the Blessed One, and he prepared a bed between two sāl trees with the head to the north.

Then the Blessed One lay down on his right side as a lion does, covering one foot with the other, mindful and fully aware. Now at that time those two sāl trees were all abloom with flowers out of season, and they rained down their blossoms in worship of the Tathāgata, showering and covering his body. Divine *mandārava* flowers too fell from the sky, raining down in worship of the Tathāgata, showering and covering his body—likewise divine sandalwood powder. Divine instruments were sounded in the sky in 138
worship of the Tathāgata, and divine songs were being sung.

The Blessed One spoke to the venerable Ānanda, 'The two sāl trees, all abloom with flowers out of season, are raining down their blossoms in worship of the Tathāgata, showering and covering his body. Divine *mandārava* flowers too are falling from the sky, raining down in worship of the Tathāgata, showering and covering his body—likewise divine sandalwood powder. Divine instruments are sounding in the sky in honour of the Tathāgata, and divine songs are being sung. Yet this does not amount to the showing of respect, honour, reverence, worship, or recognition to the Tathāgata: the one who respects, honours, reveres, and worships the Tathāgata with the ultimate worship is the monk or nun, the layman or laywoman, who lives practising the teaching and its subtleties, conducting him or herself properly, living in accordance with the Truth. Therefore, Ānanda, you should undertake the training with the thought, "We shall live practising the teaching and its subtleties, conducting ourselves properly, living in accordance with the Truth."'

Now at that time the venerable Upavāṇa was standing in front of the Blessed One, fanning him. And the Blessed One rebuked him: 'Move away, monk. Do not stand in front of me.'

Then the venerable Ānanda thought: 'The venerable Upavāṇa has 139
long been an attendant of the Blessed One, staying close, keeping near by, yet now in his final hour the Blessed One rebukes him, telling him to move away and not stand in front of him. What is the reason for the Blessed One's rebuke? What is the cause?'

So the venerable Ānanda spoke to the Blessed One: 'Sir, the venerable Upavāṇa has long been an attendant of the Blessed One, staying close, keeping near by, yet now in your final hour the Blessed One rebukes him, telling him to move away and not stand in front of him. What is the reason for the Blessed One's rebuke? What is the cause?'

'Ānanda, most of the gods of the ten world systems are assembled here to see the Tathāgata: for twelve leagues around Upavattana, the sāl grove of the Mallas at Kusinārā, there is no spot the size of a point at the tip of a hair not crowded with powerful gods. And the gods are complaining: "We have come from afar to see the Tathāgata, for Tathāgatas, perfectly awakened arahats, appear in the world only once in a while, and tonight in the last watch his final nibbana will take place, but this powerful monk is standing in front of the Blessed One preventing us from getting a view of the Tathāgata in his final hour." '

'But, sir, what sort of beings are these gods that the Blessed One is aware of?'

'There are the gods who conceive of the earth in space: with dishevelled hair they spread their arms wide and call out; they fall to
140 the ground, broken, and roll back and forth: "All too soon will the Blessed One attain final nibbana! All too soon will the Happy One attain final nibbana! All too soon will the eye of the world disappear!" There are the gods who conceive of the earth in earth: with dishevelled hair they spread their arms wide and call out; they fall to the ground, broken, and roll back and forth: "All too soon will the Blessed One attain final nibbana! All too soon will the Happy One attain final nibbana! All too soon will the eye of the world disappear!" But those gods who are without greed are mindful and fully aware; they accept that conditioning forces are impermanent, so how else could it be?'

'In the past, sir, monks who had spent the rainy season in the different regions used to come to see the Tathāgata. We received them as cherished monks who had come to see and show their devotion, but after the Blessed One has gone we cannot receive those monks.'

'There are these four places, Ānanda, that should be seen by a faithful man of family that will stir his heart. Which four? Where the Tathāgata was born is a place that should be seen by a faithful man of family that will stir his heart. Where the Tathāgata awakened to unsurpassed perfect awakening is a place that should be seen by a faithful man of family that will stir his heart. Where the Tathāgata turned the unsurpassed wheel of Truth is a place that should be seen by a faithful man of family that will stir his heart. Where the Tathāgata attained nibbana by the element of nibbana without any

remnant of attachment is a place that should be seen by a faithful man of family that will stir his heart.* . . . Monks and nuns, laymen 141
and laywomen will come, thinking: "Here is where the Tathāgata was born, and here is where he awakened to unsurpassed perfect awakening, and here is where he turned the unsurpassed wheel of Truth, and here is where he attained nibbana by the element of nibbana without any remnant of attachment." All those who die with faithful hearts while they are on pilgrimage to a shrine will at the breaking up of the body after death be born in a happy realm, a heaven world.'

'Sir, how shall we conduct ourselves with regard to women?'

'By not looking, Ānanda.'

'But when we look, sir, how shall we conduct ourselves?'

'By not talking, Ānanda.'

'But when we talk, sir, how shall we conduct ourselves?'

'Mindfulness must be established, Ānanda.'

'How shall we treat the Tathāgata's body?'

'Ānanda, don't concern yourselves with the Tathāgata's funeral.* You should strive for the true goal, you should be devoted to the true goal, you should live applying yourselves to the true goal, determined, attentive. There are knowledgeable rulers, knowledgeable brahmans, and knowledgeable householders too who are committed to the Tathāgata—they will conduct the Tathāgata's funeral.'

'But, sir, how shall we treat the Tathāgata's body?'

'Ānanda, the Tathāgata's body should be treated as people treat the body of a wheel-turning king.'*

'And how, sir, do people treat the body of a wheel-turning king?'

'First they wrap the body in unused cloth, then in teased cotton, then again in unused cloth. And when in this manner they have 142
wrapped the body in five hundred double layers, they place it in an iron coffin full of oil. This they enclose in another iron coffin. Then they make a funeral pyre of all kinds of incense and cremate the body. Afterwards they build a stupa* for the wheel-turning king where four roads meet. This is how people treat the body of a wheel-turning king. As people treat the body of a wheel-turning king, so the Tathāgata's body should be treated. A stupa should be built for the Tathāgata where four roads meet. When people place a garland, fragrance, or paste* there, or make respectful salutations or bring

peace to their hearts, that will contribute to their long-lasting welfare and happiness.

'These four are worthy of a stupa. Which four? A Tathāgata who is an arahat and perfectly awakened buddha is worthy of a stupa, a one-off buddha,* a realized disciple of a Tathāgata, and a wheel-turning king are worthy of a stupa. And what is the reason why a Tathāgata is worthy of a stupa? With the thought, "This is the stupa of a Tathāgata," people bring peace to their hearts, and by bringing peace to their hearts, at the breaking up of the body after death they are born in a happy realm, a heaven world. This is the reason why a Tathāgata is worthy of a stupa. And what is the reason why a one-off
143 buddha . . . a realized disciple . . . a wheel-turning king is worthy of a stupa? With the thought, "This is the stupa of a one-off buddha . . . of a realized disciple . . . of a wheel-turning king," people bring peace to their hearts, and by bringing peace to their hearts, at the breaking up of the body after death they are born in a happy realm, a heaven world . . .'

Then the venerable Ānanda entered the monks' dwelling and stood leaning against the gatepost, weeping: 'Here I am a trainee with work still to do, but my teacher, the one who shows me sympathy, is about to attain final nibbana.'

Then the Blessed One asked the monks, 'Where is Ānanda?'

'The venerable Ānanda has entered the monks' dwelling and is standing leaning against the gatepost, weeping: "Here I am, a trainee with work still to do, but my teacher, the one who shows me sympathy, is about to attain final nibbana."'

Then the Blessed One said to a monk, 'Go, monk, and call Ānanda
144 in my name, saying, "Venerable Ānanda, the Teacher calls you"'

'Yes, sir,' replied that monk to the Blessed One.

And he went to the venerable Ānanda and said to him: 'Venerable Ānanda, the Teacher calls you.'

'Yes,' replied the venerable Ānanda to the monk.

And he went to the Blessed One, saluted him respectfully, and sat down to one side.

Once the venerable Ānanda was seated, the Blessed One said to him: 'Enough, Ānanda! Do not grieve and lament. Have I not warned about this before: we must lose and be deprived of and separated from everything pleasant and dear? So how else could it be? That something that is born, come into being, conditioned, and of a nature to decay should not decay—this cannot happen. For a long time, Ānanda, you have attended on the Tathāgata acting in body kindly, helpfully, gladly, honestly, without limits. For a long time you have attended on the Tathāgata acting in speech . . . in thought kindly, helpfully, gladly, honestly, without limits. You have made merit, Ānanda. Keep on applying yourself and very soon you will be free of the taints.'

Then the Blessed One addressed the monks: 'Those Blessed Ones who were perfectly awakened arahats in the past also had their special attendants, just as I have Ānanda. Those Blessed Ones who will be perfectly awakened arahats in the future will also have their special attendants, just as I have Ānanda. Monks, Ānanda is skilled, he knows when is the right time for monks to come and see the
Tathāgata, when is the right time for nuns . . . for laymen . . . for 145
laywomen . . . for a king, for royal ministers, for religious leaders, for their disciples.

'These four remarkable and extraordinary qualities are found in Ānanda. Which four? If a group of monks comes to see Ānanda, they are pleased by seeing him. If Ānanda then relates the teaching, they are pleased by what he says, but dissatisfied when he is silent. If a group of nuns . . . a group of laymen . . . a group of laywomen comes to see Ānanda, they are pleased by seeing him. If Ānanda then relates the teaching, they are pleased by what he says, but dissatisfied when he is silent. These are the four remarkable and extraordinary qualities found in Ānanda.

'These four remarkable and extraordinary qualities are found in a wheel-turning king. Which four? If a group of rulers . . . a group of brahmans . . . a group of householders . . . a group of ascetics comes to see a wheel-turning king, they are pleased by seeing him. If the wheel-turning king then speaks, they are pleased by
what he says, but dissatisfied when he is silent. In exactly the same 146
way, four remarkable and extraordinary qualities are found in Ānanda . . . '

When he had said this, the venerable Ānanda spoke to the Blessed One: 'Sir, the Blessed One should not attain final nibbana in this mud-wall town, this remote, provincial town. Sir, there are other important cities such as Campā, Rājagaha, Sāvatthī, Sāketa, Kosambī, and Benares—the Blessed One should attain final nibbana in one of these. In these cities there are many wealthy rulers, brahmans, and householders who are committed to the Tathāgata—they will conduct the Tathāgata's funeral.'

'Ānanda, do not say that this is a mud-wall town, a remote, provincial town. Long ago there was a king called Mahāsudassana—a wheel-turning king, a righteous king of Truth, a sovereign of the four quarters who maintained the stability of the country. This town of Kusinārā was the royal city of King Mahāsudassana and was called Kusāvatī. Twelve leagues in length on the east and west sides and seven leagues across on the north and south sides, the royal city of
147 Kusāvatī was successful and prosperous with many inhabitants, full of people and well provided with food—just as Āḷakamandā, the royal city of the gods, is successful and prosperous with many inhabitants, full of divine beings, and well provided with food. Day and night the royal city of Kusāvatī was filled with the ten sounds: the sound of elephants, horses, carriages, kettle drums, tabors, vīṇās, singing, cymbals, gongs, and lastly the sound of the cries of, "Eat, drink, and be merry!"

'Ānanda, go into Kusinārā and tell the Mallas there that tonight, in the last watch, the final nibbana of the Tathāgata will happen. Tell them that they must come and not later regret that, although the Tathāgata attained final nibbana in the vicinity of their village, they didn't get to see him in his last hours.'

'Yes, sir,' replied the venerable Ānanda to the Blessed One.

Then he put on his outer robes and, taking his bowl, went into Kusinārā with a companion. At that time the Mallas of Kusinārā had sat down together in the meeting hall to deal with some matter. So the venerable Ānanda went to the meeting hall and told them: 'Tonight, in the last watch, the final nibbana of the Tathāgata will happen. Vāseṭṭhas, you must come. Do not later regret that, although the Tathāgata attained final nibbana in the vicinity of your village,
148 you didn't get to see him in his last hours.'

When they had heard this news from the venerable Ānanda, the Mallas and their sons and daughters and their wives felt wretched and unhappy, and were overcome with sadness. With dishevelled hair some spread their arms wide and called out; they fell to the ground, broken, and rolled back and forth: 'All too soon will the Blessed One attain final nibbana! All too soon will the Happy One attain final nibbana! All too soon will the eye of the world disappear!'

Then the Mallas and their sons and daughters and their wives, feeling wretched and unhappy, and overcome with sadness, went to Upavattana, the sāl grove of the Mallas, and approached the venerable Ānanda. Ānanda thought: 'If I present the Mallas one by one to pay their respects to the Blessed One, it will be getting light and still they will not have finished paying their respects. I had better divide them into various family groups and then present them to the Blessed One to pay their respects, announcing that a Malla of such and such a name along with his sons, his wives, his retinue, and his friends bows down at the feet of the Blessed One.'

So the venerable Ānanda divided the Mallas of Kusinārā into various family groups and presented them to the Blessed One to pay their respects, announcing that a Malla of such and such a name along with his sons, his wives, his retinue, and his friends bowed down at the feet of the Blessed One. In this way he presented the Mallas to the Blessed One to pay their respects in the first watch.

Now at that time a wanderer called Subhadda was living in Kusinārā, and when he heard people say that the final nibbana of the ascetic
Gotama would take place in the last watch of that very night he 149
thought: 'I have heard senior and elder wanderers, the teachers of teachers, say that only once in a while does a Tathāgata who is a perfectly awakened arahat appear in the world, and tonight in the last watch the final nibbana of the ascetic Gotama will take place. A particular doubt has arisen in me, but I feel confident the ascetic Gotama can teach me the Truth in a way that will allow me to get rid of this doubt.'

So the wanderer Subhadda went to Upavattana, the sāl grove of the Mallas, and approached the venerable Ānanda and said to him: 'I have heard . . . wanderers . . . say that only once in a while does a Tathāgata who is a perfectly awakened arahat appear in the world . . . A particular doubt has arisen in me, but I feel confident the ascetic Gotama can teach me the Truth in a way that will allow me to get rid of this doubt. Good Ānanda, I should like to be permitted to see the ascetic Gotama.'

At this the venerable Ānanda said to Subhadda: 'Enough, Subhadda. Do not bother the Tathāgata. The Blessed One is tired.'

A second . . . and a third time the wanderer Subhadda said to him: 'I have heard . . . wanderers . . . say that only once in a while does a
Tathāgata . . . appear in the world . . . I should like to be permitted 150
to see the ascetic Gotama.'

A third time too the venerable Ānanda said to Subhadda: 'Enough, Subhadda. Do not bother the Tathāgata. The Blessed One is tired.'

The Blessed One heard this conversation between the venerable Ānanda and the wanderer Subhadda.

Then he spoke to Ānanda: 'Enough, Ānanda. Do not refuse Subhadda. He should be allowed to see the Tathāgata. Everything Subhadda will ask me, he will ask only out of a concern to understand, not to bother me. And once I am asked, whatever I shall explain to him he will quickly understand.'

Then the venerable Ānanda said to the wanderer Subhadda: 'Go, Subhadda. The Blessed One gives you his permission.'

Then the wanderer Subhadda approached the Blessed One, and having approached, he saluted the Blessed One respectfully, exchanging pleasing and polite words with him, before sitting down to one side.

Once seated, he said to the Blessed One: 'There are ascetics and brahmans who have communities and followings and are the teachers of those followings; who are well known and of some repute, who have found a way across and are thought holy by many—for example, Pūraṇa Kassapa, Makkhali Gosāla, Ajita of the Blanket of Hair, Pakudha Kaccāyana, Sañjaya Belaṭṭhiputta, and Nigaṇṭha Nātaputta. Now have all of these achieved direct knowledge as
151 they claim, or has none achieved it, or have some achieved it and some not?'

'Enough, Subhadda. This question of whether all of these have achieved direct knowledge as they claim, or whether none has or some have and some have not can wait. I shall teach you the Truth, Subhadda. Listen and pay careful attention to what I shall say.'

'Yes, sir,' replied the wanderer Subhadda to the Blessed One.

The Blessed One said: 'In a system of teaching and discipline where the noble eightfold path is not found, the ascetic is also not found, and neither are the second, third, and fourth ascetics.* But in a system of teaching and discipline where the noble eightfold path is found, the ascetic is also found, and so too are the second, third, and fourth ascetics. Now in this system of teaching and discipline the noble eightfold path *is* found, and certainly the ascetic is found here, and the second, third, and fourth ascetics. Other contrary systems are empty of ascetics, but if the monks here live properly, the world should not be empty of arahats.

I was twenty-nine years of age, Subhadda,
When I went forth in search of what is good.
Now it is more than fifty years
Since I went forth, Subhadda,
To abide in the realm of the way of Truth,
Outside which there is no ascetic— 152

nor the second, nor the third, nor the fourth ascetic. Other contrary systems are empty of ascetics, but if the monks here live properly, the world should not be empty of arahats.'

At this Subhadda the wanderer said to the Blessed One: 'Excellent, sir! Excellent! As if someone were to set upright what had been knocked down, or reveal what had been hidden, or point out the way to someone who was lost, or hold a lamp up in the dark so that those with eyes could see—just so the Blessed One has made the Truth clear in various ways. Sir, I go to the Blessed One for refuge, and to the Teaching and the Community of monks. I should like to receive the going-forth ordination in the presence of the Blessed One. I should like to receive higher ordination.'*

'Subhadda, someone who was previously a follower of another religious school and who wants to receive the going-forth and higher ordinations in this system of teaching and discipline should wait four months. After four months, when the monks are satisfied in their minds, they will bestow the going-forth and higher ordinations to make him a monk. But in this particular case I recognize that people can be different.'

'Sir, if those who were previously the followers of another religious school and who want to receive the going-forth and higher ordinations in this system of teaching and discipline should wait four months, and after four months, when the monks are satisfied in their minds, they will bestow the going-forth and higher ordinations to make them monks, then I shall wait four years, and after four years, when the monks are satisfied in their minds, they may bestow the going-forth and higher ordinations to make me a monk.'

Then the Blessed One spoke to the venerable Ānanda: 'Therefore, Ānanda, you should bestow on the wanderer Subhadda the going-forth ordination.'

'Yes, sir,' replied the venerable Ānanda to the Blessed One.

And Subhadda said to the venerable Ānanda: 'It is something that counts for you, Ānanda, something very advantageous to you that you have been anointed as pupils in the presence of the
153 Teacher.'

So Subhadda the wanderer received the going-forth and higher ordinations in the presence of the Blessed One. Straight after he had been ordained, the venerable Subhadda withdrew alone, and living attentive, determined, and resolute, he soon lived here and now having attained the ultimate goal of the spiritual life, experiencing it for himself through direct knowledge—the goal for the sake of which sons of families properly go forth from the household life into homelessness. He understood: 'Birth is destroyed, the spiritual life lived, done is what was to be done—there is nothing further required to this end!'

So the venerable Subhadda became one of the arahats—
154 He was the last of the direct disciples of the Blessed One.

[*Sixth section for recitation*]

Then the Blessed One spoke to the venerable Ānanda: 'Perhaps you will think that there is no longer a teacher to give instruction, that you have no teacher. But you should not look at it in this way, Ānanda. The teaching and discipline that I have taught you and explained to you—that is your teacher after I have gone. After I have gone you should not address each other as "friend" as you do now. A more senior monk should address a junior monk by his name or family or as "friend"; a more junior monk should address a senior monk as "sir" or as "the venerable one". After I have gone the community may, if it wishes, abolish the minor rules of training. After I have gone, the monk Channa* should be subject to the full punishment.'

'But what is the full punishment?'

'The monk Channa can say what he likes, Ānanda, but monks are strictly not to speak to him, nor give him advice or instruction.'

Then the Blessed One addressed the monks: 'Perhaps some monk has doubt or is confused about the Buddha, the teaching, the community, the path, or the practice. Ask your questions, monks. Do not
155 later regret that, although your teacher was right in front of you, you were not able to put your questions to the Blessed One.'

At this the monks were silent. A second time . . . and a third time the Blessed One addressed the monks: 'Perhaps some monk has doubt or is confused . . . Ask your questions. Do not later regret that, although your teacher was right in front of you, you were not able to put your questions to the Blessed One.'

A third time the monks were silent. The Blessed One said to the monks: 'Perhaps you do not ask your questions out of respect for the teacher. Let one companion tell another his questions.'

At this the monks were silent. The venerable Ānanda said to the Blessed One: 'This is remarkable, sir, this is extraordinary—such is my confidence in the Blessed One: there is not a single monk in this community who has doubt or is confused about the Buddha, the teaching, the community, the path, or the practice.'

'You say this out of deep faith, Ānanda. The Tathāgata has knowledge of this: there is not a single monk in this community who has doubt or is confused about the Buddha, the teaching, the community, the path, or the practice. For the least of these five hundred monks has entered the stream and is beyond affliction, destined to full awakening for sure.'

Then the Blessed One addressed the monks: 'Well, monks, now 156
I take my leave of you: it is of the nature of things to decay, but if you are attentive you will succeed!'

These were the Tathāgata's last words. Then the Blessed One entered the first absorption. Emerging from that, he entered the second absorption. Emerging from that, he entered the third absorption. Emerging from that, he entered the fourth absorption. Emerging from that, he entered the sphere of infinity of space. Emerging from that, he entered the sphere of infinity of consciousness. Emerging from that, he entered the sphere of nothingness. Emerging from that, he entered the sphere of neither consciousness nor unconsciousness. Emerging from that, he entered the cessation of conception and feeling. Then the venerable Ānanda said to the venerable Anuruddha: 'The Blessed One has attained final nibbana, Anuruddha.'

'The Blessed One has not attained final nibbana, Ānanda. He has entered the cessation of conception and feeling.'

Then emerging from the cessation of conception and feeling, the Blessed One entered the sphere of neither consciousness nor unconsciousness. Emerging from that, he entered the sphere of nothingness. Emerging from that, he entered the sphere of infinity of consciousness. Emerging from that, he entered the sphere of infinity of space. Emerging from that, he entered the fourth absorption. Emerging from that, he entered the third absorption. Emerging from that, he entered the second absorption. Emerging from that, he entered the first absorption. Emerging from that, he entered the second absorption. Emerging from that, he entered the third absorption. Emerging from that, he entered the fourth absorption. Emerging from the fourth absorption, the Blessed One directly attained final nibbana.

And when the Blessed One attained final peace, with his final nibbana, the earth quaked, frightening, making the hairs stand on
157 end, and claps of thunder rent the sky. And when the Blessed One
attained final peace, with his final nibbana, Brahmā, Lord of the Earth,* uttered this verse:

'All beings in the world must lay their bodies aside—
So such a Teacher as this, the person without equal in the world,
The Tathāgata, powerful and perfectly awakened, has attained
final nibbana!'

And when the Blessed One attained final peace, with his final nibbana, Sakka, chief of the gods, uttered this verse:

'Impermanent are conditioned things! It is their nature to arise
and fall.
Having arisen, they cease. Their stilling is happy.'

And when the Blessed One attained final peace, with his final nibbana, the venerable Anuruddha uttered these verses:

'There was no in-breath and no out-breath when such a man's
mind was steady.
Undisturbed and set on peace the sage died.
He endured pain, undismayed in heart.
The freeing of his mind was like the blowing out of a lamp.'

And when the Blessed One attained final peace some of the monks who had not yet got rid of greed spread their arms wide and called out; they fell to the ground, broken, and rolled back and forth: 'All
158 too soon has the Blessed One attained final nibbana! All too soon
has the Happy One attained final nibbana! All too soon has the eye of the world disappeared!' But the monks who were without greed

remained mindful and fully aware, accepting that conditioning forces are impermanent, so how else could it be?

Then the venerable Anuruddha spoke to the monks: 'Enough, sirs! Do not grieve and lament. Has not the Blessed One warned you about this before: we must lose and be deprived of and separated from everything pleasant and dear? So how else could it be? That something that is born, come into being, conditioned, and of a nature to decay should not decay—this cannot happen. Sirs, the gods disapprove.'

'But what sorts of gods does the venerable Anuruddha have in mind?'*

'There are, Ānanda, the gods who conceive of the earth in space: with dishevelled hair they spread their arms wide and call out; they fall to the ground, broken, and roll back and forth: "All too soon has the Blessed One attained final nibbana! All too soon has the Happy One attained final nibbana! All too soon has the eye of the world disappeared!" There are the gods who conceive of the earth in earth: with dishevelled hair they spread their arms wide and call out; they fall to the ground, broken, and roll back and forth: "All too soon has the Blessed One attained final nibbana! All too soon has the Happy One attained final nibbana! All too soon has the eye of the world disappeared!" But those gods who are without greed are mindful and fully aware; they accept that conditioning forces are impermanent, so how else could it be?'

So the venerable Anuruddha and the venerable Ānanda spent the rest of the night in discussion about the teaching. Then the venerable Anuruddha said to the venerable Ānanda: 'Ānanda, go into Kusinārā and tell the Mallas there that the Blessed One has attained final nibbana; it is now time for them to do as they think fit.'

'Yes, sir,' replied the venerable Ānanda to the venerable Anuruddha. Then, early in the morning he put on his outer robes
and, taking his bowl, went into Kusinārā with a companion. At that 159
time the Mallas of Kusinārā had sat down together in the meeting hall to deal with some matter. So the venerable Ānanda went to the meeting hall and told them: 'The Blessed One has attained final nibbana, Vāseṭṭhas. It is now time for you to do as you think fit.'

When they had heard this news from the venerable Ānanda, the Mallas and their sons and daughters and their wives felt wretched and unhappy, and were overcome with sadness. With dishevelled hair some spread their arms wide and called out; they fell to the ground, broken, and rolled back and forth: 'All too soon has the Blessed One attained final nibbana! All too soon has the Happy One attained final nibbana! All too soon has the eye of the world disappeared!'

Then the Mallas of Kusinārā instructed their people to gather together in Kusinārā incense and garlands and all kinds of musical instrument. Then, taking the incense, garlands, and musical instruments, and five hundred sets of garments, they went to the body of the Blessed One in Upavattana, the sāl grove of the Mallas. There they paid their respects to the body, honouring, revering, and worshipping it with dances, songs, music, garlands, and incense, making awnings and preparing pavilions. In this way they passed the day. Then the Mallas thought: 'It is too late to cremate the Blessed One's body today, we shall cremate it tomorrow.'

Then the Mallas passed a second day, and a third, fourth, fifth, and sixth day paying their respects to the body, honouring, revering, and worshipping it with dances, songs, music, garlands, and incense, making awnings and preparing pavilions. On the seventh day the
160 Mallas thought: 'While continuing to pay our respects to the Blessed One's body, while honouring, revering, and worshipping it with dances, songs, music, garlands, and incense, let us carry it round by the south of the town,* keeping outside, and then cremate it there to the south.'

Thereupon eight eminent Mallas bathed their heads, put on new clothes, and tried to lift the Blessed One's body but were unable to do so. Then the Mallas of Kusinārā asked the venerable Anuruddha what was the cause, what was the reason why these eight eminent Mallas, who had bathed their heads and put on new clothes, were unable to lift the Blessed One's body when they tried to do so.

'You have one plan, but the gods have another.'

'Sir, what plan do the gods have?'

'Vāseṭṭhas, your plan is, while continuing to pay your respects to the Blessed One's body . . . to carry it round by the south of the town, keeping outside, and then cremate it there to the south of the town. The gods' plan is, while continuing to pay their respects to the Blessed One's body . . . to carry it round by the north of the town and enter the town by the north gate, then having carried it through the middle of the town to go out by the east gate to the shrine of the

Mallas called Makuṭabandhana to the east of the town, and to cremate the body there.'

'Sir, let things happen according to the gods' plan.'

At that time Kusinārā was strewn knee-deep with *mandārava* flowers, including the alleys for waste and rubbish. And so the gods and the Mallas of Kusinārā, while paying their respects to the Blessed One's body, while honouring, revering, and worshipping it 161
with dances, songs, music, garlands, and incense both human and divine, carried it round by the north of the town and entered the town by the north gate. Then, having carried it through the middle of the town, they went out by the east gate to the shrine of the Mallas called Makuṭabandhana to the east of the town. There they laid out the Blessed One's body. Then the Mallas asked the venerable Ānanda: 'Ānanda, sir, how shall we treat the Tathāgata's body?'

'Vāseṭṭhas, the Tathāgata's body should be treated, as people treat the body of a wheel-turning king.'

'And how do people treat the body of a wheel-turning king?'

'First they wrap the body in unused cloth, then in teased cotton, then again in unused cloth. And when in this manner they have wrapped the body in five hundred double layers, they place it in an iron coffin full of oil. This they enclose in another iron coffin. Then they make a funeral pyre of all kinds of incense and cremate the body. Afterwards they build a stupa for the wheel-turning king where four roads meet. This is how people treat the body of a wheel-turning king. As people treat the body of a wheel-turning king, so the Tathāgata's body should be treated. A stupa should be built for the Tathāgata where four roads meet. When people place a garland, fragrance, or paste there, make respectful salutations or bring peace to their hearts, it will contribute to their long-lasting welfare and happiness.'

Then the Mallas of Kusinārā instructed their people to fetch teased cotton for them. And they wrapped the body in unused cloth, then in teased cotton . . . When they had made a funeral pyre of all 162
kinds of incense, they lifted the Blessed One's body onto it.

At that time the venerable Mahākassapa was travelling on the main road from Pāvā to Kusinārā with a large community of five hundred monks. He left the road and sat down at the root of a tree. At the same time an Ājīvika, who had collected a *mandārava* flower in Kusinārā, was making his way along the road towards Pāvā. When the venerable

Mahākassapa saw him coming in the distance he said to the Ājīvika: 'Are you familiar with our teacher?'

'Yes, I am. A week ago today the ascetic Gotama attained final nibbana. That is how I got this *mandārava* flower.'

The monks there who had not yet got rid of greed spread their arms wide and called out; they fell to the ground, broken, and rolled back and forth: 'All too soon has the Blessed One attained final nibbana! All too soon has the Happy One attained final nibbana! All too soon has the eye of the world disappeared!' But the monks who were without greed remained mindful and fully aware, accepting that conditioning forces are impermanent, so how else could it be?

At that time the one called Subhadda,* who had gone forth in old age, was seated in the assembly. He said to the monks: 'Enough, sirs! Do not grieve and lament. We are well free of the great ascetic! We were oppressed by his "this you are allowed, this you are not allowed," but now we can do what we like and what we don't like we don't have to do.'

The venerable Mahākassapa spoke to the monks: 'Enough, sirs!
163 Do not grieve and lament. Did not the Blessed One warn you about this before: we must lose and be deprived of and separated from everything pleasant and dear? So how else could it be? That something that is born, come into being, conditioned, and of a nature to decay should not decay—this cannot happen.'

At that time four eminent Mallas who had bathed their heads and put on new clothes, tried to light the Blessed One's funeral pyre, but were unable to do so. Then the Mallas of Kusinārā asked the venerable Anuruddha what was the cause, what was the reason why these four eminent Mallas, who had bathed their heads and put on new clothes, were unable to light the Blessed One's funeral pyre when they tried to do so.

'You have one plan, but the gods have another.'

'Sir, what plan do the gods have?'

'Vāseṭṭhas, the gods' plan is that the Blessed One's funeral pyre should not catch fire until the venerable Mahākassapa, who is travelling on the main road from Pāvā to Kusinārā with a large community of five hundred monks, has bowed down touching the feet of the Blessed One with his head.'

'Sir, let things happen according to the gods' plan.'

Then the venerable Mahākassapa arrived at Makuṭabandhana, the shrine of the Mallas at Kusinārā, and approached the Blessed One's funeral pyre. Then he arranged his outer robe on one shoulder, bowed with cupped hands, and, keeping it to his right, walked three times round the funeral pyre. Then he uncovered the feet and bowed down, touching the feet of the Blessed One with his head. Those five hundred monks also arranged their outer robes on one shoulder, bowed with cupped hands, and, keeping it to their right, walked three times round the funeral pyre. Then they too bowed down,
touching the feet of the Blessed One with their heads. And when the 164
venerable Mahākassapa and the five hundred monks had finished paying their respects the Blessed One's funeral pyre caught fire by itself.

Now when the Blessed One's body was cremated, no cinders or ash at all were formed from what had been the layers of skin, flesh, sinews, and oil of the joints, only the bones remained as relics. Just as when ghee or oil burns, no cinders or ash are formed at all, in exactly the same way when the Blessed One's body was cremated, no cinders or ash were formed at all . . . only the bones remained as relics. And of those five hundred double layers of cloth, two—the innermost and the outermost—were in fact not burnt up.* And when the Blessed One's body had been burnt up, a shower of water came from the sky and extinguished the funeral pyre, and water also burst forth from the sāl trees to extinguish the pyre, while the Mallas too extinguished it with perfumed water. Then the Mallas made a fence of spears and set up a wall of bows, and for seven days they paid their respects to the relics in their meeting hall, honouring,* revering, and worshipping them with dances, songs, music, garlands, and incense.

Now when the King Ajātasattu of Magadha, son of the princess of Videha, heard people say that the Blessed One had attained final nibbana at Kusinārā, he sent a messenger to the Mallas at Kusinārā, saying: 'The Blessed One was of the Ruler class, I too am a Ruler. I deserve a share of the relics of the Blessed One. I shall build a stupa for the relics and hold a festival.'

And when the Licchavis of Vesālī heard people say that the Blessed One had attained final nibbana at Kusinārā, they also sent a messenger to the Mallas, saying: 'The Blessed One was of the
Ruler class, we too are Rulers. We deserve a share of the relics 165

of the Blessed One. We shall build a stupa for the relics and hold a festival.'

And when the Sakyas of Kapilavatthu heard people say that the Blessed One had attained final nibbana at Kusinārā, they also sent a messenger to the Mallas, saying: 'The Blessed One was the best of our kinsmen. We deserve a share of the relics . . .'

And when the Bulis of Allakappa . . . [and] the Koliyas of the village of Rāma heard . . . they also sent a messenger to the Mallas, saying: 'The Blessed One was of the Ruler class, we too are Rulers. We deserve a share of the relics . . .'

And when a brahman of Veṭhadīpa heard . . . he also sent a messenger to the Mallas, saying: 'The Blessed One was of the Ruler class, and I am of the Brahman class. I deserve a share of the relics . . .'

And when the Mallas of Pāvā heard . . . they also sent a messenger . . . saying: 'The Blessed One was of the Ruler class, we too are Rulers. We deserve a share of the relics . . .'

166 At this, the Mallas of Kusinārā said to the assembled crowds: 'The Blessed One attained final nibbana in the territory of our village. We will not give away any part of his relics.'

When they had said this the Brahman Doṇa spoke to the assembled crowds:

'Good sirs, please listen to a word from me:
Our Buddha's was a teaching of tolerance.
That there should be a quarrel about the division of the relics
Of the greatest of men—certainly that is not right.
United and with all in agreement, good sirs,
Let us rejoice together and make a division into eight portions.
There can be stupas spread in the different directions:
Many people will have deep faith in this man of vision.'

'Then, brahman, you may carefully divide the relics into eight equal portions.'

'Yes, good sirs,' replied the Brahman Doṇa to the assembled crowds, and when he had carefully divided the relics into eight equal portions, he said to them: 'Good sirs, may you give the urn to me. I shall make a stupa for the urn and hold a festival.'

So they gave the Brahman Doṇa the urn. And when the Moriyas of Pipphalivana . . . also sent a messenger . . . saying that . . . they too deserved a share of the relics . . . they were told: 'There is no share of the relics left. They have been divided up. You can take charcoal from the pyre.' So they took charcoal.

Then King Ajātasattu of Magadha built a stupa and held a
festival for the relics at Rājagaha. And the Licchavis . . . at Vesālī; the 167
Sakyas . . . at Kapilavatthu; the Bulis . . . at Allakappa; the Koliyas . . . in the village of Rāma; the brahman . . . at Veṭhadīpa; the Mallas of Pāvā . . . at Pāvā; and the Mallas of Kusinārā . . . at Kusinārā. The Brahman Doṇa built a stupa and held a festival for the urn, and the Moriyas of Pipphalivana built a stupa and held a festival for the charcoal at Pipphalivana. This is how it happened in former times.

* * *

There were eight portions of the relics of the man of vision:
Seven portions they venerate in India,
And one portion of the greatest of men
The Nāga kings venerate in Rāma's village.
One tooth is worshipped by the gods in heaven,
One is venerated in the city of Gandhāra,
Yet another in the realm of the Kaliṅga King,
And the Nāga kings worship one more.
Because of their majesty this bounteous earth,
Is adorned with the best of offerings.
So these relics of the man of vision
Are well honoured by those who are themselves honoured. 168
Worshipped by the chiefs of gods, nāgas, and men,
Just so they are worshipped by the best of humans.
Holding out your cupped hands you should make your offering:
In hundreds of aeons a buddha is indeed hard to find.*

KING MAHĀSUDASSANA

MAHĀSUDASSANA-SUTTA (D II 169–199)

Introduction

The *Mahāsudassana-sutta* is presented as the full version of a narrative given in brief in the *Mahāparinibbāna-sutta*. Ānanda urges the Buddha not to die in the tiny, insignificant town of Kusinārā, whereupon the Buddha recounts how in ages long past Kusinārā was the fabulous royal capital of a *cakkavattin* (Skt: *cakravartin*), a 'wheel-turning king', Mahāsudassana. The expression 'wheel-turning king' perhaps originally referred to a king's exercising authority over a particular sphere of influence (*cakra*) or territory. In Indian mythology a wheel-turning king is a type of universal and ideal king who rules in perfect justice—an equivalent in British mythology might be King Arthur. Buddhist tradition relates how, after Gotama's birth, brahman seers identify his body as possessing thirty-two marks of a 'great man' (*mahāpurisa/mahāpuruṣa*), indicating that his fate will either be that of a buddha or a wheel-turning king. The *Mahāsudassana-sutta* relates how in fact in previous lives the Buddha had been a wheel-turning king. The sutta is thus a type of *jātaka*, a story of a previous life of the being who eventually became the Buddha.

The type of mythic narrative presented in the *Mahāsudassana-sutta* has sometimes been read as providing the model and inspiration for the ideal Buddhist ruler, but it can also be seen as a complete mythic narrative of the Buddhist path which itself becomes a kind of meditation for the listener.

At the beginning of the sutta Mahāsudassana is established within his city within his kingdom where everything is well. The first half of the sutta emphasizes Mahāsudassana's perfect conduct (*sīla*) and the way in which he provides for his citizens—his generosity (*dāna*). He then constructs a 'Palace of Truth' (*dhamma-pāsāda*) and withdraws into it. Within the palace Mahāsudassana enters its inner room, renouncing all thoughts of sensual desire, hostility, and malice. He then achieves the four 'meditations' (*jhāna*). On entering the palace, Mahāsudassana left behind all his possessions (fourteen lots of 84,000 possessions are enumerated), but these come to remind him of their existence. Dressed in all their finery, his 84,000 wives stream into the Palace of Truth, knocking on the door of the inner room. The chief queen then urges Mahāsudassana to arouse desire for all his possessions and for life, but he reprimands her: while they may have come to him as the result of his past good actions, continued attachment to them is an obstacle to his progress along the spiritual path. The long list of Mahāsudassana's various possessions is repeated in full a total of six times in the second half of the sutta, providing the listener with a meditation on the beauties and splendours of the world and, crucially, their impermanence.

The story of Mahāsudassana's life and death forms a literary counterpoint to the story of the Buddha's death. Mahāsudassana's withdrawal from the outer city into its inner sanctum, the Palace of Truth, is also something of a mythic equivalent of a Buddhist monk's withdrawal from the household life; the king's entering the Palace of Truth effectively marks the beginning of a life as a celibate ascetic removed from his possessions and his wives.

This is a very straightforward and clear narrative of the Buddhist path: generosity (*dāna*) and good conduct (*sīla*) are followed by meditation (*bhāvanā*), consisting of the practice of calm (*samatha*), in the form of happy and peaceful absorptions (*jhāna*), and then of insight (*vipassanā*) into impermanence, achieved by contemplating the death of the king and the disappearance of his fabulous city. The listener (and reader) is also led along that path by the narrative. The slow, unhurried description of the city with its groves of jewelled trees with tinkling bells and its lotus ponds, of the palace with its jewelled rooms and couches, evokes vivid images which bring a sense of well-being and calm. The story of the king's conversation with his queen and of his death is a story of letting go, of the passing of the things to which we are deeply attached—the passing even of the Buddha himself. For further references and a longer discussion see R. Gethin, 'Mythology as Meditation: From the Mahāsudassana Sutta to the Sukhāvatīvyūha Sūtra', *Journal of the Pali Text Society*, 28 (2006), 63–110.

[*First section for recitation*]

This is what I have heard. Once the Blessed One was staying at 169
Kusinārā, in the Upavattana sāl grove of the Mallas, between the two sāl trees at the time of his final nibbana. Now the venerable Ānanda approached the Blessed One, and having approached he saluted the Blessed One respectfully and sat down to one side.

Once seated, he said to the Blessed One: 'Sir, the Blessed One should not enter final nibbana in this mud-wall town, this remote, provincial town. Sir, there are other important cities such as Campā, Rājagaha, Sāvatthī, Sāketa, Kosambī, and Benares—the Blessed One should enter final nibbana in one of these. In these cities there are many wealthy nobles, brahmans, and householders who have great faith in the Tathāgata and who will pay due honour to the remains of the Tathāgata.'

'Ānanda, do not say that this is a mud-wall town, a remote, provincial town. Long ago there was a king called Mahāsudassana. He was an anointed prince, a sovereign of the four quarters who main-
170 tained the stability of the country. This town of Kusinārā was the royal city of King Mahāsudassana and was called Kusāvatī. Twelve leagues in length on the east and west sides and seven leagues across on the north and south sides, the royal city of Kusāvatī was successful and prosperous, with many inhabitants, full of people and well provided with food—just as Āḷakamandā, the royal city of the gods, is successful and prosperous, with many inhabitants, full of divine beings and well provided with food. Day and night the royal city of Kusāvatī was filled with the ten sounds: the sound of elephants, horses, carriages, kettle drums, tabors, vīnās, singing, cymbals, gongs, and lastly the sound of the cries of "Eat, drink, and be merry!"

'The city was encircled by seven walls: one of gold, one of silver, one of beryl, one of crystal, one of ruby, one of emerald, and one of all kinds of gems. And it had gates of four colours: one of gold,
171 one of silver, one of beryl, one of crystal. At each gate seven pillars were set into the ground, three times the height of a man in circumference and in height four times that of a man.* One pillar was of gold, one of silver, one of beryl, one of crystal, one of ruby, one of emerald, one of all kinds of gems. The royal city of Kusāvatī was encircled by seven rows of palm trees: one of gold, one of silver, one of beryl, one of crystal, one of ruby, one of emerald, one of all kinds of gems. The trunks of the gold palm trees were gold, the leaves and fruits silver; the trunks of the silver palm trees were silver, the leaves and fruits gold; the trunks of the beryl palm trees were beryl, the leaves and fruits crystal; the trunks of the crystal palm trees were crystal, the leaves and fruits beryl; the trunks of the ruby palm trees were ruby, the leaves and fruits emerald; the trunks of the emerald palm trees were emerald, the leaves and fruits ruby; the trunks of the palm trees of all kinds of gems were of all kinds of gems, the leaves and fruits of all kinds of gems. And the sound of those trees when stirred by the wind was lovely, delightful, charming, enchanting—like the sound of the five kinds of musical instrument when well

played by musicians skilled in the arts of musicianship. And at that 172
time those in the royal city of Kusāvatī who were revellers, fond of drink, keen drinkers, danced round* to the sound of the trees stirred by the wind.

'Now, Ānanda, King Mahāsudassana possessed seven treasures and was especially fortunate in four ways. What were the seven treasures? On the full-moon observance day on the fifteenth of the month, when King Mahāsudassana had bathed his head and gone up onto the roof of his fine palace to keep the observance day, there appeared to him the heavenly wheel-treasure, complete with a thousand spokes, rim and hub. When he saw this the king thought: "I have heard that when a king, an anointed prince, who has bathed his head goes up onto the roof of his fine palace on the observance day on the fifteenth to keep the observance day and there appears to him the heavenly wheel-treasure complete with a thousand spokes, and furnished with a rim and hub, then that king is a wheel-turning king. Would that I were indeed a wheel-turning king!" Then, Ānanda, King Mahāsudassana got up from his seat and, having arranged his robe over one shoulder, took a golden vessel in his left hand and sprinkled the wheel treasure with his right: "May the wheel-treasure roll on! May the wheel-treasure be victorious!"

'Then the wheel-treasure rolled forward to the east, with King Mahāsudassana and his fourfold army following behind. And in
whatever country the wheel-treasure came to rest, there King 173
Mahāsudassana took up residence with his fourfold army. And all the rival princes in the east approached King Mahāsudassana and said: "Come, your majesty, you are welcome. It is yours, your majesty. Instruct us!"

'King Mahāsudassana said: "Do not kill living beings. Do not take what is not given. Do not indulge in sexual misconduct. Do not tell lies. Do not drink intoxicants. Govern as you have governed."* And so the rival princes in the east became obedient to King Mahāsudassana.

'Then, Ānanda, the wheel-treasure plunged down into the eastern ocean, rose out again, and rolled on to the south . . . Then it plunged down into the southern ocean, rose out again and rolled on to the west . . . Then it plunged down into the western ocean, rose out again, and rolled on to the north, with King Mahāsudassana and his fourfold army following behind. And in whatever country the wheel-treasure came to rest, there King Mahāsudassana took up residence with his fourfold army. And all the rival princes in the north approached King Mahāsudassana and said: "Come, your majesty, you are welcome. It is yours, your majesty. Instruct us!"

'King Mahāsudassana said: "Do not kill living beings. Do not take
174 what is not given. Do not indulge in sexual misconduct. Do not tell
lies. Do not drink intoxicants. Govern as you have governed." And so the rival princes in the north became obedient to King Mahāsudassana.

'And when, Ānanda, the wheel-treasure had conquered the entire earth to the edge of the ocean, it returned to the royal city of Kusāvatī and stopped as if fixed to an axle in front of the court at the entrance to King Mahāsudassana's inner apartments, which it adorned. Such was the wheel-treasure that appeared to King Mahāsudassana.

'Next, Ānanda, there appeared to King Mahāsudassana the elephant-treasure, all white, firm in seven ways, with magic powers, flying through the air, a king of elephants, called Changes of the Moon.* And when the king saw him his heart was inspired with confidence: "What an excellent mount! If only he would submit to control!" And then, just like a fine, thoroughbred elephant that has been well trained for a long time, that elephant-treasure submitted to control. And long ago, in order to test the elephant-treasure, King Mahāsudassana mounted him in the early dawn and travelled across the land to the edge of the ocean, returning to the royal city of Kusāvatī to take his breakfast. Such was the elephant-treasure that appeared to King Mahāsudassana.

'Next, Ānanda, there appeared to King Mahāsudassana the horse-treasure, all white, with a black head and fine mane,* with magic powers, flying through the air, a king of horses, called Thunder-cloud.* And when the king saw him his heart was inspired with
confidence: "What an excellent mount! If only he would submit to
175 control!" And then, just like a fine, thoroughbred horse that has been
well trained for a long time, that horse-treasure submitted to control. And long ago, in order to test the horse-treasure, King Mahāsudassana mounted him in the early dawn and travelled across the land to the edge of the ocean, returning to the royal city of Kusāvatī to take his breakfast. Such was the horse-treasure that appeared to King Mahāsudassana.

'Next, Ānanda, there appeared to King Mahāsudassana the gem-treasure. This was a beautiful beryl, pure, expertly cut with eight facets, bright, clear, without flaw, perfect in every respect. Its brilliance spread out for a league round about. And long ago, in order to test the gem-treasure, King Mahāsudassana summoned his fourfold army and, fixing the gem on the top of his standard, went out in the dark of the night. And because of the gem's brilliance the villagers from round about thought it was day and started their work. Such was the gem-treasure that appeared to King Mahāsudassana.

'Next, Ānanda, there appeared to King Mahāsudassana the woman-treasure. Beautiful, of wonderful looks, and graceful, she had the most lovely appearance. She was neither too tall, nor too short; neither too fat, nor too thin; neither too dark, nor too fair. She had a beauty which was more than human, like that of a goddess. And the touch of the woman-treasure's body was just like cotton or cotton wool; in the cool season her limbs felt warm, in the hot season cool; from her body wafted the scent of sandalwood, and from her mouth the scent of lotus. She got up before the king and went to bed after him; she waited for his instructions, was pleasing in her conduct, and 176
gracious in her speech. And the woman-treasure was not even unfaithful to the king in thought, let alone in deed. Such was the woman-treasure that appeared to King Mahāsudassana.

'Next, Ānanda, there appeared to King Mahāsudassana the steward-treasure. As a result of his past actions he possessed a godlike vision with which he could see hidden treasure, whether belonging to people or not. And he approached King Mahāsudassana and said to him: "You need have no worries, lord. I will manage your wealth properly." And long ago, in order to test the steward-treasure, King Mahāsudassana boarded a boat and went out into the current in the middle of the River Ganges. And then he said to the steward-treasure: "Steward, I need gold coins."

' "Then let the boat go to one bank."

' "But, steward, it is right here that I need gold coins."

'Then the steward reached down into the water with both hands and drew out a pot full of gold coins.

' "Is that enough, your majesty? Have I done what you wished?" he asked.

' "That is enough, steward. You have done what I wished. You have served me as I wished," said the king. 177

'Such was the steward-treasure that appeared to King Mahāsudassana.

'Next Ānanda, there appeared to King Mahāsudassana the adviser-treasure, a learned, clever, and wise man who knew when to advise the king to advance, when to advise him to retreat, and when to advise him to stand still. And he approached King Mahāsudassana and said to him: "You need have no worries, lord. I will advise you." Such was the adviser-treasure that appeared to King Mahāsudassana.

'These, then, were the seven treasures possessed by King Mahāsudassana. Furthermore, Ānanda, King Mahāsudassana was blessed with good fortune in four ways. Handsome, of wonderful looks, and graceful, the king had the most lovely appearance, surpassing that of other men. This was the first way in which he was blessed with good fortune. Again, he was long-lived, living longer than other men. This was the second way in which he was blessed with good fortune. Again, he was of good health, suffering little pain, with good, balanced digestion, without excessive heat or cold, surpassing that of other men. This was the third way in which he was
178 blessed with good fortune. Again, he was loved and cherished by brahmans and householders, just as a father is loved and cherished by his sons. And brahmans and householders were loved and cherished by the king, just as sons are loved and cherished by a father. Long ago, Ānanda, King Mahāsudassana went out into the park with his fourfold army, and the brahmans and householders came up to him and said: "Go slowly, lord, so that we can look at you for longer." And the king too said to his charioteer: "Drive slowly, so that I can look at the brahmans and householders for longer." This was the fourth way in which King Mahāsudassana was blessed with good fortune. So King Mahāsudassana was blessed with good fortune in these four ways.

'Now King Mahāsudassana thought: "Why don't I have lotus ponds built in the spaces between these palms* at every hundred-bows' length?" So he had lotus ponds built in the spaces between those palms at every hundred-bows' length. The lotus ponds were lined with tiles of four colours: some were of gold, some were of silver, some were of beryl, and some were of crystal. And each lotus pond had four flights of steps: one of gold, one of silver, one of beryl,
179 and one of crystal. The gold flights of steps had gold balustrades,

with silver crossbars and handrail; the silver flights of steps had silver balustrades, with gold crossbars and handrail; the beryl flights of steps had beryl balustrades, with crystal crossbars and handrail; the crystal flights of steps had crystal balustrades, with beryl crossbars and handrail. The lotus ponds were surrounded by two railings: one of gold, and one of silver. The gold railing had gold posts, with silver crossbars and handrail; the silver railing had silver posts, with gold crossbars and handrail.

'Now King Mahāsudassana thought: "Why don't I have different kinds of water lilies and lotuses for all seasons planted in these lotus ponds—blue lotuses, red lotuses, and white lotuses*—so that everyone can have garlands?"* So the king had lotuses for all seasons planted in those lotus ponds—blue lotuses, red lotuses, and white lotuses—so that everyone could have garlands.

'Then the king thought: "Why don't I have bath attendants placed at the edge of these lotus ponds who can bathe people that come?" So the king had bath attendants placed at the edge of the lotus ponds who could bathe people that came.

'Then the king thought: "Why don't I arrange for the giving out of different things at the edge of these lotus ponds: food for those who need food, drink for those who need drink, clothing for those who need clothing, transport for those who need transport, beds for those who need beds, wives for those who need wives, money and
gold for those who need money and gold?" So the king arranged for 180
the giving out of different things at the edge of the lotus ponds: food for those who needed food, drink for those who needed drink, clothing for those who needed clothing, transport for those who needed transport, beds for those who needed beds, wives for those who needed wives, money and gold for those who needed money and gold.

'Then the brahmans and householders came to the king with a great sum of money, and said: "Lord, we have brought this great sum of money for your use. Please accept it."

' "Good sirs, enough! I have a great deal of money collected through proper taxation. You should keep this, and take away some more."

'When they were refused by the king they withdrew to one side and considered together: "It is not right for us take this money back to our homes again. Why don't we have a house built for King Mahāsudassana?"

'So they approached the king and said: "Lord, we will have a house built for you."

'And by his silence the king agreed. 'Then, Ānanda, Sakka, lord of the gods, knowing in his mind King Mahāsudassana's thoughts, spoke to the god Vissakamma:* "Come now, friend Vissakamma. You must build a house for King Mahāsudassana, a palace called 'Truth'."

181 '"Such good fortune for you!" replied Vissakamma to Sakka, and then, just as a strong man might straighten his bent arm or bend his straightened arm, he disappeared from the realm of the Thirty-Three Gods and appeared before King Mahāsudassana.

'Then he said to the king: "Lord, I shall build a house for you, a palace called 'Truth'."

'And by his silence the king agreed. So the god Vissakamma built a house for King Mahāsudassana, a palace called "Truth". The Palace of Truth was one league in length on the east and west sides, and half a league across on the north and south sides. The ground floor of the palace was faced to a height three times that of a man with tiles of four colours: some were of gold, some were of silver, some were of beryl, and some were of crystal. It had 84,000 columns of four colours: some of gold, some of silver, some of beryl, and some of crystal. It was covered with boards* of four colours: some of gold, some of silver, some of beryl, and some of crystal. It had twenty-four staircases of four colours: some of gold, some of silver, some of beryl, and some of crystal. The gold staircases had gold balustrades, with silver crossbars and handrail; the silver staircases had silver balustrades, with gold crossbars and handrail; the beryl staircases
182 had beryl balustrades, with crystal crossbars and handrail; the crystal staircases had crystal balustrades, with beryl crossbars and handrail.

'There were 84,000 chambers of four colours in the palace: some were of gold, some were of silver, some were of beryl, and some were of crystal. The golden chambers were furnished with silver couches, the silver chambers with golden couches; the beryl chambers were furnished with ivory couches, the crystal chambers with ebony couches. And at the doors to the golden chambers there stood silver palms with trunks of silver and leaves and fruits of gold; at the doors to the silver chambers there stood golden palms with trunks of gold and leaves and fruits of silver; at the doors to the beryl chambers there stood crystal palms with trunks of crystal and leaves and fruits of beryl; at the doors to the crystal chambers there stood beryl palms with trunks of beryl and leaves and fruits of crystal.

'Then King Mahāsudassana thought: "Why don't I have a grove of completely golden palm trees made at the door to the Room of the Great Array so that I can sit and spend the day there?" So the king had a grove of completely golden palm trees made at the door to the Room of the Great Array so he could sit and spend the day there.

'The Palace of Truth was encircled by two railings: one of gold, 183
and one of silver. The gold railing had gold posts, with silver crossbars and handrail; the silver railing had silver posts, with gold crossbars and handrail. It was also hung right round with two strings of bells: one of gold, and one of silver. The gold string had silver bells; the silver string had gold bells. And the sound of those strings of bells when stirred by the wind was lovely, delightful, charming, enchanting—like the sound of the five kinds of musical instrument when well played by musicians skilled in the arts of musicianship. And at that time those in the royal city of Kusāvatī who were revellers, fond of drink, keen drinkers, danced round to the sound of the strings of bells stirred by the wind.

'Ānanda, when the Palace of Truth was finished it was hard to look at, dazzling one's eyes—just as in the last month of the rainy season at the beginning of autumn the sun, rising above the morning mist into a clear and cloudless sky, is hard to look at and dazzles one's eyes.

'Then King Mahāsudassana thought: "Why don't I have a lotus 184
pond called Truth built in front of the Palace of Truth?" So the king had a lotus pond called Truth built in front of the Palace of Truth. The Lotus Pond of Truth was one league in length on the east and west sides, and half a league across on the north and south. It was lined with tiles of four colours: some were of gold, some were of silver, some were of beryl, and some were of crystal. It had twenty-four flights of steps: some of gold, some of silver, some of beryl, and some of crystal. The gold flights of steps had gold balustrades, with silver crossbars and handrail; the silver flights of steps had silver balustrades, with gold crossbars and handrail; the beryl flights of steps had beryl balustrades, with crystal crossbars and handrail; the crystal flights of steps had crystal balustrades, with beryl crossbars and handrail. The Lotus Pond of Truth was encircled by two railings: one of gold, and one of silver. The gold railing had gold posts, with

silver crossbars and handrail; the silver railing had silver posts, with gold crossbars and handrail.

'The Lotus Pond of Truth was encircled by seven rows of palm trees: one of gold, one of silver, one of beryl, one of crystal, one of ruby, one of emerald, one of all kinds of gems. The trunks of the gold
185 palm trees were gold, the leaves and fruits silver; the trunks of the silver palm trees were silver, the leaves and fruits gold; the trunks of the beryl palm trees were beryl, the leaves and fruits crystal; the trunks of the crystal palm trees were crystal, the leaves and fruits beryl; the trunks of the ruby palm trees were ruby, the leaves and fruits emerald; the trunks of the emerald palm trees were emerald, the leaves and fruits ruby; the trunks of the palm trees of all kinds of gems were of all kinds of gems, the leaves and fruits of all kinds of gems. And the sound of those trees when stirred by the wind was lovely, delightful, charming, enchanting—like the sound of the five kinds of musical instrument when well played by musicians skilled in the arts of musicianship. And at that time those in the royal city of Kusāvatī who were revellers, fond of drink, keen drinkers, danced round to the sound of the trees stirred by the wind.

'Ānanda, when the Palace and Lotus Pond of Truth were finished, King Mahāsudassana provided those of the ascetics and brahmans of that time who were well known with all that they wanted and then went up into the Palace of Truth.'

[*Second section for recitation*]

'Then, Ānanda, King Mahāsudassana thought: "It is as a fruit and result of what kind of action that I now have such great fortune and
186 power?" Then he thought: "It is as a fruit and result of three kinds of action, namely giving, control, and restraint,* that I now have such great fortune and power."

'Then the king approached the Room of the Great Array, and standing at the door he breathed a sigh: "Stop here, thoughts of sensual desire! Stop here, thoughts of hostility! Stop here, thoughts of malice! This is far enough, thoughts of sensual desire! This is far enough, thoughts of hostility! This is far enough, thoughts of malice!"*

'Then King Mahāsudassana went into the Room of the Great Array and sat down on the golden couch. Secluded from sense desires and unwholesome qualities, he attained and remained in the joy and happiness of the first absorption, which is accompanied by thinking and examining, and born of seclusion. By stilling thinking and examining, he attained and remained in the joy and happiness of second absorption, a state of inner clarity and mental unification that is without thinking and examining, and is born of concentration. And then, by having no desire for joy, he remained equanimous, mindful, and fully aware; he experienced the bodily happiness of which the noble one speak, saying "equanimous and mindful, one lives happily"; and so he attained and remained in the third absorption. By letting go of happiness and unhappiness, as a result of the earlier disappearance of pleasure and pain, he attained and remained in the pure equanimity and mindfulness of the fourth absorption, which is free of happiness and unhappiness.

'Then King Mahāsudassana came out of the Room of the Great Array, and went into a golden chamber. And, seated on a silver couch, he stayed, pervading the first quarter with a mind full of friendliness, likewise the second, third, and fourth quarters. In the same way he stayed completely pervading the whole world, above, below, around, everywhere, with a mind full of friendliness—a mind abundant, great, measureless, free from hostility, free from affliction. He stayed, pervading the first quarter with a mind full of compassion . . . with a mind full of sympathetic joy . . . with a mind of full equanimity, 187
likewise the second, third and fourth quarters. In the same way he stayed completely pervading the whole world, above, below, around, everywhere, with a mind full of equanimity—a mind abundant, great, measureless, free from hostility, free from affliction.*

'Ānanda, King Mahāsudassana had 84,000 cities, the chief of which was the royal city of Kusāvatī. He had 84,000 palaces, the chief of which was the Palace of Truth. He had 84,000 chambers, the chief of which was the Room of the Great Array. He had 84,000 couches of gold, silver, ivory, and ebony,* spread with blankets and cloths, with antelope covers, canopies, and red pillows at each end. He had 84,000 elephants, decorated with gold, with golden banners and with drapes embroidered with golden thread, the chief of which was the king of elephants, Changes of the Moon. He had 84,000 horses, decorated with gold, with golden banners and with drapes embroidered with golden thread, the chief of which was the king of horses, Thundercloud. He had 84,000 chariots with coverings of lion-skin, tiger-skin, leopard-skin, and pale cloth, decorated with

gold, with golden banners and with drapes embroidered with golden thread; the chief of these was the chariot Flag of Victory. He had 84,000 gems, the chief of which was the gem-treasure. He had 84,000
188 wives, the chief of whom was Queen Subhaddā. He had 84,000 stewards, the chief of whom was the steward-treasure. He had 84,000 loyal princes, the chief of whom was the adviser-treasure. He had 84,000 cows with jute tethers and bronze milking pails.* He had 84,000 myriads of garments of the finest linen, cotton, silk, and wool. He had 84,000 plates for the serving of rice every evening and morning.

'Now at that time, Ānanda, the 84,000 elephants used to come to be of service to the king every evening and morning. And the king thought: "These 84,000 elephants come to be of service to me every morning and evening, but what if they should come in two groups of 42,000, one every hundred years?" So the king addressed the adviser-treasure: "These 84,000 elephants come to be of service to me every morning and evening, but, friend, let them come in two groups of
189 42,000, one every hundred years." "Yes, lord," replied the adviser-treasure to the king. And from that time they came in two groups of 42,000 elephants, one every hundred years.

'Now after many hundreds, many hundreds of thousands of years, Queen Subhaddā thought: "I have not seen King Mahāsudassana for a long time. What if I should go and see him?" So she addressed the court women: "Come, wash your hair and put on new clothes! We have not seen the king for a long time, so let's go and see him." "Yes, lady," they replied to the queen. And when they had washed their hair and put on new clothes they went to the queen, and she addressed the adviser-treasure: "Friend Adviser-Treasure, get ready the fourfold army. We have not seen the king for a long time, so we shall go and see him." "Yes, lady," replied the adviser-treasure. And when he had got ready the fourfold army he announced to the queen: "The fourfold army is ready for you, lady. Now it is time for you to
190 do as you think fit."

'So Queen Subhaddā, accompanied by the fourfold army, went with the women of the court to the Palace of Truth, and there she went up into the palace to the Room of the Great Array, where she stood leaning by the door. And the king thought: "What is that noise, like a great crowd of people?" And coming out he saw Queen Subhaddā leaning by the door. When he saw her, he said: "Stay right there, lady! Do not come in." Then he addressed one of his men: "Come, sir, bring out the golden couch from the Room of the Great Array and make it ready in the grove of completely golden palms." "Yes, lord," replied the man to the king. And he brought out the golden couch from the Room of the Great Array and made it ready in the grove of completely golden palms. Then the king lay down on his right side like a lion with one foot resting on the other, mindful and fully aware.

'Then Queen Subhaddā thought, "How serene King Mahāsudassana's senses are! How pure and clear the colour of his skin!* Surely it can't be that the king is dying!"

'Then she said to the king: "Lord, you have 84,000 cities, the chief of which is the royal city of Kusāvatī. Arouse your desire for them! Awaken your longing for life! You have 84,000 palaces, the chief of 191
which is the Palace of Truth. Arouse your desire for them! Awaken your longing for life! You have 84,000 chambers, the chief of which is the Room of the Great Array. Arouse your desire for them! Awaken your longing for life! You have 84,000 couches of gold, silver, ivory, and ebony, spread with blankets and cloths, with antelope covers, canopies, and red pillows at each end. Arouse your desire for them! Awaken your longing for life! You have 84,000 elephants, decorated with gold, with golden banners and with drapes embroidered with golden thread, the chief of which is the king of elephants, Changes of the Moon. Arouse your desire for them! Awaken your longing for life! You have 84,000 horses, decorated with gold, with golden banners and with drapes embroidered with golden thread, the chief of which is the king of horses, Thundercloud. Arouse your desire for them! Awaken your longing for life! You have 84,000 chariots with coverings of lion-skin, tiger-skin, leopard-skin, and pale cloth, decorated with gold, with golden banners and with drapes embroidered with golden thread, the chief of which is the chariot Flag of Victory. Arouse your desire for them! Awaken your longing for life! You have 84,000 gems, the chief of which is the gem-treasure. Arouse your desire for them! Awaken your longing for life! You have 84,000 wives, the chief of whom is the woman-treasure. Arouse your desire for them! Awaken your longing for life! You have 84,000 stewards, the chief of whom is the steward-treasure. Arouse your desire for them! Awaken your longing for life! You have 84,000 loyal princes, the chief of whom is the adviser-treasure. Arouse your

desire for them! Awaken your longing for life! You have 84,000 cows with jute tethers and bronze milking pails. Arouse your desire for
192 them! Awaken your longing for life! You have 84,000 myriads of garments of the finest linen, cotton, silk, and wool. Arouse your desire for them! Awaken your longing for life! You have 84,000 plates for the serving of rice every evening and morning. Arouse your desire for them! Awaken your longing for life!"

'At these words King Mahāsudassana said to Queen Subhaddā: "Lady, for a long time you have spoken to me with words that are welcome, dear, and agreeable, but now in these last hours you speak to me with words that are not welcome, not dear, disagreeable."

'"Then how should I speak to you, lord?"

'"Lady, speak to me like this: 'We must lose and be deprived of everything pleasant and dear. Lord, you should not die with longing. Unhappy and dishonourable is the death of one who dies with longing. Lord, you have 84,000 cities, the chief of which is the royal city of Kusāvatī. Let go of your desire for them! Do not long after life! You have 84,000 palaces, the chief of which is the Palace of Truth.
193 Let go of your desire for them! Do not long after life! You have 84,000 chambers, the chief of which is the Room of the Great Array. Let go of your desire for them! Do not long after life! You have 84,000 couches of gold, silver, ivory, and ebony, spread with blankets and cloths, with antelope covers, canopies, and red pillows at each end. Let go of your desire for them! Do not long after life! You have 84,000 elephants, decorated with gold, with golden banners and with drapes embroidered with golden thread, the chief of which is the king of elephants, Changes of the Moon. Let go of your desire for them! Do not long after life! You have 84,000 horses, decorated with gold, with golden banners and with drapes embroidered with golden thread, the chief of which is the king of horses, Thundercloud. Let go of your desire for them! Do not long after life! You have 84,000 chariots with coverings of lion-skin, tiger-skin, leopard-skin, and pale cloth, decorated with gold, with golden banners and with drapes embroidered with golden thread, the chief of which is the chariot Flag of Victory. Let go of your desire for them! Do not long after life! You have 84,000 gems, the chief of which is the gem-treasure. Let go of your desire for them! Do not long after life! You have 84,000 wives, the chief of whom is Queen Subhaddā. Let go of your desire for them! Do not long after life! You have 84,000 stewards, the chief

of whom is the steward-treasure. Let go of your desire for them! Do not long after life! You have 84,000 loyal princes, the chief of whom is the adviser-treasure. Let go of your desire for them! Do not long after life! You have 84,000 cows with jute tethers and bronze milking pails. Let go of your desire for them! Do not long after life! You have 194
84,000 myriads of garments of the finest linen, cotton, silk, and wool. Let go of your desire for them! Do not long after life! You have 84,000 plates for the serving of rice every evening and morning. Let go of your desire for them! Do not long after life!'"

'At these words Queen Subhaddā wept and shed tears. Then, wiping away her tears she spoke to King Mahāsudassana: "We must lose and be deprived of everything pleasant and dear. Lord, you should not die with longing. Unhappy and dishonourable is the death of one who dies with longing. Lord, you have 84,000 cities, the chief of which is the royal city of Kusāvatī. Let go of your desire for them! Do not long after life! You have 84,000 palaces, the chief of which is the Palace of Truth. Let go of your desire for them! Do not long after life! You have 84,000 chambers, the chief of which is the Room of the Great Array. Let go of your desire for them! Do not long after life! You have 84,000 couches of gold, silver, ivory, and ebony, spread with blankets and cloths, with antelope covers, canopies, and red pillows at each end. Let go of your desire for them! Do not long after life! You have 84,000 elephants, decorated with gold, with golden banners and with drapes embroidered with golden thread, the chief of which is the king of elephants, Changes of the Moon. Let go of your desire for them! Do not long after life! You have 84,000 horses, decorated with gold, with golden banners and with drapes embroidered with golden thread, the chief of which is the king of horses, Thundercloud. Let go of your desire for them! Do not long after 195
life! You have 84,000 chariots with coverings of lion-skin, tiger-skin, leopard-skin, and pale cloth, decorated with gold, with golden banners and with drapes embroidered with golden thread, the chief of which is the chariot Flag of Victory. Let go of your desire for them! Do not long after life! You have 84,000 gems, the chief of which is the gem-treasure. Let go of your desire for them! Do not long after life! You have 84,000 wives, the chief of whom is the woman-treasure. Let go of your desire for them! Do not long after life! You have 84,000 stewards, the chief of whom is the steward-treasure. Let go of your desire for them! Do not long after life!

You have 84,000 loyal princes, the chief of whom is the adviser-treasure. Let go of your desire for them! Do not long after life! You have 84,000 cows with jute tethers and bronze milking pails. Let go of your desire for them! Do not long after life! You have 84,000 myriads of garments of the finest linen, cotton, silk, and wool. Let go of your desire for them! Do not long after life! You have 84,000 plates for the serving of rice every evening and morning. Let go of your desire for them! Do not long after life!"

'Not long after, Ānanda, King Mahāsudassana died. And the feeling he had when he died was just like the contentment* a householder or a householder's son feels when he has eaten a wonderful
196 meal. When he died he was reborn in a happy place, the Brahma world. For 84,000 years King Mahāsudassana enjoyed the carefree life of a young prince; for 84,000 years he was viceroy; for 84,000 years he ruled the kingdom; for 84,000 years he followed the spiritual life as a householder in the Palace of Truth. Having cultivated the four sublime ways of living, at the breaking up of the body after death he was born in the Brahma world.

'Now you might think, Ānanda, that at that time King Mahāsudassana was someone else, but you should not look at it in that way, Ānanda. I was King Mahāsudassana at that time. Those 84,000 cities, the chief of which was the royal city of Kusāvatī, were mine. Those 84,000 palaces, the chief of which was the Palace of Truth, were mine. Those 84,000 chambers, the chief of which was the Room of the Great Array, were mine. Those 84,000 couches of gold, silver, ivory, and ebony, spread with blankets and cloths, with antelope covers, canopies, and red pillows at each end, were mine. Those 84,000 elephants, decorated with gold, with golden banners and with drapes embroidered with golden thread, the chief of which was the king of elephants, Changes of the Moon, were mine. Those 84,000 horses, decorated with gold, with golden banners and with drapes embroidered with golden thread, the chief of which was the
197 king of horses, Thundercloud, were mine. Those 84,000 chariots with coverings of lion-skin, tiger-skin, leopard-skin, and pale cloth, decorated with gold, with golden banners and with drapes embroidered with golden thread, the chief of which was the chariot Flag of Victory, were mine. Those 84,000 gems, the chief of which was the gem-treasure, were mine. Those 84,000 wives, the chief of whom was Queen Subhaddā, were mine. Those 84,000 stewards, the

chief of whom was the steward-treasure, were mine. Those 84,000 loyal princes, the chief of whom was the adviser-treasure, were mine. Those 84,000 cows with jute tethers and bronze milking pails were mine. Those 84,000 myriads of garments of the finest linen, cotton, silk, and wool were mine. Those 84,000 plates for the serving of rice every evening and morning were mine.

'Of those 84,000 cities, I lived in just one at that time, namely the royal city of Kusāvatī. Of those 84,000 palaces, I lived in just one at that time, namely the Palace of Truth. Of those 84,000 chambers, I lived in just one at that time, namely the Room of the Great Array. Of those 84,000 couches of gold, silver, ivory, and ebony, I used just one at that time, namely one of gold, silver, ivory, or ebony. Of those 84,000 elephants, I rode just one at that time, namely the king of elephants, Changes of the Moon. Of those 84,000 horses, I rode just 198
one at that time, namely the king of horses, Thundercloud. Of those 84,000 chariots, I rode in just one at that time, namely the chariot Flag of Victory. Of those 84,000 wives, just one wife used to attend on me at that time, namely a woman of the Ruler class or a *velāmikānī*. Of those 84,000 myriads of garments, I wore just one set of garments at that time, namely one made of the finest linen, cotton, silk, or wool. Of those 84,000 plates, I ate at most a portion of rice with a suitable amount of curry from just one plate.

'See, Ānanda, how all those conditioned things have gone, ceased, changed. Conditioned things are like that, Ānanda: they are impermanent, not lasting, unreliable. Therefore one should be disenchanted with all conditioned things; one should have no desire for them, one should be free of them.

'I recall laying aside the body in this place six times when living as a wheel-turning king, a righteous king of Truth, sovereign of the four quarters, maintaining the stability of the country, possessing the seven treasures. This is the seventh laying aside of the body.* But I do not see any place in this world with its gods, its Māra and Brahmā, 199
in this generation with its ascetics and brahmans, its princes and peoples, where the Tathāgata might lay aside an eighth body.'

This is what the Blessed One said. And when the Happy One had said this, the Teacher spoke again:

'Impermanent are conditioned things! It is their nature to arise and fall.
Having arisen, they cease. Their stilling is happy.'

THE ORIGIN OF THINGS

AGGAÑÑA-SUTTA (D III 80–98)

Introduction

In this sutta the Buddha is approached by two novice Buddhist monks who were born into the Brahman class (*vaṇṇa/varṇa*). They report to the Buddha that brahmans now look down on them for having deserted their class, claiming that the brahman class is the highest of the four classes of ancient Indian society since its members were originally born of Brahmā's mouth, and that for a brahman to become a Buddhist monk is to fall in with inferiors, descended not from Brahmā's mouth but his feet. This claim is a reference to a brahmanical idea expressed in a hymn of the Ṛg Veda, the 'Hymn of the Man' (*Puruṣa-sūkta*) (10.90) which states that the four classes were born from the body of a primordial man (subsequently identified with Brahmā, as here) in the course of an original sacrificial act which in effect brought the world as we know it into existence: the mouth of this original man became the brahmans (*brāhmaṇa*), his arms the rulers (*khattiya/kṣatriya*), his thighs the traders (*vessa/vaiśya*), and his feet the servants (*sudda/śūdra*). The Buddha counters by asserting that true status is not a matter of the class into which one is born but of how one behaves. He then offers an alternative account of the origin of the world, society, and, in particular, the four classes. This account is a clever piece of one-upmanship suggesting that if one must put one's trust in birth, then the ruler class (into which the Buddha was born) is in fact the superior class, and that the brahmans of the Buddha's day are mere shadows of the ancient brahmans, who in fact lived a life devoted to meditation, rather similar to that followed by Buddhist monks.

Some modern commentators, most notably Richard Gombrich, have suggested that this alternative account was not originally intended to be read as a straight-faced and literal account of the evolution of the world (as the subsequent Buddhist tradition has tended to read it), but as a humorous parody and pastiche of brahmanical methods and theories. Certainly we find the device of seeing in words and expressions a deeper significance beneath their surface meaning put to effective use here. Yet it is possible that this is just intended as a serious attempt to better the brahmans at their own game. The fact that irony and humour may be used here to subvert brahmanical claims, does not of itself necessarily mean that the account was intended, or understood, as anything other than a true account of the evolution of the world and society. For detailed discussions see R. Gombrich, 'The Buddha's Book of Genesis?', *Indo-Iranian Journal*, 35 (1992), 159–78, and S. Collins, 'The Discourse on What is Primary (Aggañña-Sutta)', *Journal of Indian Philosophy*, 21 (1993), 301–93; more generally on Buddhist cosmology see R. Gethin, 'Cosmology and Meditation: From the Aggañña Sutta to the Mahāyāna', *History of Religions*, 36 (1997), 183–219.

This is what I have heard. Once the Blessed One was staying in Sāvatthī, in the Eastern Park, in the grand building built by Migāra's mother. At that time Vāseṭṭha and Bhāradvāja who hoped to become monks were living with the monks there. Now towards sunset, when he had finished his solitary meditation, the Blessed One had come out from the building and was walking up and down outside in its shade. Now Vāseṭṭha saw the Blessed One . . . walking up and down outside in the shade of the building, and on seeing this he said to Bhāradvāja, 'Friend Bhāradvāja, there is the Blessed One. He has finished his solitary meditation and come out from the building and is walking up and down outside in its shade. Come, Bhāradvāja! We should approach the Blessed One. We might get to hear a talk on the teaching directly from the Blessed One.'

'That's so,' replied Bhāradvāja to Vāseṭṭha.

So Vāseṭṭha and Bhāradvāja approached the Blessed One, and when they had approached they saluted him respectfully and began walking up and down with him. Then the Blessed One spoke to Vāseṭṭha. 81

'Vāseṭṭha,* you two are brahmans by birth from brahman families who have left behind your brahman family and gone forth from home into homelessness. I hope that brahmans don't insult and reprimand you.'

'Brahmans certainly do insult and reprimand us, sir—with their personal reprimands and in full measure.'

'So, Vāseṭṭha, how do they insult and reprimand you with their personal reprimands and in full measure?'

'"The Brahman class," they say, "is the best; the other classes are inferior. The brahman class is fair, the other classes are dark. Only brahmans can be pure, not non-brahmans. Only brahmans are true sons of Brahmā, born from his mouth, coming from Brahmā, created by Brahmā, heirs of Brahmā. You have given up the best class and joined an inferior class, that of those pathetic, shaven-headed, extravagant ascetics, the dark descendants of our ancestor's feet.* It is not good, it is not becoming that you have given up the best class and joined an inferior class, that of those pathetic, shaven-headed, extravagant ascetics, the dark descendants of our ancestor's feet." This is how they insult and reprimand us with their personal reprimands and in full measure.'

'Vāseṭṭha, your brahmans are certainly not being mindful of the past when they say that the brahman class is the best . . . and that only brahmans are true sons of Brahmā, born from his mouth, coming from Brahmā, created by Brahmā, heirs of Brahmā. On the contrary,
82 brahman women are seen ovulating, getting pregnant, giving birth, and breast-feeding. And yet these very same brahmans who were born from the womb say the brahman class is the best . . . and that only brahmans are true sons of Brahmā, born from his mouth, coming from Brahmā, created by Brahmā, heirs of Brahmā. They are insulting Brahmā,* telling lies, and producing a lot of demerit.

'Vāseṭṭha, there are these four classes: Rulers, Brahmans, Traders, and Servants. Sometimes someone of the Ruler class kills living creatures, takes what is not given, practises sexual misconduct, tells lies, speaks maliciously, speaks unkindly, chatters idly, is given to longing, has hostility in his heart, holds wrong views. In that case qualities that are unwholesome and understood as such, that are blameworthy and understood as such, that should not be pursued and are understood as such, that do not deserve the name noble and are understood as such, dark and with dark result, condemned by the wise—these qualities are seen in someone of the Ruler class. Sometimes someone of the Brahman class too . . . Sometimes someone of the Trader class too . . . Sometimes someone of the Servant class too kills living creatures, takes what is not given, practises sexual misconduct, tells lies, speaks maliciously, speaks unkindly, chatters idly, is given to longing, has hostility in his heart, holds wrong views. In that case qualities that are unwholesome and understood as such, that are blameworthy and understood as such, that should not be pursued and are understood as such, that do not deserve the name noble and are understood as such, dark and with dark result, condemned by the wise—these qualities are seen in someone of the Servant class too.

'Sometimes someone of the Ruler class refrains from killing living creatures, refrains from taking what is not given, refrains from

practising sexual misconduct, refrains from telling lies, refrains from speaking maliciously, refrains from speaking unkindly, refrains from chattering idly, is not given to longing, does not have hostility in his heart, does not hold wrong views. In that case qualities that are wholesome and understood as such, that are not blameworthy and understood as such, that should be pursued and are understood as such, that do deserve the name noble and are understood as such, bright and with bright result, praised by the wise—these qualities are seen in someone of the Ruler class. Sometimes someone of the Brahman class too . . . Sometimes someone of the Trader class too . . . Sometimes someone of the Servant class too refrains from killing living creatures, refrains from taking what is not given, refrains from practising sexual misconduct, refrains from telling lies, refrains from speaking maliciously, refrains from speaking unkindly,
refrains from chattering idly, is not given to longing, does not have 83
hostility in his heart, does not hold wrong views. In that case qualities that are wholesome and understood as such, that are not blameworthy and understood as such, that should be pursued and are understood as such, that do deserve the name noble and are understood as such, bright and with bright result, praised by the wise—these qualities are seen in a Servant too.

'Given that these bad and good qualities, which are condemned and praised by the wise, are both found distributed among these four classes, then the wise are not going to approve the brahmans' claim that the Brahman class is the best . . . and that only brahmans are true sons of Brahmā, born from his mouth, coming from Brahmā, created by Brahmā, heirs of Brahmā. And why not? Because it is the monk, of any of these four classes, who is an arahat and has destroyed the taints, lived the spiritual life, done what was to be done, put down the burden, reached the true goal, destroyed the fetters of existence, and is freed through faultless knowledge—it is such a one who, in accordance with good practice, not bad practice,* is called the foremost. For it is Truth, Vāseṭṭha, that is best in the world, both here and now and for the future.

'And that Truth is best in the world, both here and now and for the future, can be seen from the following example. King Pasenadi of Kosala is fully aware that the ascetic Gotama has gone forth from the Sakya family, a family of similar rank to his own. Yet the Sakyas are subjects of King Pasenadi of Kosala. They bow down before him,

salute him respectfully, stand up, bow with cupped hands, and are at
his service. All this bowing down, respectful salutation, standing up,
bowing with cupped hands, and service the Sakyas do for King
84 Pasenadi of Kosala, he does for the Tathāgata, thinking, "Surely the
ascetic Gotama is well born, while I am of ill birth; the ascetic
Gotama is strong while I am weak; the ascetic Gotama inspires faith,
while I am threatening; the ascetic Gotama commands great respect,
while I command little." Now it is precisely Truth that King
Pasenadi of Kosala honours, Truth that he respects, Truth that he
esteems, Truth that he worships, Truth that he serves, when he
bows down before the Tathāgata, salutes him respectfully, stands up,
bows with cupped hands, and is at his service. So from this example
it can be seen that Truth is best in the world, both here and now and
for the future.

'Vāseṭṭha, you are people of different birth,* with different names, from different lineages and families, who have gone forth from home into homelessness. When you are asked who you are, you should affirm, "We are ascetics, the sons of the Sakya." When someone has gained faith in the Tathāgata that has taken root and become established, firm, and incapable of being swayed by any ascetic, brahman, or god, by Māra or Brahmā or anyone else in the world, then it is right that he should say, "I am the Blessed One's true son, born of his mouth, born of Truth, created by Truth, an heir of Truth." Why is this? Because "the one whose body is Truth", "the one whose body is the highest", "the one who is Truth", "the one who is the highest" are all designations of the Tathāgata.*

'Now there comes a time, Vāseṭṭha, when, at some point, after a
long period of time this world contracts. When the world contracts
beings for the most part go up to the realm of the Radiant. There
they exist made of mind, feeding on joy, self-luminous, moving
through the air, always beautiful. They remain like this for a long,
long time. Then there comes a time, Vāseṭṭha, when, at some point,
after a long period of time this world evolves. When the world
evolves beings for the most part fall from the realm of the Radiant
85 and come here to this world; and they exist made of mind, feeding on
joy, self-luminous, moving through the air, always beautiful. They
remain like this for a long, long time.

'At that time there is only water, and darkness—unseeing darkness. No sun and moon are distinguished, no constellations of the stars, no night and day, no months and half-months, no seasons and years, no males and females. Beings are just counted as beings.

'Now at some point, Vāseṭṭha, after a long period of time, the essence of earth spread out* over the water to those beings, just like a skin forming on the surface of boiled milk* as it cools. Its look, smell, and taste were excellent: like the finest ghee or butter in colour, like pure honey in taste. Then a being of greedy disposition thought, "I say, what do we have here!" and using his finger he tasted that essence of earth. He liked what he tasted and was overcome by craving. Other beings, following his example, also used their fingers to taste the essence of earth. They liked what they tasted and were overcome by craving. Then beings set about eating the essence of earth, taking lumps in both hands. And when they set about eating 86
the essence of earth like this, their self-luminosity disappeared. Once their self-luminosity had disappeared, the sun and moon appeared. And once the sun and moon had appeared, the constellations of the stars appeared. And once they had appeared, night and day were distinguished, then months and half-months, and seasons and years were also distinguished. Thus far, Vāseṭṭha, this world had once more evolved.

'For a long time, Vāseṭṭha, those beings remained eating the essence of earth, consuming it and feeding on it. The more they continued to consume and feed on it, the more their bodies were overtaken by coarseness, and good and bad looks could be distinguished: on the one hand there were beings with good looks, on the other there were beings who were ugly. Then the beings with good looks looked down on the ugly beings, thinking, "We are better-looking than they are! They are uglier than we are!" As a result of their pride in their looks the essence of earth disappeared from those proud and conceited beings. And when the essence of earth had disappeared they gathered together lamenting, "Oh, the taste! Oh, the taste!" So still today, when people get something tasty, they say "Oh, tasty! Oh, tasty!"* They are repeating this same ancient, original expression, yet they do not understand its meaning.

'Vāseṭṭha, when the essence of earth had disappeared a soil crust 87
appeared for beings—just like a mushroom appearing. Its look, smell, and taste were excellent: like the finest ghee or butter in colour, like pure honey in taste. Then beings set about eating the soil crust. For a long time beings remained eating the soil crust, consuming

it and feeding on it. The more they continued to consume and feed
on it the more their bodies were increasingly overtaken by coarseness, and their good and bad looks became distinguished: on the one
hand there were beings with good looks, on the other there were
beings who were ugly. The beings with good looks looked down on
the ugly beings, thinking, "We are better-looking than they are!
They are uglier than we are!" As a result of their pride in their looks
the soil crust disappeared from those beings. When it had disappeared a creeper appeared for beings—just like a waterweed appearing. Its look, smell, and taste were excellent: like the finest ghee or
butter in colour, like pure honey in taste. Then beings set about eating the creeper. For a long time beings remained eating the creeper,
consuming it and feeding on it. The more they continued to consume and feed on it the more their bodies were increasingly overtaken by coarseness, and their good and bad looks became
88 distinguished . . . The beings with good looks looked down on the
ugly beings . . . As a result of their pride in their looks the creeper
disappeared from those beings. And when the creeper had disappeared they gathered together, lamenting, "Alas, it was ours, but
alas, the creeper failed us!" So still today, when people are affected
by some painful circumstance, they say, "Alas, it was ours, but alas,
it has failed us!" They are repeating this same ancient, original
expression, yet they do not understand its meaning.

'Vāseṭṭha, when the creeper had disappeared rice appeared for
beings, growing wild, with no bran or husk, sweet-smelling, ready to
use. Whatever they gathered in the evening for the evening meal had
by morning grown back ripe; whatever they gathered in the morning
for the morning meal had by evening grown back ripe—harvesting
was unknown. For a long time beings remained eating that wild rice,
consuming it and feeding on it. The more they continued to consume
and feed on it the more their bodies were increasingly overtaken by
coarseness, and their good and bad looks became distinguished: the
female characteristics appeared in woman and male characteristics
in man, and then a woman looked at a man with uncontrolled
longing, and a man at a woman. And as they looked at each other
like this, desire arose in them, and their bodies were overtaken by
burning lust. As a result of this burning lust they engaged in sexual
practice. Of those beings who saw them engaging in sexual practice
89 at that time, some threw soil, some ash, some cow dung, saying,

"Perish, impure one! Perish, impure one! How can one being do such a thing to another!" So still today, in some areas, when a bride is being led out some people throw soil, some ash, some cow dung. They are repeating this same ancient, original custom, yet they do not understand its meaning.* Vāseṭṭha, what was considered improper practice at that time is today considered proper practice. At that time beings who engaged in sexual practice were not allowed to enter a town or village for one or two months. Because beings at that time became uncontrollably intoxicated with wrong practice, they set about building houses in order to hide that wrong practice.

'Now, Vāseṭṭha, it occurred to one being of lazy disposition, "Oh, I am fed up with collecting rice in the evening for the evening meal and in the morning for the morning meal. Why shouldn't I collect rice just once for the evening and morning meals?" So that being collected rice just once for the evening and morning meals. Then, when another being came to him and said, "Come, we need to go and collect rice," he replied, "I don't need to, I have already collected rice for the evening and morning meals." So that other being, following his example, collected rice just once for two days, saying, "This is certainly a good idea, friend." Then, when another being came to *this*
being and said, "Come, we need to go and collect rice," he replied, 90
"I don't need to, I have already collected rice for two days." So that other being, following his example, collected rice just once for four days, saying, "This is certainly a good idea, friend." Then, when another being came to *this* being and said, "Come, we need to go and collect rice," he replied, "I don't need to, I have already collected rice for four days." So that other being, following his example, collected rice just once for eight days, saying, 'This is certainly a good idea, friend." Because beings set about eating rice that they had stored, the grain became covered with bran and a husk, what had been cut did not grow back again, harvesting appeared, and the rice plants stood in clusters.

'Then those beings gathered together, lamenting, "Alas, bad practices have appeared among beings. For we used to exist made of mind, feeding on joy, self-luminous, moving through the air, always beautiful. For a long, long time we remained like that. Then at some point, after a long period of time, the essence of earth spread out over the water to us, its look, smell, and taste were excellent. We set about eating the essence of earth, taking lumps in both hands.

And when we did so our self-luminosity disappeared, and then the
sun and moon appeared. And once the sun and moon had appeared,
91 the constellations of the stars appeared. And once they had appeared,
night and day were distinguished, then months and half-months, and
seasons and years were also distinguished. For a long time we continued eating the essence of earth, consuming it and feeding on it, but because of the appearance of our bad, unwholesome practices the essence of earth disappeared. When the essence of earth had disappeared a soil crust appeared. Its look, smell, and taste were excellent, and we set about eating the soil crust. For a long time we remained eating the soil crust, consuming it and feeding on it, but because of the appearance of our bad, unwholesome practices the soil crust disappeared. When it had disappeared a creeper appeared. Its look, smell, and taste were excellent, and we set about eating the creeper. For a long time we remained eating the creeper, consuming it and feeding on it, but because of the appearance of our bad, unwholesome practices the creeper disappeared. When the creeper had disappeared rice appeared for beings, growing wild, with no bran or husk, sweet-smelling, ready to use. Whatever we gathered in the evening for the evening meal had by morning grown back ripe; whatever we gathered in the morning for the morning meal had by evening grown back ripe—harvesting was unknown. For a long time we remained eating that wild rice, consuming it and feeding on it, but because of the appearance of our bad, unwholesome practices, the grain has
became covered with bran and a husk, what has been cut does not
92 grow back again, harvesting has appeared, and the rice plants stand
in clusters. What if we were to divide up the rice into fields and establish boundaries?" So, Vāseṭṭha, beings divided up the rice into fields and established boundaries.

'Then one being of greedy disposition, while still keeping his own share, took another share which he had not been given and ate it. Then they seized him and said, "This is a bad thing that you do—keeping your own share, and then taking another share which you have not been given and eating that. Don't ever do such a thing again!" He agreed that he would not, but a second time and a third time that being, while still keeping his own share, took another share which he had not been given and ate it. They seized him and said, "This is a bad thing that you do . . . Don't ever do such a thing again!" Some hit him with their hands, some with stones, some with sticks.

From then on taking what is not given, chastising, lying, and punishment became known.

'Then those beings gathered together, lamenting, "Alas, bad practices have appeared among beings, for certainly where taking what is not given becomes known, chastising, lying, and punishment will also become known. Suppose we were to agree on one being: he could accuse whoever deserved to be accused for us, he could reprimand whoever deserved to be reprimanded, he could banish whoever deserved to be banished, while we would hand over a share of rice to him." 93

'Then those beings approached the most handsome, best-looking, most graceful and most commanding being among them and said to him, "Come, good being, accuse whoever deserves to be accused, reprimand whoever deserves to be reprimanded, banish whoever deserves to be banished, while we will hand over a share of rice to you." And having agreed to their request, that being accused whoever deserved to be accused, reprimanded whoever deserved to be reprimanded, banished whoever deserved to be banished, while they handed over a share of rice to him.

'Vāseṭṭha, "Mahāsammata" means "agreed on by all people* (*mahā-jana-sammata*)"; it was "Agreed Great" that was the first expression that appeared. "Ruler (*khattiya*)" means "lord of the fields (*khettānaṃ pati*)"; it was Ruler that was the second expression that appeared. "King (*rājan*)" means "he pleases (*rañjeti*) others by his truth"; it was "King" that was the third expression that appeared. In this way, Vāseṭṭha, in accordance with the ancient original expression, the circle of Rulers came into being—made up of those very same beings, not other beings, of beings who were just like them, not different in kind, in accordance with good practice, not bad practice. For Truth is best in the world, both here and now and for the future.

'Then some of those same beings thought, "Alas, bad practices have appeared among beings, for certainly where taking what is not given becomes known, chastising, lying, punishment, and banishment will also become known. Suppose we were to do away with bad, unwholesome practices." So they did away with bad, unwholesome practices. Vāseṭṭha, "Brahmans" means "they do away with 94
(*bāhenti*) bad, unwholesome practices"; it was "Brahmans" that was the first expression that appeared.* They made huts of leaves out in the forests and meditated in them; without coals and smoke, having

laid down the pestle,* evening and morning they went into villages, towns, and royal cities in search of food for the evening and morning meals. When they had got food they once again meditated in the forest in their leaf huts. When people saw this they said, "These beings have made huts of leaves out in the forests and meditate in them; . . . they go into villages, towns, and royal cities in search of food . . . When they have got food they once again meditate in the forest in their leaf huts." Vāseṭṭha, "keepers of a sacrificial fire (*jhāyaka*)" means "they meditate* (*jhāyanti*)"; it was "meditators" that was the second expression that appeared.

'Then some of those same beings, when they were unsuccessful in their meditation out in the forest in leaf huts, moved close to villages and towns where they sat about composing texts. When people saw this they said, "These beings who were unsuccessful in their meditation out in the forest in leaf huts have moved close to villages and towns where they sit about composing texts. They no longer meditate." Vāseṭṭha, "Students of the Vedas (*ajjhāyaka*)" means "they no longer meditate (*na dān'ime jhāyanti*)"; it was "non-meditators (*ajjhāyaka*)" that was the third expression that appeared. For what was considered inferior at that time is today considered superior. In this way, Vāseṭṭha, in accordance with the ancient, original expression, the circle of Brahmans came into being—made up of those
95 very same beings, not other beings, of beings who were just like them, not different in kind, in accordance with good practice, not bad practice. For Truth is best in the world, both here and now and for the future.

'Some of those same beings took up sexual practice and engaged in domestic business.* Vāseṭṭha, "Traders (*vessa*)" means "they take up sexual practice and engage in domestic (*vissu*) business"; it was "Traders" that was the expression that appeared. In this way, Vāseṭṭha, in accordance with the ancient, original expression, the circle of Traders came into being—made up of those very same beings, not other beings, of beings who were just like them, not different in kind, in accordance with good practice, not bad practice. For Truth is best in the world, both here and now and for the future.

'The beings that remained from these beings led cruel lives. Vāseṭṭha, "Servants (*sudda*)" means "they led cruel (*ludda*) lives and mean (*khudda*) lives"; it was "Servants" that was the expression that appeared. In this way, Vāseṭṭha, in accordance with the ancient, original expression, the circle of Servants came into being—made up of those very same beings, not other beings, of beings who were just like them, not different in kind, in accordance with good practice, not bad practice. For Truth is best in the world, both here and now and for the future.

'Now there came a time when someone of the Ruler class, despising his own practice, went forth from home into homelessness with the idea of becoming an ascetic. Likewise someone of the Brahman class . . . of the Trader class . . . of the Servant class, despising his 96
own practice, went forth from home into homelessness with the idea of becoming an ascetic. In this way, Vāseṭṭha, from the four circles the circle of Ascetics came into being—made up of those very same beings, not other beings, of beings who were just like them, not different in kind, in accordance with good practice, not bad practice. For Truth is best in the world, both here and now and for the future.

'Someone of the Ruler class who has behaved badly in body, in speech, and in thought, whose views are mistaken, will, as a result of engaging in these actions and of his mistaken views, at the breaking up of the body after death be reborn in a state of misfortune, an unhappy destiny, a state of affliction, hell. Likewise, someone of the Brahman class . . . of the Trader class . . . of the Servant class who has behaved badly in body, in speech and in thought, whose views are mistaken, will, as a result of engaging in these actions and of his mistaken views, at the breaking up of the body after death be reborn in a state of misfortune, an unhappy destiny, a state of affliction, hell.

Someone of the Ruler class who has behaved well in body, in speech, and in thought, whose views are right, will, as a result of engaging in these actions and of his right views, at the breaking up of the body after death be reborn in a happy destiny, a heaven world. Likewise, someone of the Brahman class . . . of the Trader class . . . of the Servant class who has behaved well in body, in speech, and in thought, whose views are right, will, as a result of engaging in these actions and of his right views, at the breaking up of the body after death be reborn in a happy destiny, a heaven world.

Someone of the Ruler class who has behaved both badly and well in body, in speech, and in thought, whose views are of both kinds, will, as a result of engaging in these actions and of his mixed views, at the breaking up of the body after death have both pleasurable and

97 painful experiences. Likewise, someone of the Brahman class . . . of the Trader class . . . of the Servant class who has behaved both badly and well in body, in speech, and in thought, whose views are of both kinds, will, as a result of engaging in these actions and of his mixed views, at the breaking up of the body after death have both pleasurable and painful experiences.

Someone of the Ruler class who is restrained in body, in speech, and in thought will, when he cultivates the seven qualities that contribute to awakening, attain full nibbana right here and now. Likewise, someone of the Brahman class . . . of the Trader class . . . of the Servant class who is restrained in body, in speech, and in thought will, when he cultivates the seven qualities that contribute to awakening,* attain full nibbana right here and now.

'It is the monk, of any of these four classes, who is an arahat and has destroyed the taints, lived the spiritual life, done what was to be done, put down the burden, reached the true goal, destroyed the fetters of existence, and is freed through faultless knowledge—it is such a one who, in accordance with good practice, not bad practice, is called the foremost. For it is truth, Vāseṭṭha, that is best in the world, both here and now and for the future.

'Vāseṭṭha, this verse has been uttered by Brahmā Ever-Youthful:

> "The Ruler is best among people who rely on lineage;
> One accomplished in knowledge and conduct is best among
> gods and men."

'This verse which Brahmā Ever-Youthful has uttered is well sung, not ill sung, well spoken, not ill spoken, profitable, not unprofitable—
98 I approve it. I too say this, Vāseṭṭha:

> The Ruler is best among people who rely on lineage;
> One accomplished in knowledge and conduct is best among
> gods and men.'

This is what the Blessed One said. Gladdened, Vāseṭṭha and Bhāradvaja felt joy at the Blessed One's words.

ADVICE TO SIGĀLA

SIGĀLOVĀDA-SUTTA (D III 180–193)

Introduction

This sutta gives an account of how the Buddha reinterprets an Indian ritual: in effect, what is potentially an empty ritual is given meaning by being recast in terms of everyday actions and relationships. This method of recasting what were originally concrete brahmanical rituals is characteristic of early Buddhism's approach to the brahmanical tradition, though it is not entirely without a certain precedent in the Vedic tradition itself, where external rituals are reconceived by those in the know as something internal, such as breathing, the digestion, and the sexual act.[1] In Buddhist terms the emphasis in the sutta is on conduct (*sīla*) rather than on meditation and knowledge. And this conduct is recommended on the grounds not that it will bring freedom from the round of rebirth in the form of nibbana, but that it will bring happiness and well-being in this life and rebirth in a heaven world. The commentary identifies the sutta as 'the householder's discipline' (*gihi-vinaya*), the laity's equivalent of the monastic rule.

The sutta's ethics share much in common with general ancient Indian conceptions of good conduct, including the *dhamma* set out and recommended by the great 'Buddhist' emperor Aśoka in his third-century BCE edicts. This is one of the reasons why a simple equation of Aśokan *dhamma* with Buddhist *dhamma* becomes problematic. Equally though, the fact that, like Aśoka's edicts, the *Sigālovada-sutta* contains no mention of specific Buddhist teachings such as the four noble truths and the eightfold path, and focuses on rebirth in heaven with no mention of reaching nibbana, makes it harder to insist categorically that Aśoka's *dhamma* is *not* Buddhist. The sutta is perhaps a reminder that throughout history, for most Buddhists in most places, 'Buddhism' has meant aspiring to the kind of behaviour outlined here and to a favourable rebirth in heaven rather than the attainment of nibbana.

The sutta is also a nice example of a mnemonic numerical structure: four defilements of action, four causes of doing bad deeds, six ways of losing belongings (each with six dangers), four false friends (each for four reasons), four true friends (each for four reasons), and covering the six directions (each in five ways).

---

[1] On the internalization of the sacrifice see Gavin Flood, *An Introduction to Hinduism* (Cambridge, 1996), 83–4.

180 This is what I have heard. Once the Blessed One was staying in the Squirrels' Feeding Ground in the Bamboo Grove at Rājagaha. On that occasion Sigāla,* a householder's son, had got up early and left Rājagaha, and was honouring each of the directions, bowing with cupped hands to the east, the south, the west, the north, the direction below, and the direction above, his clothes and hair all wet.*

Now the Blessed One, having dressed at dawn, took his robe and bowl and went into Rājagaha for alms. And he saw Sigāla . . . honouring each of the directions, bowing with cupped hands to the east, the south, the west, the north, the direction below, and the direction above, his clothes and hair all wet.

Seeing him, the Blessed One said: 'Young householder, why . . .
181 are you honouring each of the directions, bowing with cupped hands to the east, the south, the west, the north, the direction below, and the direction above, your clothes and hair all wet?'

'Sir, when my father was dying he said to me, "Son, you should honour the directions." So out of consideration for my father's words which I revere, value, and respect, I have got up early and left Rājagaha, and am honouring each of the directions, bowing with cupped hands to the east, the south, the west, the north, the direction below, and the direction above, my clothes and hair all wet.'

'But, young householder, this is not the way to honour the six directions in the discipline of a noble one.'

'So how then, sir, should one honour the six directions in the discipline of a noble one? Could the Blessed One please teach me the right way* to honour the six directions in the discipline of a noble one?'

'Then listen, young householder, and pay careful attention to what I shall say.'

'Yes, sir,' replied Sigāla the householder's son, and the Blessed One began to speak.

'Young householder, when the disciple of the noble ones has given up four defilements of action, does no bad deed from four causes, does not pursue six ways of losing his belongings—when he avoids these fourteen bad ways, it is then that he covers the six directions. He is set to be victorious in both worlds: he gains the success of both this world and the next world, and at the breaking up of the body after death he is born in a happy realm, a heaven world. What are the four defilements of action that he gives up? Killing living creatures is a defilement of action, taking what is not given is a defilement of action, sexual misconduct is a defilement of action, telling lies is a defilement of action. He gives up these four defilements of action.'

This is what the Blessed One said. And when the Happy One had said this, the Teacher spoke again: 182

'Killing living beings, taking what is not given, and telling lies;
Going with another's wife—these things wise men do not commend.'

'What are the four causes from which he does no bad deed? People do bad deeds motivated by desire, they do bad deeds motivated by hatred, they do bad deeds motivated by delusion, and they do bad deeds motivated by fear. In that the noble disciple does no bad deed motivated by desire, does no bad deed motivated by hatred, does no bad deed motivated by delusion, and does no bad deed motivated by fear, he does no bad deed from these four causes.'

This is what the Blessed One said. And when the Happy One had said this, the Teacher spoke again:

'When desire, hatred, fear, and delusion lead someone to offend against Truth,
Then his reputation vanishes like the moon waning in the black night.
When desire, hatred, fear, and delusion, do not lead someone to offend against Truth,
Then his reputation grows like the moon waxing bright.

'What are the six ways of losing one's belongings that he does not pursue? Young householder, being devoted to the recklessness of strong drink and spirits is a way of losing one's belongings; wandering in the streets at unseemly hours is a way of losing one's belongings; frequenting fairs is a way of losing one's belongings; being devoted to the recklessness of gambling is a way of losing one's belongings; being devoted to bad friends is a way of losing one's belongings; being habitually idle is a way of losing one's belongings.

'Young householder, there are these six dangers in being devoted to the recklessness of strong drink and spirits: the diminishing of any wealth, increased quarrelling, a whole range of illnesses, ill repute, exposing oneself, and weakening of the intellect as the sixth. 183

'Young householder, there are these six dangers in wandering in the streets at unseemly hours: one is defenceless and without protection, one's wife and children are defenceless and without protection, one's property is defenceless and without protection, one is suspected of being up to no good, false accusations are made against one, one encounters all sorts of misfortunes.

'Young householder, there are these six dangers in frequenting fairs: one is always asking, "Where is there dancing? Where is there singing? Where are they playing music? Where are they giving recitations? Where are the cymbals? Where are the drums?"

'Young householder, there are these six dangers in being devoted to the recklessness of gambling: if one wins one engenders hatred, if one loses one bemoans the things lost, one's wealth diminishes, one's word has no authority in an assembly, one is despised by one's friends and companions, one is not considered a desirable marriage partner, since the gambling man does not have the means to support a wife.

'Young householder, there are these six dangers in being devoted to bad friends: one has friends and associates who are gamblers,
184 drinkers, drunks, cheats, liars, and ruffians.

'Young householder, there are these six dangers in being habitually idle: one thinks, "It's too cold" and does no work; one thinks, "It's too hot" and does no work; one thinks, "It's too early" and does no work; one thinks, "It's too late" and does no work; one thinks, "I'm too hungry" and does no work; one thinks, "I'm too full" and does no work. And with all one's tasks still undone, one does not get what one does not have, and what one has dwindles away.'

This is what the Blessed One said. And when the Happy One had said this, the Teacher spoke again:

'There is the drinking companion, the one who is always saying, "My good friend!",
But the one who is a companion when there are things to do, he is the comrade.
Sleeping when the sun is high, chasing others' wives, being full of enmity and causing hurt,
Bad friends and much meanness—these are six things that ruin a man.
With bad friends and bad companions, occupied in harmful deeds
A man loses both this world and the next world.

Dice and women, drink, and song and dance, sleeping by day
and roaming by night,
Bad friends and much meanness—these are six things that ruin
a man.
They play the dice, drink strong drink, go with women who are
other men's wives, 185
Pursuing ruin rather than prosperity, waning like the moon in
the black night.
Penniless and destitute with his drink, the drinker given to drink
Sinks into the depths of debt and will soon find himself with no
family.
One given to sleeping by day, and finding his occupation by
night,
Who is always crazed with drink is not able to keep a home.
It's too cold, too hot, too early, they say,
And in this way their work piles up, and opportunities pass them
by.
But thinking of the cold and the heat as no more than straw,
One gets on with one's tasks and does not let happiness slip
away.

'Young householder, these four should be seen as false friends in the guise of friends: one who is all take should be seen as a false friend in the guise of a friend; one who is all talk should be seen as a false friend in the guise of a friend; one who always says what is pleasing should be seen as a false friend in the guise of a friend; one who is a companion in squandering should be seen as a false friend in the guise of a friend.

186 'There are four reasons why one who is all take should be seen as a false friend in the guise of a friend: he is all take, he expects a lot in exchange for little, he only acts when there is some threat to himself, he looks after his own interests.

'There are four reasons why one who is all talk should be seen as a false friend in the guise of a friend: he professes his past goodwill, he professes his future goodwill, he makes meaningless professions of goodwill, when there are things that actually need to be done he mentions some problem.

'There are four reasons why one who always says what is pleasing should be seen as a false friend in the guise of a friend: he approves of one's bad actions, and he approves of one's good actions,* he praises one to one's face, he disparages one to others.

'There are four reasons why one who is a companion in squandering should be seen as a false friend in the guise of a friend: he is a companion in one's devotion to the recklessness of strong drink and spirits; he is a companion in one's devotion to wandering in the streets at unseemly hours; he is a companion in one's frequenting of fairs; he is a companion in one's devotion to the recklessness of gambling.'

This is what the Blessed One said. And when the Happy One had said this, the Teacher spoke again:

> 'The friend who is all take, the friend who is all talk,
> The friend who says what is pleasing, the fellow in ways of
> squandering—
> These four are false friends. Recognizing this, a wise man
> 187 Keeps well away, as from a dangerous path.

'Young householder, these four should be seen as true friends: the helper should be seen as a true friend; one who is the same in happiness and adversity should be seen as a true friend; one who gives good advice should be seen as a true friend; one who is sympathetic should be seen as a true friend.

'There are four reasons why the helper should be seen as a true friend: he looks after one when one is reckless, he looks after one's belongings when one is reckless, he is a comfort when one is afraid, he offers twice as much as one needs when there are things to be done.

'There are four reasons why one who is the same in happiness and adversity should be seen as a true friend: he tells one his own secrets, he does not reveal one's secrets to others, he does not abandon you in times of trouble, he even gives up his life for one's sake.

'There are four reasons why one who gives good advice should be seen as a true friend: he keeps one from doing wrong, he encourages one in what is good, he tells one of things one has not heard, he explains the way to heaven.

'There are four reasons why one who is sympathetic should be seen as a true friend: he does not rejoice in one's misfortune, he rejoices in one's fortune, he stops those who speak badly of one, he commends those who speak well of one.'

This is what the Blessed One said. And when the Happy One had said this, the Teacher spoke again: 188

'The friend who is a helper, and the friend in happiness and adversity,
The friend who gives good advice, and the sympathetic friend—
These four are friends. Recognizing this, a wise man
Should honour them respectfully, like a mother her true son.
The wise man accomplished in conduct shines like a burning beacon.
While he collects goods, like the never still bee,
Goods accumulate, piling up like an anthill.
Collecting his goods like this, the householder brings success to his family.
He should divide his goods in four and keep his friends together:*
One portion of his goods he should enjoy, two portions he should make use of,
The fourth portion he should put aside in case of troubles.

'And how, young householder, does the noble disciple cover the six directions? These six directions should be seen as follows: the east
should be seen as one's mother and father, the south as one's teach- 189
ers, the west as one's wife and children, the north as one's friends and companions, the direction below as servants and workers, the direction above as ascetics and brahmans.

'A son should look after the eastern direction as his mother and father in five respects: "As I have been supported by them I shall give my support; I shall look after their affairs; I shall maintain the family's traditions; I shall prove worthy of my inheritance, and I shall make offering for them when they are dead and departed." When a son cares for his mother and father as the eastern direction in these five respects, then they show him sympathy in five respects: they keep him from what is bad; they encourage him in what is good; they see that he is trained in a craft; they find him a suitable wife; they hand over his inheritance at the proper time. When a son cares for his mother and father as the eastern direction in these five respects, then they show him sympathy in these five respects, and in this way the east is covered by him and kept safe from danger.

'A pupil should look after the southern direction as his teachers in

five respects: by getting up, by waiting on them, by obedience, by service, by being properly appreciative of what he is taught. When a pupil looks after the southern direction as his teachers in these five respects, then they show him sympathy in five respects: they teach him proper behaviour; they make sure he understands what he has learnt; they fully explain all the branches of knowledge; they introduce him* to friends and companions, they provide security in
190 all quarters. When a pupil looks after the southern direction as his teachers in these five respects, then they show him sympathy in these five respects, and in this way the south is covered by him and kept safe from danger.

'A husband should look after the western direction as his wife in five respects: by being respectful, by not being disrespectful,* by not being unfaithful, by relinquishing authority, by providing her with adornment. When a husband looks after the western direction as his wife in these five respects, then she shows him sympathy in five respects: she attends to her work properly, she treats the servants well, she is not unfaithful, she looks after the family's wealth, she is skilled and tireless in her duties. When a husband looks after the western direction as his wife in these five respects, then she shows him sympathy in these five respects, and in this way the west is covered by him and kept safe from danger.

'A son of a good family should look after the northern direction as his friends and companions in five respects: by being generous, by talking kindly, by acting helpfully, by treating them equally,* by not breaking his promise. When a son of a good family looks after the northern direction as his friends and companions in these five respects, then they show him sympathy in five respects: they look after him when he is reckless, they look after his belongings when he is reckless, they are a comfort when he is afraid, they do not abandon him in times of trouble, they honour his descendants. When a son of a good family looks after the northern direction as his friends and companions in these five respects, then they show him sympathy in these five respects, and in this way the north is covered by him and kept safe from danger.

'A master should look after the direction below as his servants
191 and workers in five respects: by assigning work in accordance with their capabilities, by providing them with food and wages, by looking after them in sickness, by sharing rare delicacies, by giving them

leave at the proper time. When a master looks after the direction below as his servants and workers in these five respects, then they show him sympathy in five respects: they get up before him, they go to bed after him, they take only what is given, they do their work well, they spread his good reputation and name. When a master looks after the direction below as his servants and workers in these five respects, then they show him sympathy in these five respects, and in this way the direction below is covered by him and kept safe from danger.

'A son of a good family should look after the direction above as ascetics and brahmans in five respects: with friendliness in acts of body, with friendliness in acts of speech, with friendliness in acts of thought, by keeping his doors open to them, by providing them with their material needs. When a son of a good family looks after the direction above as ascetics and brahmans in these five respects, then they show him sympathy in six respects: they keep him from what is bad; they encourage him in what is good; they show their sympathy with kind thoughts; they tell him what he hasn't heard before; they clarify what he has heard before; they explain the path to heaven. When a son of a good family looks after the direction above as ascetics and brahmans in these five respects, then they show him sympathy in these six respects, and in this way the direction above is covered by him and kept safe from danger.'

This is what the Blessed One said. And when the Happy One had said this, the Teacher spoke again:

'Mother and father are the first direction, teachers the south, 192
Wife and children are the west, friends and companions the north.
Servants and workers are below, above are ascetics and brahmans.
The able householder of the family should honour these directions.
The wise man, accomplished in conduct, gentle and bright,
Unpretentious in character, without arrogance—such a one wins fame.
Rising early, tireless, he does not waver in adversity,
Faultless in his behaviour, and clever—such a one wins fame.

He brings people together and makes friends, he is welcoming and beyond stinginess,
A leader, a teacher and guide—such a one wins fame.
Generosity and kind words, helpful actions in this world,
And treating others equally in all matters and in all circumstances—
Such kindnesses in the world hold the axle of its chariot as it moves.
Should they not exist then neither mothers nor fathers
Win the respect and worship owed them by their sons.
It is because these kindnesses are what the wise hold in high
193 regard
That they achieve their greatness and deserve their praises.'

When the Blessed One had spoken these words the householder Sigāla said: 'Excellent, sir! Excellent! As if someone were to set upright what had been knocked down, or reveal what had been hidden, or point out the way to someone who was lost, or hold a lamp up in the dark so that those with eyes could see—just so the Blessed One has made the Truth clear in various ways. Sir, I go to the Blessed One for refuge, and to the Teaching and the Community of monks. Let the Blessed One accept me as a lay follower who has taken refuge from this day for as long as I live.'

FROM THE COLLECTION OF MIDDLE-LENGTH SAYINGS

(Majjhima-nikāya)

ESTABLISHING MINDFULNESS

SATIPAṬṬHĀNA-SUTTA (M I 55–63)

Introduction

This is the only sutta of the Pali canon to occur both in the Dīgha-nikāya and Majjhima-nikāya, an indication, perhaps, of its importance, although this should not be exaggerated, as many other teachings are also found repeated throughout the canon. The version translated here is from the Majjhima-nikāya, which appears identical to its Dīgha-nikāya counterpart apart from the omission towards the end of an expanded exposition of the four noble truths.

The meaning of the term *sati-paṭṭhāna* is problematic. It is used to refer to the fourfold practice of watching the (1) body, (2) feelings, (3) mind, and (4) mental qualities. It is perhaps most often translated as 'foundation' (*paṭṭhāna*) of 'mindfulness' (*sati*), which might suggest that *sati-paṭṭhāna* refers to the body, feelings mind and qualities as 'the foundations', in the sense of objects of mindfulness. While Buddhist tradition certainly allows such an interpretation, more often it tends to interpret the expression in the light of such phrases as 'causing mindfulness to stand near' (*satiṃ upaṭṭhapetvā*), and sees it as directly characterizing mindfulness as a mental state that has the quality of 'standing near' or 'standing in attendance'; using an English idiom, we might say that *sati* is defined as 'presence of mind'. A *sati-(u) paṭṭhāna* is thus the 'presence of mind' (*upaṭṭhāna*) that is mindfulness; the four *satipaṭṭhānas* are then 'four practices in which the quality of presence of mind is found in the form of mindfulness'. However, the precise significance of the expression in the earliest Buddhist texts remains unclear. The present translation—'four ways of establishing mindfulness'—is merely an attempt to convey something of its meaning while avoiding an overly clumsy English phrase.

After setting out in basic terms the four contemplations that constitute 'establishing mindfulness'—watching the body, feelings, mind, and qualities—the sutta continues by providing a detailed exposition of each.

In the account of watching the body there are fourteen basic sections: (1) the monk is mindful when breathing in and out; (2) he knows his different postures; (3) he acts with clear comprehension in his various activities; (4) he reflects on the body as full of different kinds of impurity; (5) he reflects on the body as constituted by the elements of earth, water, fire, and wind; (6–14) he compares his body to a corpse in nine different states of putrefaction. Appended to the description of each of these fourteen practices is an expanded description of the exercise of establishing mindfulness, culminating in the statement that 'the monk lives independently, not holding on to anything in the world'.

The practice of watching feelings and mind are each dealt with in just one section, in both cases followed by the expanded formula. Lastly, watching qualities (*dhamma*) is dealt with in five sections: the monk watches qualities with regard to (1) the five hindrances, (2) the five aggregates, (3) the six internal and external spheres of sense, (4) the seven constituents of awakening, and (5) the four noble truths. Once again, each of these five sections concludes with the expanded formula.

The sutta closes with an extended statement indicating that if anyone should practise these four ways of establishing mindfulness, awakening or something very close to awakening must be the result.

The expanded formula (though it is lost in the abbreviations of the text) thus occurs a total of twenty-one times. The Pali commentaries take 'living independently and not holding onto anything in the world' as indicating the possibility of awakening, and thus characterize the sutta as 'the teaching that culminates in arahatship in twenty-one places'.

The sutta is often read today as describing a pure form of insight (*vipassanā*) meditation that bypasses calm (*samatha*) meditation and the four absorptions (*jhāna*), as outlined in the description of the Buddhist path found, for example, in the *Sāmaññaphala-sutta* (also translated in this volume). The earlier tradition, however, seems not to have always read it this way, associating accomplishment in the exercise of establishing mindfulness with abandoning of the five hindrances and the first absorption (Rupert Gethin, *The Buddhist Path to Awakening: A Study of the Bodhi-Pakkhiyā Dhammā* (Leiden, 1992; repr: Oxford, 2001), 47–53, 58–9). Significantly, neither the term *vipassanā* nor its associated verbal forms occur in the sutta. A simple bifurcation between 'calm' and 'insight' is, anyway, probably inappropriate in the context of much of the Nikāya material.

A recent comprehensive study of 'establishing of mindfulness' is Anālayo, *Satipṭṭhāna: The Direct Path to Realization* (Birmingham, 2003).

This is what I have heard. Once the Blessed One was staying in the country of the Kurus in a small town belonging to the Kurus called Kammāsadamma.

There the Blessed One addressed the monks: 'Monks.'

'Yes, sir,' the monks replied to the Blessed One.

'Monks, this is a path leading directly* to the purification of
56 beings—to passing beyond sorrow and grief, to the disappearance

of pain and discontent, to finding the proper way, to the direct experience of nibbana—namely the four ways of establishing mindfulness.

'What four? Here, a monk* lives watching the body as body; he is determined, fully aware, mindful, overcoming his longing for and discontent with the world. He lives watching feelings as feelings; he is determined, fully aware, mindful, overcoming his longing for and discontent with the world. He lives watching mind as mind; he is determined, fully aware, mindful, overcoming his longing for and discontent with the world. He lives watching qualities* as qualities; he is determined, fully aware, mindful, overcoming his longing for and discontent with the world.

'And how does a monk live watching the body as body? Here, a monk sits down in the forest, or at the root of a tree, or in some deserted house; he crosses his legs, straightens his body, and establishes mindfulness in front of him. Just mindful, he breathes in. Just mindful, he breathes out. As he breathes in a long breath, he knows he is breathing in a long breath; as he breathes out a long breath, he knows he is breathing out a long breath. As he breathes in a short breath, he knows he is breathing in a short breath; as he breathes out a short breath, he knows he is breathing out a short breath. He practises so that he can breathe in, experiencing the whole body; he practises so that he can breathe out, experiencing the whole body. He practises so that he can breathe in, tranquillizing the activity of the body; he practises so that he can breathe out, tranquillizing the activity of the body.*

'Just as a skilled turner or his apprentice, in making a long stroke, knows he is making a long stroke, or in making a short stroke, knows he is making a short stroke,* in exactly the same way, as the monk breathes in a long breath, he knows he is breathing in a long breath . . . He practises so that he can breathe out, tranquillizing the activity of the body.

'In this way he lives watching the body within as body, or he lives watching the body without as body, or he lives watching the body within and without as body.* He lives watching the way things arise in the case of the body; or he lives watching the way things pass in the case of the body; or he lives watching the way things arise and pass in the case of the body. Furthermore, his mindfulness that there is body is established so that there is knowledge and recollection in full degree; he lives independently, not holding on to anything in the world. This is how a monk lives watching the body as body.

'Again, monks, when a monk is walking, he knows he is walking;
57 when he is standing, he knows he is standing; when he is sitting, he knows he is sitting; when he is lying down, he knows he is lying down. In whatever posture his body is, he knows it is in that posture.

'In this way he lives watching the body within as body, or he lives watching the body without as body, or he lives watching the body within and without as body. He lives watching the way things arise in the case of the body; or he lives watching the way things pass in the case of the body; or he lives watching the way things arise and pass in the case of the body. Furthermore his mindfulness that there is body is established so that there is knowledge and recollection in full degree; he lives independently, not holding on to anything in the world. This is how a monk lives watching the body as body.

'Again, monks, in moving forward and turning back, a monk acts with full awareness; in looking ahead and looking around, he acts with full awareness; in bending and straightening his limbs, he acts with full awareness; in wearing his inner and outer robes and carrying his alms bowl, he acts with full awareness; in eating, drinking, chewing, and swallowing, he acts with full awareness; in defecating and urinating, he acts with full awareness; in walking, standing, sitting, falling asleep, waking up, speaking, and keeping silent, he acts with full awareness.

'In this way he lives watching the body within as body . . . This is how a monk lives watching the body as body.

'Again, monks, a monk reviews this body from the soles of his feet upwards and from the ends of the hair on his head downwards, as enveloped in skin and full of various kinds of impurity: "Here in this body there are head hairs, body hairs, nails, teeth, skin, flesh, sinews, bones, bone marrow, kidneys, heart, liver, diaphragm, spleen, lungs, large intestine, small intestine, gorge, faeces, bile, phlegm, pus, blood, sweat, fat, tears, grease, saliva, snot, oil of the joints, and urine."* As if there were a sack with an opening at either end full of various sorts of grain, which a man with good eyes should review thus: "Here are rice grains,* here mung beans, here kidney beans, here sesame seeds." In exactly the same way, a monk reviews this body from the soles of his feet upwards and from the ends of the hair on his head downwards as enveloped in skin and full of various kinds of impurity . . .

'In this way he lives watching the body within as body . . . This is how a monk lives watching the body as body.

'Again, monks, a monk reviews this body, whatever its position, whatever its posture, by way of the elements: "In this body there is the earth element, the water element, the fire element, the wind element."
As if a skilled butcher or his apprentice were to slaughter a cow and 58
sit down at a crossroads, having divided it up into portions. In exactly the same way a monk reviews this body, whatever its position, whatever its posture, by way of the elements . . .

'In this way he lives watching the body within as body . . . This is how a monk lives watching the body as body.

'Again, monks, a monk considers this body as though he were looking at a body left in a charnel ground,* one, two, or three days dead, bloated, livid, and festering: "This body is of the same nature, of the same constitution, it has not got beyond this."

'In this way he lives watching the body within as body . . . This is how a monk lives watching the body as body.

'Again, monks, a monk considers this body as though he were looking at a body left in a charnel ground, eaten by crows, hawks, vultures, dogs, jackals, or other animals: "This body is of the same nature, of the same constitution, it has not got beyond this."

'In this way he lives watching the body within as body . . . This is how a monk lives watching the body as body.

'Again, monks, a monk considers this body as though he were looking at a body left in a charnel ground, a skeleton with flesh and blood, held together with sinews . . . a skeleton with no flesh but smeared with blood and held together with sinews . . . a skeleton without flesh or blood, held together with sinews . . . disconnected bones scattered around, a hand-bone here, a foot-bone here, a leg-bone here, a rib-bone here, a hip-bone here, a back-bone here, the skull here:* "This body is of the same nature, of the same constitution, it has not got beyond this."

'In this way he lives watching the body within as body . . . This is how a monk lives watching the body as body.

'Again, monks, a monk considers this body as though he were looking at a body left in a charnel ground, white bones looking like shells . . . piled-up bones, more than a year old . . . rotten crumbling
bones: "This body is of the same nature, of the same constitution, it 59
has not got beyond this."

'In this way he lives watching the body within as body, or he lives watching the body without as body, or he lives watching the body within and without as body. He lives watching the way things arise in the case of the body; or he lives watching the way things pass in the case of the body; or he lives watching the way things arise and pass in the case of the body. Furthermore, his mindfulness that there is body is established so that there is knowledge and recollection in full degree; he lives independently, not holding on to anything in the world. This is how a monk lives watching the body as body.

'And how does a monk live watching feelings as feelings? Here, when a monk feels a happy feeling, he knows he is feeling a happy feeling; when he feels an unhappy feeling, he knows he is feeling an unhappy feeling; when he feels a neither happy nor unhappy feeling, he knows he is feeling a neither happy nor unhappy feeling. When he feels a happy feeling connected with the world, he knows he is feeling a happy feeling connected with the world; when he feels a happy feeling unconnected with the world, he knows he is feeling a happy feeling unconnected with the world.* When he feels an unhappy feeling connected with the world, he knows he is feeling an unhappy feeling connected with the world; when he feels an unhappy feeling unconnected with the world, he knows he is feeling an unhappy feeling unconnected with the world. When he feels a neither happy nor unhappy feeling connected with the world, he knows he is feeling a neither happy nor unhappy feeling connected with the world; when he feels a neither happy nor unhappy feeling unconnected with the world, he knows he is feeling a neither happy nor unhappy feeling unconnected with the world.

'In this way he lives watching feelings within as feelings, or he lives watching feelings without as feelings, or he lives watching feelings within and without as feelings. He lives watching the way things arise in the case of feelings; or he lives watching the way things pass in the case of feelings; or he lives watching the way things arise and pass in the case of feelings. Furthermore, his mindfulness that there are feelings is established so that there is knowledge and recollection in full degree; he lives independently, not holding on to anything in the world. This is how a monk lives watching feelings as feelings.

'And how does a monk live watching mind as mind? Here, a monk knows a mind affected with desire as a mind affected with desire; he knows a mind unaffected with desire as a mind unaffected with desire. He knows a mind affected with hate as a mind affected with hate; he knows a mind unaffected with hate as a mind unaffected with hate. He knows a mind affected with delusion as a mind affected with delusion; he knows a mind unaffected with delusion as a mind unaffected with delusion. He knows a dull mind as a dull mind; he knows a distracted mind as a distracted mind. He knows a higher mind as a higher mind; he knows a lower mind as a lower mind. He knows an inferior mind as an inferior mind; he knows a superior mind as a superior mind. He knows a concentrated mind as a concentrated mind; he knows an unconcentrated mind as an unconcentrated mind. He knows a mind that is freed as a mind that is freed; he knows a mind that is not freed as a mind that is not freed.

'In this way he lives watching mind within as mind, or he lives watching mind without as mind, or he lives watching mind within
and without as mind. He lives watching the way things arise in the 60
case of mind; or he lives watching the way things pass in the case of mind; or he lives watching the way things arise and pass in the case of mind. Furthermore, his mindfulness that there is mind is established so that there is knowledge and recollection in full degree; he lives independently, not holding on to anything in the world. This is how a monk lives watching mind as mind.

'And how does a monk live watching qualities as qualities? Here, a monk lives watching qualities as qualities in terms of the five hindrances. How? When sense desire is present in him, a monk knows it is present in him, and when it is not present in him he knows it is not present in him. And so, when it has not arisen, he knows how sense desire arises; when it has arisen, he knows how it is abandoned; and when it has been abandoned, he knows how it will not arise in the future.

'When hostility is present in him, a monk knows it is present in him, and when it is not present in him he knows it is not present in him. And so, when it has not arisen, he knows how hostility arises; when it has arisen, he knows how it is abandoned; and when it has been abandoned, he knows how it will not arise in the future.

'When dullness and lethargy are present in him, a monk knows dullness and lethargy are present in him, and when they are not present in him he knows they are not present in him. And so, when they have not arisen, he knows how dullness and lethargy arise; when they have arisen, he knows how they are abandoned; and when they have been abandoned, he knows how they will not arise in the future.

'When agitation and worry are present in him, a monk knows they are present in him, and when they are not present in him he knows they are not present in him. And so, when they have not arisen, he knows how agitation and worry arise; when they have arisen, he knows how they are abandoned; and when they have been abandoned, he knows how they will not arise in the future.

'When doubt is present in him, a monk knows it is present in him, and when it is not present in him he knows it is not present in him. And so, when it has not arisen, he knows how doubt arises; when it has arisen, he knows how it is abandoned; and when it has been abandoned, he knows how it will not arise in the future.

'In this way he lives watching qualities within as qualities, or he lives watching qualities without as qualities, or he lives watching qualities within and without as qualities. He lives watching the way things arise in the case of qualities; or he lives watching the way things pass in the case of qualities; or he lives watching the way things arise and pass in the case of qualities. Furthermore, his mindfulness that there are qualities is established so that there is knowledge and recollection in full degree; he lives independently, not holding on to anything in the world. This is how a monk lives watching qualities as qualities in terms of the five hindrances.

61 'Again, monks, a monk lives watching qualities as qualities in terms of the five aggregates of attachment. How? Here a monk thinks, "Such is physical form, such its arising, such its disappearance; such is feeling, such its arising, such its disappearance; such is conceiving, such its arising, such its disappearance; such are volitional forces, such their arising, such their disappearance; such is consciousness, such its arising, such its disappearance."

'In this way he lives watching qualities within as qualities . . . This is how a monk lives watching qualities as qualities in terms of the five aggregates of attachment.

'Again, monks, a monk lives watching qualities as qualities in terms of the six internal and external spheres of sense. How? Here, a monk knows the eye and he knows visible forms; he also knows the fetter that arises dependent on the two. And so he knows how a fetter which has not arisen arises, he knows how a fetter that has arisen is abandoned, he knows how a fetter that has been abandoned will not arise in the future. A monk knows the ear and he knows sounds . . . A monk knows the nose and he knows smells . . . A monk knows the tongue and he knows tastes . . . A monk knows the body and he knows objects of touch . . . A monk knows the mind and he knows ideas; he also knows the fetter that arises dependent on the two. And so he knows how a fetter which has not arisen arises, he knows how a fetter that has arisen is abandoned, he knows how a fetter that has been abandoned will not arise in the future.

'In this way he lives watching qualities within as qualities . . . This is how a monk lives watching qualities as qualities in terms of the six internal and external spheres of sense.

'Again, monks, a monk lives watching qualities as qualities in terms of the seven constituents of awakening. How? When mindfulness is present in him as a constituent of awakening a monk knows it is present in him, and when it is not present in him he knows it is not present in him. And so, when it has not arisen, he knows how mind- 62
fulness arises as a constituent of awakening; when it has arisen, he knows how it is brought to full development.

'When investigation of qualities is present in him as a constituent of awakening a monk knows it is present in him, and when it is not present in him he knows it is not present in him. And so, when it has not arisen, he knows how investigation of qualities arises as a constituent of awakening; when it has arisen, he knows how it is brought to full development.

'When energy is present in him as a constituent of awakening a monk knows it is present in him, and when it is not present in him he knows it is not present in him. And so, when it has not arisen, he knows how energy arises as a constituent of awakening; when it has arisen, he knows how it is brought to full development.

'When joy is present in him as a constituent of awakening, a monk knows it is present in him, and when it is not present in him he knows it is not present in him. And so, when it has not arisen, he knows how joy arises as a constituent of awakening; when it has arisen, he knows how it is brought to full development.

'When tranquillity is present in him as a constituent of awakening, a monk knows it is present in him, and when it is not present in him he knows it is not present in him. And so, when it has not arisen, he knows how tranquillity arises as a constituent of awakening; when it has arisen, he knows how it is brought to full development.

'When concentration is present in him as a constituent of awakening, a monk knows it is present in him, and when it is not present in him he knows it is not present in him. And so, when it has not arisen, he knows how concentration arises as a constituent of awakening; when it has arisen, he knows how it is brought to full development.

'When equanimity is present in him as a constituent of awakening, a monk knows it is present in him, and when it is not present in him he knows it is not present in him. And so, when it has not arisen, he knows how equanimity arises as a constituent of awakening; when it has arisen, he knows how it is brought to full development.

'In this way he lives watching qualities within as qualities . . . This is how a monk lives watching qualities as qualities in terms of the seven constituents of awakening.

'Again, monks, a monk lives watching qualities as qualities in terms of the four noble truths. How? Here, a monk truly understands what suffering is, he truly understands what the arising of suffering is, he truly understands what the cessation of suffering is, he truly understands what the practice leading to the cessation of suffering is.

'In this way he lives watching qualities within as qualities, or he lives watching qualities without as qualities, or he lives watching qualities within and without as qualities. He lives watching the way things arise in the case of qualities; or he lives watching the way things pass in the case of qualities; or he lives watching the way things arise and pass in the case of qualities. Furthermore his mindfulness that there are qualities is established so that there is knowledge and recollection in full degree; he lives independently, not holding on to anything in the world. This is how a monk lives watching qualities as qualities in terms of the four noble truths.

'Now, monks, if anyone should cultivate these four ways of establishing mindfulness in this way for seven years, one of two results can be expected for him: knowledge here and now, or, if some trace of attachment still remains, the state of non-return. Let alone seven
63 years, if anyone should cultivate these four ways of establishing mindfulness in this way for six years . . . for five years . . . for four years . . . for three years . . . for two years . . . for one year. Let alone one year, if anyone should cultivate these four ways of establishing mindfulness in this way for seven months, one of two results can be expected for him: knowledge here and now, or, if some trace of attachment still remains, the state of non-return. Let alone seven months, if anyone should cultivate these four ways of establishing mindfulness in this way for six months . . . for five months . . . for

four months . . . for three months . . . for two months . . . for one month . . . for a fortnight . . . Let alone a fortnight, if anyone should cultivate these four ways of establishing mindfulness in this way for seven days,* one of two results can be expected for him: knowledge here and now, or, if some trace of attachment still remains, the state of non-return.

'This is the reason it was said that this is a path leading directly to the purification of beings—to passing beyond sorrow and grief, to the disappearance of pain and discontent, to finding the proper way, to the direct experience of nibbana—namely, the four ways of establishing mindfulness.'

This is what the Blessed One said. Gladdened, those monks felt joy at the Blessed One's words.

THE STILLING OF THOUGHTS

VITAKKASAṆṬHĀNA-SUTTA (M I 118–122)

Introduction

This short sutta is one of relatively few that give specific advice on the techniques of meditation practice. For the most part the specific techniques of meditation practice seem assumed, and the Nikāyas describe meditation practice in general terms by reference to the various subjects and attainments. Thus, in the *Sāmaññaphala-sutta* (also included in this volume) we are simply told that the monk establishes mindfulness, abandons the five hindrances, and attains the four absorptions (*jhāna*); there is no real indication of how this is actually accomplished. Of course, suttas such as the *Satipaṭṭhāna-sutta* (also included in this volume) and the *Ānāpānasati-sutta* (not included in this volume) on mindfulness of breathing do give some general indication of how to set about meditation practice, but probably, in keeping with the general Indian attitude to the communication of learning, specific instruction was considered best given by a teacher face to face with his pupils.

The present sutta apparently assumes a meditator who is trying to develop concentration by focusing his attention on a particular, but unspecified, object, and who has to deal with distracting thoughts. A series of techniques is suggested. For a modern discussion see Padmal de Silva, 'A Psychological Analysis of the Vitakkasaṇṭhāna Sutta', *Buddhist Studies Review*, 18 (2001), 65–72.

This is what I have heard. Once the Blessed One was staying at Sāvatthī, in Jeta's grove, in Anāthapiṇḍika's park.*

There the Blessed One addressed the monks: 'Monks.'

119 'Yes, sir,' the monks replied to the Blessed One.

'A monk who is intent on meditation must from time to time direct his attention to five types of sign. Which five? In this case, monks, if, when a monk is directing his attention to a particular sign, bad, unwholesome thoughts associated with desire, hatred, and delusion arise in connection with that sign, then he should direct his attention to a different sign, one that is associated with what is wholesome. As he directs his attention to this different sign associated with what is wholesome, those bad, unwholesome thoughts associated with desire, hatred and delusion are abandoned, they go away. As a result of their being abandoned, his mind becomes still within, settles down, and becomes unified and concentrated. It is as if a skilled carpenter or his apprentice were to knock out, take out, and remove a rough peg with a fine one. In exactly the same way, when a monk . . . directs his attention to this different sign . . . his mind becomes still within, settles down, and becomes unified and concentrated.

'But if, as he directs his attention to this different sign associated with what is wholesome, those bad, unwholesome thoughts associated with desire, hatred, and delusion continue to arise, then that monk should consider the danger of those thoughts: how they are unwholesome, how they are blameworthy, how their results are unpleasant. As he considers the danger of those thoughts . . . those bad, unwholesome thoughts associated with desire, hatred, and delusion are abandoned, they go away. As a result of their being abandoned, his mind becomes still within, settles down, and becomes unified and concentrated. It is as if a young and youthful man or woman who was given to adornment would be upset, shamed, and disgusted by the remains of a dead snake, dog, or man being hung 120
around their neck. In exactly the same way, when a monk . . . considers the danger of those thoughts . . . his mind becomes still within, settles down, and becomes unified and concentrated.

'But if, as he considers the danger of those thoughts, the bad, unwholesome thoughts associated with desire, hatred, and delusion continue to arise, then the monk should practise not being aware of those thoughts, not directing his attention to them. As he practises not being aware of those thoughts, not directing his attention to them, those bad, unwholesome thoughts associated with desire, hatred, and delusion are abandoned, they go away. As a result of their being abandoned, his mind becomes still within, settles down, and becomes unified and concentrated. It is as if a person with good eyes, not wanting to look at the visible forms that had come into view, were to close his eyes or look away. In exactly the same way, when a monk . . . practises not being aware of those thoughts, not directing his attention to them . . . his mind becomes still within, settles down, and becomes unified and concentrated.

'But if, as he practises not being aware of those thoughts, not directing his attention to them, the bad, unwholesome thoughts associated with desire, hatred, and delusion continue to arise, then the monk should direct his attention to stilling the process of thought creating those thoughts. As he directs his attention to stilling the process of thought creating those thoughts, those bad, unwholesome thoughts associated with desire, hatred, and delusion are abandoned, they go away. As a result of their being abandoned, his mind becomes still within, settles down, and becomes unified and concentrated. It is as if a person who was walking fast should ask himself, "Why am I walking fast? Suppose I walk slowly," and when he was walking slowly should ask himself, "Why am I walking slowly? Suppose I stand still," and when he was standing still should ask himself, "Why am I standing? Suppose I sit down," and when he was sitting down, should ask himself, "Why am I sitting? Suppose I lie down." In this way that person would gradually give up active postures for quieter and quieter postures. In exactly the same way, when a monk . . . directs his attention to stilling the process of thought creating those thoughts . . . his mind becomes still within, settles down, and becomes unified and concentrated.

'But if, as he directs his attention to stilling the process of thought creating those thoughts, the bad, unwholesome thoughts associated with desire, hatred, and delusion continue to arise, then gritting his teeth and pressing his tongue against the roof of his mouth, the monk
121 should mentally hold down his mind, crush it, and overwhelm it. As he mentally holds down his mind, crushes it, and overwhelms it, gritting his teeth and pressing his tongue against the roof of his mouth, those bad, unwholesome thoughts associated with desire, hatred, and delusion are abandoned, they go away. As a result of their being abandoned, his mind becomes still within, settles down and becomes unified and concentrated. It is as if a strong man, grabbing a weaker man by the head or the shoulders, were to hold him down, crush him, and overwhelm him. In exactly the same way, when a monk . . . gritting his teeth and pressing his tongue against the roof of his mouth, mentally holds down his mind, crushes it, and overwhelms it . . . his mind becomes still within, settles down and becomes unified and concentrated.

'So when a monk is directing his attention to a particular sign, and bad, unwholesome thoughts . . . arise in connection with that sign, he directs his attention to a different sign associated with what is wholesome, and those bad, unwholesome thoughts associated with

desire, hatred, and delusion are abandoned, they go away; as a result of their being abandoned, his mind becomes still within, settles down, and becomes unified and concentrated. He also considers the danger of those thoughts . . . he also practises not being aware of those thoughts, not directing his attention to them . . . he also directs his attention to stilling the process of thought creating those thoughts . . . he also mentally holds down his mind, crushes it, and overwhelms it, gritting his teeth and pressing his tongue against the roof of his mouth, and those bad, unwholesome thoughts associated with desire, hatred, and delusion are abandoned, they go away; as a result of their being abandoned, his mind becomes still within, settles down, and becomes unified and concentrated. Because of this such a monk is 122
called a master of the ways and courses of thought: the thoughts he wants to think, he thinks; the thoughts he does not want to think, he does not think. He has cut off craving, removed the fetter, and by rightly seeing through conceit he has made an end of suffering.'

This is what the Blessed One said. Gladdened, those monks felt joy at the Blessed One's words.

THE SIMILE OF THE SNAKE

ALAGADDŪPAMA-SUTTA (M I 130–142)

Introduction

The overall theme of this sutta appears to be the holding of 'mistaken views' (*micchādiṭṭhi*), that is, fixed views or opinions that misrepresent in particular what the Buddha teaches.

The sutta falls into two parts. The first part concerns the monk Ariṭṭha, who holds the view that 'those practices said by the Blessed One to be obstacles, need not be obstacles for someone pursuing them'. Although the specifics of this view are not spelt out in the sutta itself, the commentary understands that they pertain to sexual activity. In short, Ariṭṭha seems to hold the view that if one remains free of attachment, then there is no harm in enjoying sexual activity. Developed Buddhist psychological theory as found in the Abhidhamma commentaries would argue that such a view presents something of a psychological contradiction: it is simply not possible to simultaneously enjoy sexual activity and yet have no attachment; the kind of pleasure associated with sexual activity is intrinsically bound up with greed. The commentary's understanding of the nature of Ariṭṭha's view gains some plausibility from the fact that the response to it on the part of the monks who hear it is to point out that the Buddha has spoken about the dangers of sense pleasures at length.

The Buddha's response is to reprimand Ariṭṭha and give two similes (of the eponymous snake and of the raft) which illustrate different ways in which someone might miss the point of his teachings. He then switches to issues connected with views of the self. The sutta proceeds to give a relatively full account of the Buddhist teaching that within the five aggregates of physical and mental phenomena that define our individual experience of the world it is not possible to identify a basis for a 'self' (*attan/ātman*), understood as some kind of underlying unchanging subject of our changing experiences; in short, whatever we experience is 'not self' (*anattan*). In part this teaching seems certainly directed against some such theories of the self or *ātman* as found in the Upaniṣads. Yet the precise implications of the Buddhist understanding of what is 'not self' have been the subject of much discussion, both within the Buddhist world and in modern scholarly literature. It appears from the present sutta that even during the Buddha's lifetime, it prompted some to accuse him of nihilism, a charge which he denies.

The single most comprehensive scholarly study of 'not self' remains S. Collins, *Selfless Persons: Imagery and Thought in Theravāda Buddhism* (Cambridge, 1982); for further references see also R. Gethin, *The Foundations of Buddhism* (Oxford, 1998), 133–62, 312.

This is what I have heard. Once the Blessed One was staying at 130
Sāvatthī, in Jeta's grove, in Anāthapiṇḍika's park. At that time the following harmful view had come up for a monk, the former vulture killer,* called Ariṭṭha: 'This is how I understand the practice taught by the Blessed One: those practices* said by the Blessed One to be obstacles, need not be obstacles for someone pursuing them.'

When a number of monks heard it said that this harmful view had come up for a monk . . . called Ariṭṭha . . . they went to him and asked him: 'Is it true what people say—that this harmful view has come up for you . . . ?'

'Yes, this is how I understand the practice taught by the Blessed One: those practices said by him to be obstacles, need not be obstacles for someone pursuing them.'

Then those monks, wishing to make him give up this harmful view, together reprimanded, reproved, and rebuked him: 'Ariṭṭha, friend, do not say this. Do not misrepresent the Blessed One. It is certainly not good to misrepresent him and this is certainly not what he would say. For in many ways, Ariṭṭha, have the practices been said by the Blessed One to be obstacles, and necessarily obstacles for someone pursuing them. The Blessed One has said that sense pleasures bring little enjoyment and much pain and trouble—great is the danger in them. He has said that, like a skeleton, sense pleasures bring much pain and trouble—great is the danger in them . . . He has said that, like a lump of meat . . . like a grass torch . . . like a pit of coals . . . like a dream . . . like something borrowed . . . like a fruit tree . . . like a butcher's knife and chopping block . . . like a sword and stake . . . like a snake's head, sense pleasures bring much pain and trouble—great is the danger in them.'*

But when those monks together reprimanded, reproved, and rebuked him, the monk Ariṭṭha expressed exactly the same harmful view, holding firmly to it and insisting on it: 'This is how I understand the practice taught by the Blessed One: those practices said by him to be obstacles, need not be obstacles for someone pursuing them.'

131 Since those monks were unable to make the monk Ariṭṭha give up this harmful view, they approached the Blessed One, and having saluted him respectfully, they sat down to one side.

Once seated, those monks said to the Blessed One: 'Sir, the following harmful view has come up for a monk, the former vulture killer, called Ariṭṭha: ". . . those practices said by the Blessed One to be obstacles, need not be obstacles for someone pursuing them." When we heard it said that this harmful view had come up for . . . Ariṭṭha . . . we went to him and asked him if it was true . . . Then, wishing to make him give up this harmful view, together we reprimanded, reproved, and rebuked him . . . But . . . Ariṭṭha expressed exactly the same harmful view, holding firmly to it and insisting on it . . . Since we were unable to make the monk Ariṭṭha give up his harmful view, we are telling the Blessed One about this matter.'

Then the Blessed One said to a monk: 'Go, monk, and call the monk Ariṭṭha in my name saying, "Ariṭṭha friend, the Teacher calls
132 you."'

'Yes, sir,' replied that monk to the Blessed One.

And he went to the monk Ariṭṭha and said to him: 'Ariṭṭha, friend, the Teacher calls you.'

'Yes, friend,' replied the monk Ariṭṭha, and he went to the Blessed One, and having saluted him respectfully, he sat down to one side.

Once the monk Ariṭṭha was seated the Blessed One said to him: 'Is it true what people say—that this harmful view has come up for you . . . ?'

'Yes, this is how I understand the practice taught by the Blessed One: those practices said by him to be obstacles, need not be obstacles for someone pursuing them.'

'Foolish man, who are you* to understand that this is the practice I have taught? For have I not in many ways stated that those practices are obstacles, and necessarily obstacles for someone pursuing them? I have said that sense pleasures bring much pain and trouble—great is the danger in them. I have said that, like a skeleton, sense pleasures bring much pain and trouble—great is the danger in them . . . I have said that, like a lump of meat . . . a grass torch . . . a pit of coals . . . a dream . . . things borrowed . . . a fruit tree . . . a butcher's knife and chopping block . . . a sword and stake . . . a snake's head, sense pleasures bring much pain and trouble—great is the danger in them. But because of your wrong grasp of this, foolish man, you misrepresent us, you damage yourself, and you produce great misfortune. Certainly it will cause you harm and suffering for a long time.'

Then the Blessed One addressed the monks: 'What do you think about this, monks? Has the monk Ariṭṭha, the former vulture killer, got even a glimmer of understanding in this system of teaching and discipline?'

'How could that be, sir? Certainly not.'

At this, the monk Ariṭṭha became silent and confused; he sat there with drooping shoulders, looking down, deep in thought, and not saying anything in response. Seeing him like that, the Blessed One said to him: 'Foolish man, you will be remembered for this harmful view of yours. I shall ask the monks about it.'

Then the Blessed One addressed the monks: 'Is this how you 133
understand the practice taught by me, like this monk Ariṭṭha, who, because of his wrong grasp of things, misrepresents us, damages himself, and produces great misfortune?'

'Certainly not, sir, for in many ways has the Blessed One stated those practices to be obstacles, and necessarily obstacles for someone pursuing them. The Blessed One has said that sense pleasures bring much pain and trouble—great is the danger in them . . . like a skeleton . . . like a snake's head, they bring much pain and trouble—great is the danger in them.'

'Good, monks. It is good that this is how you understand the practice that I have taught, for in many ways have I told you that there are practices that are obstacles, and necessarily obstacles for someone pursuing them . . . But this monk Ariṭṭha, because of his wrong grasp of things, misrepresents us, damages himself, and produces great misfortune. Certainly it will cause this foolish man harm and suffering for a long time. That one can pursue sense pleasures without desire for them, without experiencing sense desire, without thoughts of sense desire—this is impossible.

'Monks, some foolish men learn the teaching—the sayings, chants, analyses, verses, utterances, traditions, birth stories, marvels, and dialogues. Yet after they have learnt the teaching they do not use wisdom to consider the purpose of those teachings. And when they do not use wisdom to consider their purpose the teachings don't succeed in bearing deep reflection: the only benefit those people get from learning the teaching is the ability to argue and counter criticism;

the point of their learning the teaching is missed by them. Teachings that they have a wrong grasp of cause them harm and suffering for a long time. Why is that? Because of their wrong grasp of the teachings. It is as if a man needing and requiring a snake went around searching for one, and when he saw a large snake, were to take hold of it by one of its coils or its tail. That snake would turn around
134 and bite him on his hand or arm or one of his limbs, and as a result he would suffer death or the pain of death. Why is that? Because of his wrong grasp of the snake. In exactly the same way, some foolish men learn the teaching . . . Yet . . . the point of their learning the teaching is missed by them . . . Because of their wrong grasp of the teachings.

'Monks, some sons of good family learn the teaching—the sayings, chants, analyses, verses, utterances, traditions, birth stories, marvels, and dialogues. After they have learnt the teaching they do use wisdom to consider the purpose of those teachings. And when they use wisdom to consider their purpose, the teachings succeed in bearing deep reflection: the benefit those people get from learning the teaching is not the ability to argue and counter criticism; the point of their learning the teaching is gained by them. Teachings that they have a correct grasp of bring them good and happiness for a long time. Why is that? Because of their correct grasp of the teachings. It is as if a man needing and requiring a snake went around searching for one, and when he saw a large snake, were to hold it down correctly with a cleft stick and then to take hold of it correctly by its neck. Although the snake might wrap its coils around his hand or his arm or one of his limbs, he would not as a result suffer death or the pain of death. Why is that? Because of his correct grasp of the snake. In exactly the same way, some sons of good family learn the teaching . . . the point of their learning the teaching is gained by them . . . Because of their correct grasp of the teachings. Therefore, monks, if you understand the meaning of what I have said, then you can preserve it in accordance with that understanding, but if you do not understand the meaning, you should either ask me about it, or the monks who are experienced.

'Monks, I shall teach you how the practice is like a raft, for the purpose of crossing over and not for the purpose of holding on to. Listen. Pay careful attention to what I shall say.'

'Yes, sir,' replied the monks to the Blessed One.

This is what he said: 'It is as if there were a man who had set out on a long journey. He might see a great river in flood, the near shore fearful and dangerous, the far shore safe and free of danger, but there might be no ferry or bridge for crossing from one side to the other. And this man might think: "This is a great river in flood. The near 135
shore is fearful and dangerous, the far shore safe and free of danger, but there is no ferry or bridge to cross from one side to the other. What if I were to gather together grass, sticks, branches, and foliage and bind together a raft, and then using that raft, striving with my hands and feet, cross over safely to the further shore?" Thereupon that man might gather together grass, sticks, branches, and foliage and bind together a raft, and then using that raft, striving with his hands and feet, he might cross over safely to the further shore. Once he had crossed over it might occur to him: "This raft has been very useful to me. Using this raft, striving with my hands and feet, I have crossed over safely to the further shore. What if I were now to lift it onto my head or hoist it onto my back and go off where I please?" What do you think of this, monks? If the man did this would he be doing what is appropriate with the raft?'

'Certainly not, sir.'

'But what should this man do in order to do what is appropriate with the raft? In this case, once he had crossed over it might occur to him, "This raft has been very useful to me. Using this raft, striving with my hands and feet, I have crossed over safely to the further shore. What if I were now to beach this raft on the shore or sink it in the water and go off where I please?" The man who did this would be doing what is appropriate with the raft. In exactly the same way, monks, I have taught you how the practice is like a raft—for the purpose of crossing over and not for the purpose of holding on to. Monks, those who understand its similarity to a raft must let go of even good practices, let alone bad practices.*

'Monks, there are these six points of view. Which six? Here the uninformed, ordinary person, who takes no notice of the noble ones, who has no experience of and no acquaintance with their practice, who takes no notice of wise people, who has no experience of and no acquaintance with their practice, looks on physical form as his, as what he is, as his self. He looks on feeling as his, as what he is, as his self. He looks on conceiving as his, as what he is, as his self. He looks on volitional forces as his, as what he is, as his self. He looks on what

he has seen, heard, sensed, known, experienced, pursued, and pondered in his mind as his, as what he is, as his self. And there is also this point of view: "The world and the self are the same, and after death this is what I shall be—permanent, enduring, eternal, not
136 liable to change, and I shall remain like that for all eternity."* This point of view too he looks on as his, as what he is, as his self.

'But the informed noble disciple, who takes notice of the noble ones, who has experience of and acquaintance with their practice, who takes notice of wise people, who has experience of and acquaintance with their practice, does not look on physical form as his, as what he is, as his self. He does not look on feeling as his, as what he is, as his self. He does not look on conceiving as his, as what he is, as his self. He does not look on volitional forces as his, as what he is, as his self. He does not look on what he has seen, heard, sensed, known, experienced, pursued, and pondered in his mind as his, as what he is, as his self. And the point of view, "The world and the self are the same—after death this is what I shall be: permanent, enduring, eternal, not liable to change; I shall remain like that for all eternity"—this point of view too he does not look on as his, as what he is, as his self. When he looks on things in this way, he does not get anxious about what doesn't exist.'

At this, one monk asked the Blessed One: 'Sir, can there be anxiety about something that doesn't exist outside?'

'There can, monk,' said the Blessed One. 'For example, someone thinks, "Alas, what I used to have, I have no longer! Alas, what I would have, I can't get!" He grieves and is distraught; he laments and wails, beating his chest; he falls into complete confusion. This is how there is anxiety about something that doesn't exist outside.'

'But, sir, can there be no anxiety about something that doesn't exist outside?'

'There can, monk,' said the Blessed One. 'For example, someone does not think, "Alas, what I used to have, I have no longer! Alas, what I would have, I can't get!" He does not grieve and is not distraught; he does not lament and wail, beating his chest; he does not fall into complete confusion. This is how there is no anxiety about something that doesn't exist outside.'

'Sir, can there be anxiety about something that doesn't exist inside?

'There can, monk,' said the Blessed One. 'For example, someone has the view that the world and the self are the same, and that after death this is what he will be, permanent, enduring, eternal, not liable to change, and that he will remain like that for all eternity. He hears the Tathāgata or a disciple of the Tathāgata teaching the practice for doing away with fixing on views, viewpoints, and positions, for doing away with the latent tendency to insist on those, for the stilling of all volitional forces, for the letting go of all attachments, for the destruction of craving, for dispassion, cessation, nibbana. Then he thinks,
"It is clear I shall be annihilated! I shall be destroyed! I shall no 137
longer exist!" He grieves and is distraught; he laments and wails, beating his chest; he falls into complete confusion. This is how there is anxiety about something that doesn't exist inside.'

'But, sir, can there be no anxiety about something that doesn't exist inside?

'There can, monk,' said the Blessed One. 'For example, someone does not have the view that the world and the self are the same, that after death this is what he will be, permanent, enduring, eternal, not liable to change, and that he will remain like that for all eternity. He hears the Tathāgata or a disciple of the Tathāgata teaching the practice for doing away with fixing on views, viewpoints, and positions, for doing away with the latent tendency to insist on those, for the stilling of all volitional forces, for the letting go of all attachments, for the destruction of craving, for dispassion, cessation, nibbana. He does not then think, "It is clear I shall be annihilated! I shall be destroyed! I shall no longer exist!" He does not grieve and is not distraught; he does not lament and wail, beating his chest; he does not fall into complete confusion. This is how there is no anxiety about something that doesn't exist inside.

'Monks, the possession that could be one's permanent, enduring, eternal possession, not liable to change, and that would remain like that for all eternity—that is a possession you ought to have. But do you see such a possession?'

'Certainly we do not, sir.'

'Good, monks. I too do not perceive the possession that could be one's permanent, enduring, eternal possession, not liable to change, and that would remain like that for all eternity. Monks, if taking up a theory of self did not bring about grief, sorrow, suffering, unhappiness, and distress for the one taking it up, then you ought to take up that theory of self. But do you see such a theory of self?'

'Certainly we do not, sir.'

'Good, monks. I too do not perceive a theory of self where taking it up would not bring about grief, sorrow, suffering unhappiness, and distress for the one taking it up. Monks, if relying on a view did not bring about grief, sorrow, suffering unhappiness, and distress for the one relying on it, then you ought to rely on that view. But do you see such a view?'

'Certainly we do not, sir.'

138 'Good, monks. I too do not perceive a view where relying on it would not bring about grief, sorrow, suffering unhappiness, and distress for the one relying on it. Monks, if there existed a self, one could talk of what belonged to one's self.'

'Yes, sir.'

'And if there existed what belonged to one's self, one could talk of one's self.'

'Yes, sir.'

'But if both the self and what belongs to the self are not in actual fact found, then the point of view that the world and the self are the same and that after death this is what one will be, permanent, enduring, eternal, not liable to change, and one will remain like that for all eternity, is a totally and completely foolish idea.'

'How could it be other than this, sir?'

'What do you think about this, monks? Is physical form permanent or impermanent?'

'Impermanent, sir.'

'But is what is impermanent, painful or pleasurable?'

'Painful, sir.'

'But is it right to look on what is painful and liable to change as yours, as what you are, as your self?'

'Certainly not, sir.'

'What do you think about this, monks? Is feeling . . . is conceiving . . . are volitional forces . . . is consciousness permanent or impermanent?'

'Impermanent, sir.'

'But is what is impermanent, painful or pleasurable?'

'Painful, sir.'

'But is it right to look on what is painful and liable to change as yours, as what you are, as your self?'

'Certainly not, sir.'

'In that case, monks, all physical form whatsoever—whether past, present, or future, whether inside or outside, gross or subtle, 139
inferior or refined, far or near—should be seen with proper understanding as it is: "This is not mine, I am not this, this is not my self." All feeling . . . conceiving . . . volitional forces . . . consciousness whatsoever—whether past, present, or future, whether inside or outside, gross or subtle, inferior or refined, far or near—should be seen with proper understanding as it is: "This is not mine, I am not this, this is not my self."

'When the informed noble disciple sees things in this way he becomes disenchanted with physical form; he becomes disenchanted with feeling; he becomes disenchanted with conceiving; he becomes disenchanted with volitional forces; he becomes disenchanted with consciousness. Being disenchanted, he becomes dispassionate. Through dispassion, he is freed: of that which is freed, there is knowledge that it is freed. He knows: "Birth is destroyed, the spiritual life lived, done is what was to be done—there is nothing further required to this end!"

'This monk is called "one who has lifted up the crossbar," "one who has filled in the trench," "one who has removed the post," "one who has no bolt," "a noble one who has lowered the banner, put down the burden, unfettered". In what way is this monk "one who has lifted up the crossbar"? In this case the monk has abandoned ignorance—with its roots cut off, it is like the dead stump of a palm, finished, without the capacity to arise in the future. In this way he is "one who has lifted up the crossbar".

'In that way is this monk "one who has filled in the trench"? In this case the monk has abandoned the round of birth with its repeated existences—with its roots cut off, it is like the dead stump of a palm, finished, without the capacity to arise in the future. In this way he is "one who has filled in the trench". In what way is this monk "one who has removed the post"? In this case the monk has abandoned craving—with its roots cut off, it is like the dead stump of a palm, finished, without the capacity to arise in the future. In this way he is "one who has removed the post". In what way is this monk "one who has no bolt"? In this case the monk has abandoned the five lower fetters—with their roots cut off, they are like the dead stump of a palm, finished, without the capacity to arise in the future. In this way

he is "one who has no bolt". In what way is this monk "a noble
one who has lowered the banner, put down the burden, unfettered"?
In this case the monk has abandoned the conceit "I am"—
with its root cut off, it is like the dead stump of a palm, finished,
140 without the capacity to arise in the future. In this way he is
"a noble one who has lowered the banner, put down the burden,
unfettered".

'When the gods, including Inda, Brahmā, Pajāpati, go searching for a monk whose mind has been freed in this way, they do not come across anything of which they can say, "This is what supports the consciousness of one who is like that."* What is the reason for this? I say that one like that is untraceable in the here and now. When I speak like this, when I talk like this, some ascetics and brahmans falsely, mistakenly, wrongly, and incorrectly misrepresent me, saying, "The ascetic Gotama is a nihilist. He teaches the annihilation, the destruction, and non-existence of the being that exists." In saying this they falsely, mistakenly, wrongly, and incorrectly accuse me of being what I am not, and of teaching what I do not. Monks, previously and now I teach just suffering and the cessation of suffering. If others are abusive, and criticize and get angry with the Tathāgata for this, then the Tathāgata does not feel hostility and disappointment, and get disheartened. If others respect, honour, revere, and worship the Tathāgata for this, then the Tathāgata does not feel delight and pleasure, and get excited. If others respect, honour, revere and worship the Tathāgata for this, then the Tathāgata thinks, "Such acts are done to this, which previously has been fully understood."* In which case, monks, if others are also abusive, and criticize and get angry with you, then you should not feel hostility and disappointment, and get disheartened. If others also respect, honour, revere, and worship you, then you should not feel delight and pleasure, and get excited. If others also respect, honour, revere, and worship you, then you should think, "Such acts are done to this, which previously has been fully understood."

'Therefore, monks, abandon what is not yours—your abandoning
it will bring you good and happiness for a long time. And what is it
that is not yours? Physical form is not yours. Abandon it—your
abandoning it will bring you good and happiness for a long time.
141 Feeling is not yours . . . Conceiving is not yours . . . Volitional forces
are not yours . . . Consciousness is not yours. Abandon it—your
abandoning it will bring you good and happiness for a long time.

What do you think about this, monks? People might collect the grass, sticks, branches, leaves here in the Jeta grove, or burn them or do with them as they want. Would it occur to you that people were collecting you, or burning you, or doing with you as they want?'

'No it would not, sir. What is the reason for this? This is clearly neither our self nor what belongs to our self.'

'In exactly the same way, monks, abandon what is not yours . . . Physical form is not yours . . . Feeling is not yours . . . Conceiving is not yours . . . Volitional forces are not yours . . . Consciousness is not yours. Abandon it—your abandoning it will bring you good and happiness for a long time.

'Monks, in this way I have properly stated the teaching: it is laid bare, open, clear, plain to see. In this teaching that I have properly stated in this way, that is laid bare, open, clear, plain to see, for those monks who are arahats, who have destroyed the taints, lived the spiritual life, done what was to be done, put down the burden, reached the true goal, destroyed the fetters of existence, and are freed through faultless knowledge, there is no further occurrence to declare. Monks, in this way I have properly stated the teaching . . . In this teaching . . . all those monks who have abandoned the five lower fetters are reborn purely and will attain final nibbana in that world and not return from there. Monks, in this way I have properly stated the teaching . . . In this teaching . . . all those monks who have abandoned three fetters and weakened greed, hatred' and delusion, are once-returners—having returned once to this world they will make an end of suffering. Monks, in this way I have properly stated the teaching . . . In this teaching . . . all those monks who have abandoned three fetters, are stream-enterers, beyond affliction, destined 142
to full awakening for sure. Monks, in this way I have properly stated the teaching . . . In this teaching . . . all those monks who follow in Truth, who follow in faith, are destined to full awakening. Monks, in this way I have properly stated the teaching . . . In this teaching . . . all those who have a degree of faith in me, a degree of affection for me are destined for heaven.'*

This is what the Blessed One said. Gladdened, those monks felt joy at the Blessed One's words.

THE SHORT DIALOGUE WITH MĀLUṄKYA

CŪḶA-MĀLUṄKYA-SUTTA (M I 426–432)

Introduction

This sutta focuses on the 'unexplained' or 'undetermined' (*avyākata*) questions. Why did the Buddha refuse to give categorical answers to these questions? It has been claimed by some modern scholars that the Buddha was simply not interested in metaphysical questions and that he wished to leave these matters open. Yet it is possible that the Buddha's refusal to answer has a philosophically more interesting basis. It is stated in this sutta that one reason he did not explain these matters was because they were not connected with the goal of the Buddhist path, namely the cessation of suffering. This leaves no doubt as to the practical intent of the Buddha's teaching, but what precisely is being said about these questions when it is declared that their explanation does not conduce to the cessation of suffering? Was the Buddha suggesting that he simply did not know the answers to these questions? The Buddha of the Nikāyas certainly never straightforwardly admits to not knowing the answers. Alternatively, the Buddha might have had answers to these questions which he simply refused to divulge on the stated grounds that they would not help his followers in their progress along the path. A third possibility would seem to be that these questions are somehow by their very nature unanswerable. The reason for this is because they assume categories and concepts—the world, the soul, the self, the Tathāgata—that the Buddha and the Buddhist tradition do not accept or at least criticize or understand in particular ways. That is, from the Buddhist perspective these questions are ill-formed and misconceived. To answer 'yes' or 'no' to any one of them is to be drawn into accepting the validity of the question and the terms in which it is couched—rather like answering 'yes' or 'no' to a question such as, 'Are Martians green?' One's answer may be construed in ways one had not intended. See Collins, *Selfless Persons*, 131–8; for a discussion of some contemporary scholarly interpretations of the 'unanswered questions' see R. Hayes, 'Nāgārjuna's Appeal', *Journal of Indian Philosophy*, 22 (1994), 299–378 (at 356–61).

This is what I have heard. Once the Blessed One was staying at Sāvatthī, in Jeta's grove, in Anāthapiṇḍika's park. Now, while the venerable Māluṅkyāputta was alone in quiet meditation the following thought arose in his mind: 'The Blessed One has left the following points of view unexplained, he has set them aside and refused them—whether the world is eternal, whether it is not eternal, whether it is finite, whether it is infinite, whether the soul and the body are one and the same thing, whether the soul is one thing and the body another, whether after death a Tathāgata exists, whether after death he does not exist, whether after death he both exists and does not exist, whether after death he neither exists nor does not exist. That the Blessed One does not explain these points to me is disagreeable and unacceptable to me. I shall go to the Blessed One and ask him about this. I shall tell him that if he will explain to me whether the world is eternal . . . whether it is finite . . . whether the soul and the body are one and the same thing . . . whether the Tathāgata exists . . . whether he neither exists nor does not exist, then I shall continue to practise the spiritual life with him. But if he will not explain whether the world is eternal . . . whether the Tathāgata neither exists nor does not exist, then I shall give up the training and return to ordinary life.'

Then, at dusk, the venerable Māluṅkyāputta got up from his 427
meditation and approached the Blessed One. Having approached, he saluted him respectfully and sat down to one side.

Once seated, he said to the Blessed One: 'Now, while I was alone in quiet meditation the following thought arose in my mind: "The Blessed One has left the following points of view unexplained, he has set them aside and refused them—whether the world is eternal, whether it is not eternal . . . whether after death he neither exists nor does not exist. That the Blessed One does not explain these points to me is disagreeable and unacceptable to me. I shall go to the Blessed One and ask him about this. I shall tell him that if he will explain whether the world is eternal . . . whether the Tathāgata neither exists nor does not exist, then I shall continue to practise the spiritual life with him. But if he will not explain whether the world is eternal . . . whether the Tathāgata neither exists nor does not exist, then I shall give up the training and return to ordinary life."

'If the Blessed One knows that the world is eternal, then let the Blessed One explain to me that the world is eternal. If the Blessed One knows that the world is not eternal, then let the Blessed One explain to me that the world is not eternal. But if the Blessed One does not know whether the world is eternal or not, then the only honest thing for someone who does not know or see to do is to say, "I don't know, I don't see."

'If the Blessed One knows that the world is finite, then let the Blessed One explain that to me . . . But if the Blessed One does not know . . . then the only honest thing . . . is to say, "I don't know, I don't see."

'If the Blessed One knows that the soul and the body are one and the same thing, then let the Blessed One explain that to me . . . But if the Blessed One does not know . . . then the only honest thing . . . is to say, "I don't know, I don't see."

'If the Blessed One knows that after death a Tathāgata exists, then
428 let the Blessed One explain that to me . . . But if the Blessed One does not know . . . then the only honest thing . . . is to say, "I don't know, I don't see."

'If the Blessed One knows that after death he both exists and does not exist, then let the Blessed One explain that to me . . . But if the Blessed One does not know . . . then the only honest thing . . . is to say, "I don't know, I don't see." '

'Have I ever said to you, Māluṅkyāputta, that you should come and practise the spiritual life with me and I shall explain to you whether the world is eternal . . . whether the Tathāgata neither exists nor does not exist?'

'You have not, sir.'

'And have you ever said to me that you will come and practise the spiritual life with the Blessed One and he will explain to you whether the world is eternal . . . whether the Tathāgata neither exists nor does not exist?'

'I have not, sir.'

'So apparently, neither have I ever said to you that you should come and practise the spiritual life with me and I shall explain to you whether the world is eternal . . . whether the Tathāgata neither exists nor does not exist, nor have you said to me that you will come and practise the spiritual life with the Blessed One and he will explain to you whether the world is eternal . . . whether the Tathāgata neither exists nor does not exist. In which case, foolish man, who are you to challenge whom?

'If someone were to say that he would not practise the spiritual life with the Blessed One so long as the Blessed One did not explain
429 to him whether the world was eternal . . . whether the Tathāgata

neither existed nor did not exist, that person would die and still the Tathāgata would not have explained this.

'It is as if, Māluṅkyāputta, there were a man struck by an arrow that was smeared thickly with poison; his friends and companions, his family and relatives would summon a doctor to see to the arrow. And the man might say, "I will not draw out this arrow so long as I do not know whether the man by whom I was struck was of the Brahman, Ruler, Trader, or Servant class" . . . or . . . "so long as I do not know his name and his family . . . whether he was tall, short or of medium height . . . whether he was black, brown or light-skinned . . . whether he comes from this or that village, town or city . . . whether the bow . . . was a *cāpa* type or a *kodaṇḍa* type . . . whether the bow-string . . . was of the *akka* plant, reed, sinew, hemp, or the milk-leaf tree . . . whether the shaft . . . was taken from the wild or cultivated* . . . whether the shaft . . . was fitted with the feathers of a vulture, heron, falcon, peacock, or *sithilahanu**. . . whether the shaft . . . was bound with the sinews of a cow, buffalo, antelope, or monkey . . . whether the arrowhead . . . was a barb, a razor-point, a *vekaṇḍa* type, iron, a 'calf-tooth', or an 'oleander leaf'."* 430

'That person would die and still he would not know this. Exactly so, Māluṅkyāputta, if someone were to say that he would not practise the spiritual life with the Blessed One so long as the Blessed One did not explain to him whether the world was eternal . . . that person would die and still the Tathāgata would not have explained this.

'It is not the case, Māluṅkyāputta, that by holding the view that the world is eternal, one would live the spiritual life. Nor is it the case that by holding the view that the world is not eternal, one would live the spiritual life. Whether one holds the view that the world is eternal or the view that it is not eternal, there is still birth, ageing, death, grief, despair, pain, and unhappiness—and it is the destruction of these here and now that I declare.

'It is not the case, Māluṅkyāputta, that by holding the view that the world is finite . . . by holding the view that the world is infinite, one would live the spiritual life. Whether one holds the view that the world is finite or the view that it is infinite, there is still birth, ageing, death, grief, despair, pain, and unhappiness—and it is the destruction of these here and now that I declare.

'It is not the case, Māluṅkyāputta, that by holding the view that the soul and the body are one and the same thing . . . that the soul is

one thing and the body another . . . that after death a Tathāgata
431 exists . . . that after death he does not exist . . . that after death he both exists and does not exist . . . that after death he neither exists nor does not exist, one would live the spiritual life. Whether one holds the view that after death he both exists and does not exist or the view that after death he neither exists nor does not exist, there is still birth, ageing, death, grief, despair, pain, and unhappiness—and it is the destruction of these here and now that I declare.

'Therefore, Māluṅkyāputta, remember what I have not explained as what is unexplained, and what I have explained as what is explained. So what is it that I have not explained? That the world is eternal, I have not explained. That it is not eternal . . . That it is finite . . . That it is infinite . . . That the soul and the body are one and the same thing . . . That the soul is one thing and the body another . . . That after death a Tathāgata exists . . . That after death he does not exist . . . That after death he both exists and does not exist . . . That after death he neither exists nor does not exist, I have not explained. And why have I not explained this? Because it is not relevant to the goal, it is not fundamental to the spiritual life, it does not lead to disenchantment, to dispassion, to cessation, to peace, to direct knowledge, to full awakening, to nibbana. Therefore I have not explained this.

'And what is it that I have explained? What suffering is, I have explained. What the origin of suffering is . . . What the cessation of suffering is . . . What the practice leading to the cessation of suffering is, I have explained. And why have I explained this? Because it is relevant to the goal, it is fundamental to the spiritual life, it leads to disenchantment, to dispassion, to cessation, to peace, to direct knowledge, to full awakening, to nibbana. Therefore I have explained
432 this. And so, Māluṅkyāputta, remember what I have not explained as what is unexplained, and what I have explained as what is explained.'

This is what the Blessed One said. Gladdened, the venerable Māluṅkyāputta felt joy at the Blessed One's words.

THE DIALOGUE WITH PRINCE BODHI

BODHIRĀJAKUMĀRA-SUTTA (M II 91–97)

Introduction

This sutta gives the single fullest account of Gotama's quest for awakening found in the Pali Nikāyas. The various elements that make up the narrative are found in other suttas in the Nikāyas, but are here brought together to produce a single, extended, first-person narrative. The sutta is found in the middle of the second set of fifty suttas of the 152 suttas that constitute the Majjhima-nikāya. Because it combines and repeats material that is found earlier in different suttas, the *Bodhirājakumāra-sutta* is somewhat overlooked, being largely reduced to cross-references to two other suttas (the *Mahāsaccaka-* and *Ariyapariyesana-suttas*), in the two complete English translations of the Majjhima-nikāya (by I. B. Horner, and Bhikkhu Ñāṇamoli and Bhikkhu Bodhi); this is also the case with the Pali Text Society's edition of the Pali text, but not with other editions.[1] Some schools of ancient Indian Buddhism included their version of this text in their collection of long sayings (Dīrghāgama).[2]

What prompts the Buddha to give an account of his own spiritual quest is Prince Bodhi's idea that 'happiness can only be reached through pain'. The Buddha recounts how he left home to become a wandering ascetic and, having initially followed two different teachers in succession, took up the practice of painful austerities. When these failed to bring him the final freedom from suffering he was seeking, he recalled his own previous attainment of 'the joy and happiness of the first absorption' (*jhāna*); realizing that he had nothing to fear from a 'happiness that has nothing to do with sense pleasures, nothing to do with unwholesome qualities', he decided to pursue this as the basis for the final attainment of awakening—with success. The Buddha

[1] Thus the introducory and concluding sections of this sutta follow the Pali text of M II 91–7; the two sections dealing with (1) the bodhisatta's going forth and practice under Āḷāra Kālāma and Uddaka Rāmaputta and (2) his hesitation and then decision to teach following Brahmā's request follow M I 61–73 from the *Ariyapariyesana-sutta*; the section in the middle describing his practice of austerities and his awakening follows M I 240–9 from the *Mahāsaccaka-sutta*.

[2] See Jens-Uwe Hartmann, 'The Contents and Structure of the Dīrghāgama of the (Mūla-)Sarvāstivādins', *Annual Report of the International Research Institute for Advanced Buddhology at Soka University*, 7 (2004), 119–37.

goes on to tell of how the great god Brahmā himself requested him to teach what he had discovered, and how as a result he first set the wheel of Truth (*dhamma-cakka*) in motion in the animal park outside Benares. Prince Bodhi finally asks how quickly one might attain awakening, and reaffirms that he goes to the Buddha, Dhamma, and Sangha as refuge.

No indication is given here that the Buddha was born the son of a great king, a prince who enjoyed a sumptuously wealthy youth and who was prompted to renounce his wealth by his encounter with an old man, a sick man, a corpse, and ascetic; in the four Nikāyas this famous story is only related in the mythic account of a previous buddha, Vipassin (D II 21–31). For further discussion and suggestions for further reading see Gethin, *Foundations of Buddhism*, 7–34, 306–7.

This is what I have heard. Once the Blessed One was staying in the Bhagga country at Suṃsumāragira, in the Bhesakaḷā grove in the animal park. At that time Prince Bodhi had recently had built a building called Kokanada, but it had not yet been occupied by any ascetic or brahman or by any human being.

Then Prince Bodhi spoke to the brahman student Sañjikāputta: 'My good Sañjikāputta, go to the Blessed One, and having approached him bow down at his feet with your head in my name and ask if he is free of sickness and disease, if he is in good health and strong, if he lives at ease, saying, "Sir, Prince Bodhi bows down at your feet with his head and asks if you are free of sickness and disease, if you are in good health and strong, if you live at ease." And then say, "Sir, may the Blessed One along with the community of monks accept Prince Bodhi's invitation for tomorrow's meal."'

'Yes, sir,' replied the brahman student Sañjikāputta.

Then he approached the Blessed One. Having approached, he saluted the Blessed One respectfully, and exchanged pleasing and polite words with him, before sitting down to one side.

Once seated, he said to the Blessed One: 'Gotama sir,* Prince Bodhi bows down at Gotama's feet with his head and asks if you are free of sickness and disease, if you are in good health and strong, if you live at ease. He asks further whether Gotama along with the community of monks might accept Prince Bodhi's invitation for tomorrow's meal.'

By his silence the Blessed One accepted. Understanding that he had accepted the invitation, the brahman student Sañjikāputta got up from his seat and approached Prince Bodhi.

Having approached he said to him: 'I have conveyed your message to Gotama as you asked . . . The ascetic Gotama has accepted your invitation.' 92

Then, when the night was over, Prince Bodhi had fine foods of different sorts prepared in his own home, and had the Kokanada building spread with white cloths down to the lowest step of the stairs.

Then he said to the brahman student Sañjikāputta: 'My good Sañjikāputta, go to the Blessed One, and inform him that it is time: the meal is ready.'

'Yes, sir,' replied the brahman student Sañjikāputta.

Then he approached the Blessed One, and having approached, he informed him that it was time, the meal was ready. Then, early in the morning, the Blessed One put on his outer robes and, taking his bowl, went together with the community of monks to Prince Bodhi's home. At that time the Prince was standing in the outer porch waiting for the Blessed One. When he saw him he went out to salute him respectfully, and then, letting the Blessed One walk ahead, he approached the Kokanada building.

By the lowest step the Blessed One stopped, and Prince Bodhi said to him: 'Sir, may the Blessed One step on the cloths, may the Happy One step on the cloths, in order that it will contribute to my long-lasting welfare and happiness.'

At this the Blessed One was silent.

A second time Prince Bodhi said to him: 'Sir, may the Blessed One step on the cloths . . .'

A second time the Blessed One was silent.

A third time Prince Bodhi said to him: 'Sir, may the Blessed One step on the cloths . . .'

Then the Blessed One looked towards the venerable Ānanda.

The venerable Ānanda said to the prince: 'Gather up your cloths, prince. The Blessed One will not walk on strips of cloth. The Tathāgata has regard for later generations.'*

So Prince Bodhi had the cloths gathered up and had seats prepared on the upper floor of the Kokanada building. Then the Blessed One went up into the building with the company of monks and they sat down on the appointed seats. And Prince Bodhi waited on the Blessed One and the community of monks, serving them with the fine foods with his own hands. And when the Blessed One had finished eating and washed his hands and bowl, Prince Bodhi brought a low seat and sat down to one side.

Once seated, he said to the Blessed One: 'Sir, my idea is this: happiness cannot be reached through happiness, it can only be reached through pain.'

'Prince, before my awakening, when I was not fully awakened but merely intent on awakening,* I too had the idea that happiness could not be reached through happiness, but could only be reached through
I 163 pain. So after some time, while still a young man with a head of black hair and the advantages of being in the first flush of youth, against the wishes of my mother and father, who wept, their faces covered with tears, I shaved off my hair and beard, put on ochre robes, and went forth from home into homelessness. Once I had gone forth like this in search of what is wholesome, in quest of the ultimate state of sublime peace, I approached Āḷāra Kālāma. Having approached, I said to Āḷāra: "My friend Kālāma, I wish to follow the spiritual life according to this teaching and discipline."

'At this, Āḷāra Kālāma said to me: "Let the venerable sir stay
164 here. This teaching is one in which a clever person can quite soon come to live, experiencing and attaining for himself through direct knowledge what the teacher has understood." So I quite soon, quite quickly, learnt his teaching.* As far as mere mouthing of the words, mere repeating of what had been repeated to me, I declared my knowledge and assurance;* I—like the others—claimed, "I know, I see." But then it occurred to me that Āḷāra Kālāma did not declare himself just by faith alone to live, having experienced and attained this teaching for himself through direct knowledge; certainly he must live knowing and seeing this teaching. So I approached Āḷāra Kālāma, and having approached I said to him: "Friend Kālāma, this teaching that you declare, how far have you experienced and attained it for yourself through direct knowledge?"* In response Āḷāra Kālāma declared the sphere of nothingness.*

'Then it occurred to me: "Āḷāra Kālāma is not the only one to have faith, I too have faith; he is not the only one to have energy, I too have energy; he is not the only one to have mindfulness, I too have mindfulness; he is not the only one to have concentration, I too have concentration; he is not the only one to have wisdom, I too have wisdom. Why shouldn't I apply myself to experiencing that same teaching which he declares that he lives, having experienced and attained for himself through direct knowledge?"

'So I quite soon, quite quickly, came to live, experiencing and attaining that teaching for myself through direct knowledge. Then I approached Āḷāra Kālāma, and having approached I asked him: "Friend Kālāma, this teaching that you declare, is it this far that you have experienced and attained it for yourself through direct knowledge?"

'"It is this far . . ."

'"Friend Kālāma, this far I too live experiencing and attaining this teaching for myself through direct knowledge."

'"This is a gain for us, friend, a fortunate gain for us, that we should live to see such a companion in the spiritual life. The teaching which I declare, having experienced and attained for myself through direct knowledge, is the one you live, having experienced and attained for yourself through direct knowledge. And the teaching which you 165
live having experienced and attained for yourself through direct knowledge is the one I declare, having experienced and attained for myself through direct knowledge. The teaching I know is the one you know; the teaching you know is the one I know. You are as I am, and I am as you are. Come, friend, the two of us together should look after this community now."

'So Āḷāra Kālāma, who was my teacher, placed me, his pupil, on the exact same level as him, and showed me the highest respect. But it occurred to me that that teaching did not conduce to disenchantment, nor dispassion, nor cessation, nor peace, nor direct knowledge, nor awakening, nor nibbana, but only to rebirth in the sphere of nothingness. Finding no satisfaction in that teaching, I lost my enthusiasm for it, and left.

'In search of what is wholesome, in quest of the ultimate state of sublime peace, I approached Uddaka Rāmaputta. Having approached, I said to Uddaka: "My friend, I wish to follow the spiritual life according to this teaching and discipline."

'At this, Uddaka Rāmaputta said to me: "Let the venerable sir stay here. This teaching is one in which a clever person can quite soon come to live, experiencing and attaining for himself through direct knowledge what the teacher has understood." So I quite soon, quite quickly, learnt his teaching. As far as mere mouthing of the words, mere repeating of what had been repeated to me, I declared my knowledge and assurance; I—like the others—claimed, "I know, I see." But then it occurred to me that Rāma had not declared himself just by faith alone to live, having experienced and attained this teaching for himself through direct knowledge; certainly he must have lived knowing and seeing this teaching. So I approached Uddaka Rāmaputta, and having approached I said to him: "Friend, this teaching that he declared, how far did Rāma* experience and attain for himself through direct knowledge?" In response, Uddaka Rāmaputta declared the sphere of neither consciousness nor unconsciousness.*

'Then it occurred to me: "Rāma was not the only one to have faith,
166 I too have faith; he was not the only one to have energy, I too have energy; he was not the only one to have mindfulness, I too have mindfulness; he was not the only one to have concentration, I too have concentration; he was not the only one to have wisdom, I too have wisdom. Why shouldn't I apply myself to experiencing that same teaching which he declared that he lived, having experienced and attained for himself through direct knowledge?"

'So I quite soon, quite quickly, came to live, experiencing and attaining that teaching for myself through direct knowledge. Then I approached Uddaka Rāmaputta, and having approached I asked him: "Friend, this teaching that he declared, is it this far that Rāma experienced and attained for himself through direct knowledge?"

'"It is this far . . ."

'"Friend, this far I too live, experiencing and attaining this teaching for myself through direct knowledge."

'"This is a gain for us, friend, a fortunate gain for us, that we should live to see such a companion in the spiritual life. The teaching which Rāma declared, having experienced and attained for himself through direct knowledge, is the one you live, having experienced and attained for yourself through direct knowledge. And the teaching which you live, having experienced and attained for yourself through direct knowledge, is the one he declared, having experienced and attained for himself through direct knowledge. The teaching he knew, is the one you know; the teaching you know, is the one he knew. You are as he was, and he was as you are. Come, friend, you should look after this community now."

'So Uddaka Rāmaputta, who was my companion in the spiritual life, placed me in the position of teacher, and showed me the highest respect. But it occurred to me that that teaching did not conduce to disenchantment, nor dispassion, nor cessation, nor peace, nor direct knowledge, nor awakening, nor nibbana, but only to rebirth in the sphere of neither consciousness nor unconsciousness. Finding no satisfaction in that teaching, I lost my enthusiasm for it, and left.

'In search of what is wholesome, in quest of the ultimate state of
sublime peace, I continued on my journey through Magadha until
I came to the army township of Uruvelā. There I saw a delightful 167
place, a pleasing grove of trees, a river flowing with clear water with
easy access to its banks, and all around delightful villages for seeking
alms. And it occurred to me that here was a delightful place . . . that
was exactly what a son of family intent on striving needed for that
striving. So I sat down right there with the idea that it was exactly
the place for striving. Moreover, three similes, unheard of previously, I 240
spontaneously came to mind. Suppose there were a wet, uncured piece
of wood that had been left in water and someone should come along
with a fire-drill and get the idea that he would light a fire and produce
heat. What do you think, prince? Would he, taking his fire-drill and
turning it on that wet, uncured piece of wood that had been left in
water, manage to light a fire and produce heat?'

'Definitely not, sir. And why not? Clearly because the wood was
wet and uncured and moreover had been left in water, and that per- 241
son's only reward would be weariness and frustration.'

'In exactly the same way, prince, there are some, whether ascetics or brahmans, who live without having withdrawn themselves from sense pleasures either physically or mentally. And their desire and fondness for, their infatuation with, their thirst and passion for sense pleasures—this is not properly relinquished, not properly stilled within. And if these ascetics and brahmans experience feelings of sharp, violent, severe pain as a result of their practices, they are not ready for knowing and seeing, for the highest awakening. And if they don't experience feelings of sharp, violent, severe pain as a result of their practices, they are still not ready for knowing and seeing, for the highest awakening. Prince, this was the first simile, unheard of previously, that spontaneously came to mind.

'Furthermore, this second simile, unheard of previously, spontaneously came to mind. Suppose there were a wet, uncured piece of wood that had been left on dry ground far from the water and someone should come along with a fire-drill and get the idea that he would light a fire and produce heat. What do you think, prince? Would he, taking his fire-drill and turning it on that wet, uncured piece of wood that had been left on dry ground far from the water, manage to light a fire and produce heat?'

'Definitely not, sir. And why not? Clearly because the wood was wet and uncured, even though it had been left on dry ground far from the water, and that person's only reward would be weariness and frustration.'

'In exactly the same way, prince, there are some, whether ascetics or brahmans, who live having withdrawn themselves from sense pleasures either physically or mentally. Yet their desire and fondness for, their infatuation with, their thirst and passion for sense pleasures—this is not properly relinquished, not properly stilled within. And if these ascetics and brahmans experience feelings of sharp, violent, severe pain as a result of their practices, they are not ready for knowing and seeing, for the highest awakening. And if they don't experience feelings of sharp, violent, severe pain as a result of their practices, they are still not ready for knowing and seeing, for the highest awakening. Prince, this was the second simile, unheard of previously, that spontaneously came to mind.

242 'Furthermore, this third simile, unheard of previously, spontaneously came to mind. Suppose there were a dry, hollow piece of wood that had been left on dry ground far from the water, and someone should come along with a fire-drill and get the idea that he would light a fire and produce heat. What do you think, prince? Would he, taking his fire-drill and turning it on that dry, hollow piece of wood that had been left on dry ground far from the water, manage to light a fire and produce heat?'

'Definitely, sir. And why? Clearly because the wood was dry and hollow and moreover had been left on dry ground far from the water.'

'In exactly the same way, prince, there are some, whether ascetics or brahmans, who live having withdrawn themselves from sense pleasures either physically or mentally. Moreover their desire and fondness for, their infatuation with, their thirst and passion for sense pleasures—this is properly relinquished, properly stilled within. And if these ascetics and brahmans experience feelings of sharp, violent, severe pain as a result of their practices, they are ready for knowing and seeing, for the highest awakening. And if they don't experience feelings of sharp, violent, severe pain as a result of their practices, they are still ready for knowing and seeing, for the highest awakening. Prince, this was the third simile, unheard of previously, that spontaneously came to mind.

'So then it occurred to me that I might grit my teeth and, pressing my tongue against the roof of my mouth, I might mentally hold down my mind, crush it, and overwhelm it. So I mentally held down my mind. I crushed it and overwhelmed it, gritting my teeth and pressing my tongue against the roof of my mouth, with the sweat pouring from my armpits. It was as if a strong man, grabbing a weaker man by the head or the shoulders, were to hold him down, crush him and overwhelm him . . . Yet while the energy I put into this was unremitting, and the mindfulness I established was free of
any confusion, I was overcome by the effort of this painful exertion 243
and ended up with a body that was without stillness.

'So then it occurred to me that I might practise only the absorption without breathing. So I stopped breathing in and out through my mouth and nose. Then, once I had stopped breathing through my mouth and nose, there was the terrible noise of winds coming out from my ears, like the terrible noise that comes from a smith's bellows being blown . . . Yet while the energy I put into this was unremitting, and the mindfulness I established was free of any confusion, I was overcome by the effort of this painful exertion and ended up with a body that was without stillness.

'Still it occurred to me that I might practise only the absorption without breathing. So I stopped breathing in and out through my mouth, my nose, and my ears. Then, once I had stopped breathing through my mouth, nose, and ears, I had terrible winds pushing up in my head, as if a strong man were twisting a sharp knife in my head . . . Yet while the energy I put into this was unremitting, and the mindfulness I established was free of any confusion, I was overcome by the effort of this painful exertion and ended up with a body that was without stillness.

'Still it occurred to me that I might practise only the absorption without breathing. So I stopped breathing in and out through my mouth, my nose, and my ears. Then, once I had stopped breathing through my mouth, nose, and ears, I had terrible sensations in
my head, as if a strong man were fastening a turban round my head 244
with a tough leather strap . . . Yet while the energy I put into this was

unremitting, and the mindfulness I established was free of any confusion, I was overcome by the effort of this painful exertion and ended up with a body that was without stillness.

'Still it occurred to me that I might practise only the absorption without breathing. So I stopped breathing in and out through my mouth, my nose, and my ears. Then, once I had stopped breathing through my mouth, nose, and ears, I had terrible winds cutting through my abdomen, as if a skilled butcher or his apprentice were cutting through the abdomen with a sharp butcher's knife . . . Yet while the energy I put into this was unremitting, and the mindfulness I established was free of any confusion, I was overcome by the effort of this painful exertion and ended up with a body that was without stillness.

'Still it occurred to me that I might practise only the absorption without breathing. So I stopped breathing in and out through my mouth, my nose, and my ears. Then, once I had stopped breathing through my mouth, nose, and ears, I had a terrible burning in my body, as if two strong men were to grab a weaker man by his two arms and roast him right through in a pit of hot coals . . . Yet while the energy I put into this was unremitting, and the mindfulness I established was free of any confusion, I was overcome by the effort of this painful exertion and ended up with a body that was without stillness.

245 'Moreover, when gods saw me they said: "The ascetic Gotama is dead." But some gods said: "The ascetic Gotama isn't dead, but he's dying." And some gods said: "The ascetic Gotama isn't dead, nor is he dying. He's an arahat. This is exactly the way arahats live."

'It occurred to me that I might take on the practice of cutting out food entirely. Then gods asked me not to take on the practice of cutting out food entirely. They told me that if I did they would feed me through the pores with divine nourishment, and that I would be sustained by that. Then I thought that if I claimed to be keeping a strict fast, yet gods were feeding me through the pores with divine nourishment and I was being sustained by that, then I would be lying. So I refused those gods and told them there was no need.

'So it occurred to me that I might take very little food, just a morsel at a time, whether of mung-bean soup, lentil soup, chickpea soup, or pea soup. So I took very little food, just a morsel at a time

of mung-bean, lentil, chickpea, or pea soup. And when I did this my body became extremely emaciated: my limbs became like the jointed stems of creepers or bamboo because of eating so little; my backside became like a buffalo's hoof; my backbone, bent or straight, became like corded beads; my ribs jutted and stuck out like the jutting and broken rafters of an old house; the pupils of my eyes when glimpsed sunk deep in their sockets were like the glint of water seen deep down at the bottom of a deep well; my scalp became withered and
shrivelled like a fresh bitter gourd that has been withered and 246
shrivelled by the wind and sun. When I wanted to touch the skin of my belly I felt my backbone, and when I wanted to touch my backbone I felt the skin of my belly; in fact the skin of my belly stuck to my backbone because of eating so little. When I wanted to urinate or defecate I fell over right there on my face because of eating so little. I stroked my limbs with my hand in order to soothe my body, but because of eating so little, as I rubbed my limbs with my hand, the hairs, whose roots had grown rotten, dropped from my body. Moreover, when non-human beings saw me they said: "The ascetic Gotama is black." But some non-human beings said: "The ascetic Gotama isn't black, he's brown." And some non-human beings said: "The ascetic Gotama isn't black, nor is he brown. His skin is sallow." So much had my skin lost its clear complexion because of eating so little.

'And it occurred to me that whoever in the past were ascetics or brahmans who experienced feelings of sharp, violent, severe, pain as a result of their practices, it was not beyond this extreme. Whoever in the future will be ascetics or brahmans who will experience feelings of sharp, violent, severe pain as a result of their practices, it will not be beyond this extreme. Whoever in the present are ascetics or brahmans who experience feelings of sharp, violent, severe pain as a result of their practices in the present, it is not beyond this extreme. And yet by means of this severe, harsh practice* I had achieved no special knowledge and insight beyond the capacity of human beings and worthy of the noble ones: might there in fact be another path to awakening? Then it occurred to me that I remembered that when I was sitting in the cool shade of a rose apple tree while my Sakyan father was engaged in work, I had spent time having attained the joy and happiness of the first absorption, which is accompanied by thinking and examining, and is born of seclusion: might this in fact

be the path to awakening? Then immediately following that memory I became aware that this was indeed the path to awakening. I asked
247 myself why I feared this happiness, which was a happiness that had nothing to do with sense pleasures, nothing to do with unwholesome qualities. Then I decided that I would not fear this happiness, which was a happiness that had nothing to do with sense pleasures, nothing to do with unwholesome qualities.

'It occurred to me that it would not be easy to achieve this happiness with a body that had become so extremely emaciated, so I thought I should take some solid food, some rice gruel. Then I took solid food, some rice gruel. Now at that time there were five monks with me, who thought: "The ascetic Gotama* will inform us of any Truth he achieves." But after I had taken some solid food, some rice gruel, those five monks lost their enthusiasm for me and left, thinking: "The ascetic Gotama is one for excess. He has given up the struggle and reverted to a life of excess."

'Once I had taken solid food and regained my strength, I lived completely secluded from sense desires and unwholesome qualities of mind, having attained the joy and happiness of the first absorption, which is accompanied by thinking and examining, and born of seclusion. Then, by stilling thinking and examining, I lived having attained the joy and happiness of the second absorption, a state of inner clarity and mental unification without thinking and examining, and born of concentration. By having no desire for joy, I lived equanimously, mindful and fully aware; I experienced the bodily happiness of which the noble ones speak, saying "equanimous and mindful, one lives happily", and so I lived, having attained the third absorption. By letting go of happiness and unhappiness, as a result of the earlier disappearance of pleasure and pain, I lived having attained the pure equanimity and mindfulness of the fourth absorption, which is free of happiness and unhappiness.

'Once my mind was concentrated in this way, once it was thoroughly purified and cleansed—stainless, without defilements, having become sensitive, workable, and steady, reaching a state that
248 is unshakeable—I applied and directed my mind towards the knowledge of recollection of previous lives. I remembered my numerous previous lives: one birth, two births, three, four, five births; ten, twenty, thirty, forty, fifty births; a hundred, a thousand, a hundred thousand births; over many periods of expansion of the universe,

over many periods of contraction, over many periods of expansion and contraction. I remembered, "In that life I had that name, belonged to that family, that class, had that food, experienced that unhappiness, that happiness, and met my end in that way. When I died there I was born in that place. There I had that name, belonged to that family, that class, had that food, experienced that unhappiness, that happiness, and met my end in that way. When I died there I was born here." In this way I remembered the various circumstances and details of my many previous lives. Prince, this was the first knowledge I achieved in the first watch of the night: ignorance was dispelled, knowledge arose, darkness was dispelled, light arose, as I lived attentive, determined, applying myself to this.

'Once my mind was concentrated in this way, once it was thoroughly purified and cleansed—stainless, without defilements, having become sensitive, workable, and steady, reaching a state that is unshakeable—I applied and directed my mind towards the knowledge of the death and birth of beings. With the godlike vision that is purified, surpassing that of men, I saw beings dying and being born. I understood how beings are inferior or superior, fair or ugly, fortunate or unfortunate, according to their actions: "These beings behaved badly in body, badly in speech, badly in thought; disparaging the noble ones, they held wrong views and performed the sorts of action that follow from wrong view. At the breaking up of the body after death they were born in hell, a realm of loss, misfortune, and torment. These beings, on the other hand, behaved well in body, well in speech, well in thought; not disparaging the noble ones, they held right views and performed the sorts of action that follow from right view. At the breaking up of the body after death they were born in a happy heaven world." In this way, with the godlike vision that is purified, surpassing that of men, I saw beings dying and being born. I understood how beings are inferior or superior, fair or ugly, fortunate or unfortunate, according to their actions. Prince, this was the second knowledge I achieved in the second watch of the
night: ignorance was dispelled, knowledge arose, darkness was dis- 249
pelled, light arose, as I lived attentive, determined, applying myself to this.

'Once my mind was concentrated in this way, once it was thoroughly purified and cleansed—stainless, without defilements, having become sensitive, workable, and steady, reaching a state that is

unshakeable—I applied and directed my mind towards the knowledge of the destruction of taints. I truly knew what suffering is, I truly knew what the arising of suffering is, I truly knew what the cessation of suffering is, I truly knew what the practice leading to the cessation of suffering is. I truly knew what taints are, I truly knew what the arising of taints is, I truly knew what the cessation of taints is, I truly knew what the practice leading to the cessation of taints is. In the course of knowing this and seeing this, my mind was freed from the taint of sense desire, my mind was freed from the taint of being, my mind was freed from the taint of ignorance. And when it was freed, there was knowledge that it was freed: I understood, "Birth is destroyed. The spiritual life has been lived. Done is what should be done. There is nothing further required to this end." Prince, this was the third knowledge I achieved in the third watch of the night: ignorance was dispelled, knowledge arose, darkness was dispelled, light arose, as I
I 167 lived attentive, determined, applying myself to this.

'Then it occurred to me that the Truth I had found was profound, hard to see, hard to understand; it was peaceful, sublime, beyond the sphere of mere reasoning, subtle, to be experienced by the wise. But this generation takes delight in belongings, is delighted by belongings, enjoys belongings. And because it takes delight in belongings, is delighted by belongings, enjoys belongings it is hard for this generation to see the possibility of things having specific causes and arising in dependence on things; it is hard for this generation to see the possibility of stilling all volitional forces, of relinquishing all attachments,
168 of destroying craving, of dispassion, cessation, nibbana. If I were to teach the Truth, others would not understand me, and that would be distressing and hurtful for me. Moreover these verses, unheard of previously, spontaneously came to mind:

> With difficulty I have made this discovery, there is no need
> now to explain it;
> Those overwhelmed by greed and hatred will not easily wake
> up to this Truth.
> Going against the stream, subtle, profound, hard to see, fine—
> Those impassioned by greed, enveloped in a thick darkness,
> will not see it.

So, Prince, as I reflected in this way my mind inclined to the least discomfort, not to teaching the Truth.

'Then, Prince, when Brahmā, Lord of the Earth, understood in his mind what I was thinking, he thought, "The world is lost! The world is finished! For here is the Tathāgata, an arahat, perfectly awakened, and his mind inclines to the least discomfort, not to teaching the Truth." Then, just as a strong man might straighten his bent arm or bend his straightened arm, Brahmā, Lord of the Earth, disappeared from the world of Brahmā and appeared in front of me. Having arranged his robe over one shoulder, he bowed to me with cupped hands and said: "Sir, let the Blessed One teach the Truth!* Let the Happy One teach the Truth! There are beings with little dust in their eyes who will be lost if they do not hear the Truth. They will understand the Truth."

'This is what Brahmā, Lord of the Earth, said. And then he spoke further:

' "There appeared in Magadha previously a Truth that was impure, conceived by those who are tarnished.
Open the door to the deathless! Let them hear the Truth that the one who is untarnished has awakened to.

Like standing on a rock on a mountain peak and seeing the people all around,
The palace made of Truth is so, wise one. Ascend it, all seeing one.
People are immersed in grief—let he who has left grief behind observe them, overcome by birth and death. 169

Rise up, a hero, the victor in battle, leader of the caravan, owing nothing, wanderer in the world!
Let the Blessed One teach the Truth, there will be those who understand."

'Aware of Brahmā's request, and out of compassion for beings, I surveyed the world with the vision of one awakened. As I surveyed the world I saw beings with little dust in their eyes and with much dust in their eyes, with keen faculties and with dull faculties, of good habits and of bad habits, easy to teach and difficult to teach, some who lived seeing the danger in wrongdoing for the next world, some who lived without seeing the danger in wrongdoing for the next world. As where there is a clump of blue lotuses, red lotuses, or white lotuses, some of those blue, red, or white lotuses sprout in the water, grow in the water, and do not rise out of the water but thrive while still immersed in it; some of those blue, red, or white lotuses sprout in the water, grow in the water, and do not rise out of the water but remain level with the surface of the water; some of those blue, red, or white lotuses sprout in the water, grow in the water, and then rise out of the water and remain untouched by any water. In exactly the same way, when I surveyed the world I saw beings with little dust in their eyes and with much dust in their eyes . . . Then I responded to Brahmā, Lord of the Earth, with a verse:

> '"The doors to the deathless are open! Let those who will listen take heart!
> Brahmā, thinking of the hurt, I did not utter the excellent and subtle Truth among men."

'Then Brahmā, Lord of the Earth, knowing that he had created the circumstances for the Blessed One to teach the Truth, saluted me respectfully and, keeping me to his right, he disappeared right there.

'Then I considered to whom I should first teach the Truth, who
would quickly understand this Truth. Then I thought of Āḷāra the
Kālāma: he was wise, clever, learned, someone who had long had
170 little dust in his eyes. Suppose I were to teach him the Truth first.
He would quickly understand this Truth. Then gods approached
and told me that Āḷāra the Kālāma had died seven days ago. And
then the knowledge, the vision came to me: Āḷāra the Kālāma had
died seven days ago. I thought: "Great is Āḷāra the Kālāma's loss: if
he had heard this Truth, he would have quickly understood it."

'So again I considered to whom I should first teach the Truth, who would quickly understand this Truth. Then I thought of Uddaka Rāmaputta: he was wise, clever, learned, someone who had long had little dust in his eyes. Suppose I were to teach him the Truth first. He would quickly understand this Truth. Then gods approached and told me that Uddaka Rāmaputta had died the previous night. And then the knowledge, the vision came to me: Uddaka Rāmaputta had died the previous night. I thought: "Great is Uddaka Rāmaputta's loss: if he had heard this Truth, he would have quickly understood it."

'So again I considered to whom I should first teach the Truth, who would quickly understand this Truth. Then I thought of the group of five monks: they had been very helpful to me when they were with me while I applied myself to the struggle. Suppose I were to teach the group of five monks the Truth first. Then I considered where the group of five monks might now be living. With the godlike vision that is purified, surpassing that of men, I saw the group of five monks were now living in Benares, in the animal park at Isipatana. So, having stayed at Uruvelā as long as I wanted, I set out to walk to Benares.

'On the road between the place of awakening and Gayā, Upaka, an Ājīvika,* saw me. When he saw me he said: "How serene your senses are, friend! How pure and clear the colour of your skin! Friend, under whom have you gone forth? Who is your teacher? Whose
Truth do you follow?" When he had said this, I responded with these 171
verses:

'"I have overcome all, I know all.
Where there are all qualities, I am unmarked.
Letting go of all, in the destruction of craving I am freed.
When I have direct knowledge by myself, to whom should I
refer?
I have no teacher, none like me is found
In the world with its gods, no person is my equal.
I am the one who is worthy, I am the incomparable teacher in the
world;
I alone am perfectly awakened, cooled, satisfied.
To turn the wheel of Truth, I go to the city of Kāsi.
In this world that is blind I will beat the drum for the deathless!"

'"According to your claim, friend, you must be conqueror* of the infinite."

'"Like me, indeed, the conquerors are those who have achieved
the destruction of taints.
I have conquered bad qualities, therefore, Upaka, I am a
conqueror!"

'At this, Upaka the Ājīvika said: "Maybe, friend. Maybe." Then, shaking his head, he left, taking some other path.*

'Then I made my way in stages to the animal park at Isipatana in Benares, where I approached the group of five monks. They saw me coming in the distance, and when they saw me they agreed with one another: "Here is the ascetic Gotama coming. He is one for excess; he gave up the struggle and reverted to a life of excess. We will not salute him respectfully, we will not get up for him, we will not take his bowl and robe. But we will allow him a seat: if he wants to, he can sit down."

'Yet as I came nearer that group of five monks was unable to stick to their agreement: several came forward to meet me, several showed me to a seat, several set out water for my feet. However, they did address me by name and the title "friend". At this I told the group of five monks: "Monks, do not address one who is like this (*tathāgata*) by name and the title friend. The one who is like this is an arahat,
172 perfectly awakened. Listen! The deathless is achieved. I will give instruction, I will teach the Truth. If you practise as instructed then soon you will come to live, having experienced and attained here and now for yourselves through direct knowledge the ultimate goal of the spiritual life, for the sake of which the sons of families quite rightly go forth from home into homelessness."

'At this the group of five monks replied: "Friend Gotama, by means of your conduct, by means of your practice, by means of your severe, harsh practice you achieved no special knowledge and insight beyond the capacity of human beings and worthy of the noble ones. And now you are one for excess, who has given up the struggle and reverted to a life of excess, so how will you achieve special knowledge and insight beyond the capacity of human beings and worthy of the noble ones?"

'When they had said this, I said to that group of five monks: "Monks, the Tathāgata is not one for excess, he has not given up the struggle and reverted to a life of excess. The Tathāgata is an arahat, perfectly awakened. Listen! The deathless is achieved. I will give instruction, I will teach the Truth. If you practise as instructed then soon you will come to live, having experienced and attained here and now for yourselves through direct knowledge the ultimate goal of the spiritual life for the sake of which the sons of families quite rightly go forth from home into homelessness."

'Then for a second time the group of five monks replied: "Friend Gotama, by means of your . . . severe, harsh practice you achieved no special knowledge and insight . . . And now you are one for excess, who has given up the struggle and reverted to a life of excess, so how will you achieve special knowledge and insight beyond the capacity of human beings and worthy of the noble ones?"

'Then for a second time I said to that group of five monks: "Monks, the Tathāgata is not one for excess . . . I will give instruction, I will teach the Truth. If you practise as instructed then soon you will come to live, having experienced and attained here and now for yourselves through direct knowledge the ultimate goal of the spiritual life for the sake of which the sons of families quite rightly go forth from home into homelessness."

'Then for a third time the group of five monks replied: "Friend Gotama, by means of your . . . severe, harsh practice you achieved no special knowledge and insight . . . And now you are one for excess who has given up the struggle and reverted to a life of excess, so how will you achieve special knowledge and insight beyond the capacity of human beings and worthy of the noble ones?"

'At this I said to that group of five monks: "Monks, do you recall my having announced something like this before now?"

' "Indeed not, sir."*

' "Monks, the Tathāgata is not one for excess . . . I will give instruction, I will teach the Truth. If you practise as instructed then soon you will come to live, having experienced and attained for yourselves through direct knowledge the ultimate goal of the spiritual life for the sake of which the sons of families quite rightly go forth from home into homelessness." 173

'Prince, I was able to convince that group of five monks. I would advise two monks while the other three went to get alms, and the six of us managed on what the three brought back. I would advise three monks while the other two went to get alms, and the six of us managed on what the two brought back. In this way that group of five II 94
monks was advised and instructed by me, and quite soon they lived, having experienced and attained here and now for themselves through direct knowledge the ultimate goal of the spiritual life for the sake of which the sons of families quite rightly go forth from home into homelessness.'

At this Prince Bodhi asked: 'Sir, when a monk has a Tathāgata to direct him, how soon could he come to live, having experienced and attained here and now for himself through direct knowledge the ultimate goal of the spiritual life for the sake of which the sons of families quite rightly go forth from home into homelessness?'

'Then, prince, I shall ask you a related question in return. You should answer it as seems appropriate to you. What do you think, prince? Are you skilled in the art of handling a goad for elephant riding?'

'Certainly, sir. I am skilled in this art.'

'What do you think, prince? A man might come along here with the idea that Prince Bodhi understands the art of handling a goad for elephant riding and that he could learn this art from you. If he lacked faith, then he would not achieve as much as can be achieved by one who has faith. If he was often sick, then he would not achieve as much as can be achieved by one who is seldom sick. If he was dishonest and cunning, then he would not achieve as much as can be achieved by one who is honest and straight. If he was lazy, then he would not achieve as much as can be achieved by one who puts in effort. If he was dim-witted, then he would not achieve as much as can be achieved by one who is clever. What do you think, prince? Could this man learn the art of handling a goad for elephant riding from you?'

'Sir, a man who had any one such quality could not learn the art of handling a goad for elephant riding from me, never mind someone with all five.'

95 'What do you think, prince? A man might come along here with the idea that Prince Bodhi understands the art of handling a goad for elephant riding and that he could learn this art from you. If he had faith, then he would achieve as much as can be achieved by one who has faith. If he was seldom sick, then he would achieve as much as can be achieved by one who is seldom sick. If he was honest and straight, then he would achieve as much as can be achieved by one who is honest and straight. If he put in effort, then he would achieve as much as can be achieved by one who puts in effort. If he was clever, then he would achieve as much as can be achieved by one who is clever. What do you think, prince? Could this man learn the art of handling a goad for elephant riding from you?'

'Sir, a man who had any one such quality could learn the art of handling a goad for elephant riding from me, never mind someone with all five.'

'In exactly the same way, prince, there are these five qualities associated with striving. Which five? A monk has faith, he gains faith in the awakening of the Tathāgata, that for the following reasons he is the Blessed One: he is an arahat, a perfect buddha, accomplished in knowledge and conduct, happy, one who understands the world, an unsurpassed charioteer of men to be tamed, teacher of gods and men, a blessed buddha. He is seldom sick, seldom ill: he has stable digestion, neither too cold nor too hot, balanced and suited to striving. He is honest and straight: he is open about himself both with the teacher and with his experienced companions in the spiritual life. He lives putting in effort: he is firm, forceful in his endeavour to abandon unwholesome qualities and arouse wholesome qualities; he is not one to drop the task when it comes to wholesome qualities. He has wisdom: he possesses the wisdom that understands the rise and fall of things, that is noble, penetrating, leads to the proper destruction of suffering.

'Prince, a monk with these five qualities associated with striving who had a Tathāgata to direct him could in seven years come to live, having experienced and attained here and now for himself through direct knowledge the ultimate goal of the spiritual life for the sake of which the sons of families quite rightly go forth from home into homelessness. Let alone seven years, a monk with these five qual- 96
ities . . . could in six years come to live, having experienced and attained here and now for himself through direct knowledge the ultimate goal of the spiritual life . . . Let alone six years, a monk with these five qualities . . . could in five years. . . in four years . . . in three years . . . in two years . . . in one year . . . Let alone one year, a monk with these five qualities . . . could in seven months come to live, having experienced and attained here and now for himself through direct knowledge the ultimate goal of the spiritual life . . . Let alone seven months, a monk with these five qualities . . . could in six months. . . in five months . . . in four months . . . in three months . . . in two months . . . in one month . . . in a fortnight . . . Let alone a fortnight, a monk with these five qualities . . . could in seven days and nights come to live, having experienced and attained here and now for himself through direct knowledge the ultimate goal of the spiritual life . . . Let alone seven days and nights, a monk with these five qualities . . . could in six days and nights . . . in five days and nights . . . in four days and nights . . . in three days and nights . . . in two days and nights . . . in one day and night come to live, having experienced and attained here and now for himself through direct knowledge the ultimate goal of the spiritual life . . . Let alone one day and night, a monk with these five qualities who had a Tathāgata to direct him will when instructed in the evening attain distinction in the morning, and when instructed in the morning attain distinction in the evening.'

At this, Prince Bodhi said to the Blessed One: 'The Buddha! The Teaching! How the Teaching has been well proclaimed when someone instructed in the evening will attain distinction in the morning, and when someone instructed in the morning will attain distinction in the evening!'

When he said this, the brahman student Sañjikāputta said to Prince Bodhi: 'The honourable Bodhi announces: "The Buddha! The Teaching! How the Teaching has been well proclaimed . . .", but not that he goes to the honourable Gotama and to the Community of monks for refuge.'

'Do not speak so, good Sañjikāputta. Do not speak so. I have heard this directly from my mother, I have learnt this directly from her.
97 Once the Blessed One was staying at the Ghosita park in Kosambī. Then my mother, who was pregnant, approached the Blessed One. Having approached, she saluted him respectfully and sat down to one side.

Once seated, she said to the Blessed One: "Sir, whether it is a prince or princess in my womb, the child goes to the Blessed One for refuge, and to the Teaching and the Community of monks. Let the Blessed One accept the child as a lay follower who has taken refuge from this day for as long as it lives." Once the Blessed One was staying right here in the Bhagga country at Suṃsumāragira, in the Bhesakaḷā grove in the animal park. Then my nurse, who was carrying me on her hip, approached the Blessed One. Having approached, she saluted him respectfully and stood to one side. Standing there, she said to the Blessed One: "Sir, the Prince Bodhi goes to the Blessed One for refuge, and to the Teaching and the Community of monks. Let the Blessed One accept him as a lay follower who has taken refuge from this day for as long as he lives." So, good Sañjikāputta, for a third time I go to the Blessed One for refuge, and to the Teaching and the Community of monks. Let the Blessed One accept me as a lay follower who has taken refuge from this day for as long as I live.'

THE ANALYSIS OF ACTS

MAHĀ-KAMMAVIBHAṄGA-SUTTA (M III 207–215)

Introduction

This sutta, the 'great' (*mahā*) dialogue on the analysis of acts, forms a pair with the sutta that immediately precedes it in the Majjhima-nikāya, the 'small' (*cūḷa*) dialogue on the analysis of acts (*Cūḷa-Kammavibhaṅga-sutta*),[1] which is not included in the present volume. The subject of both suttas is actions and their results, that is, what is generally referred to in Indian thought as 'karma'. According to the general Indian theory our actions (*kamma/karman*) bear fruit both in this life and, most significantly, in subsequent lives: bad actions bear pleasant fruit and good actions unpleasant. The beginnings of a theory of karma are found in the Vedic texts such as the Upaniṣads. Subsequent Indian thought develops the theory in various ways. The different traditions—Jain, Buddhist, Hindu—all have distinctive notions of precisely what constitutes a good or bad action and of the manner in which actions yield their karmic results.

The Buddhist understanding is that it is intentional actions that are significant—actions motivated either by greed, hatred, and delusion or by non-attachment, friendliness, and wisdom. In the *Cūḷa-Kammavibhaṅga-sutta* the Buddha gives a straightforward explanation of how bad actions result in rebirth in unfortunate and unpleasant circumstances. In the *Mahā-Kammavibhaṅga-sutta* he explains that in practice things are not quite as simple as this: in short, the acts do not always bear their fruits in strict order, and a person's state of mind at the time of death is also significant in determining rebirth. Thus, it is possible that someone who commits bad actions in one life may be reborn in the immediately following life in pleasant circumstances, and vice versa.

The sutta anticipates ideas that are developed and articulated in considerable technical detail in later Buddhist systematic thought; see R. Gethin, '*Bhavaṅga* and Rebirth According to the Abhidhamma', in Tadeusz Skorupski and Ulrich Pagel (eds.), *The Buddhist Forum*, vol. 3 (London: School of Oriental and African Studies, 1994), 11–35. For the notion of karma more generally in Indian thought see W. Doniger (ed.), *Karma and Rebirth in Classical Indian Traditions* (Berkeley, 1980).

---

[1] M III 202–6.

This is what I have heard. Once the Blessed One was staying at Rājagaha, in the Squirrels' Feeding Ground in the Bamboo Grove.* At that time the venerable Samiddhi was living in a forest hut. Now the wanderer Potaliputta, who was on the move, walking and roaming about, approached the venerable Samiddhi. Having approached, he saluted him respectfully, exchanging pleasing and polite words with him before sitting down to one side.

Once seated, he said to the venerable Samiddhi: 'I have heard this directly from the ascetic Gotama, I have learnt this directly from him: acts of the body are futile, acts of speech are futile, acts of the mind are alone real. And also that there is an attainment in which a person who attains it experiences nothing!'

'Don't speak in this way, friend Potaliputta! Don't speak in this way! Don't misrepresent the Blessed One. It is not good to misrepresent the Blessed One. Certainly he wouldn't say that acts of the body and speech are futile, and that acts of the mind are alone real. And in fact there is an attainment in which a person who attains it experiences nothing.'

'How long is it since you went forth, friend Samiddhi?'

'Not long. Three years.'

'Now why should we speak to the senior monks when a junior monk thinks his teacher can be defended in this way? Samiddhi, when one performs an act intentionally by body, speech, or mind, what does one experience?'

'When one performs an act intentionally by body, speech, or mind, one experiences pain.'

Thereupon the wanderer Potaliputta neither agreed nor disagreed with the venerable Samiddhi's words, but simply got up from his seat and went away. Not long after Potaliputta had left, the venerable
208 Samiddhi approached the venerable Ānanda. Having approached, he saluted him respectfully, exchanging pleasing and polite words with him before sitting down to one side. Once seated, the venerable Samiddhi told the venerable Ānanda in full of the discussion he had had with the wanderer Potaliputta.

When he had finished, the venerable Ānanda said: 'Friend Samiddhi, the subject raised in your conversation is a reason for visiting the Blessed One. Come, friend Samiddhi, let us approach the Blessed One. Having approached him, we should tell him about this, and then we can remember how he explains the matter.'

'Yes, friend,' replied the venerable Samiddhi to the venerable Ānanda.'

Then the venerable Samiddhi and the venerable Ānanda approached the Blessed One. Having approached, they sat down to one side. Once seated, the venerable Ānanda told the Blessed One in full of the discussion the venerable Samiddhi had had with the wanderer Potaliputta.

When Ānanda had finished, the Blessed One said: 'Certainly I do not remember meeting the wanderer Potaliputta, so how could such a conversation between us have taken place? But this confused person Samiddhi has responded to the wanderer Potaliputta's question categorically when it should have been answered after analysis.'

At this, the venerable Udāyin said to the Blessed One: 'But perhaps the venerable Samiddhi said what he did with reference to the fact that whatever is experienced counts as pain.'

'See, Ānanda, how this confused person Udāyin has jumped to a conclusion! I knew just now that he was trying to come up with something and that he would come up with the wrong idea! From the start the wanderer Potaliputta was asking about the three feelings. If this confused Samiddhi had explained to the wanderer Potaliputta 209
as follows when he had been asked this question—that when one performs an act intentionally by body, speech, or mind that is to be experienced as pleasure, one experiences pleasure; when one performs an act intentionally by body, speech, or mind that is to be experienced as pain, one experiences pain; when one performs an act intentionally by body, speech, or mind that is to be experienced as neither pleasure nor pain, one experiences neither pleasure nor pain—then this confused Samiddhi would have explained the matter correctly. And yet which of these childish and foolish followers of another school would understand the Tathāgata's full analysis of action? But what if you, Ānanda, were to listen to the Tathāgata as he sets out the full analysis of action?'

'It is the time for this, Blessed One. It is the time for this, Happy One—time for the Blessed One to set out the full analysis of action. What the monks hear from the Blessed One they will remember.'

'Then listen, Ānanda. Pay careful attention to what I shall say.'

'Yes, sir,' replied Ānanda to the Blessed One.

This is what the Blessed One said: 'These four kinds of person are found in the world. Which four? Here in this life, some person harms living creatures, takes what is not given, behaves improperly sexually, says what is untrue, talks maliciously and unkindly, chatters idly, is greedy, hateful, and has mistaken views. At the breaking up of the body, after death, he is reborn in a state of misfortune, an unhappy destiny, a state of affliction, hell.

'Another person harms living creatures, takes what is not given, behaves improperly sexually, says what is untrue, talks maliciously and unkindly, chatters idly, is greedy, hateful, and has mistaken views. At the breaking up of the body, after death, he is reborn in a happy destiny, a heaven world.

'Another person refrains from harming living creatures, taking
what is not given, behaving improperly sexually, saying what is
210 untrue, talking maliciously and unkindly, chattering idly; is not
greedy, nor hateful, and has right views. At the breaking up of the
body, after death, he is reborn in a happy destiny, a heaven world.

'Another person refrains from harming living creatures, taking what is not given, behaving improperly sexually, saying what is untrue, talking maliciously and unkindly, chattering idly; is not greedy, nor hateful, and has right views. At the breaking up of the body, after death, he is reborn in a state of misfortune, an unhappy destiny, a state of affliction, hell.

'Then some ascetic or brahman, as a consequence of his energy, application, practice, and attentiveness; as a consequence of properly directing his attention, reaches that state of concentration where, with his mind concentrated, he sees with the godlike vision, purified and surpassing that of men, some person who here in this life harmed living creatures, took what is not given, behaved improperly sexually, spoke what is untrue, talked maliciously and unkindly, chattered idly, was greedy, hateful, and had mistaken views; and he sees that at the breaking up of the body, after death, that person has been reborn in a state of misfortune, an unhappy destiny, a state of affliction, hell. And that ascetic or brahman speaks as follows: "Bad actions certainly do exist. Bad conduct has its result. Indeed, I have seen that person who here in this life harmed living creatures, took what is not given, behaved improperly sexually, spoke what is untrue, talked maliciously . . . and had mistaken views; and I have seen that at the breaking up of the body, after death, that person was reborn in a state of misfortune, an unhappy destiny, a state of affliction, hell." He speaks as follows: "Everyone who here in this life harms living creatures, takes what is not given . . . and has mistaken views, at the breaking up of the body, after death, will be reborn in a state of misfortune, an unhappy destiny, a state of affliction, hell. Those whose understanding is like this understand correctly; those whose understanding is different have a mistaken understanding." In this way he obstinately holds to and insists on just what he has known, seen, and experienced himself, claiming that this alone is the truth, the rest is useless.

'But some other ascetic or brahman, as a consequence of his 211
energy, application, practice, and attentiveness; as a consequence of properly directing his attention, reaches that state of concentration where, with his mind concentrated, he sees with the godlike vision, purified and surpassing that of men, some person who here in this life harmed living creatures, took what is not given . . . and had mistaken views; and he sees that at the breaking up of the body, after death, that person has been reborn in a happy destiny, a heaven world. And that ascetic or brahman speaks as follows: "Bad actions certainly do *not* exist. Bad conduct has *no* result. Indeed, I have seen that person who here in this life harmed living creatures, took what is not given . . . and had mistaken views; and I have seen that at the breaking up of the body, after death, that person was reborn in a happy destiny, a heaven world." He speaks as follows: "Everyone who here in this life harms living creatures, takes what is not given . . . and has mistaken views, at the breaking up of the body, after death, will be reborn in a happy destiny, a heaven world. Those whose understanding is like this understand correctly; those whose understanding is different have a mistaken understanding." In this way he obstinately holds to and insists on just what he has known, seen, and experienced himself, claiming that this alone is the truth, the rest is useless.

'Yet another ascetic or brahman, as a consequence of his energy, application, practice, and attentiveness; as a consequence of properly directing his attention, reaches that state of concentration where, with his mind concentrated, he sees with the godlike vision, purified and surpassing that of men, some person who here in this life refrained from harming living creatures, taking what is not given, behaving improperly sexually, speaking what is untrue, talking maliciously and unkindly, chattering idly; who was not greedy, not hateful, and who had right views; and he sees that at the breaking up of the body, after death, that person has been reborn in a happy destiny, a heaven world. And that ascetic or brahman speaks as follows: "Beautiful actions certainly do exist. Good conduct has its result. Indeed, I have seen that person who here in this life refrained from harming living creatures, taking what is not given . . . and who had right views; and I have seen that at the breaking up of the body, after death, that person was reborn in a happy destiny, a heaven world." He speaks as follows: "Everyone who here in this life refrains from harming living creatures, taking what is not given . . . and has right views, at the breaking up of the body, after death, will be reborn in a happy destiny, a heaven world. Those whose understanding is like this understand correctly; those whose understanding is different have a mistaken understanding." In this way he obstinately holds to and insists on just what he has known, seen, and experienced himself, claiming that this alone is the truth, the rest is useless.

'Yet another ascetic or brahman, as a consequence of his energy, application, practice, and attentiveness; as a consequence of properly directing his attention, reaches that state of concentration where, with
212 his mind concentrated, he sees with the godlike vision, purified and surpassing that of men, some person who here in this life refrained from harming living creatures, taking what is not given, behaving improperly sexually, speaking what is untrue, talking maliciously and unkindly, chattering idly; who was not greedy, not hateful, and who had right views; and he sees that at the breaking up of the body, after death, that person has been reborn in a state of misfortune, an unhappy destiny, a state of affliction, hell. And that ascetic or brahman speaks as follows: "Beautiful actions certainly do *not* exist. Good conduct has *no* result. Indeed, I have seen that person who here in this life refrained from harming living creatures, taking what is not given . . . and who had right views; and I have seen that at the breaking up of the body, after death, that person was reborn in a state of misfortune, an unhappy destiny, a state of affliction, hell." He speaks as follows: "Everyone who here in this life refrains from harming living creatures, taking what is not given . . . and has right views, at the breaking up of the body, after death, will be reborn in a state of misfortune, an unhappy destiny, a state of affliction, hell. Those whose understanding is like this understand correctly; those whose understanding is different have a mistaken understanding." In this way he obstinately holds to and insists on just what he has known, seen, and experienced himself, claiming that this alone is the truth, the rest is useless.

'With regard to this, Ānanda, when an ascetic or brahman says that bad actions certainly exist, that bad conduct has its result, I go along with him in this. When he also says that, indeed, he has seen some person who here in this life harmed living creatures, took what is not given . . . and had mistaken views; and he has seen that at the breaking up of the body, after death, that person was reborn in a state of misfortune, an unhappy destiny, a state of affliction, hell, again I go along with him in this. But when he says that everyone who here in this life harms living creatures, takes what is not given . . . and has mistaken views, at the breaking up of the body, after death, will be reborn in a state of misfortune, an unhappy destiny, a state of affliction, hell, I do *not* go along with him in this. And when he also says that those whose understanding is like this understand correctly, while those whose understanding is different have a mistaken understanding, again I do *not* go along with him in this. And when he also obstinately holds to and insists on just what he has known, seen, and experienced himself, claiming that this alone is the truth, the rest useless, again I do *not* go along with him in this. Why is this? Because, Ānanda, the Tathāgata's understanding of the full analysis of actions is otherwise.

'With regard to this, Ānanda, when an ascetic or brahman says that bad actions certainly do not exist, that bad conduct has no result, I do *not* go along with him in this. But when he says that, indeed, he has seen some person who here in this life harmed living creatures, took what is not given . . . and had mistaken views; and he has seen that at the breaking up of the body, after death, that person was reborn in a happy destiny, a heaven world, I *do* go along with him in this. But when he says that everyone who here in this life harms living creatures, takes what is not given . . . and has mistaken views, at the breaking up of the body, after death, will be reborn in a happy destiny, a heaven world, I do *not* go along with him in this. And when 213
he also says that those whose understanding is like this understand correctly, while those whose understanding is different have a mistaken understanding, again I do *not* go along with him in this. And when he also obstinately holds to and insists on just what he has known, seen, and experienced himself, claiming that this alone is the truth, the rest useless, again I do *not* go along with him in this. Why is this? Because, Ānanda, the Tathāgata's understanding of the full analysis of actions is otherwise.

'With regard to this, Ānanda, when an ascetic or brahman says that beautiful actions certainly exist, that good conduct has its result, I go along with him in this. And when he also says that, indeed, he has seen some person who here in this life refrained from harming living creatures, taking what is not given . . . and had right views; and he has seen that at the breaking up of the body, after death, that person was reborn in a happy destiny, a heaven world, again I go along with him in this. But when he says that everyone who here in this life refrains from harming living creatures, taking what is not given . . . and has right views, at the breaking up of the body, after death, will be reborn in a happy destiny, a heaven world, I do *not* go along with him in this. And when he also says that those whose understanding is like this understand correctly, while those whose understanding is different have a mistaken understanding, again I do *not* go along with him in this. And when he also obstinately holds to and insists on just what he has known, seen, and experienced himself, claiming that this alone is the truth, the rest useless, again I do *not* go along with him in this. Why is this? Because, Ānanda, the Tathāgata's understanding of the full analysis of actions is otherwise.

'With regard to this, Ānanda, when an ascetic or brahman says that beautiful actions certainly do not exist, that good conduct has no result, I do *not* go along with him in this. But when he says that, indeed, he has seen some person who here in this life refrained from harming living creatures, taking what is not given . . . and had right views; and he has seen that at the breaking up of the body, after death, that person was reborn in a state of misfortune, an unhappy destiny, a state of affliction, hell, I do go along with him in this. But when he says that everyone who here in this life refrains from harming living creatures, taking what is not given . . . and has right views, at the breaking up of the body, after death, will be reborn in a state of misfortune, an unhappy destiny, a state of affliction, hell, I do *not* go along
214 with him in this. And when he also says that those whose understanding is like this understand correctly, while those whose understanding is different have a mistaken understanding, again I do *not* go along with him in this. And when he also obstinately holds to and insists on just what he has known, seen, and experienced himself, claiming that this alone is the truth, the rest useless, again I do *not* go along with him in this. Why is this? Because, Ānanda, the Tathāgata's understanding of the full analysis of actions is otherwise.

'With regard to this, Ānanda, when a person who here in this life harms living creatures, takes what is not given . . . and has mistaken views is at the breaking up of the body, after death, reborn in a state of misfortune, an unhappy destiny, a state of affliction, hell, then either before or afterwards he has done a bad act whose result is to be experienced as painful; or else at the time of death he has taken on and adopted some mistaken view. Therefore, at the breaking up of the body, after death, he has been reborn in a state of misfortune, an unhappy destiny, a state of affliction, hell. And in that here in this life he harms living creatures, takes what is not given . . . and has mistaken views, he experiences the result of that either in this very life or when he is reborn in further future existences.*

'With regard to this, Ānanda, when a person who here in this life harms living creatures, takes what is not given . . . and has mistaken views is at the breaking up of the body, after death, reborn in a happy destiny, a heaven world, then either before or afterwards he has done a beautiful act whose result is to be experienced as pleasant; or else at the time of death he has taken on and adopted a right view. Therefore, at the breaking up of the body, after death, he has been reborn in a happy destiny, a heaven world. And in that here in this life he harms living creatures, takes what is not given . . . and has mistaken views, he experiences the result of that either in this very life or when he is reborn in further future existences.

'With regard to this, Ānanda, when a person who here in this life
refrains from harming living creatures, taking what is not given . . .
and has right views is at the breaking up of the body, after death,
reborn in a happy destiny, a heaven world, then either before or afterwards he has done a beautiful act whose result is to be experienced as
pleasant; or else at the time of death he has taken on and adopted a
right view. Therefore, at the breaking up of the body, after death, he
has been reborn in a happy destiny, a heaven world. And in that here
in this life he refrains from harming living creatures, taking what is 215
not given . . . and has right views, he experiences the result of that
either in this very life or when he is reborn in further future existences.

'With regard to this, Ānanda, when a person who here in this life refrains from harming living creatures, taking what is not given . . . and has right views is at the breaking up of the body, after death, reborn in a state of misfortune, an unhappy destiny, a state of affliction, hell, then either before or afterwards he has done a bad act whose result is to be experienced as painful; or else at the time of death he has taken on and adopted some mistaken view. Therefore, at the breaking up of the body, after death, he has been reborn in a state of misfortune, an unhappy destiny, a state of affliction, hell. And in that here in this life he refrains from harming living creatures, taking what is not given . . . and has right views, he experiences the result of that either in this very life or when he is reborn in further future existences.

'In this way, Ānanda, there is action that is unfortunate and appears unfortunate; there is action that is unfortunate but appears fortunate; there is action that is both fortunate and appears fortunate; there is action that is fortunate but appears unfortunate.'

This is what the Blessed One said. Gladdened, the venerable Ānanda felt joy at the Blessed One's words.

FROM THE COLLECTION OF GROUPED SAYINGS

(Saṃyutta-nikāya)

Introduction

The Saṃyutta-nikāya or 'collection of grouped sayings' arranges its suttas into fifty-six groups (*saṃyutta*) according to topic; these groups of sayings are then further arranged by way of five main divisions: (1) *Sagātha-vagga* (the Chapter of Suttas with Verses), (2) *Nidāna-vagga* (the Chapter on Causes), (3) *Khandha-vagga* (the Chapter on the Aggregates), (4) *Saḷāyatana-vagga* (the Chapter on the Six Senses), (5) *Mahā-vagga* (the Great Chapter). The *Nidāna-*, *Khandha-*, and *Saḷāyatana-vaggas* are each named after the particular group of suttas that dominates them, and which accounts for around half the material in each of these vaggas: the groups of suttas on causes (*nidāna-saṃyutta*), aggregates (*khandha-saṃyutta*), and the six senses (*saḷāyatana-saṃyutta*) respectively. The 'with verses' chapter is a miscellaneous collection of grouped suttas that all contain verses. The final 'Great Chapter', while not dominated by a single group, nevertheless centres on a particular set of seven groups: suttas on the path (*magga-saṃyutta*), the constituents of awakening (*bojjhaṅga-saṃyutta*), the establishing of mindfulness (*satipaṭṭhāna-saṃyutta*), the faculties (*indriya-saṃyutta*), right application (*sammappadhāna-saṃyutta*), the powers (*bala-saṃyutta*), the bases of accomplishment (*iddhipāda-saṃyutta*). These seven sets are, in a number of places in the Nikāyas (such as the *Mahā-Parinibbāna-sutta*, also included in this volume), presented as encapsulating the Buddhist path to awakening. Later Buddhist tradition identifies the individual items that constitute these seven sets as collectively the thirty-seven 'qualities that contribute to awakening' (*bodhi-pakkhiya-dhamma/bodhi-pākṣika-dharma*).[1] The Great Chapter also includes the group of suttas on the four noble truths (*sacca-saṃyutta*).

What is evident is that the Saṃyutta-nikāya is structured around a basic list (*mātikā*) of fundamental items of Buddhist teaching:[2] The current selection is intended to reflect this overall structure of the Saṃyutta-nikāya. We begin with one sutta from the *Sagātha-vagga*, and then have two suttas each from the principal groups of the remaining four chapters. The selection is necessarily somewhat arbitrary, but is intended to exemplify something of the flavour of the generally shorter pieces that characterize this Nikāya.

[1] R. Gethin, *The Buddhist Path to Awakening: A Study of the Bodhi-Pakkhiyā Dhammā*, 2nd edn. (Oxford, 2001).

[2] R. Gethin, 'The Mātikās: Memorization, Mindfulness and the List', in J. Gyatso (ed.), *In The Mirror of Memory: Reflections on Mindfulness and Remembrance in Indian and Tibetan Buddhism* (Albany, NY, 1992), 149–72.

In the case of the *Mahā-vagga* or Great Chapter, the second sutta in each case is an example of one of the 'repetition' (*peyyāla*) sections, although in three of the groups the repetition sections are all there is, so it is the only sutta. These repetition sections are characteristic of the Saṃyutta-nikāya generally and the Great Chapter in particular. Modern editors and translators have not always looked kindly on these repetitions, but they remain integral to Pali literature. A 'repetition' works by setting down a basic pattern in the form of an initial sutta and then repeats the sutta changing one element in that pattern each time. The repetition section chosen for the present volume is the 'Ganges repetition' (*Gaṅgā-peyyāla*), which, if recited in full, would involve the recitation of forty-eight separate suttas (6×2×4):

> Just as the river (1) Ganges, (2) Yamunā, (3) Aciravatī, (4) Sarabhū, (5) Mahī, (6) great rivers incline[s] to (1) the east, (2) the ocean, so a monk who cultivates the eight constituents of the path (1) based on seclusion . . . (2) ending in the removal of greed . . . (3) immersed in the deathless . . . (4) inclining to nibbana . . ., himself inclines to nibbana.

All manuscripts, editions, and translations abbreviate such repetitions, though some more than others. Such repetitions seem to have a number of effects. In the first place the doctrinal and practical importance of the items that are the subject of the repetitions is highlighted and enhanced. Moreover, in the case of the Ganges repetition as applied to various qualities that contribute to awakening, something of the depth and richness of the awakening experience is evoked. This kind of repetition also requires and develops a certain mental alertness and agility that goes beyond mere rote repetition, such that it can be considered a practice for developing the Buddhist meditative virtues of mindfulness and concentration. It is a meditation in itself for reciter, listener, and reader.[3]

A set of five repetitions beginning with the Ganges repetition is applied in eight of the Great Chapter's twelve groups of suttas: the eighth group in addition to the groups mentioned above is the 'absorption' (*jhāna*) group, indicating a close relationship between the cultivation of the ways of establishing mindfulness, the ways of right application, the bases of accomplishment, the faculties, the powers, the constituents of awakening, and the eightfold path on the one hand and the four absorptions on the other.

In the Saṃyutta-nikāya, the names of suttas are not as fixed by the tradition as in the Dīgha- and Majjhima-nikāyas, and I introduce them by the usually single terms that are used as something of a mnemonic tag but which are not always consistent in the manuscripts and editions.

[3] See R. Gethin, 'What's in a Repetition? On Counting the Suttas of the Saṃyutta-nikāya', *Journal of the Pali Text Society*, 29 (2007), 365–87.

The structure of the Saṃyutta-nikāya

Group of suttas	Chapter
12 links (*nidāna*) of dependent arising (*paṭicca-samuppāda*)	*Nidāna-vagga*
5 aggregates (*khandha*)	*Khandha-vagga*
6 sense spheres (*āyatana*)	*Saḷāyatana-vagga*
4 truths (*sacca*)	
4 ways of establishing mindfulness (*sati-paṭṭhāna*)	
4 ways of right application (*samma-ppadhāna*)	
4 bases of accomplishment (*iddhi-pāda*)	
5 faculties (*indriya*)	*Mahā-vagga*
5 powers (*bala*)	
7 constituents of awakening (*bojjhaṅga*)	
8 constituents of the path (*magga*)	

FROM THE CHAPTER WITH VERSES

SAGĀTHA-VAGGA

Rohitassa (S I 61–62)

This is what I have heard. Once the Blessed One was staying at Sāvatthī, in Jeta's grove, in Anāthapiṇḍika's park. Then, well into the night, a god, Rohitassa, of surpassing beauty approached the Blessed One, illuminating the whole Jeta grove. When he had approached, he saluted the Blessed One respectfully and stood to one side. Standing there, the god Rohitassa spoke to the Blessed One.

'Sir, by travelling is it possible to know or see or reach the end of the world, where one is not born, does not grow old, does not die, does not fall away, is not reborn?'

'Friend, I say that not by travelling could one know or see or reach the end of the world, where one is not born, does not grow old, does not die, does not fall away, is not reborn.'

'It is remarkable, extraordinary, sir, how this is well put by the Blessed One when you say that not by travelling could one know or see or reach the end of the world, where one is not born, does not grow old, does not die, does not fall away, is not reborn.

'Once in the past I was a seer called Rohitassa, a pupil of Bhoja's,
who had the power to travel through the sky. As when a steady 62

archer—well trained, practised, skilled, and experienced—shoots a swift arrow across the shadow of a palm tree, such was my speed. As from the eastern to the western ocean, such was my stride. This wish arose in me: "By travelling I shall reach the end of the world." Possessing such speed and such a stride, having a life of a hundred years, and living a hundred years, I travelled for a hundred years, only stopping to eat, drink, and take meals, to defecate and urinate, to relieve my tiredness in sleep, and still I died on the way without reaching the end of the world.

'It is remarkable, extraordinary, sir, how this is well put by the Blessed One when you say that not by travelling could one know or see or reach the end of the world, where one is not born, does not grow old, does not die, does not fall away, is not reborn.'

'And yet, friend, I say that there is no making an end to suffering without reaching the end of the world. But it is in this fathom-long body which has a mind and conceives, that I declare the world, the arising of the world, the ceasing of the world, and the practice leading to the ceasing of the world.

'By travelling, the end of the world will never be reached;
But without reaching its end, from suffering there is no release.
And so the wise one, knowing the world,
Dwelling in the spiritual life goes to the end of the world,
And knowing the world's end, he is still,
Not wishing for this world nor another.'

FROM THE CHAPTER ON CAUSES

NIDĀNA-VAGGA

Analysis (S II 2–4)

This is what I have heard. Once the Blessed One was staying at Sāvatthī, in Jeta's grove, in Anāthapiṇḍika's park.

'I shall teach you, monks, dependent arising and I shall analyse it. Listen. Pay careful attention to what I shall say.'

'Yes, sir,' replied those monks to the Blessed One.

This is what the Blessed One said: 'And what is dependent arising? Conditioned by ignorance there are volitional forces, conditioned by volitional forces there is consciousness, conditioned by consciousness there is mind-and-body, conditioned by mind-and-body there are the six senses, conditioned by the six sense spheres there is stimulation, conditioned by stimulation there is feeling, conditioned by feeling there is craving, conditioned by craving there is attachment, conditioned by attachment there is existence, conditioned by becoming there is birth, conditioned by birth there is old-age and death—grief, lamentation, pain, sorrow, and despair come into being. And so there is the arising of this whole mass of suffering.

'What is old-age and death? Of whatever being in whatever kind of existence—its old-age, aging, decrepitude, greying, wrinkling, loss of vitality, deterioration of the faculties. This is called old-age. Of whatever being from whatever kind of existence—its fall, falling 3
away, breaking up, disappearance, death, dying, completing its time, breaking up of the aggregates, laying aside of the body. This is called death. And these two together, monks, are called old-age and death.

'What is birth? Of whatever being in whatever kind of existence—its birth, being born, conception, production, appearance of the aggregates, acquisition of the spheres of sense. This, monks, is called birth.

'What is existence? There are these three kinds of existence: existence in the sense world, existence in the form world, existence in the formless world. This, monks, is called existence.

'What is attachment? There are these four kinds of attachment: attachment to the objects of the senses, attachment to views, attachment to precepts and vows, attachment to the doctrine of a self. This, monks, is called attachment.

'What is craving? There are these six classes of craving: craving for visible forms, craving for sounds, craving for smells, craving for tastes, craving for touch, craving for the objects of thought. This, monks, is called craving.

'What is feeling? There are these six classes of feeling: feeling produced by stimulation of the eye, feeling produced by stimulation of the ear, feeling produced by stimulation of the nose, feeling produced by stimulation of the tongue, feeling produced by stimulation of the body, feeling produced by stimulation of the mind. This, monks, is called feeling.

'What is stimulation? There are these six classes of stimulation: stimulation of the eye, stimulation of the ear, stimulation of the nose, stimulation of the tongue, stimulation of the body, stimulation of the mind. This, monks, is called stimulation.

'What are the six sense spheres? The sphere of the eye, the sphere of the ear, the sphere of the nose, the sphere of the tongue, the sphere of the body, the sphere of the mind. These, monks, are called the six sense spheres.

'What is mind-and-body? Feeling, conceiving, volition, stimula-
4 tion, and attention are called mind. The four principal elements and
physical form that is dependent on these four elements are called body. And these two together, monks, are called mind-and-body.

'What is consciousness? There are these six classes of consciousness: eye consciousness, ear consciousness, nose consciousness, tongue consciousness, body consciousness, mind consciousness. This, monks, is called consciousness.

'What are volitional forces? There are these three kinds of volitional force: the volitional force of bodily action, the volitional force of speech, the volitional force of thought. These, monks, are called volitional forces.

'What is ignorance? Misunderstanding about suffering, misunderstanding about the arising of suffering, misunderstanding about the ceasing of suffering, misunderstanding about the practice leading to the ceasing of suffering. This, monks, is called ignorance.

'So it is that, conditioned by ignorance there are volitional forces, conditioned by volitional forces there is consciousness, conditioned by consciousness there is mind-and-body, conditioned by mind-and-body there are the six senses, conditioned by the six sense spheres there is stimulation, conditioned by stimulation there is feeling, conditioned by feeling there is craving, conditioned by craving there is attachment, conditioned by attachment there is existence, conditioned by becoming there is birth, conditioned by birth there is old-age and death—grief, lamentation, pain, sorrow, and despair come into being. And so there is the arising of this whole mass of suffering.

'But with the utter fading away and ceasing of ignorance there is the ceasing of volitional forces, with the ceasing of volitional forces there is the ceasing of consciousness, with the ceasing of consciousness there is the ceasing of mind-and-body, with the ceasing of mind-and-body there is the ceasing of the six sense spheres, with the ceasing of the six sense spheres there is the ceasing of stimulation, with the ceasing of stimulation there is the ceasing of feeling, with the ceasing of feeling there is the ceasing of craving, with the ceasing of craving there is the ceasing of attachment, with the ceasing of attachment there is the ceasing of existence, with the ceasing of existence there is the ceasing of birth, with the ceasing of birth there is the ceasing of old-age and death—grief, lamentation, pain, sorrow, and despair cease. And so there is the ceasing of this entire mass of suffering.'

This is what the Blessed One said. Gladdened, those monks felt joy at the Blessed One's words.

Specific Basis (S II 29–32)

This is what I have heard. Once the Blessed One was staying at Sāvatthī, in Jeta's grove, in Anāthapiṇḍika's park.

'I say that it is when one knows, when one sees that one destroys the taints, not when one does not know, when one does not see. But knowing what, seeing what, does one destroy the taints? How physical form is, how it arises, how it comes to an end; how feeling is . . . how conceiving is . . . how volitional forces are . . . how consciousness is, how it arises, how it comes to an end. Knowing this, seeing this, one destroys the taints. 30

'With regard to this destruction, I say that one's knowledge of the destruction has a specific basis, and is not without a specific basis. And what is the specific basis for that knowledge? The answer should be that it is "freedom".

'I also say that freedom has a specific basis, and is not without a specific basis. And what is the specific basis for freedom? The answer should be that it is "dispassion".

'I also say that dispassion has a specific basis, and is not without a specific basis. And what is the specific basis for dispassion? The answer should be that it is "disenchantment".

'I also say that disenchantment has a specific basis, and is not without a specific basis. And what is the specific basis for disenchantment? The answer should be that it is "knowing and seeing things as they are".

'I also say that knowing and seeing things as they are has a specific basis, and is not without a specific basis. And what is the specific basis for knowing and seeing things as they are? The answer should be that it is "deep concentration".

'I also say that deep concentration has a specific basis, and is not without a specific basis. And what is the specific basis for deep concentration? The answer should be that it is "happiness".

'I also say that happiness has a specific basis, and is not without a specific basis. And what is the specific basis for happiness? The answer should be that it is "tranquillity".

'I also say that tranquillity has a specific basis, and is not without a specific basis. And what is the specific basis for tranquillity? The answer should be that it is "joy".

'I also say that joy has a specific basis, and is not without a specific basis. And what is the specific basis for joy? The answer should be that it is "gladness".

'I also say that gladness has a specific basis, and is not without a specific basis. And what is the specific basis for gladness? The answer should be that it is "faith".

'I also say that faith has a specific basis, and is not without a specific basis. And what is the specific basis for faith? The answer should be that it is "suffering".

'I also say that suffering has a specific basis, and is not without a specific basis. And what is the specific basis for suffering? The answer should be that it is "birth".

'I also say that birth has a specific basis, and is not without a
31 specific basis. And what is the specific basis for birth? The answer should be that it is "existence".

'I also say that existence has a specific basis, and is not without a specific basis. And what is the specific basis for existence? The answer should be that it is "attachment".

'I also say that attachment has a specific basis, and is not without a specific basis. And what is the specific basis for attachment? The answer should be that it is "craving".

'I also say that craving has a specific basis, and is not without a specific basis. And what is the specific basis for craving? The answer should be that it is "feeling".

'I also say that feeling has a specific basis, and is not without a specific basis. And what is the specific basis for feeling? The answer should be that it is "stimulation".

'I also say that stimulation has a specific basis, and is not without a specific basis. And what is the specific basis for stimulation? The answer should be that it is "the six spheres of the senses".

'I also say that the six spheres of the senses have a specific basis, and are not without a specific basis. And what is the specific basis for the six spheres of the senses? The answer should be that it is "mind-and-body".

'I also say that mind-and-body has a specific basis, and is not without a specific basis. And what is the specific basis for mind-and-body? The answer should be that it is "consciousness".

'I also say that consciousness has a specific basis, and is not without a specific basis. And what is the specific basis for consciousness? The answer should be that it is "volitional forces".

'I also say that volitional forces have a specific basis, and are not without a specific basis. And what is the specific basis for volitional forces? The answer should be that it is "ignorance".

'So it is that volitional forces have as their specific basis ignorance, consciousness has as its specific basis volitional forces, mind-and-body has as its specific basis consciousness, the six spheres of the senses have as their specific basis mind-and-body, stimulation has as its specific basis the six spheres of the senses, feeling has as its specific basis stimulation, craving has as its specific basis feeling, attachment has as its specific basis craving, existence has as its specific basis attachment, birth has as its specific basis existence, suffering has as its specific basis birth, faith has as its specific basis suffering, gladness has as its specific basis faith, joy has as its specific basis gladness, tranquillity has as its specific basis joy, happiness has as its specific basis tranquillity, deep concentration has as its specific basis happiness, knowing and seeing things as they are has as its specific basis deep concentration, disenchantment has as its specific basis knowing and seeing things as they are, dispassion has as its specific basis disenchantment, freedom has as its specific basis dispassion, knowledge of the destruction has as its specific basis freedom.

'Monks, it is just as when the god brings rain in huge drops upon a mountain-top, and the water runs down the slope, filling up the mountain crevices, clefts, and gullies; when the mountain crevices, clefts, and gullies are full, they fill up the pools; when the pools are full, they fill up the lakes; when the lakes are full, they fill up the streams; when the streams are full, they fill up the rivers; when the rivers are full, they fill up the great ocean and seas. In exactly the same way, monks, volitional forces have as their specific basis ignorance, consciousness . . . volitional forces, mind-and-body . . . consciousness, the six spheres of the senses . . . mind-and-body, stimulation . . . the six spheres of the senses, feeling . . . stimulation, craving . . . feeling, attachment . . . craving, existence . . . attachment, birth . . . existence, suffering . . . birth, faith . . . suffering, gladness . . . faith, joy . . . gladness, tranquillity . . . joy, happiness . . . tranquillity, deep concentration . . . happiness, knowing and seeing things as they are . . . deep concentration, disenchantment . . . knowing and seeing things as they are, dispassion . . . disenchantment, freedom . . . dispassion, knowledge of the destruction . . . freedom.'

This is what the Blessed One said. Gladdened, those monks felt joy at the Blessed One's words.

FROM THE CHAPTER ON THE AGGREGATES

KHANDHA-VAGGA

Nakulapitar (S III 1–5)

This is what I have heard. Once the Blessed One was staying in the Bhagga country at Suṃsumāragira, in the Bhesakaḷā grove in the animal park. Now the householder Nakulapitar approached the Blessed One. Having approached, he sat down to one side.

Once seated, he said to the Blessed One: 'Sir, I am old, getting on, of a venerable age and experienced in life. Having reached a great age, I am sick in body and frequently ill. So I cannot always get to see the Blessed One or revered monks. Sir, could the Blessed One please direct me, please instruct me, as this would contribute to my welfare and happiness for a long time to come?'

'This is the way it is, householder. This is the way it is. Your body is sick, oppressed,* and afflicted. For how could anyone carrying around this body claim freedom from disease for even a second, unless, that is, he was being childish? Therefore you should practise so that although your body is sick your mind will not be sick. This is how you should practise.'

2 When the householder Nakulapitar had enjoyed and expressed his appreciation of what the Blessed One said, he got up from his seat, respectfully saluted the Blessed One, keeping him on his right, and then approached the venerable Sāriputta. Having approached,

he saluted the venerable Sāriputta respectfully and sat down to one side.

Once seated, the venerable Sāriputta said to him: 'How serene your senses are, householder! How pure and clear the colour of your face! Surely today you got to hear a talk on the teaching directly from the Blessed One.'

'And why should it not be so? Just now, sir, I was blessed with the nectar of the Blessed One's talk on the Truth.'

'So how then were you blessed with the nectar of the Blessed One's talk on Truth?'

'Well, sir, I approached the Blessed One . . . I said to the Blessed One: "Sir, I am old . . . I am sick in body and frequently ill . . . Sir, could the Blessed One please direct me . . . ?" At this the Blessed One said to me: "This is the way it is, householder . . . Therefore you should practise so that although your body is sick your mind will not be sick. This is how you should practise." This, sir, is how I was blessed with the nectar of the Blessed One's talk on Truth.'

'But, householder, did it not occur to you to question the Blessed One further, to ask him how it is that one is both sick in body and sick in mind, how it is that one is sick in body yet not sick in mind?' 3

'I would come from afar to learn the significance of what has been said directly from the venerable Sāriputta. Certainly it would be good if the significance of what has been said might be clear to the venerable Sāriputta.'

'Then listen, householder. Pay careful attention to what I shall say.'

'Yes, sir,' replied the householder Nakulapitar to the venerable Sāriputta.

This is what the venerable Sāriputta said: 'How is it, then, that one is both sick in body and sick in mind? Here the uninformed, ordinary person, who takes no notice of the noble ones, who has no experience of and no acquaintance with their practice, who takes no notice of wise people, who has no experience of and no acquaintance with their practice, looks on physical form as the self, or the self as something that possesses physical form, or physical form as in the self, or the self as in physical form. He becomes fixated on the idea that he is physical form, that physical form is his. And then the physical form of this person who is fixated on the idea that he is physical form, the idea that physical form is his, changes and alters;

as a result of that change and alteration in physical form grief, lamentation, pain, sorrow, and despair come into being for him.

'He looks on feeling as the self, or the self as something that possesses feeling, or feeling as in the self, or the self as in feeling. He becomes fixated on the idea that he is feeling, that feeling is his. And then the feeling of this person who is fixated on the idea that he is feeling, the idea that feeling is his, changes and alters; as a result of that change and alteration in feeling grief, lamentation, pain, sorrow, and despair come into being for him.

'He looks on conceiving as the self, or the self as something that possesses conceiving, or conceiving as in the self, or the self as in conceiving. He becomes fixated on the idea that he is conceiving, that conceiving is his. And then the conceiving of this person who is fixated on the idea that he is conceiving, the idea that conceiving is his, changes and alters; as a result of that change and alteration in conceiving grief, lamentation, pain, sorrow, and despair come into being for him.

'He looks on volitional forces as the self, or the self as something
that possesses volitional forces, or volitional forces as in the self, or the
self as in volitional forces. He becomes fixated on the idea that he is
volitional forces, that volitional forces are his. And then the volitional
forces of this person who is fixated on the idea that he is volitional
4 forces, the idea that volitional forces are his, change and alter; as a
result of that change and alteration in volitional forces grief, lamentation, pain, sorrow, and despair come into being for him.

'He looks on consciousness as the self, or the self as something that possesses consciousness, or consciousness as in the self, or the self as in consciousness. He becomes fixated on the idea that he is consciousness, that consciousness is his. And then the consciousness of this person who is fixated on the idea that he is consciousness, the idea that consciousness is his, changes and alters; as a result of that change and alteration in consciousness grief, lamentation, pain, sorrow, and despair come into being for him. It is in this way that one is both sick in body and sick in mind.

'How is it, then, that one is sick in body and yet not sick in mind? Here the informed, ordinary person, who takes notice of the noble ones, who has experience of and acquaintance with their practice, who takes notice of wise people, who has experience of and acquaintance with their practice, *does not* look on physical form as the self, or the self as something that possesses physical form, or physical form as in the self, or the self as in physical form. He *does not* become fixated on the idea that he is physical form, that physical form is his. And then the physical form of this person who is not fixated on the idea that he is physical form, the idea that physical form is his, changes and alters; as a result of that change and alteration in physical form grief, lamentation, pain, sorrow, and despair *do not* come into being for him.

'He *does not* look on feeling as the self, or the self as something that possesses feeling, or feeling as in the self, or the self as in feeling. He *does not* become fixated on the idea that he is feeling, that feeling is his. And then the feeling of this person who is not fixated on the idea that he is feeling, the idea that feeling is his, changes and alters; as a result of that change and alteration in feeling grief, lamentation, pain, sorrow, and despair *do not* come into being for him.

'He *does not* look on conceiving as the self, or the self as something that possesses conceiving, or conceiving as in the self, or the self as in conceiving. He *does not* become fixated on the idea that he is conceiving, that conceiving is his. And then the conceiving of this person who is not fixated on the idea that he is conceiving, the idea that conceiving is his, changes and alters; as a result of that change and alteration in conceiving grief, lamentation, pain, sorrow, and despair *do not* come into being for him. 5

'He *does not* look on volitional forces as the self, or the self as something that possesses volitional forces, or volitional forces as in the self, or the self as in volitional forces. He *does not* become fixated on the idea that he is volitional forces, that volitional forces are his. And then the volitional forces of this person who is not fixated on the idea that he is volitional forces, the idea that volitional forces are his, change and alter; as a result of that change and alteration in volitional forces grief, lamentation, pain, sorrow, and despair *do not* come into being for him.

'He *does not* look on consciousness as the self, or the self as something that possesses consciousness, or consciousness as in the self, or the self as in consciousness. He *does not* become fixated on the idea that he is consciousness, that consciousness is his. And then the consciousness of this person who is not fixated on the idea that he is consciousness, the idea that consciousness is his, changes and alters; as a result of that change and alteration in consciousness grief, lamentation, pain, sorrow, and despair *do not* come into being for him. It is in this way that one is sick in body and yet not sick in mind.'

This is what the venerable Sāriputta said. Gladdened, the householder Nakulapitar felt joy at the venerable Sāriputta's words.

Foam (S III 140–143)

This is what I have heard. Once the Blessed One was staying in Ayojjhā, on the banks of the River Ganges.

There the Blessed One addressed the monks: 'It is as if, monks, this River Ganges were to carry down a large ball of foam, which a person with good eyes might see, study, and carefully scrutinize. On doing so, it would become apparent to him that it was something quite empty, quite worthless, with no substance at all. For could there be any substance in a ball of foam? In exactly the same way, monks, a monk sees, studies, and carefully scrutinizes physical form—whether past, present, or future, whether inside or outside, gross or subtle, inferior or refined, far or near. On doing so, it becomes apparent to him that it is something quite empty, quite worthless, with no substance at all.
141 For could there be any substance in a physical form?

'It is just as, monks, when the god brings rain in the autumn in huge drops and a bubble appears on the surface of the water and just vanishes. A person with good eyes might see, study, and carefully scrutinize it. On doing so, it would become apparent to him that it was something quite empty, quite worthless, with no substance at all. For could there be any substance in a bubble? In exactly the same way, monks, a monk sees, studies, and carefully scrutinizes feeling—whether past, present, or future, whether inside or outside, gross or subtle, inferior or refined, far or near. On doing so, it becomes apparent to him that it is something quite empty, quite worthless, with no substance at all. For could there be any substance in feeling?

'It is just as, monks, when in the last month of the hot season at midday a mirage appears, shimmering.* A person with good eyes might see, study, and carefully scrutinize it. On doing so, it would become apparent to him that it was something quite empty, quite worthless, with no substance at all. For could there be any substance in a mirage? In exactly the same way, monks, a monk sees, studies, and carefully scrutinizes conceiving—whether past, present, or future, whether inside or outside, gross or subtle, inferior or refined, far or near. On doing so, it becomes apparent to him that it is something quite empty, quite worthless, with no substance at all. For could there be any substance in conceiving?

'It is as if, monks, a person in need of heartwood, seeking heartwood, wandering about in search of heartwood, might take a sharp axe and enter the forest. There he might see the trunk of a big banana tree, straight, fresh, without any bud. He might cut that trunk at the root, then split it at the top and peel back the outer layer. Yet when he peeled back the outer layer he would not get any outer wood, let alone heartwood. A person with good eyes might see, study, and carefully scrutinize it. On doing so, it would become apparent to him 142
that it was something quite empty, quite worthless, with no substance at all. For could there be any substance in the trunk of a banana tree? In exactly the same way, monks, a monk sees, studies, and carefully scrutinizes volitional forces—whether past, present, or future, whether inside or outside, gross or subtle, inferior or refined, far or near. On doing so, it becomes apparent to him that they are something quite empty, quite worthless, with no substance at all. For could there be any substance in volitional forces?

'It is as if, monks, a magician or a magician's pupil were to make an illusion appear at a crossroads. A person with good eyes might see, study, and carefully scrutinize it. On doing so, it would become apparent to him that it was something quite empty, quite worthless, with no substance at all. For could there be any substance in an illusion? In exactly the same way, monks, a monk sees, studies, and carefully scrutinizes consciousness—whether past, present, or future, whether inside or outside, gross or subtle, inferior or refined, far or near. On doing so, it becomes apparent to him that it is something quite empty, quite worthless, with no substance at all. For could there be any substance in consciousness?

'When the informed noble disciple sees this he becomes disenchanted with physical form, disenchanted with feeling, conceiving, volitional forces, and consciousness. Being disenchanted, he becomes dispassionate. Through dispassion he is freed: of what is freed, there is knowledge that it is freed. He knows: "Birth is destroyed, the spiritual life lived, done is what was to be done—there is nothing further required to this end!"'

This is what the Blessed One said. And when the Happy One had said this, the Teacher spoke again:

'Like a ball of foam is physical form, and feeling is like a bubble;
Like a mirage is conceiving, and the forces of volition are like a banana tree;
Like an illusion is consciousness—the kinsman of the sun has explained.
However one studies these, carefully scrutinizing,
That they are empty, quite worthless, is how one accurately sees them.
Of this body, the one of broad wisdom has taught,
When three qualities are lost, see how physical form is discarded:
Vitality, heat, and consciousness, when these leave this body
Then it lies thrown away, senseless, food for others.
Such is this stream, an illusion that makes us babble like fools;
It is proclaimed a killer, no substance is found here.
A monk should look on the aggregates thus, summoning his strength,
Whether by day or night, fully aware, always mindful.
He should give up all that ties him, making himself his refuge.
He should act as if his head was burning away, and aim for the place that is imperishable.'

FROM THE CHAPTER ON THE SIX SENSE SPHERES

SAḶĀYATANA-VAGGA

Burning (S IV 19–20)

This is what I have heard. Once the Blessed One was staying in Gayā at Gayā Head with a thousand monks.*

There the Blessed One addressed the monks: 'All is burning,* monks. And what is the all that is burning, monks? The eye is burning, visible forms are burning, eye consciousness is burning, stimulation of the eye is burning, and also whatever happy, unhappy, or neither happy nor unhappy feeling that comes about conditioned by stimulation of the eye, that too is burning. Burning with what? I say it is burning with the fire of greed, the fire of hatred, the fire of delusion; burning with birth, with old-age, with death, with grief, with lamentation, with pain, with sorrow, with despair.

'The ear is burning . . . The nose is burning . . . The tongue is burning . . . The body is burning . . . The mind is burning, ideas are burning, mind consciousness is burning, stimulation of the mind is burning, and also whatever happy, unhappy, or neither happy nor unhappy feeling that comes about conditioned by stimulation of the mind, that too is burning. Burning with what? I say it is burning with the fire of greed, the fire of hatred, the fire of delusion; burning with birth, with old-age, with death, with grief, with lamentation, with pain, with sorrow, with despair.

'When the informed noble disciple sees this, he becomes disenchanted with the eye, disenchanted with visible forms, disenchanted with eye consciousness, disenchanted with stimulation of the eye; also whatever happy, unhappy, or neither happy nor unhappy feeling that comes about conditioned by stimulation of the eye, with that too he becomes disenchanted.

'When the informed noble disciple sees this, he becomes disenchanted with the ear . . . he becomes disenchanted with the nose . . . he becomes disenchanted with the tongue . . . he becomes disenchanted with the body . . .

'When the informed noble disciple sees this, he becomes disenchanted with the mind, disenchanted with ideas, disenchanted with mind consciousness, disenchanted with stimulation of the mind; also whatever happy, unhappy, or neither happy nor unhappy feeling that comes about conditioned by stimulation of the mind, with that too he becomes disenchanted.

'Being disenchanted he becomes dispassionate. Through dispassion he is freed: of what is freed, there is knowledge that it is freed. He knows directly: "Birth is destroyed, the spiritual life lived, done is what was to be done—there is nothing further required to this end!"'

This is what the Blessed One said. Gladdened, those monks felt joy at the Blessed One's words. And even while this explanation was being spoken, the minds of those thousand monks were freed from the taints as a result of not grasping.

Illness (S IV 46–47)

This is what I have heard. Once the Blessed One was staying at Sāvatthī, in Jeta's grove, in Anāthapiṇḍika's park. Now a certain monk approached the Blessed One, and having saluted him respectfully sat down to one side.

Once seated, that monk said to the Blessed One: 'Sir, in our residence there is a young monk, not well known, who is ill, in pain, seriously ill. Sir, it would be good if the Blessed One out of kindness could go to this monk.'

Then the Blessed One, as soon as he heard it said that he was young and that he was ill, and realizing that he was not well known, went to that monk. That monk saw the Blessed One coming in the distance, and when he saw him he tried to get up from his bed. Then the Blessed One said to that monk: 'Wait! Don't try to get up from your bed. There are seats that have been prepared. I can sit there.'

When the Blessed One had sat down on a prepared seat, he said to the monk: 'I hope you are coping, monk. I hope you are managing. I hope that the pains are getting better and not getting worse, that there are signs of their getting better, not of their getting worse.'

'I am not coping, sir. I am not managing. My pains are severe and getting worse; they are not getting better. There are signs of their getting worse, not of their getting better.'

'I hope you do not feel any remorse, monk. I hope you do not feel any regret.'

'In fact, sir, I have considerable remorse. I have considerable
47 regret.'

'Then I hope that nothing to do with your conduct is preying on your conscience, monk.'

'Not this, sir.'

'But if, as you say, nothing to do with your conduct is preying on your conscience, monk, then what is it that you feel remorse about, what is it that you feel regret about?'

'It is not for the sake of purifying conduct that the Blessed One has taught the practice as I understand it.'

'If, as you say, you understand that it is not for the sake of purifying conduct that I have taught the practice, then tell me for the sake of what do you understand I have taught the practice.'

'As I understand it, the Blessed One has taught the practice for the sake of the fading away of greed.'

'Good, good, monk. It is good that you understand that I have taught the practice for the sake of the fading away of greed. I have indeed, monk, taught the practice for the sake of the fading away of greed. What do you think about this, monk? Is the eye permanent or impermanent?'

'Impermanent, sir.'

'But is what is impermanent painful or pleasurable?'

'Painful, sir.'

'But is it right to look on what is painful and subject to change as yours, as what you are, as your self?'

'Certainly not, sir.'

'What do you think about this, monk? Is the ear . . . is the nose . . . is the tongue . . . is the body . . . is the mind permanent or impermanent?'

'Impermanent, sir.'

'But is what is impermanent painful or pleasurable?'

'Painful, sir.'

'But is it right to look on what is painful and subject to change as yours, as what you are, as your self?'

'Certainly not, sir.'

'When the informed noble disciple sees things in this way he becomes disenchanted with the eye; he becomes disenchanted with the ear; he becomes disenchanted with the nose; he becomes disenchanted with the tongue; he becomes disenchanted with the body; he becomes disenchanted with the mind. Being disenchanted, he becomes dispassionate. Through dispassion he is freed: of what is freed, there is knowledge that it is freed. He knows directly: "Birth is destroyed, the spiritual life lived, done is what was to be done—there is nothing further required to this end!"'

This is what the Blessed One said. Gladdened, that monk felt joy at the Blessed One's words. And even while this explanation was being spoken, the spotless and stainless vision of the Truth came to that monk: everything whose nature it is to arise has the nature to cease.

FROM THE GREAT CHAPTER

MAHĀ-VAGGA

[*Grouped Sayings on the Path*]

Ignorance (S V 1–2)

This is what I have heard. Once the Blessed One was staying at Sāvatthī, in Jeta's grove, in Anāthapiṇḍika's park.

There the Blessed One addressed the monks: 'Monks.'

'Yes, sir,' the monks replied to the Blessed One.

This is what the Blessed One said: 'Ignorance, monks, comes first in the acquiring of unwholesome qualities, followed by shamelessness and lack of conscience. In someone who is given to ignorance and is unwise, wrong view thrives. In someone with wrong view, wrong resolve thrives. In someone with wrong resolve, wrong speech thrives. In someone with wrong speech, wrong action thrives. In someone with wrong action, wrong livelihood thrives. In someone with wrong livelihood, wrong effort thrives. In someone with wrong effort, wrong mindfulness thrives. In someone with wrong mindfulness, wrong concentration thrives.

'Knowledge, monks, comes first in the acquiring of wholesome qualities, followed by self respect and conscience. In someone who is
2 given to knowledge and is wise, right view thrives. In someone with right view, right resolve thrives. In someone with right resolve, right speech thrives. In someone with right speech, right action thrives. In someone with right action, right livelihood thrives. In someone with right livelihood, right effort thrives. In someone with right effort, right mindfulness thrives. In someone with right mindfulness, right concentration thrives.'

The Ganges Repetition (S V 38–41, etc.)

This is what I have heard . . .*

'Just as, monks, the River Ganges tends to the east, inclines to the east, slides to the east, in exactly the same way a monk who cultivates and makes much of the noble eightfold path tends to nibbana, inclines to nibbana, slides to nibbana. And how is it that a monk who cultivates and makes much of the noble eightfold path tends to nibbana, inclines to nibbana, slides to nibbana? Here, monks, he cultivates right view that has its basis in seclusion, in dispassion, in cessation, in release. He cultivates right resolve . . . right speech . . . right action . . . right livelihood . . . right effort . . . right mindfulness . . . right concentration that has its basis in seclusion, in dispassion, in cessation, in release. It is in this way that a monk who cultivates and makes much of the noble eightfold path tends to nibbana, inclines to nibbana, slides to nibbana.'

* * *

This is what I have heard . . .

'Just as, monks, the River Yamunā . . . Aciravatī . . . Sarabhū . . . Mahī . . . Just as the great rivers incline, tend, slide to the east . . . to the sea, in exactly the same way a monk who cultivates and makes much of the noble eightfold path tends to nibbana, inclines to nibbana, slides to nibbana. And how is it that a monk who cultivates and makes much of the noble eightfold path tends to nibbana, inclines to nibbana, slides to nibbana? Here, monks, he cultivates right view that has its basis in seclusion, in dispassion, in cessation, in release. He cultivates right resolve . . . right speech . . . right action . . . right livelihood . . . right effort . . . right mindfulness . . . right concentration that has its basis in seclusion, in dispassion, in cessation, in release . . .

'He cultivates right view that ends in the removal of greed, in the removal of hatred, in the removal of delusion. He cultivates right resolve . . . right speech . . . right action . . . right livelihood . . . right effort . . . right mindfulness . . . right concentration that ends in the removal of greed, in the removal of hatred, in the removal of delusion . . .

'He cultivates right view that is immersed in the deathless,* is destined for the deathless, ends in the deathless. He cultivates right resolve . . . right speech . . . right action . . . right livelihood . . . right effort . . . right mindfulness . . . right concentration that is immersed in the deathless, is destined for the deathless, ends in the deathless . . .

'He cultivates right view that inclines, tends, slides to nibbana. He cultivates right resolve . . . right speech . . . right action . . . right livelihood . . . right effort . . . right mindfulness . . . right concentration that inclines, tends, slides to nibbana. It is in this way that a monk who cultivates and makes much of the noble eightfold path tends to nibbana, inclines to nibbana, slides to nibbana.'

[*Grouped Sayings on the Seven Constituents of Awakening*]

Fire (S V 112–115)

This is what I have heard. Once the Blessed One was staying at Sāvatthī . . .

Now in the morning a considerable number of monks, having dressed, took their robes and bowls and went into Sāvatthī in search of alms. Then it occurred to those monks that since it was still too early to be collecting alms, they might go to the park of the wanderers belonging to another school. So they approached their park, and having approached, they saluted the wanderers of the other school respectfully, exchanging pleasing and polite words with them before sitting down to one side.

Once the monks were seated, the wanderers said to them: 'Friends, the ascetic Gotama teaches the following practice to his disciples: "Come, monks, abandon the five hindrances that come as defilements of the mind weakening wisdom, and truly cultivate the seven constituents of awakening." We too teach our disciples this practice . . . So what is the distinction, what is the difference, between the ascetic Gotama's teaching or instruction and ours or of our teaching or instruction and the ascetic Gotama's? What makes them unlike each other?'

The monks neither agreed nor disagreed with the words of the wanderers of the other school, but simply got up from their seats and went away, thinking, 'We will get to understand the significance of what has been said when we see the Blessed One.'

Then, after they had collected alms, eaten their meal, and returned from the alms round, the monks approached the Blessed One. Having approached, they saluted him respectfully and sat down to one side.

Once seated, those monks said to the Blessed One: 'Sir, this morning, having dressed, we took our robes and bowls and went into Sāvatthī in search of alms. Then it occurred to us that since it was still too early to be collecting alms, we might go to the park of the wanderers belonging to another school . . . the wanderers told us that . . . they too teach their disciples the practice of abandoning the five hindrances . . . and truly cultivating the seven constituents of awakening. So what, they asked, is the distinction, what is the difference between the ascetic Gotama's teaching or instruction and theirs . . . ? We neither agreed nor disagreed with their words . . . thinking that we would get to understand the significance of what had been said when we saw the Blessed One.'

'Monks, when the wanderers of another school talk like that, this should be the response: "Friends, when the mind is dull, which of the constituents of awakening is it not the right time to cultivate, and which of the constituents of awakening is it the right time to cultivate? When the mind is stirred up, which of the constituents of awakening is it not the right time to cultivate, and which of the constituents of awakening is it the right time to cultivate?" When questioned in this way, the wanderers of the other school will not succeed in their response and will stray further towards failure. What is the reason for this? Because this falls beyond their reach: I do not see anyone in this world with its gods, with its Māra and Brahmā, or in this generation with its ascetics and brahmans, its princes and peoples, who could satisfy the mind with his explanation of these questions, unless it was the Tathāgata or a disciple of the Tathāgata or someone who had heard it from them.

'When the mind is dull, then it is not the right time to cultivate tranquillity as a constituent of awakening, concentration as a constituent of awakening, and equanimity as a constituent of awakening. What is the reason for this? It is difficult to enliven a mind that is dull by means of these qualities. It's as if there were a person who wanted to make a small fire flare up and he were to throw on it wet grass, wet cow dung, and wet sticks, and then spray water on it and scatter sand over it. Would that person manage to make the small fire flare up?'

'Certainly not, sir.'

'In exactly the same way, monks, when the mind is dull, then it is not the right time to cultivate tranquillity, concentration, and equanimity as constituents of awakening . . . However, when the mind is dull, then it is the right time to cultivate investigation of qualities as a constituent of awakening, energy as a constituent of awakening, and joy as a constituent of awakening. What is the reason for this? It is easy to enliven a mind that is dull by means of these qualities. It's as if there were a person who wanted to make a small fire flare up and he were to throw on it dry grass, dry cow dung, and dry sticks, and then blow on it and not scatter sand over it. Would that person manage to make the small fire flare up?'

'Certainly, sir.'

'In exactly the same way, monks, when the mind is dull, then it is the right time to cultivate investigation of qualities, energy, and joy as constituents of awakening . . .

'When the mind is stirred up, then it is not the right time to cultivate investigation of qualities as a constituent of awakening, energy as a constituent of awakening, and joy as a constituent of awakening. What is the reason for this? It is difficult to still a mind that is stirred up by means of these qualities. It's as if there were a person who wanted to put out a blazing fire and he were to throw on it dry grass, dry cow dung, and dry sticks, and then blow on it and not scatter sand over it. Would that person manage to put out the blazing fire?'

'Certainly not, sir.'

'In exactly the same way, monks, when the mind is stirred up, then it is not the right time to cultivate investigation of qualities, energy, and joy as constituents of awakening . . . When the mind is stirred up, then it is the right time to cultivate tranquillity as a constituent of awakening, concentration as a constituent of awakening, and equanimity as a constituent of awakening. What is the reason for this? It is easy to still a mind that is stirred up by means of these qualities. It's as if there were a person who wanted to put out a blazing fire and he were to throw on it wet grass, wet cow dung, and wet sticks, and then spray water on it and scatter sand over it. Would that person manage to put out the blazing fire?'

'Certainly, sir.'

'In exactly the same way, monks, when the mind is stirred up, then it is the right time to cultivate tranquillity, concentration, and equanimity as constituents of awakening . . . But mindfulness I say is beneficial in all circumstances.'

The Ganges Repetition (S V 134, 137)

This is what I have heard . . .

'Just as, monks, the River Ganges tends to the east, inclines to the east, slides to the east, in exactly the same way a monk who cultivates and makes much of the seven constituents of awakening tends to nibbana, inclines to nibbana, slides to nibbana. And how is it that a monk who cultivates and makes much of the seven constituents of awakening tends to nibbana, inclines to nibbana, slides to nibbana? Here, monks, he cultivates mindfulness as a constituent of awakening, having its basis in seclusion, in dispassion, in cessation, in release. He cultivates investigation of qualities as a constituent of awakening . . . energy as a constituent of awakening . . . joy as a constituent of awakening . . . tranquillity as a constituent of awakening . . . concentration as a constituent of awakening . . . equanimity as a constituent of awakening, having its basis in seclusion, in dispassion, in cessation, in release. It is in this way that a monk who cultivates and makes much of the seven constituents of awakening tends to nibbana, inclines to nibbana, slides to nibbana.'

* * *

This is what I have heard . . .

'Just as, monks, the River Yamunā . . . Aciravatī . . . Sarabhū . . . Mahī . . . Just as the great rivers incline, tend, slide to the east . . . to the sea, in exactly the same way a monk who cultivates and makes much of the seven constituents of awakening tends to nibbana, inclines to nibbana, slides to nibbana. And how is it that a monk who cultivates and makes much of the seven constituents of awakening tends to nibbana, inclines to nibbana, slides to nibbana? Here, monks, he cultivates mindfulness as a constituent of awakening, having its basis in seclusion, in dispassion, in cessation, in release. He cultivates investigation of qualities as a constituent of awakening . . . energy as a constituent of awakening . . . joy as a constituent of awakening . . . tranquillity as a constituent of awakening . . . concentration as a constituent of awakening . . . equanimity as a constituent of awakening, having its basis in seclusion, in dispassion, in cessation, in release . . .

'He cultivates mindfulness as a constituent of awakening that ends in the removal of greed, in the removal of hatred, in the removal of delusion. He cultivates investigation of qualities as a constituent of awakening . . . energy as a constituent of awakening . . . joy as a constituent of awakening . . . tranquillity as a constituent of awakening . . . concentration as a constituent of awakening . . . equanimity as a constituent of awakening that ends in the removal of greed, in the removal of hatred, in the removal of delusion . . .

'He cultivates mindfulness as a constituent of awakening that is immersed in the deathless, is destined for the deathless, ends in the deathless. He cultivates investigation of qualities as a constituent of awakening . . . energy as a constituent of awakening . . . joy as a constituent of awakening . . . tranquillity as a constituent of awakening . . . concentration as a constituent of awakening . . . equanimity as a constituent of awakening that is immersed in the deathless, is destined for the deathless, ends in the deathless . . .

'He cultivates mindfulness as a constituent of awakening that inclines, tends, slides to nibbana. He cultivates investigation of qualities as a constituent of awakening . . . energy as a constituent of awakening . . . joy as a constituent of awakening . . . tranquillity as a constituent of awakening . . . concentration as a constituent of awakening . . . equanimity as a constituent of awakening that inclines, tends, slides to nibbana. It is in this way that a monk who cultivates and makes much of the seven constituents of awakening tends to nibbana, inclines to nibbana, slides to nibbana.'

[*Grouped Sayings on the Four Ways of Establishing Mindfulness*]

The Monkey (S V 148–150)

This is what I have heard . . .

'Monks, in the Himalaya, king of mountains, there are inaccessible and rugged places where neither monkeys nor human beings roam. In the Himalaya, king of mountains, there is inaccessible and rugged country where monkeys roam, but not human beings. In the Himalaya, king of mountains, there are level parts which are delightful where both monkeys and human beings roam. There hunters spread monkey lime* along the trails of the monkeys in order to trap them. Now those monkeys who are by nature not so foolish, not so impulsive, see the lime and pass round it, keeping their distance. But a monkey who is foolish and impulsive comes up to the lime and grasps it with his paw; then he is trapped by his paw. Thinking that he can free his paw, he grasps the lime with his second paw. Then he is trapped by that. Thinking that he can free both his paws, he grasps the lime with his foot. Then he is trapped by that. Thinking that he can free both his paws and also his foot, he grasps the lime with his second foot. Then he is trapped by that.

Thinking that he can free both his paws and both his feet, he grasps the lime with his muzzle. Then he is trapped by that. So, monks, caught at five points, that monkey lies there screeching. He has met with ruin and disaster, and the hunter will do whatever he wants with him. The 149
hunter spears him and, fastening him to that same piece of wood,* goes off where he wants. Monks, this is what happens when one strays beyond one's own range into the territory of others.

'Therefore, monks, do not stray beyond your own range into the territory of others. Māra will find a way of getting to those who stray beyond their own range into the territory of others; he will get a hold on them. So what, monks, is not the range of a monk, but the territory of others? It is the five kinds of object of sense desire. Which five? Visible forms experienced through the eye that are desirable, attractive, agreeable, pleasing, seductive, appealing; sounds experienced through the ear . . . smells experienced through the nose . . . tastes experienced through the tongue . . . the objects of touch experienced through the body that are desirable, attractive, agreeable, pleasing; seductive, appealing. These are not the range of a monk, but the territory of others.

'You should keep to your range, your own accepted territory, monks. Māra will not find a way of getting to those who keep to their range, their own accepted territory; he will not get a hold on them. So what is your range, your own accepted range? The four ways of establishing mindfulness. Which four? Here a monk lives watching the body as body; he is determined, fully aware, mindful, overcoming his longing for and discontent with the world. He lives watching feelings as feelings; he is determined, fully aware, mindful, overcoming his longing for and discontent with the world. He lives watching mind as mind; he is determined, fully aware, mindful, overcoming his longing for and discontent with the world. He lives watching qualities as qualities; he is determined, fully aware, mindful, overcoming his longing for and discontent with the world.'

The Ganges Repetition (S V 189)

This is what I have heard . . .

'Just as, monks, the River Ganges tends to the east, inclines to the east, slides to the east, in exactly the same way a monk who cultivates and makes much of the four ways of establishing mindfulness tends to nibbana, inclines to nibbana, slides to nibbana. And how is it that a monk who cultivates and makes much of the four ways of establishing mindfulness tends to nibbana, inclines to nibbana, slides to nibbana? Here, a monk lives watching the body as body; he is determined, fully aware, mindful, overcoming his longing for and discontent with the world. He lives watching feelings as feelings . . . mind as mind . . . qualities as qualities; he is determined, fully aware, mindful, overcoming his longing for and discontent with the world. It is in this way that a monk who cultivates and makes much of the four ways of establishing mindfulness tends to nibbana, inclines to nibbana, slides to nibbana.'

* * *

This is what I have heard . . .

'Just as, monks, the River Yamunā . . . Aciravatī . . . Sarabhū . . . Mahī . . . Just as the great rivers incline, tend, slide to the east . . . to the sea, in exactly the same way a monk who cultivates and makes much of the four ways of establishing mindfulness tends to nibbana, inclines to nibbana, slides to nibbana. And how is it that a monk who cultivates and makes much of the four ways of establishing mindfulness tends to nibbana, inclines to nibbana, slides to nibbana? Here, a monk lives watching the body . . . feelings . . . mind . . . qualities . . . It is in this way that a monk who cultivates and makes much of the four ways of establishing mindfulness tends to nibbana, inclines to nibbana, slides to nibbana.'

[*Grouped Sayings on the Five Faculties*]

Sāketa (S V 219–220)

This is what I have heard. Once the Blessed One was staying at Sāketa in the Añjana Grove, in the animal park.

There the Blessed One addressed the monks: 'Is there, monks, a way of exposition according to which the five faculties are the five powers, and the five powers are the five faculties?'

'Sir, the Blessed One is our source for such matters, the Blessed One is our guide, the Blessed One is the one we turn to. It is certainly proper when the significance of this question is clear only to the Blessed One. What we have heard from the Blessed One we will remember.'

'There is, monks, a way of exposition according to which the five faculties are the five powers, and the five powers are the five faculties. And what is that way of exposition . . . ? That which is the 220 faculty of faith is the power of faith, and that which is the power of faith is the faculty of faith. That which is the faculty of energy is the power of energy, and that which is the power of energy is the faculty of energy. That which is the faculty of mindfulness is the power of mindfulness, and that which is the power of mindfulness is the faculty of mindfulness. That which is the faculty of concentration is the power of concentration, and that which is the power of concentration is the faculty of concentration. That which is the faculty of wisdom is the power of wisdom, and that which is the power of wisdom is the faculty of wisdom.

'It is as if, monks, there were a river tending, inclining, and sliding eastwards, and in the middle an island. There is a way of exposition according to which the stream of that river is counted as just one. Then again there is a way of exposition according to which the stream of that river is counted as two. And what, monks, is the way of exposition according to which the stream of that river is counted as just one? In that there is water both to the eastern end of the island and also to the western end: this is the way of exposition according to which the stream of that river is counted as just one. And what, monks, is the way of exposition according to which the stream of that river is counted as two? In that there is water both to the northern side of the island, and also to the southern side: this is the way of exposition according to which the stream of that river is counted as two.

'As a result of cultivating and making much of these five faculties, with destruction of the taints a monk lives, having experienced and attained for himself through direct knowledge here and now the freedom of mind and understanding that is without any taint.'

The Ganges Repetition (S V 239, 241)

This is what I have heard . . .

'Just as, monks, the River Ganges tends to the east, inclines to the east, slides to the east, in exactly the same way a monk who cultivates and makes much of the five faculties tends to nibbana, inclines to nibbana, slides to nibbana. And how is it that a monk who cultivates and makes much of the five faculties tends to nibbana, inclines to nibbana, slides to nibbana? Here, monks, he cultivates the faculty of faith having its basis in seclusion, in dispassion, in cessation, in release. He cultivates the faculty of energy . . . the faculty of mindfulness . . . the faculty of concentration . . . the faculty of wisdom having its basis in seclusion, in dispassion, in cessation, in release. It is in this way that a monk who cultivates and makes much of the five faculties tends to nibbana, inclines to nibbana, slides to nibbana.'

* * *

This is what I have heard . . .

'Just as, monks, the River Yamunā . . . Aciravatī . . . Sarabhū . . . Mahī . . . Just as the great rivers incline, tend, slide to the east . . . to the sea, in exactly the same way a monk who cultivates and makes much of the five faculties tends to nibbana, inclines to nibbana, slides to nibbana. And how is it that a monk who cultivates and makes much of the five faculties tends to nibbana, inclines to nibbana, slides to nibbana? Here, monks, he cultivates the faculty of faith having its basis in seclusion, in dispassion, in cessation, in release. He cultivates the faculty of energy . . . the faculty of mindfulness . . . the faculty of concentration . . . the faculty of wisdom having its basis in seclusion, in dispassion, in cessation, in release . . .

'He cultivates the faculty of faith that ends in the removal of greed, in the removal of hatred, in the removal of delusion. He cultivates the faculty of energy . . . the faculty of mindfulness . . . the faculty of concentration . . . the faculty of wisdom that ends in the removal of greed, in the removal of hatred, in the removal of delusion . . .

'He cultivates the faculty of faith that is immersed in the deathless, is destined for the deathless, ends in the deathless. He cultivates the faculty of energy . . . the faculty of mindfulness . . . the faculty of concentration . . . the faculty of wisdom that is immersed in the deathless, is destined for the deathless, ends in the deathless . . .

'He cultivates the faculty of faith that inclines, tends, slides to nibbana. He cultivates the faculty of energy . . . the faculty of mindfulness . . . the faculty of concentration . . . the faculty of wisdom that inclines, tends, slides to nibbana. It is in this way that a monk who cultivates and makes much of the five faculties tends to nibbana, inclines to nibbana, slides to nibbana.'

[*Grouped Sayings on the Four Ways of Right Application*]

The Ganges Repetition (S V 244–245)

This is what I have heard . . .

'Just as, monks, the River Ganges tends to the east, inclines to the east, slides to the east, in exactly the same way a monk who cultivates and makes much of the four ways of right application tends to nibbana, inclines to nibbana, slides to nibbana. And how is it that a monk who cultivates and makes much of the four ways of right application tends to nibbana, inclines to nibbana, slides to nibbana? Here, a monk generates purpose, strives, initiates effort, takes hold of his mind, applies himself in order that unwholesome qualities that have not arisen should not arise. He generates purpose, strives, initiates effort, takes hold of his mind, applies himself in order that unwholesome qualities that have arisen should be abandoned. He generates purpose, strives, initiates effort, takes hold of his mind, applies himself in order that wholesome qualities that have not arisen should arise. He generates purpose, strives, initiates effort, takes hold of his mind, applies himself in order that wholesome qualities that have arisen should remain, not be lost, become more, become abundant, develop, come to fulfilment. It is in this way that a monk who cultivates and makes much of the four ways of right application tends to nibbana, inclines to nibbana, slides to nibbana.'

* * *

This is what I have heard . . .

'Just as, monks, the River Yamunā . . . Aciravatī . . . Sarabhū . . . Mahī . . . Just as the great rivers incline, tend, slide to the east . . . to the sea, in exactly the same way a monk who cultivates and makes much of the four ways of right application tends to nibbana, inclines to nibbana, slides to nibbana. And how is it that a monk who cultivates and makes much of the four ways of right application tends to nibbana, inclines to nibbana, slides to nibbana? Here, a monk generates purpose, strives, initiates effort, takes hold of his mind, applies himself in order that unwholesome qualities that have not arisen should not arise . . . in order that unwholesome qualities that have arisen should be abandoned . . . in order that wholesome qualities that have not arisen should arise . . . in order that wholesome qualities that have arisen should remain . . . It is in this way that a monk who cultivates and makes much of the four ways of right application tends to nibbana, inclines to nibbana, slides to nibbana.'

[*Grouped Sayings on the Five Powers*]

The Ganges Repetition (S V 249, 251)

This is what I have heard . . .

'Just as, monks, the River Ganges tends to the east, inclines to the east, slides to the east, in exactly the same way a monk who cultivates and makes much of the five powers tends to nibbana, inclines to nibbana, slides to nibbana. And how is it that a monk who cultivates and makes much of the five powers tends to nibbana, inclines to nibbana, slides to nibbana? Here, monks, he cultivates the power of faith having its basis in seclusion, in dispassion, in cessation, in release. He cultivates the power of energy . . . the power of mindfulness . . . the power of concentration . . . the power of wisdom having its basis in seclusion, in dispassion, in cessation, in release. It is in this way that a monk who cultivates and makes much of the five powers tends to nibbana, inclines to nibbana, slides to nibbana.'

* * *

This is what I have heard . . .

'Just as, monks, the River Yamunā . . . Aciravatī . . . Sarabhū . . . Mahī . . . Just as the great rivers incline, tend, slide to the east . . . to the sea, in exactly the same way a monk who cultivates and makes much of the five powers tends to nibbana, inclines to nibbana, slides to nibbana. And how is it that a monk who cultivates and makes much of the five powers tends to nibbana, inclines to nibbana, slides to nibbana? Here, monks, he cultivates the power of faith having its basis in seclusion, in dispassion, in cessation, in release. He cultivates the power of energy . . . the power of mindfulness . . . the power of concentration . . . the power of wisdom having its basis in seclusion, in dispassion, in cessation, in release . . .

'He cultivates the power of faith that ends in the removal of greed, in the removal of hatred, in the removal of delusion. He cultivates the power of energy . . . the power of mindfulness . . . the power of concentration . . . the power of wisdom that ends in the removal of greed, in the removal of hatred, in the removal of delusion . . .

'He cultivates the power of faith that is immersed in the deathless, is destined for the deathless, ends in the deathless. He cultivates the power of energy . . . the power of mindfulness . . . the power of concentration . . . the power of wisdom that is immersed in the deathless, is destined for the deathless, ends in the deathless . . .

'He cultivates the power of faith that inclines, tends, slides to nibbana. He cultivates the power of energy . . . the power of mindfulness . . . the power of concentration . . . the power of wisdom that inclines, tends, slides to nibbana. It is in this way that a monk who cultivates and makes much of the five powers tends to nibbana, inclines to nibbana, slides to nibbana.'

[*Grouped Sayings on the Four Bases of Accomplishment*]

Moggallāna (S V 269–271)

This is what I have heard. Once the Blessed One was staying at Sāvatthī, in the eastern park in the grand building built by Migāra's mother. Now at that time a lot of the monks who lived on the lower floor of the building were agitated, uncontrolled, restless, talkative, conversing about this and that; with their minds astray, they were not fully aware, not concentrated; their thoughts wandered and their senses were uncontrolled. So the Blessed One talked to the venerable Moggallāna the Great.*

'Moggallāna, these companions in the spiritual life living on
the lower floor . . . are agitated, uncontrolled, restless . . . their 270
thoughts wander and their senses are uncontrolled. Go and shake those monks up!'*

'Yes, sir,' the venerable Moggallāna the Great replied to the Blessed One.

So he contrived an act of accomplishment in meditation such that with his big toe he made the building of Migāra's mother shake, shudder, and quake. Then those monks were shaken and their hair stood on end; they remained at one end saying, 'This is remarkable, this is extraordinary—there is no wind and the building built by

Migāra's mother has deep-dug foundations; it can't move or shake, but still it shook, shuddered, and quaked.'

Then the Blessed One approached those monks and asked them, 'Monks, why do you remain at one end, shaken, with your hair standing on end?'

'It is remarkable, it is extraordinary, sir—there is no wind and the building built by Migāra's mother has deep-dug foundations; it can't move or shake, but still it shook, shuddered, and quaked.'

'The monk Moggallāna wanted to shake you up, so with his big toe he made the building of Migāra's mother shake, shudder, and quake. What do you think, monks? Which qualities has Moggallāna the Great cultivated and made much of with the result that he has such great accomplishments, such great power?

'Sir, the Blessed One is our source for such matters, the Blessed One is our guide, the Blessed One is the one we turn to. It is certainly proper when the significance of this question is clear only to the Blessed One. What we have heard from the Blessed One we will
271 remember.'

'Then listen. The monk Moggallāna has cultivated and made much of the four bases of accomplishment, with the result that he has such great accomplishments, such great power. Which four? Here, the monk Moggallāna cultivates the basis for accomplishment that consists of concentration gained by way of a desire to act and the forces of application, so that his desire to act will not be too slack nor too tight; it will not be constrained within nor dispersed without; aware of what was after and what was before, he lives practising after as before, before as after, above as below, below as above, by night as by day, by day as by night. By opening up and fully uncovering mental activity in this way, he cultivates a consciousness that radiates brilliance. He cultivates the basis for accomplishment that consists of concentration gained by way of energy and the forces of application, so that his energy will not be too slack nor too tight . . . He cultivates the basis for accomplishment that consists of concentration gained by way of his state of mind and the forces of application, so that his state of mind will not be too slack nor too tight . . . He cultivates the basis for accomplishment that consists of concentration gained by way of investigation and the forces of application, so that his investigation will not be too slack nor too tight; it will not be constrained within nor dispersed without; aware of what was after and what was before, he lives practising after as before, before as after, above as below, below as above, by night as by day, by day as by night. By opening up and fully uncovering mental activity in this way, he cultivates a consciousness that radiates brilliance.

'The monk Moggallāna has cultivated and made much of the four bases of accomplishment with the result that he enjoys the different accomplishments in meditation: being one, he becomes many, being many, he becomes one; he appears then vanishes; he passes unhindered through house walls, through city walls, and through mountains as if through air; he rises up out of the earth and sinks down into it as if it were water; he walks on water as if it were solid like earth; he travels through the sky cross-legged as if he were a bird with wings; he touches and strokes with his hand things of such power and energy as the sun and moon; he has mastery with his body as far as the world of Brahmā.

'The monk Moggallāna has cultivated and made much of the four bases of accomplishment with the result that, with destruction of the taints, he lives, having experienced and attained for himself through direct knowledge here and now the freedom of mind and understanding that is without any taint.'

The Ganges Repetition (S V 290–1)

This is what I have heard . . .

'Just as, monks, the River Ganges tends to the east, inclines to the east, slides to the east, in exactly the same way a monk who cultivates and makes much of the four bases of accomplishment tends to nibbana, inclines to nibbana, slides to nibbana. And how is it that a monk who cultivates and makes much of the four bases of accomplishment tends to nibbana, inclines to nibbana, slides to nibbana? Here, a monk cultivates the basis for accomplishment that consists of concentration gained by way of a desire to act and the forces of application. He cultivates the basis for accomplishment that consists of concentration gained by way of energy and the forces of application. He cultivates the basis for accomplishment that consists of concentration gained by way of his state of mind and the forces of application. He cultivates the basis for accomplishment that consists of concentration gained by way of investigation and the forces of application. It is in this way that a monk who cultivates and makes much of the four bases of accomplishment tends to nibbana, inclines to nibbana, slides to nibbana.'

* * *

This is what I have heard . . .

'Just as, monks, the River Yamunā . . . Aciravatī . . . Sarabhū . . . Mahī . . . Just as the great rivers incline, tend, slide to the east . . . to the sea, in exactly the same way a monk who cultivates and makes much of the four bases of accomplishment tends to nibbana, inclines to nibbana, slides to nibbana. And how is it that a monk who cultivates and makes much of the four bases of accomplishment tends to nibbana, inclines to nibbana, slides to nibbana? Here, a monk cultivates the basis for accomplishment that consists of concentration gained by way of a desire to act . . . by way of energy . . . by way of his state of mind . . . by way of investigation . . . It is in this way that a monk who cultivates and makes much of the four bases of accomplishment tends to nibbana, inclines to nibbana, slides to nibbana.'

[*Grouped Sayings on the Four Absorptions*]

The Ganges Repetition (S V 307–308)

This is what I have heard . . .

'Just as, monks, the River Ganges tends to the east, inclines to the east, slides to the east, in exactly the same way a monk who cultivates and makes much of the four absorptions tends to nibbana, inclines to nibbana, slides to nibbana. And how is it that a monk who cultivates and makes much of the four absorptions tends to nibbana, inclines to nibbana, slides to nibbana? Here a monk, completely secluded from sense desires and unwholesome qualities, lives having attained the joy and happiness of the first absorption, which is accompanied by thinking and examining, and born of seclusion. By stilling thinking and examining, he lives having attained the joy and happiness of the second absorption, a state of inner clarity and mental unification that is without thinking and examining, and is born of concentration. By having no desire for joy a monk lives equanimously, mindful, and fully aware; he experiences the bodily happiness of which the noble ones speak, saying "equanimous and mindful, one lives happily," and so lives having attained the third absorption. By letting go of happiness and unhappiness, as a result of the earlier disappearance of pleasure and pain, he lives having attained the pure equanimity and mindfulness of the fourth absorption, which is free of happiness and unhappiness. It is in this way that a monk who cultivates and makes much of the four absorptions tends to nibbana, inclines to nibbana, slides to nibbana.'

* * *

This is what I have heard . . .

'Just as, monks, the River Yamunā . . . Aciravatī . . . Sarabhū . . . Mahī . . . Just as the great rivers incline, tend, slide to the east . . . to the sea, in exactly the same way a monk who cultivates and makes much of the four absorptions tends to nibbana, inclines to nibbana, slides to nibbana. And how is it that a monk who cultivates and makes much of the four absorptions tends to nibbana, inclines to nibbana, slides to nibbana? Here a monk, completely secluded from sense desires and unwholesome states of mind, lives having attained the joy and happiness of the first absorption . . . the joy and happiness of the second absorption . . . he experiences the bodily happiness of which the noble ones speak, saying "equanimous and mindful, one lives happily," and so lives having attained the third absorption . . . having attained the pure equanimity and mindfulness of the fourth absorption . . . It is in this way that a monk who cultivates and makes much of the four absorptions tends to nibbana, inclines to nibbana, slides to nibbana.'

[*Grouped Sayings on the Truths*]

Turning the Wheel of Truth (S V 420–424)*

This is what I have heard. Once the Blessed One was staying in Benares, at Isipatana in the animal park. 421

There the Blessed One addressed the group of five monks: 'Monks, there are two extremes that someone who has gone forth should not be involved in. Which two? The pursuit of enjoyment through indulgence in the pleasures of the senses—this is inferior, vulgar, common, ignoble, unbeneficial; and also the pursuit of physical exhaustion—this is painful, ignoble, unbeneficial. Not approaching either of these two extremes, the Tathāgata has thoroughly understood that it is the middle way of practice that brings insight and knowledge, that conduces to peace, to direct knowledge, to awakening, to nibbana.

'And what is this middle way of practice that the Tathāgata has thoroughly understood brings insight and knowledge, conduces to peace, to direct knowledge, to awakening, to nibbana? Just this eightfold path, namely, right view, right resolve, right speech, right action, right livelihood, right effort, right mindfulness, right concentration. This is the middle way of practice that the Tathāgata has thoroughly understood brings insight and knowledge, conduces to peace, to direct knowledge, to awakening, to nibbana.

422 'Monks, this is the noble truth of suffering:* birth is suffering, old-age is suffering, sickness is suffering, death is suffering, being brought together with things disliked is suffering, separation from things liked is suffering, not to get what one wants is suffering; in sum, the five aggregates of attachment are suffering.

'Monks, this is the noble truth of the cause of suffering: the craving for further existence that is associated with greed and satisfaction, that takes pleasure in this and that, namely, craving for the objects of the senses, craving for existence, craving for non-existence.

'Monks, this is the noble truth of the cessation of suffering: the complete cessation and fading away of that very craving—giving it up, letting go, being free, not tied to it.

'Monks, this is the noble truth of the practice leading to the cessation of suffering: just this eightfold path, namely, right view, right resolve, right speech, right action, right livelihood, right effort, right mindfulness, right concentration.

'Monks, insight into things not previously heard came to me—knowledge, understanding, wisdom, light: the noble truth that this was suffering. Insight . . . came to me: as to this noble truth, this suffering must be fully understood. Insight . . . came to me: as to this noble truth, this suffering has been fully understood.

'Insight with regard to things not previously heard came to me—knowledge, understanding, wisdom, light: the noble truth that this was the cause of suffering. Insight . . . came to me: as to this noble truth, this cause of suffering must be abandoned. Insight . . . came to me: as to this noble truth, this cause of suffering has been abandoned.

'Insight with regard to things not previously heard came to me—knowledge, understanding, wisdom, light: the noble truth that this was the cessation of suffering. Insight . . . came to me: as to this noble truth, this cessation of suffering must be directly experienced. Insight . . . came to me: as to this noble truth, this cessation of suffering has been directly experienced.

'Insight into things not previously heard came to me—knowledge, understanding, wisdom, light: the noble truth that this is the practice leading to the cessation of suffering. Insight . . . came to me: as to this noble truth, the practice leading to the cessation of suffering must be cultivated. Insight . . . came to me: as to this noble truth, the practice leading to the cessation of suffering has been cultivated.

'Monks, as long as my true knowledge and insight into these four noble truths in these three stages and twelve aspects* was not completely clear, I did not claim that—in this world with its gods and 423
human beings, its Brahmā and Māra, that in this generation with its ascetics and brahmans, its princes and peoples—I was one who had fully understood the unsurpassed perfect awakening. But as soon as my true knowledge and insight into these four noble truths in these three stages and twelve aspects was completely clear, then I claimed that—in this world with its gods and human beings, its Brahmā and Māra, that in this generation with its ascetics and brahmans, its princes and peoples—I was one who had fully understood the unsurpassed perfect awakening. And the knowledge and insight came to me that my freedom was unshakeable; this was my last birth; there would be no further existence.'

This is what the Blessed One said. Gladdened, the group of five monks felt joy at the Blessed One's words. And while this explanation was being given, there arose in the venerable Koṇḍañña a vision of truth without blemish, untarnished: 'The nature of everything whose nature it is to arise is to cease.'

And when the Blessed One had turned the wheel of Truth, the Gods of the Earth proclaimed: 'This wheel of Truth that the Blessed has turned in Benares, at Isipatana in the animal park, no ascetic, nor brahman, nor god, nor Māra, nor Brahmā, nor anyone in the world can stop!'

And when the Gods of the Four Kings heard their proclamation, they proclaimed: 'This wheel of Truth that the Blessed One has turned in Benares, at Isipatana in the animal park, no ascetic, nor brahman, nor god, nor Māra, nor Brahmā, nor anyone in the world can stop!'

And when the Gods of the Heaven of the Thirty-Three . . . the Yāma Gods . . . the Contented Gods . . . the Gods who Delight in Creation . . . the Gods who Master the Creations of Others heard their proclamation, they proclaimed: 'This wheel of Truth that the Blessed One has turned in Benares, at Isipatana in the animal park, no ascetic, nor brahman, nor god, nor Māra, nor Brahmā, nor anyone in the world can stop!'

Thus, at that moment, that instant, that second the proclamation reached the world of Brahmā, and this ten-thousandfold world system shook, trembled, and quaked. A boundless splendid radiance appeared in the world, surpassing the majesty of the gods.

Then the Blessed One breathed a sigh: 'Koṇḍañña has understood! Koṇḍañña has understood!'

And so it was that the venerable Koṇḍañña was known as 'Koṇḍañña Understood'.

FROM THE COLLECTION OF NUMBERED SAYINGS

(Aṅguttara-nikāya)

Introduction

The Aṅguttara-nikāya is, literally, the collection of 'progressively increasing by an item' (*aṅguttara*) sayings. Like the Saṃyutta-nikāya, it contains miscellaneous and generally shorter suttas, but in this case not arranged according to topic but simply according to the number of items discussed in a sutta, so suttas concerned with a single item are grouped first, then suttas concerned with two items, three items, and so on up to eleven items. The main focus is in principle, then, numbered lists. Such lists are characteristic of early Buddhist literature and indeed early Indian literature more generally. Such numbered lists are in part mnemonic devices, and reflect the oral origins of Buddhist literature.

Numbered lists are also a feature of the Saṃyutta-nikāya, where we find suttas on the five aggregates, six sense spheres, and so on. But for the most part the Aṅguttara-nikāya focuses on the less prominent numbered list, so that while, for example, the five aggregates are mentioned incidentally in the Aṅguttara-nikāya, we do not find a whole series of suttas on the five aggregates in 'the section of fives'. Sometimes, however, it is not obvious why a particular sutta has been placed in a particular numbered section (as in the case of 'the *Kālāma-sutta*', taken here as the representative of 'the section of threes').

Except in the case of 'the section of ones', I have taken just one sutta to represent each numbered section. As with the Saṃyutta-nikāya, the selection is inevitably somewhat arbitrary, though I have aimed at variety of subject-matter across the eleven sections. Thus we begin with five very short suttas that highlight the significance of a single quality, and then move on to the debt owed to our mothers and fathers (twos), the so-called *Kālāma-sutta* (threes), the fear of death (fours), a simile for the way the Buddha helps his pupils (fives), the relations of those who take different approaches to meditation (sixes), a series of similes for the fleetingness of our lives (sevens), the qualities that make the world go around (eights), things that it is impossible for an arahat to do (nines), the powers of the Tathāgata (tens), and the benefits of the meditation on friendliness (*mettā*) (elevens).

As in the Saṃyutta-nikāya, names of the suttas in the Aṅguttara-nikāya are not as fixed by the tradition as in the Dīgha-and Majjhima-nikāyas, and I introduce them by the usually single terms that are used as something of a mnemonic tag but are not always consistent in the manuscripts and editions.

FROM THE SECTION OF ONES

A Finger-Snap (A I 11)

This is what I have heard . . .

'Monks, if a monk pays attention to the mental state of friendliness for just a finger-snap, then he is to be called a monk: he lives as someone whose meditation is not in vain; he carries out the teacher's instruction, he responds to his advice, and his consumption of the country's alms is not useless. What can one say of the one who makes much of friendliness?'

This is what I have heard . . .

'Monks, whatever unwholesome qualities there are that contribute to and participate in the unwholesome, they all follow in the train of the mind.'

This is what I have heard . . .

'Monks, whatever wholesome qualities there are that contribute to and participate in the wholesome, they all follow in the train of the mind.'

This is what I have heard . . .

'Monks, I consider no other single quality to be so much the cause of the arising of unwholesome qualities that have not arisen and the wasting away of wholesome qualities that have arisen as this: inattentiveness. When a monk is inattentive, unwholesome qualities that have not arisen arise and wholesome qualities that have arisen waste away.'

This is what I have heard . . .

'Monks, I consider no other single quality to be so much the cause of the arising of wholesome qualities that have not arisen and the wasting away of unwholesome qualities that have arisen as this: attentiveness. When a monk is attentive, wholesome qualities that have not arisen arise and unwholesome qualities that have arisen waste away.'

FROM THE SECTION OF TWOS

Mother and Father (A I 61–62)

This is what I have heard . . . 'Monks, there are two people whom one cannot fully repay. Which two? One's mother and father. Having 62
a life of a hundred years and living a hundred years, one might carry one's mother on one shoulder and one's father on the other, anointing, bathing, massaging, and shampooing them, even while they excreted and urinated there, but still one would not have done enough, one would not have repaid them. One might establish one's mother and father as rulers of supreme authority over this whole earth with its abundance of seven treasures, but still one would not have done enough, one would not have repaid them. Why is this? Mothers and fathers do much for their children, bringing them up, feeding them, guiding them through this world.

'And yet one who brings about the fullness of faith in parents who have little faith, who directs them towards and establishes them in the fullness of faith; one who brings about the fullness of virtue in parents who have little virtue, who directs them towards and establishes them in the fullness of virtue; one who brings about the fullness of generosity in parents who are stingy, who directs them towards and establishes them in the fullness of generosity; one who brings about the fullness of wisdom in parents who have little wisdom, who directs them towards and establishes them in the fullness of wisdom—by doing these things he has done enough, he has repaid them, he has done more than enough.'

FROM THE SECTION OF THREES

Kesaputta (A I 188–193)

This is what I have heard. Once the Blessed One, when wandering on tour with a large company of monks, came to the Kālāma town called Kesaputta.* Then the Kālāmas of Kesaputta heard that the ascetic Gotama, the Sakya son who had gone forth from the Sakyan clan, had arrived in Kesaputta, and of the lovely report spread abroad concerning the Blessed Gotama: 'For the following reasons he is a Blessed One—he is an arahat, a perfect buddha, accomplished in knowledge and conduct, happy, one who understands the world, an unsurpassed charioteer of men to be tamed, teacher of gods and men, a blessed buddha.' So they approached the Blessed One, and having approached him sat down to one side, some saluting the Blessed One respectfully, some exchanging pleasing and polite words with him, some bowing down before him with cupped hands, some having their clan names announced, some remaining silent.

Once seated, the Kālāmas of Kesaputta said to the Blessed One: 'Sir, there are some ascetics and brahmans who come to Kesaputta and set out and explain only their own theories, while attacking, insulting, disparaging, and rejecting the theories of others. Then
189 other ascetics and brahmans come to Kesaputta and they too set out and explain only their own theories, while attacking, insulting, disparaging, and rejecting the theories of others. Sir, we are doubtful and uncertain about who among these recognized ascetics and brahmans are telling the truth, and who lies.'

'It is right that you should be doubtful, Kālāmas, right that you should be uncertain. Your uncertainty concerns something that is indeed a matter for doubt.

'Kālāmas, you should not go along with something because of what you have been told, because of authority, because of tradition, because of accordance with scripture, on the grounds of reason, on the grounds of logic, because of analytic thought, because of abstract theoretical pondering, because of the appearance of the speaker, or because some ascetic is your teacher. When you know for yourselves that particular qualities are unwholesome, blameworthy, censured by the wise, and lead to harm and suffering when taken on and pursued, then you should give them up, Kālāmas.

'What do you think, Kālāmas? If greed arises in a person, is it for his good or harm?'

'His harm, sir.'

'And if this greedy person, with his mind overcome and consumed by greed, kills a living creature, takes what is not given, goes with another's wife, speaks what is false, and encourages others to act likewise, that will long be to his harm and suffering?'

'Certainly, sir.'

'What do you think, Kālāmas? If hate arises in a person, is it for his good or harm?'

'His harm, sir.'

'And if this hateful person, with his mind overcome and consumed by hate, kills a living creature, takes what is not given, goes with another's wife, speaks what is false, and encourages others to act likewise, that will long be to his harm and suffering?'

'Certainly, sir.'

'What do you think, Kālāmas? If delusion arises in a person, is it for his good or harm?'

'His harm, sir.' 190

'And if this deluded person, with his mind overcome and consumed by delusion, kills a living creature, takes what is not given, goes with another's wife, speaks what is false, and encourages others to act likewise, that will long be to his harm and suffering?'

'Certainly, sir.'

'So what do you think, Kālāmas? Are these qualities wholesome or unwholesome?'

'Unwholesome, sir.'

'Blameworthy or blameless?'

'Blameworthy, sir.'

'Censured or praised by the wise?'

'Censured by the wise, sir.'

'And when taken on and pursued, do they lead to harm and suffering, or not? How is it for you* in the case of these qualities?'

'When taken on and pursued, they lead to harm and suffering. This is how it is for us in the case of these qualities.'

'So, Kālāmas, what I have said, namely, that you should not go along with something because of what you have been told, because of authority, because of tradition, because of accordance with scripture, on the grounds of reason, on the grounds of logic, because of analytic thought, because of a view's bearing deep reflection, because of the appearance of the speaker, or because some ascetic is your teacher; that when you know for yourselves that particular qualities are unwholesome, blameworthy, censured by the wise, and lead to harm and suffering when taken on and pursued, then you should give them up— I have said all this with reference to the above example.

'Kālāmas, you should not go along with something because of what you have been told, because of authority, because of tradition, because of accordance with scripture, on the grounds of reason, on the grounds of logic, because of analytic thought, because of a view's bearing deep reflection, because of the appearance of the speaker, or because some ascetic is your teacher. When you know for yourselves that particular qualities are wholesome, blameless, praised by the wise, and lead to good and happiness when taken on and pursued, then you should engage in them and live by them, Kālāmas.

'What do you think, Kālāmas? If lack of greed arises in a person, is it for his good or harm?'

'His good, sir.'

'And if this person who is not greedy, whose mind is not overcome and consumed by greed, does not kill a living creature, does not take what is not given, does not go with another's wife, does not speak
191 what is false, and does not encourage others to act in this way, that will long be to his good and happiness?'

'Certainly, sir.'

'What do you think, Kālāmas? If lack of hate arises in a person, is it for his good or harm?'

'His good, sir.'

'And if this person who is not hateful, whose mind is not overcome and consumed by hate, does not kill a living creature, does not take what is not given, does not go with another's wife, does not speak what is false, and does not encourage others to act in this way, that will long be to his good and happiness?'

'Certainly, sir.'

'What do you think, Kālāmas? If lack of delusion arises in a person, is it for his good or harm?'

'His good, sir.'

'And if this person who is not deluded, whose mind is not overcome and consumed by delusion, does not kill a living creature, does not take what is not given, does not go with another's wife, does not speak what is false, and does not encourage others to act in this way, that will long be to his good and happiness?'

'Certainly, sir.'

'So what do you think, Kālāmas? Are these qualities wholesome or unwholesome?'

'Wholesome, sir.'

'Blameworthy or blameless?'

'Blameless, sir.'

'Censured or praised by the wise?'

'Praised by the wise, sir.'

'And when taken on and pursued, do they lead to good and happiness, or not? How is it for you in the case of these qualities?'

'When taken on and pursued, they lead to good and happiness. This is how it is for us in the case of these qualities.'

'So, Kālāmas, I have said this: that you should not go along with something because of what you have been told, because of authority, because of tradition, because of accordance with scripture, on the grounds of reason, on the grounds of logic, because of analytic thought, because of abstract theoretical pondering, because of the appearance of the speaker, or because some ascetic is your teacher; that when you know for yourselves that particular qualities are wholesome, blameless, praised by the wise, and lead to good and happiness when taken on and pursued, then you should engage in
them and live by them. And I have said this with reference to the 192
above example.

'Kālāmas, the noble disciple who is thus free of longing and ill will, who is unmuddled, fully aware, and mindful remains pervading the first quarter with a mind full of friendliness, likewise the second, third, and fourth quarters. In the same way he remains completely pervading the whole world, above, below, around, everywhere, with a mind full of friendliness—a mind abundant, great, measureless, free from hostility, free from affliction. He remains pervading the first quarter with a mind full of compassion . . . with a mind full of sympathetic joy . . . with a mind full of equanimity, likewise the second, third, and fourth quarters. In the same way he remains completely pervading the whole world, above, below, around, everywhere, with a mind full of equanimity—a mind abundant, great, measureless, free from hostility, free from affliction.

'Kālāmas, the noble disciple is one whose mind is in this way free of hostility, free of affliction, free of defilement, and purified. Here and now he gains four reasons to breathe easily.

'He thinks: "If there is another world, if good and bad deeds do bear fruit and yield result, then at the breaking up of the body after death I shall be reborn in a happy realm, a heaven world." This is the first reason.

'He thinks: "But if there is no other world, if good and bad deeds do not bear fruit and yield result, then here and now I shall make myself free of hostility and affliction, happy, free of misery." This is the second reason.

'He thinks: "But if evil can be committed by one who acts, and I intend no evil to anyone, how can suffering affect me who does no evil deed?" This is the third reason.

'He thinks: "But if evil is not committed by one who acts, I shall see myself doubly purified."* This is the fourth reason to breathe easily.

'Kālāmas, the noble disciple is one whose mind is in this way free of hostility, free of affliction, free of defilement, and purified, and these are four reasons he gains here and now to breathe easily.'

'Certainly, Blessed One! Certainly, Happy One! The noble disciple is one whose mind is in this way free of hostility, free of afflic-
193 tion, free of defilement, and purified . . . and these are four reasons he gains here and now to breathe easily.

'Excellent, sir! Excellent! As if someone were to set upright what had been knocked down, or reveal what had been hidden, or point out the way to someone who was lost, or hold a lamp up in the dark so that those with eyes could see—just so the Blessed One has made the Truth clear in various ways. Sir, we go to the Blessed One for refuge, and to the Teaching and the Community of monks. Let the Blessed One accept us as lay followers who have taken refuge from this day for as long as we live.'

FROM THE SECTION OF FOURS

Jāṇussoṇi (A II 173–176)

This is what I have heard . . . Then the brahman Jāṇussoṇi approached the Blessed One. Having approached, he saluted him respectfully, exchanging pleasing and polite words with him before sitting down to one side.

Once seated, he said to the Blessed One: 'Gotama sir, my opinion, my view is this: that there is no one who is mortal who is not afraid of, not frightened of death.'

'Brahman, there are those who are mortal and who are afraid of, are frightened of, death. But there are those who are mortal and who are not afraid of, not frightened of death.

'Who is someone who is mortal and who is afraid of, is frightened of, death? Take someone who has not overcome his greed for the objects of the senses, who has not overcome his desire, liking, yearn- 174
ing, aching, and craving for them. This person is stricken by some serious illness or disease. At this he thinks: "These cherished objects of the senses are going to abandon me! I am going to abandon these cherished objects of the senses!" He grieves, frets, laments; he cries out, beating his chest; he becomes deranged. This is someone who is mortal and who is afraid of, is frightened of death.

'Again, take someone who has not overcome his greed for the body, who has not overcome his desire, liking, yearning, aching, and craving for it. This person is stricken by some serious illness or disease. At this he thinks: "This cherished body is going to abandon me! I am going to abandon this cherished body!" He grieves, frets, laments; he cries out, beating his chest; he becomes deranged. This is someone who is mortal and who is afraid of, is frightened of death.

'Again, take someone who has not done anything beautiful, not done anything wholesome, not provided himself with any refuge from danger,* but has done wrong, acting cruelly and wickedly. This person is stricken by some serious illness or disease. At this he thinks: "I have not done anything beautiful or wholesome; I have not provided myself with any refuge from danger, but have done wrong, acting cruelly and wickedly. When I die my destiny will be the destiny of those who have done wrong . . ." He grieves, frets, laments; he cries out, beating his chest; he becomes deranged. This is someone who is mortal and who is afraid of, is frightened of death.

'Again, take someone who has doubts, is undecided, is not quite sure about the true teaching. This person is stricken by some serious illness or disease. At this he thinks: "I have doubts and am undecided, not quite sure about the true teaching." He grieves, frets, laments; he cries out, beating his chest; he becomes deranged. This is someone who is mortal and who is afraid of, is frightened of death. 175

'Who is someone who is mortal but is not afraid of, not frightened of, death? Take someone who has overcome his greed for the objects of the senses, who has overcome his desire, liking, yearning, aching, and craving for them. This person is stricken by some serious illness or disease. At this he does not think:* "These cherished objects of the senses are going to abandon me! I am going to abandon these cherished objects of the senses!" He does not grieve, fret, lament; he does not cry out, beating his chest; he does not become deranged. This is someone who is mortal but is not afraid of, not frightened of death.

'Again, take someone who has overcome his greed for the body, who has overcome his desire, liking, yearning, aching, and craving for it. This person is stricken by some serious illness or disease. At this he does not think: "This cherished body is going to abandon me! I am going to abandon this cherished body!" He does not grieve, fret, lament; he does not cry out, beating his chest; he does not become deranged. This is someone who is mortal but is not afraid of, not frightened of death.

'Again, take someone who has not done wrong, not acted cruelly and wickedly, but has done beautiful things, wholesome things, and provided himself with a refuge from danger. This person is stricken by some serious illness or disease. At this he thinks: "I have not done wrong, not acted cruelly and wickedly, but have done beautiful things, wholesome things, and provided myself with a refuge from danger. When I die my destiny will be the destiny of those who have not done wrong . . ." He does not grieve, fret, lament; he does not cry out, beating his chest; he does not become deranged. This is someone who is mortal but is not afraid of, not frightened of death.

'Again, take someone who has no doubts, is decided, is quite sure about the true teaching. This person is stricken by some serious illness or disease. At this he thinks: "I have no doubts, I am decided and quite sure about the true teaching." He does not grieve, fret, lament; he does not cry out, beating his chest; he does not become
176 deranged. This is someone who is mortal but is not afraid of, not frightened of death.'

'Excellent, sir! Excellent! As if someone were to set upright what had been knocked down, or reveal what had been hidden, or point out the way to someone who was lost, or hold a lamp up in the dark so that those with eyes could see—just so the Blessed One has made the Truth clear in various ways. Sir, I go to the Blessed One for refuge, and to the Teaching and the Community of monks. Let the Blessed One accept me as a lay follower who has taken refuge from this day for as long as I live.'

FROM THE SECTION OF FIVES

Excited by the Senses (A III 5–6)

This is what I have heard . . .

'Monks, for the most part beings are excited* by the pleasures of the senses. When a son of good family lays aside his scythe and carrying-pole* and goes forth from home into homelessness, it can be said that he has gone forth out of faith. Why is this? Because pleasures of the senses of various kinds are to be enjoyed in one's youth. And all pleasures of the senses, whether they are basic, normal, or extreme, can be reckoned simply pleasures of the senses.

'As if there were a charming little baby boy lying on his back, and because of the nurse's inattentiveness he had put a stick or piece of pottery in his mouth. The nurse would immediately notice this, and as soon as she had noticed it she would remove it. But if she were unable to remove it immediately, then she would hold his head with her left hand and, hooking a finger of her right hand, remove it, even drawing blood. Why is this? It causes the boy pain, that I don't deny. Yet the nurse has to act in this way if she desires the boy's good, cares for his welfare, is kind, and motivated by kindness. But when that boy is old enough to understand himself, then the nurse need not worry; her attitude to the boy is that he will look after himself and will not be careless.

'In exactly the same way, monks, as long as a monk has not achieved what he must concerning wholesome qualities through faith, through self respect, through conscience, through energy, through wisdom, I must watch over that monk. But when a monk has achieved what he must concerning wholesome qualities through faith, through self respect, through conscience, through energy, through wisdom, then I need not worry; my attitude to that monk is that he will look after himself and will not be careless.'

FROM THE SECTION OF SIXES

Mahācunda (A III 355–356)

This is what I have heard. At one time the venerable Mahācunda was staying in the Ceti country at Sahajātī. There he addressed the monks.

'Friends!'

'Friend!' replied those monks to the venerable Mahācunda.

This is what the venerable Mahācunda said: 'Monks who are specialists in the teachings* disparage monks who are meditators: "Those meditators, they meditate and meditate, always saying, 'We are the ones who meditate!' But what do they meditate for? Why do they meditate? How exactly do they meditate?" As a result, neither the monks who are specialists in the teachings are satisfied, nor the monks who are meditators; and neither are acting in the interests of the good and happiness of the many, for the benefit, good, and happiness of the many,* of gods and men.

'On the other hand, monks who are meditators disparage monks who are specialists in the teachings: "Those specialists in the teachings, who are always saying, 'We are the ones who are specialists in the teachings!'—they are agitated, uncontrolled, restless, talkative, conversing about this and that; with their minds astray, they are not fully aware, not concentrated; their thoughts wander and their senses are uncontrolled. But what are they specialists in the teachings for? Why are they specialists in the teachings? How exactly are they specialists in the teachings?" As a result, neither the monks who are meditators are satisfied, nor the monks who are specialists in the teachings; and neither are acting in the interests of the good and happiness of the many, for the benefit, good, and happiness of the many, of gods and men.

'Monks who are specialists in the teachings only speak in praise of monks who are specialists in the teachings, and never of monks who are meditators. As a result, neither the monks who are specialists in
356 the teachings are satisfied, nor the monks who are meditators; and neither are acting in the interests of the good and happiness of the many, for the benefit, good, and happiness of the many, of gods and men.

'Monks who are meditators only speak in praise of monks who are meditators, and never of monks who are specialists in the teachings. As a result, neither the monks who are meditators are satisfied, nor the monks who are specialists in the teachings; and neither are acting in the interests of the good and happiness of the many, for the benefit, good, and happiness of the many, of gods and men.

'So, friends, you should train yourselves to think: "As monks who are specialists in the teachings we will speak in praise of monks who are meditators." Why must you train yourselves in this way? They are remarkable and difficult to find in this world, these people who live having experienced the deathless directly.

'So, friends, you should train yourselves to think: "As monks who are meditators we will speak in praise of monks who are specialists in the teachings." Why must you train yourselves in this way? They are remarkable and difficult to find in this world, these people who reach insight, having penetrated the deep significance of a term by their understanding.'

FROM THE SECTION OF SEVENS

Araka (A IV 136–139)

This is what I have heard . . .

'Monks, long ago there was a teacher called Araka, one who had found a way across and overcome greed for the pleasures of the senses. He had several hundred disciples, whom he taught the following teaching.

'"Short is the life of human beings, brahmans.* Brief and fleeting,
it is full of pain and despair. You should heed advice, do what is 137
wholesome, practise the spiritual life; there is no escape from death for one who is born. Just as a dewdrop on the tip of a blade of grass as soon as the sun comes up quickly disappears and doesn't last long; even so, like a dewdrop, the life of human beings is brief and fleeting, full of pain and despair. You should heed advice, do what is wholesome, practise the spiritual life, there is no escape from death for one who is born. Just as, when the god brings rain in the autumn in huge drops, a bubble on the surface of the water quickly disappears and

doesn't last long; even so, like a bubble on water, the life of human beings is brief and fleeting, full of pain and despair. You should heed advice . . . Just as a line drawn on water with a stick quickly disappears and doesn't last long; even so, like a line drawn on water, the life of human beings is brief and fleeting, full of pain and despair. You should heed advice . . . Just as a river that has arisen far away in the mountains and is flowing swiftly along, taking everything with it, never for a moment, a second, an instant stops, but just moves, swirls, and flows on; even so, like a river from the mountains, the life of human beings is brief and fleeting, full of pain and despair. You should heed advice . . . Just as a strong man might form a ball of spit at the tip of his tongue and simply spit it out; even so, like a ball of spit, the life of human beings is brief and fleeting, full of pain and
138 despair. You should heed advice . . . Just as a piece of meat thrown into an iron pan that has been heating all day quickly disappears and doesn't last long; even so, like a piece of meat, the life of human beings is brief and fleeting, full of pain and despair. You should heed advice . . . Just as when a cow ready for slaughter is being led to the slaughterhouse, and each step she takes brings her closer to slaughter, closer to death; even so, like a cow ready for slaughter, the life of human beings is brief and fleeting, full of pain and despair. You should heed advice, do what is wholesome, practise the spiritual life; there is no escape from death for one who is born."

'Now at that time, monks, the lifespan of human beings was 60,000 years, and young women were ready for marriage at 500 years. At that time, monks, human beings only suffered six afflictions: cold and heat, hunger and thirst, excreting and urinating. And yet this teacher Araka, even while human beings were so long-lived, lasted so long, had so few afflictions, taught his disciples this teaching: "Short is the life of human beings . . . there is no escape from death for one who is born." To speak appropriately about this nowadays, one would have to say: "Short is the life of human beings . . . there is no escape from death for one who is born."

'Nowadays, to live a long time is to live a hundred years, more or less. To live a hundred years, monks, is to live for just 300 seasons: a hundred cool seasons, a hundred hot seasons, a hundred rainy seasons. To live for 300 seasons is to live for just 1,200 months:
139 400 months of cool season, 400 months of hot season, 400 months of rainy season. To live for 1,200 months is to live for just

2,400 half-months: 600 half-months of cool season, 600 half-months of hot season, 600 half-months of rainy season. To live for 2,400 half-months is to live for just 36,000 days: 12,000 days of cool season, 12,000 days of hot season, 12,000 days of rainy season. To live for 36,000 days is to eat just 72,000 meals: 24,000 in the cool season, 24,000 in the hot season, 24,000 in the rainy season, including taking one's mother's milk and missed meals. The reasons for missing meals are these: when one is upset one does not eat, when one is in pain, sick, keeping the observance-day fast one does not eat, and also when one cannot get food. In this way, monks, I have reckoned the life of a man who lives for a hundred years—I have reckoned his lifespan, the seasons, the years, the months, the half-months, the days and nights, the meals, and the meals missed.

'Whatever a teacher, desiring his disciples' welfare, should do for them out of kindness, through kindness, this I have done for you. Here are roots of trees. Here are deserted houses. Meditate, monks! Do not later have regrets. This is my instruction to you.'

FROM THE SECTION OF EIGHTS

Worldly Qualities (A IV 157–160)

This is what I have heard . . .

'Monks, these eight worldly qualities go around with the world, and the world goes round with these eight worldly qualities. Which eight? Gain and loss, renown and disgrace, criticism and praise, happiness and unhappiness. These eight worldly qualities go around with the world, and the world goes round with these eight worldly qualities. Monks, an uninformed ordinary person will experience both gain and loss, renown and disgrace, criticism and praise, happiness and unhappiness. An informed noble disciple, too, will experience both gain and loss, renown and disgrace, criticism and praise, happiness and unhappiness. But what is the distinction between an uninformed 158
ordinary person and an informed noble disciple in this regard? What is the difference? What makes them unlike each other?'

'The Blessed One is our source for such matters, the Blessed One is our guide, the Blessed One is the one we turn to. It is certainly proper when the significance of this question is clear only to the

Blessed One. What we have heard from the Blessed One we will remember.'

'Then listen. Pay careful attention to what I shall say.'

'Yes, sir,' replied those monks to the Blessed One.

This is what the Blessed One said: 'When an uninformed ordinary person experiences gain, he does not reflect that while he may experience a particular gain, yet his gain is impermanent, painful, and liable to change; he does not understand it as it truly is. When an uninformed ordinary person experiences loss . . . renown . . . disgrace . . . criticism . . . praise . . . happiness . . . unhappiness, he does not reflect that while he may experience a particular unhappiness, yet his unhappiness is impermanent, painful, and liable to change; he does not understand it as it truly is. And so his gain . . . loss . . . renown . . . disgrace . . . criticism . . . praise . . . happiness . . . unhappiness takes hold of his mind and stays there. He embraces any gain that comes, and recoils at loss; he embraces any renown that comes, and recoils at disgrace; he embraces any praise that comes, and recoils at criticism; he embraces any happiness that comes, and recoils at unhappiness. Caught by what he likes and dislikes, he cannot free himself from birth, old-age, and death, from grief, lamentation, pain, sorrow, and despair. He cannot free himself from suffering, I declare.

'But when an informed noble disciple experiences gain, he reflects that while he may experience a particular gain, yet his gain is impermanent, painful, and liable to change; he understands it as it truly is. When an informed noble disciple experiences loss . . . renown . . . disgrace . . . criticism . . . praise . . . happiness . . . unhappiness, he reflects that while he may experience a particular unhappiness, yet his unhappiness is impermanent, painful, and liable to change; he understands it as it truly is. And so his gain . . . loss . . . renown . . . disgrace . . . criticism . . . praise . . . happiness . . . unhappiness does not take hold of his mind and stay there. He does not embrace any gain that comes, and recoil at loss; he does not embrace any renown that comes, and recoil at disgrace; he does not embrace any praise that comes, and recoil at criticism; he does not embrace any happiness that comes, and recoil at unhappiness. Having given up likes and dislikes, he frees himself from birth, old-age, and death, from grief, lamentation, pain, sorrow, and despair. He frees himself from suffering, I declare. This is the distinction between an uninformed ordinary person and an informed noble disciple in this regard. This is the difference. This is what makes them unlike each other.

'Gain and loss, renown and disgrace, criticism and praise,
happiness and unhappiness—
These qualities are impermanent in human life, inconstant,
liable to change.
But, mindful, the sage knows them; he observes how they are
liable to change.
Desirable things do not upset his mind, nor is there resistance
to the undesirable;
His likes and dislikes have vanished, gone away, and exist no
more.
Having known the place that is stainless, free of grief, he has
crossed beyond existence.'

FROM THE SECTION OF NINES

Sutavat (A IV 369–371)

This is what I have heard. Once the Blessed One was staying at Rājagaha, on the mountain called Vultures' Peak. Then the wanderer Sutavat approached the Blessed One. Having approached, he saluted him respectfully, exchanging pleasing and polite words with him before sitting down to one side.

Once seated, he said to the Blessed One: 'Once, when the Blessed One* was staying at Giribbaja right here in Rājagaha, I heard this directly from the Blessed One, I learnt this directly from the Blessed One. If anyone is an arahat and has destroyed the taints, lived the spiritual life, done what was to be done, put down the burden, 370
reached the true goal, destroyed the fetters of existence, and is freed through faultless knowledge, then there are five things that he is incapable of doing. A monk who has destroyed the taints is incapable of deliberately depriving a living being of life; he is incapable of taking what is not given such that it would be reckoned as theft; he is incapable of engaging in the sexual act; he is incapable of consciously saying what is untrue; he is incapable of amassing material

things to enjoy as he did previously when he lived in a house.* I hope I have properly understood the Blessed One, that I have fully grasped what he meant, paid full attention, and remembered it correctly.'

'You have indeed, Sutavat, properly understood this; you have fully grasped what was meant, paid full attention, and remembered it correctly. Previously and now I say this: if anyone is an arahat and has destroyed the taints, lived the spiritual life, done what was to be done, put down the burden, reached the true goal, destroyed the fetters of existence, and is freed through faultless knowledge, then there are nine things that he is incapable of doing. A monk who has destroyed the taints is incapable of deliberately depriving a living being of life; he is incapable of taking what is not given such that it would be reckoned as theft; he is incapable of engaging in the sexual act; he is incapable of consciously saying what is untrue; he is incapable of amassing material things to enjoy as he did previously when he lived in a house; he is incapable of following a course of action out of desire; he is incapable of following a course of action out of hate; he is incapable of following a course of action out of delusion; he is
371 incapable of following a course of action out of fear. Previously and now I say this, that if anyone is an arahat and has destroyed the taints . . . then he is incapable of doing these nine things.'

FROM THE SECTION OF TENS

A Lion's Roar (A V 32–36)

This is what I have heard . . .

'Monks, the lion is the king of beasts. In the evening he comes out from his lair. And when he has come out, he stretches himself. Then
133 he surveys the four quarters in full and roars his lion's roar, three times. Then, once he has roared his lion's roar, he sets off in search of food. What is the reason for this? He thinks, "Let me not bring about the death of small creatures that have wandered astray." And "lion", monks, is a term for the Tathāgata, an arahat who is a perfectly awakened buddha. And when the Tathāgata teaches the Truth in an assembly, that is his lion's roar.

'The Tathāgata, monks, has the following ten powers of a Tathāgata, and because he has these ten powers he perceives his supremacy, roars the lion's roar in assemblies, and turns the sublime wheel.* Which ten powers?

'As to this, he truly understands why what is possible is possible and why what is impossible is impossible. That he truly understands this—this is a power of the Tathāgata that the Tathāgata has, a power with reference to which he perceives his supremacy, roars the lion's roar in assemblies, and turns the sublime wheel.

'Again, he truly understands by way of its foundation and cause the result that follows from the undertaking of an action in the past, present, or future. That he truly understands this—this is a power of the Tathāgata . . .

'Again, he truly understands all forms of practice wherever they may lead. That he truly understands this—this is a power of the Tathāgata . . .

'Again, he truly understands the world that comprises many and 34
various elements. That he truly understands this—this is a power of the Tathāgata . . .

'Again, he truly understands the various dispositions of beings. That he truly understands this—this is a power of the Tathāgata . . .

'Again, he truly understands the inferior or superior state of the faculties of other beings and persons. That he truly understands this—this is a power of the Tathāgata . . .

Again, he truly understands how the absorptions, freedoms, concentrations, and attainments are liable to defects, and how to purify and emerge from them.* That he truly understands this—this is a power of the Tathāgata . . .

'Again, he remembers his numerous previous lives: one birth, two
births, three, four, five births; ten, twenty, thirty, forty, fifty births; a 35
hundred, a thousand, a hundred thousand births; over many periods of expansion of the universe, over many periods of contraction, over many periods of expansion and contraction. He remembers, "In that life I had that name, belonged to that family, that class, had that food, experienced that unhappiness, that happiness, and met my end in that way. When I died there I was born in that place. There I had that name, belonged to that family, that class, had that food, experienced that unhappiness, that happiness, and met my end in that way. When I died there I was born here." In this way he remembers

the various circumstances and details of his many previous lives. That he remembers this—this is a power of the Tathāgata . . .

'Again, with the godlike vision that is purified, surpassing that of men, he sees beings dying and being born. He understands how beings are inferior or superior, fair or ugly, fortunate or unfortunate, according to their actions: "These beings behaved badly in body, badly in speech, badly in thought; disparaging the noble ones, they held wrong views and performed the sorts of action that follow from wrong view. At the breaking up of the body after death they were born in hell, a realm of loss, misfortune, and torment. These beings, on the other hand, behaved well in body, well in speech, well in thought; not disparaging the noble ones, they held right views and performed the sorts of action that follow from right view. At the breaking up of the body after death they were born in a happy heaven world." In this way, with the godlike vision that is purified, surpassing that of men, he sees beings dying and being born. He understands how beings are inferior or superior, fair or ugly, fortunate or
36 unfortunate, according to their actions. That he understands this—this is a power of the Tathāgata . . .

'Again, with destruction of the taints he lives, having experienced and attained for himself through direct knowledge here and now the freedom of mind and understanding that is without any taint. That he lives having attained this—this is a power of the Tathāgata that the Tathāgata has, a power with reference to which he perceives his supremacy, roars the lion's roar in assemblies, and turns the sublime wheel.'

FROM THE SECTION OF ELEVENS

Friendliness (A V 342)

This is what I have heard . . .

'Monks, when freeing the mind through friendliness is practised, cultivated, made much of, made the vehicle of one's practice, made firm, pursued, built up, and fully undertaken, eleven benefits are to be expected. Which eleven? One sleeps well; one wakes up feeling happy; one does not have bad dreams; one is dear to human beings;

one is dear to non-human beings; the gods protect one; fire, poison, and weapons do not harm one; one's mind easily attains concentration; the expression on one's face is serene; one dies unconfused and, if one penetrates no further, is born in the world of Brahmā. When freeing the mind through friendliness is practised, cultivated, made much of, made the vehicle of one's practice, made firm, pursued, built up, and fully undertaken, these eleven benefits are to be expected.'

EXPLANATORY NOTES

6 *This is what I have heard*: these are traditionally regarded as the words of Ānanda as he introduced each of the Buddha's discourses at the first Buddhist 'council' at Rājagaha three months after the Buddha's death (Sv 26). Buddhist tradition recognizes two ways of punctuating the phrase. The Pali tradition prefers the punctuation that appears in my translation; the Buddhist scriptural traditions that have come down to us from North India, and China and Tibet, prefer the alternative punctuation (*This is what I heard on one occasion. The Blessed One was staying . . .*), although both traditions appear to know both ways of punctuating the phrase. There is no modern scholarly consensus on which should be regarded as the 'original' or 'correct' punctuation—nor on what difference it makes. See J. Brough, '"Thus have I heard . . ."', *Bulletin of the School of Oriental and African Studies*, 13 (1949), 416–26; B. Galloway, '"Thus Have I Heard: At One Time . . ."', *Indo-Iranian Journal*, 34 (1991), 87–104.

Jīvaka Komārabhacca: his story is found elsewhere in the Pali canon (Vin I 268–81). According to tradition, he was the son of a courtesan. Abandoned at birth, he was found and brought up in the royal household. Having studied medicine in Takkasilā (Taxila) in North-West India, he returned to Rājagaha where he became the royal physician. He also treated the Buddha, of whom he became a great supporter, donating the mango grove mentioned in the present sutta as the place where the Buddha was staying.

7 *twelve hundred and fifty monks*: the number of the Buddha's full assembly (*sannipāta*) of awakened monks or arahats (D II 6).

observance day known as White Lotus: the full moon at the end of Kattikā (October–November), the fourth month of the rainy season (*vassa*) and the time when the white lotus is said to flower; 'observance days' (*uposatha*) are the days of the new and full moon when monks traditionally recite and confess breaches of the monastic rule (*pātimokkha*) and the laity undertake additional religious observances and precepts.

son of the Princess of Videha: elsewhere (e.g. Ja II 403) we are told that Ajātasattu's mother was a princess of Kosala; Buddhaghosa, by resort to a play on *vedehi*, explains that the epithet means 'wise woman' (Sv 139); cf. *DPPN*, s.v. Vedehiputta. The epithet is given in the text every time the king's name is mentioned, though I have omitted it except at the beginning and close of the sutta.

one who has found a way across: *titthakara* (Skt: *tīrthakara*), literally one who makes a ford across a stream or river. The image refers to the way in which a great religious teacher is one who finds a way to cross the flood of existence, or to cross from this shore, which is fraught with dangers, to the safety of the far shore (cf. the Buddha's famous simile of the raft at M I 134–5). The term, like a number of other terms, including *buddha* and *jina* ('conqueror'), is common to Indian religion as a whole, although in the course of India's long religious history particular terms have come to have a special association with particular traditions, and so Buddhism talks more of *buddhas*, and Jainism (the tradition of the Jina) more of *jinas* and *tīrthakaras*.

7 *possesses the pearls of wisdom*: the term *rataññū* is traditionally taken as deriving from *rātri* ('night') and √*jñā* ('know') and as meaning 'knowing [many] nights', i.e. of some experience (Sv 143); K. R. Norman, however, has suggested a more convincing derivation from Sanskrit *ratna* ('jewel'); see *Journal of the Pali Text Society*, 9 (1981), 40–1.

8 *an arahat and perfect buddha*: both *arahat* and *buddha* are honorific titles with particular implications in Indian religious literature; the former means literally 'worthy one' and the latter 'one who has woken up [to the knowledge of the way things are]'. Both are used in Buddhist texts only of the fully realized Buddhist saint. But such terms are not exclusively Buddhist but common to various Indian religious traditions. This formula lists nine qualities of the Buddha; these form the basis of the traditional meditation practice of 'recollection of the Buddha' (*buddhānussati*); see Vism VII 1–67.

9 *my son the prince Udāyibhadda*: in fact tradition has it that Ajātasattu was eventually also murdered by his son, and he in turn by his son (Mhv IV 1–2); see also *DPPN*, s.v. Ajātasattu.

10 *with cupped hands*: the term *añjali* (q.v. MW, *CPD*, *DOP*) seems originally to have referred to a gesture of holding out the cupped hands to make an offering; it can also refer to the gesture of holding the joined palms before the chest or forehead.

11 *non-existence of action*: later Indian sources associate Pūraṇa Kassapa's name with Ājīvikism, and it seems clear that he was an early Ājīvika teacher, his antinomian ethics being consonant with Ājīvika determinism. Later Buddhist sources give what must be a largely legendary account of his life that ends in his suicide; see A. L. Basham, *History and Doctrines of the Ājīvikas* (London, 1951), 80–90. From the Buddhist point of view, Pūraṇa's denial that how we behave matters constitutes a basic 'wrong view' (*micchā-diṭṭhi*), since it denies the fundamental principle of the law of karma (Pali: *kamma*), namely, that good and bad actions have their due results (e.g. M III 72).

But how is a person like me . . . reproached?: as a good Indian king, Ajātasattu should provide for all ascetics and brahmans living in his realm.

12 *six types of existence*: these *abhijāti* are discussed by Basham, *History and Doctrine of the Ājīvikas*, 243–6, and seem to involve a classification according to a scheme of colours relating to psychological dispositions.

Nāgas: in Indian mythology, a type of serpent-demon, a being of some power, sometimes depicted as having a human face with a serpent-like body.

companions of the chief of gods: previous translators have taken *indriya* as 'faculty' or 'sense' here. This is one of its most common meanings, but in the middle of a list of what appear to be types of birth this makes little sense; I have taken it in the sense of 'belonging to Indra'.

7 transferences of the soul plus 700: following Basham, *History and Doctrine of the Ājīvikas*, 252.

14 *Nigaṇṭha Nātaputta*: the historical founder of Jainism, Mahāvīra. From a Buddhist perspective, Jainism tends to advocate rather more severe forms of ascetic practice as the path to liberation; the account of Jainism offered here is obscure and seems to be something of a Buddhist caricature. On Jainism generally see Padmanabh S. Jaini, *The Jaina Path of Purification* (Delhi, 1979) and Paul Dundas, *The Jains*, 2nd edn. (London, 2000).

15 *Aggivessana*: probably the name of the brahman clan to which Nigaṇṭha Nātaputta belonged (*DPPN*).

discipline of the four restraints: elsewhere (D III 48–9) this is explained as not killing living creatures, not taking what is not given, not saying what is false, and not pursuing the pleasures of the senses, which fits better with Jain understanding; see P. S. Jaini, '*Cātuyāma-saṃvara* in the Pāli Canon', in P. Balcerowicz and M. Marek (eds.), *Essays in Jain Philosophy and Religion* (Warsaw, 2002), 119–35.

16 *most confused*: though curiously, from one perspective Sañjaya's position might be seen as bearing a certain resemblance to the Buddha's position on the 'unanswered questions'; see the *Cūḷa-Māluṅkya-sutta* below.

17 *proper care and protection*: Ajātasattu here demonstrates that he knows his duties as a good king: he respects the vocation of the renouncer rather than demanding that his servant return to his former life.

19 *monastic rule*: *pātimokkha*, elaborated in the Vinaya-piṭaka by way of 227 precepts or, more literally, training rules (*sikkhāpada*).

accomplished in his moral behaviour: what follows are three sections detailing a monk's moral behaviour or conduct (*sīla*); the first, or 'short section', outlines the main principles of the monastic rule; the 'middle section' in effect elaborates on these by listing specific examples of the kinds of conduct a Buddhist monk refrains from, but from which other ascetics might not; the final 'long section' focuses on refraining from making a living by means of the 'childish arts' (*tiracchāna-vijjā*), which are detailed in long lists. The lists contained in the middle and long sections include many obscure single terms which can only be translated with the help of the explanations found in the commentary; it does not seem that the commentator himself always understood what the terms signified. The three sections on conduct are repeated in all thirteen suttas of the first volume of the Dīgha-nikāya, giving it its name: 'the volume with the sections on conduct' (*sīlakkhandha-vagga*).

20 *encourages*: PTS edition's *anuppādātā* = wrong reading for *anuppadātā* (see *CPD*; cf. other editions).

harming seeds and plants: according to some ancient Indian schools of thought, such as Jainism, plants are sentient beings (and thus part of the cycle of rebirth); injuring a plant is thus injuring a living being. Developed Buddhist thought did not accept that plants were sentient, but nevertheless, injuring plants was perhaps a sensitive issue among wandering ascetics. See L. Schmithausen, *The Problem of the Sentience of Plants in Earliest Buddhism* (Tokyo, 1991).

the wrong time: generally understood to mean after midday.

23 *scheming . . . pursuing gain with gain*: I follow Ñāṇamoli's translation of these terms in his *Path of Purification*, where it is explained that they refer to different ways which a monk might use to acquire donations of food, etc.; e.g. a monk might 'hint' to a lay follower with sugar cane, by saying: 'I just saw a snake on the ground that looked like sugar cane—that is a sign that it will be difficult to get alms today.' (See Vism I 42, 61–82.)

24 *glow in the skies*: *disdāha*; see MW, s.v. *digdāha*.

studying the nature of the world: *lokāyata*, which usually refers to the ancient Indian school of materialism, in Buddhist texts exemplified by the system of Ajita Kesakambalin; see introduction to the *Sāmaññaphala-sutta*.

Great One: *mahat*, which in later Indian literature refers to the primordial intelligence that, according to the Sāṃkhya system of thought, existed at the start of the universe; but there is no evidence for this concept at this early date. Buddhaghosa suggests Mahā-Brahmā, a god who might be thought of as a kind of personalized form of Mahat. Rhys Davids speculates that in fact the Earth Goddess Mahī is here referred to, which fits well with the mention of the Sun.

Sirī: (Skt: Śrī), the goddess of good fortune, the consort of the god Viṣṇu.

25 *administering emetics . . . medicines*: the point here, as with the other 'childish arts', is not so much that these practices are proscribed for the Buddhist monk per se, but that if a monk renders these services to those who give alms, then he is earning his living as a doctor and not a monk. In practice, Buddhist monks have been involved in the practice of medicine; see Kenneth G. Zysk, *Asceticism and Healing in Ancient India* (Delhi, 1998).

26 *with its wings*: a play on the word *patta*, which can mean both wing and alms bowl; the latter is included in the standard list of the basic possessions allowed a monk.

the open air: Ps II 215 appears to take *abbhokāsaṃ* as a separate item.

27 *jewellery for his wife*: *dārābharaṇāya*, but some editions read *dārabharaṇāya*, 'to support his wife', which is perhaps supported by the Sanskrit version's *dārāṇāṃ poṣanārthaṃ* (SBV 241).

28 *first absorption*: later tradition understands the absorptions (*jhāna*) as meditation attainments where the mind becomes progressively still as a

result of complete contentment with and absorption in a simple object of contemplation, such as the breath, friendliness directed towards all beings, a colour, etc. See L. S. Cousins, 'Buddhist Jhāna: Its Nature and Attainment according to the Pāli Sources', *Religion*, 3 (1973), 115–31.

29 *did not fill*: a reading with 'not' (*na*)—supported by various manuscripts and editions—seems preferable, indicating that the pool has its own deep source of cooling waters.

30 *concentrated in this way*: that is, in the way characteristic of the fourth absorption; this phrase is repeated introducing all subsequent attainments, indicating that they are achieved on the basis of the fourth absorption.

31 *accomplishments in meditation*: these kinds of powers, termed *iddhi* (Skt: *ṛddhi*), are commonly presented in the Indian traditions of meditation and yoga as acquired on the basis of deep concentration (*samādhi*); see also pp. 239–41.

34 *actions*: *kamma* (Skt: *karman*); the monk who achieves this knowledge understands directly the workings of the 'law of karma'.

taints: the *āsavas* or 'taints' represent the subtlest level of the 'defilements' (*kilesa*); with the destruction of the *āsavas* one is no longer subject to the influences of greed, hatred, and delusion; one is an awakened (*buddha*) arahat.

35 *there is nothing further required to this end*: literally 'there is nothing further for being thus/here' (*nāparaṃ itthattāya*). Most translators have taken the 'being thus/here' as referring to 'this (kind of) existence' and have then rendered the expression along the lines of 'there is no more of this (kind of) existence'; the justification for weakening the sense of the dative in this way is not clear. Context in fact suggests that 'being thus/here' refers rather to the state of having achieved the aim of the spiritual life (*brahmacariya*); the monk understands that there is nothing further required of him in order to reach his goal. The commentaries (Sp 169; Sv 226; Ps I 128, 180–1; Spk I 205; Mp II 264) offer two alternative interpretations which correspond in intent to those just outlined: (1) the monk understands that he has nothing further to do in order to know the four truths and destroy the defilements; (2) he understands that nothing more comes after the present 'arrangement' (*pakāra*) and that after the current stream of aggregates there will be no further stream.

Truth: *dhamma*.

Let the Blessed One . . . restraint: as Walshe points out (*Long Discourses of the Buddha*, 547), this is the monastic formula of confession; such monastic references in the sutta narratives have a special significance for monastic audiences; cf. S. Collins, 'The Discourse on What is Primary (Aggañña-Sutta): An Annotated Translation', *Journal of Indian Philosophy*, 21 (1993), 301–93.

36 *taken the life of his father*: killing one's father is one of five *ānantariya-kammas*, bad actions that must bear their fruits in the immediately following

existence in the form of rebirth in hell (the others are wounding a buddha, killing an arahat, causing a split in the Saṅgha, killing one's mother).

36 *vision of the Truth*: the expression *dhamma-cakkhu* is taken by the commentary (Sv I 237) to refer to the direct knowledge of the four truths that falls short of awakening but, nevertheless, transforms one into a 'noble person' (*ariya-puggala*): a 'stream-enterer', 'once-returner', or 'non-returner'. See notes to the *Mahā-Parinibbāna-sutta*.

39 *Vajjis*: the most significant of the republican tribal confederacies at the time of the Buddha; subsequently Ajātasattu was to wage war on them and annex their lands.

the Blessed One spoke to him: asked about an issue related to a potential war, it is perhaps significant that the Buddha does not address Vassakāra directly, but rather through Ānanda; cf. S. Collins, *Nirvana and Other Buddhist Felicities: Utopias of the Pali Imaginaire* (Cambridge, 1998), 444.

41 *dissension among them*: this strategy for overcoming one's enemy is one recommended in the *Arthaśāstra*, the classical Indian manual of statecraft; see A. L. Basham, *The Wonder that was India* (London, 1967), 97.

45 *he explained . . . the taint of ignorance*: this paragraph, which sums up the Buddhist path in terms of the relationship of conduct (*sīla*), concentration (*samādhi*), and wisdom (*paññā*), is repeated a number of times throughout the sutta.

Sāriputta: along with Moggallāna (see pp. 239–41), Sāriputta, 'the disciple chief in wisdom', was considered one of the two great disciples of the Buddha; this was apparently his last meeting with the Buddha; according to tradition he died before the Buddha and was not present at his death or the first communal recitation.

46 *by abandoning the five hindrances . . . constituents of awakening*: another important summary statement of the Buddhist path; the *Satipaṭṭhāna-sutta* (see below) might be read as an expansion of this summary.

49 *the seed sacks are split open*: a play on the name Pāṭaliputta: '*pāṭali* seed sacks (*puṭa*)'; in the century after the Buddha's death Pāṭaliputta became the capital of the Mauryan empire.

50 *washed his hands and bowl*: for this understanding of *onīta-patta-pāṇi* see K. R. Norman, *The Group of Discourses*, 2nd edn. (Oxford: 2001), 281 and *DOP*, s.v. *onīyati*. Previous translators have taken it as 'removed his hand from his bowl'.

make an offering: the meaning of 'offering' (*dakkhiṇā*) in this passage has been the subject of scholarly discussion; the commentary suggests it refers to the 'merit' (Sv 542: *patti*), and thus understands the passage to be recommending the sharing of the merit which comes from a good act (in this case, the offering of food to monks), which is an almost universal Buddhist practice. However, the Skt equivalent (*dakṣiṇā*) is used of a gift made to a person deserving of honour, such as an officiating brahman priest, and such a meaning cannot be excluded in this context. For a discussion of the problems and of the development of the practice of 'giving merit', see Rita Langer, *Buddhist Rituals of Death and Rebirth* (London, 2007), 166–85.

appreciation: the corollary of sharing one's own merit (see previous note) is participating in the merit of others by rejoicing and appreciation (*anumodana*); in the practice of contemporary Theravāda Buddhism, this is formally done by monks after receiving alms, and is to be cultivated more generally as an attitude when witnessing meritorious actions.

Gotama Gate: presumably why no crossing is called 'Gotama Crossing' is because, as becomes apparent, he does not use a crossing.

52 *what is their fate?*: In what follows the Buddha explains the fate of these various disciples with reference to the ten 'fetters' (*saṃyojana*) that bind beings to the round of rebirth (the view of individuality, doubt, clinging to precepts and vows, sensual desire, aversion, desire for form, desire for the formless, pride, agitation, and ignorance). By the practice of the Buddhist path these fetters are progressively weakened and then broken. By the abandoning of the first three fetters one becomes a 'stream-enterer' (*sotāpanna*), that is, one whose final awakening is assured within seven rebirths. By the abandoning of the first three and the permanent weakening of the next two, one becomes a 'once-returner' (*sakadāgāmin*), that is, one whose final awakening is assured and who will be reborn as a human being no more than once. By the complete abandoning of the five lower fetters one becomes a 'non-returner' (*anāgāmin*), that is, one who at death will not be reborn as a human being but in one of five 'pure abodes' where that being will gain final awakening and become an arahat by abandoning all ten fetters. It is noteworthy that here a number of lay disciples are mentioned as stream enterers, etc., but not as arahats.

reborn purely: they are not born from an egg, womb, or 'moisture'; they simply come into being fully grown.

53 *the Truth that is clear . . . by the Blessed One*: this formula provides the basis for 'recollection of the Dhamma' (*dhammānussati*); see Vism VII 68–88.

eight persons in four pairs: the persons who have attained the paths and fruits of stream entry, once return, non-return, and arahatship; see note to p. 52. The whole formula provides the basis for 'recollection of the Saṅgha' (*saṅghānussati*); see Vism VII 89–100.

54 *Ambapālī*: tradition has it that Ambapālī subsequently became a Buddhist nun and arahat; a vivid poem, a meditation on how her once beautiful young body has become the decrepit body of an old woman, is attributed to her (Thī 252–70).

55 *Licchavis*: an important clan of eastern India at the time of the Buddha, who formed a part of the Vajji confederacy, with their capital at Vesālī.

mango girl: a reference to Ambapālī's name: mango (*amba*).

55 *Thirty-Three*: one of the principal heavens of the gods, ruled over by Sakka or Inda (Skt: Indra).

57 *rainy season*: Buddhist monks traditionally remain resident in one place for the months of the rainy season (July to October).

58 *repairs*: R. Gombrich ('Old Bodies like Carts', *Journal of the Pali Text Society*, 11 (1987), 1–3) suggests amending *vegha* to *vedha*, and translates 'keeps going with various quakings'; but cf. K. R. Norman, *Elders' Verses* I, 2nd edn. (PTS, 2007), 172.

island of refuge: or possibly 'lamp and refuge'; the Pali *dīpa* can mean both 'island' and 'lamp', but the Sanskrit version of this text (see E. Waldschmidt, *Das Māhaparinirvāṇasūtra: Text in Sanskrit und Tibetisch* (Berlin, 1951), 200) suggests an early tradition in favour of 'island' (*dvīpa*). Note that 'island' here should not be taken as having the connotation of cutting oneself off, but rather of a place of safety when crossing the ocean of existence; cf. MW, s.v. *dvīpa*.

darkness: Rhys Davids and Walshe both translate this following the first of the commentary's interpretations, taking *tama* as an indicator of the superlative: 'at the topmost'. But the commentary (Sv 548, Spk III 205) also recognizes that *tama(s)* here might be taken as 'darkness'; *agge* might then be taken in the sense of 'in front of' (MW, s.v. *agra*).

59 *an aeon or what remains of it*: later Buddhist thought distinguishes various types of aeons (*kappa/kalpa*), all of which are fantastically long. Most commonly an aeon is the immeasurable time it takes for the universe to pass through one full cycle of expansion and contraction (see R. Gethin, *The Foundations of Buddhism* (Oxford, 1998), 112–32). Some ancient Buddhist commentators accepted the implications of the current passage; others, including Buddhaghosa, suggested, not entirely convincingly, that 'aeon' here stands for the maximum human life-span (100 years). See P. S. Jaini, 'Buddha's Prolongation of Life', *Bulletin of the School of Oriental and African Studies*, 21 (1958), 546–52; R. Gethin, *The Buddhist Path to Awakening: A Study of the Bodhi-Pakkhiyā Dhamma* (Leiden, 1992; repr. Oxford, 2001), 94–7.

61 *Balancing*: taking *tulaṃ* as a present participle, following the alternative suggestion of the commentary at Sv 557.

62 *remnant of attachment*: this comprises the mental and physical processes that continue after awakening, since their existence in different lifetimes is perpetuated through attachment or grasping (*upādāna*); only with the death of an awakened person do they finally cease. In effect, two 'attainments of nibbana' are distinguished: the initial attainment at the moment of awakening, when the defilements are extinguished (*kilesa-nibbāna*), and the final awakening at death, when the aggregates of physical and mental experience are extinguished (*khandha-nibbāna*); see Gethin, *Foundations of Buddhism*, 74–9. It has become conventional in modern writings to refer to the first as *nibbāna* and the latter as *parinibbāna*, although this strict usage is not found in the ancient texts.

63 *Bright Star*: or Venus (*sukka-tārakā*), which is called the 'medicine star' (*osadhi-tārakā*), because when it rises people gather medicines and take them (Ps III 274).

67 *you who have failed*: the Buddha thus points out to Ānanda that he had given Ānanda 'an obvious sign and hint' a total of sixteen times: ten times in the past in Rājagaha, five times in the past in Vesālī, and one last time in Vesālī.

68 *four ways of establishing mindfulness . . . eightfold path*: these seven sets of practices and qualities are taken as a complete statement of the practice leading to the cessation of suffering (the fourth of the four noble truths) and are the main focus of the fifth volume of the Saṃyutta-nikāya (see below); they are later collectively referred to as 'the thirty-seven qualities that contribute to awakening (*bodhipakkhiya-dhamma*)'; see Gethin, *Buddhist Path to Awakening*.

I take my leave of you: although the meaning 'to take leave of' is not listed in *PED* (s.v. *āmanteti*), it is given in *DOP*, is well attested in Sanskrit (see MW, s.v. *ā-mantr*), and fits the context well here.

69 *as an elephant does*: the commentary explains this as turning the whole body to look back, rather than just the neck (Sv 564–5).

71 *summary lists*: the *mātikās* are mnemonic lists of bare headings that summarize the principal points of the Buddha's teaching and monastic discipline; especially in the Abhidhamma texts they are employed as lists of contents that are subsequently expanded. See Rupert Gethin, 'The *Mātikās*: Memorization, Mindfulness and the List', in J. Gyatso (ed.), *In the Mirror of Memory: Reflections on Mindfulness and Remembrance in Indian and Tibetan Buddhism* (Albany, NY, 1992), 149–72.

72 *tender boar*: literally 'boar-softness' (*sūkara-maddava*), but what this refers to has been the subject of debate since ancient times (the soft flesh of the boar, bamboo shoots trampled (*maddita*) by boars, mushrooms that grow where boars have trampled, a life-prolonging elixir, or a kind of rice pudding); but some kind of pork dish seems the most natural understanding. That Buddhist monks were allowed to eat meat is clear (M I 368–71), and on at least one occasion the Buddha is explicitly said to have eaten boar's flesh (A III 49); see Mettanando Bhikkhu and Oskar von Hinüber, 'The Cause of the Buddha's Death', *Journal of the Pali Text Society*, 26 (2000), 105–19.

74 *Āḷāra the Kālāma*: the former teacher of the Buddha, who had died before or soon after the Buddha had attained awakening; see the *Bodhirājakumāra-sutta* below.

76 *offered both the garments . . . body*: the fact that Ānanda immediately offers the second garment to the Buddha may be connected to the tradition that Ānanda made it one of the conditions of his becoming the Buddha's attendant that the Buddha should not give him robes that had been offered to him (Ja IV 96), though the commentary to the present sutta understands that Ānanda does accept the garment because his duties as

the Buddha's attendant have come to a conclusion (Sv 570). Walshe misunderstands this passage.

77 *sāl trees*: the sāl tree (*shorea robusta*), prized for its timber, is common in the forests of eastern India and Nepal; its yellow-white flowers appear in early summer. According to some accounts, the Buddha's mother gave birth to him while holding onto the branch of a sāl tree.

Directed: reading *codito* (with the Burmese edtion) for *modito* (PTS edition).

81 *should be seen . . . stir his heart*: Gregory Schopen suggests that we should understand the emphasis on 'seeing' (*dassanīya*) here in the light of the general Indian concept of *darśan*, 'direct, intimate contact with a living presence'; see Schopen, *Bones, Stones, and Buddhist Monks* (Honolulu, 1997), 116–17.

funeral: *sarīra-pūjā*; this is sometimes interpreted as 'worshipping relics', but what appears to be meant here is the preparation of the Buddha's body in the context of the funeral. Although in the plural, the injunction 'not to concern yourselves' with *sarīra-pūjā* seems directed to Ānanda (and other monks who have yet to reach arahatship) rather than monks in general, since later Mahākassapa does become involved in *sarīra-pūjā*; see Schopen, *Bones, Stones, and Buddhist Monks*, 99–113.

wheel-turning king: see the introduction to the *Mahāsudanassa-sutta*.

stupa: Sanskrit *stūpa* and Pali *thūpa*; a monumental burial-mound or tomb enshrining relics of the deceased. In India stupa-building became particularly associated with Buddhism, and spread with Buddhism beyond India. The stupa commonly consists of three parts: the base in the form of a raised platform providing a path for ritual circumambulation; the main dome; and the summit formed by a cuboid structure topped with a spire; the whole structure is oriented to the cardinal directions by four gates. The stupa has a developed symbolism: it is at once a representation of the cosmos and of the stages of the Buddhist path. See A. L. Dallapiccola, *The Stūpa: Its Religious, Historical and Archaeological Significance* (Wiesbaden, 1980).

paste: translates *vaṇṇaka* or, following a variant reading, *cuṇṇaka*, both of which seem to refer to some form of coloured or perfumed paste used for anointing.

82 *one-off buddha*: a *pacceka-buddha* or someone who (in contrast to an arahat) has achieved awakening without hearing the teaching of a buddha and (in contrast to a perfect buddha) does not establish a buddha's tradition of instruction (*sāsana*) by teaching; in effect, a *pacceka-buddha* is a non-Buddhist who achieves awakening.

86 *the ascetic . . . fourth ascetics*: the commentary suggests that the ascetic and the second, third, and fourth ascetics are the stream-enterer, once-returner, non-returner, and arahat respectively; however, this is the only place in the

four Nikāyas where they are referred to in this manner. Perhaps the suggestion is that this is a mode of expression more familiar to Subhadda.

87 *the going-forth ordination . . . higher ordination*: the ceremony of *pabbajjā* or 'going forth' constitutes the initial stage in the ordination of a Buddhist monk; the minimum qualifying age is 7 or 8; the ordinand shaves his head, puts on monastic robes, and adopts ten precepts that include celibacy, thereby becoming a *sāmaṇera*. The candidate for *upasampadā* or 'higher ordination' must be at least 20; the ceremony confers the full status of a *bhikkhu* who must live by the 227 precepts of the monastic rule (*pāṭimokkha*).

88 *Channa*: tradition identifies him with the Channa who was the young Gotama's charioteer and who drove him out to encounter the four 'signs'—an old man, a sick and dying man, a corpse, and an ascetic—that prompted him to leave behind his comfortable life. Elsewhere in the Pali canon we are told how, when Ānanda communicated the punishment to him after the Buddha's death, Channa was immediately motivated to achieve awakening and so became an arahat (Vin II 292).

90 *Brahmā, Lord of the Earth*: who first requested the Buddha to teach; see *Bodhirājakumāra-sutta* below; as Brahmā, he resides with his retinue in the Brahma realms, beyond the more ordinary heavens, such as that of the 'Thirty-Three Gods' ruled over by Sakka, who is mentioned a few lines later.

91 *gods . . . Anuruddha have in mind?*: as one who had cultivated the accomplishment of meditation (*iddhi*), Anuruddha is apparently aware of the gods when others are not; see *DPPN*, s.v. Anuruddha.

92 *south of the town*: the south is the direction associated with Yama, the god of death.

94 *Subhadda*: apparently quite a different Subhadda from the wanderer who was the last monk to be ordained in the presence of the Buddha—certainly the later tradition is clear that this is so.

95 *not burnt up*: following the Burmese Sixth-Council and Sinhalese Buddha Jayanti editions, which have *na ḍayhiṃsu* ('were *not* burnt up'); the PTS and Royal Siam editions have 'were burnt up'. The reading *na ḍayhiṃsu* is supported by other accounts of the Buddha's funeral, including the Sanskrit *Mahāparinirvāṇa-sūtra* edited by Waldschmidt (Berlin, 1951). John Strong, *Relics of the Buddha* (Princeton, 2004), 104–5, suggests that the unburnt layers have to do with keeping the relics separate from the ashes of the fire; Strong does not mention the Pali variant. Rhys Davids and Walshe translate the sentence as indicating that all the layers were burnt up, which is hardly possible as a translation.

honouring: the PTS edition has *parikariṃsu*, but other editions have *garuṃkariṃsu*, which is usual in this standard sequence.

97 *There were eight portions . . . hard to find*: the commentary says that these final verses were added later by the elders in Ceylon (Sv 615).

100 *four times that of a man*: so the PTS edition (but mistranslated by Rhys Davids and Walshe); other editions have 'three times the height of a man in circumference, set into the ground to a depth three times the height of a man, and in height twelve times that of a man'.

101 *danced round*: Walshe has (p. 280) 'had their desires assuaged by the sound', and dismisses (p. 576) Rhys Davids's 'danced', but this is certainly how the commentary understood *paricāresuṃ*: 'with movements of their hands or feet they enjoyed themselves dancing' (Sv 617).

Govern as you have governed: for a discussion of this phrase (*yathā-bhuttaṃ bhuñjatha*) see S. Collins, 'The Lion's Roar on the Wheel-turning King', *Journal of Indian Philosophy*, 24 (1996), 426–46 (at 443 f.) and *Nirvana and Other Buddhist Felicities*, 605.

102 *Changes of the Moon*: following Rhys Davids's inspired and poetic translation of *uposatha* here, which strictly refers to the new and full-moon days.

fine mane: literally, 'with hair like muñja grass' (*muñja-kesa*); there appears to be no reason to take this as referring to colour (as do Rhys Davids and Walshe).

Thundercloud: again borrowing from Rhys Davids.

104 *those palms*: the palm trees outside the gates of the city, mentioned earlier.

105 *blue lotuses, red lotuses, and white lotuses*: four kinds are mentioned; the colours of each are not strictly fixed (both *kumuda* and *puṇḍarīka* are usually considered white) and it is not possible to convey the distinction in translation.

everyone can have garlands: literally, 'a garland is not-closed (i.e. available) to everyone', reading *anāvaṭaṃ* with the Burmese edition as suggested by *CPD* (s.v. *anāvaṭa*).

106 *Vissakamma*: the 'all-maker', the divine architect who resides in the Heaven of the Thirty-Three along with Sakka (Indra).

covered with boards: *phalaka* (also mentioned in the Sanskrit versions); while MW gives 'a wooden bench' (which explains Rhys Davids's 'seats'), a 'flat board or surface' seems to be the general meaning.

108 *giving, control, and restraint*: the commentary (Sv 630) says that 'control' (*dama*) should here be understood as observing the new and full-moon days (*uposatha-kamma*); 'restraint' (*saṃyama*) is proper conduct (*sīla*). So far in the sutta we have thus had the first stages of the Buddhist path: generosity (*dāna*) and proper conduct (*sīla*); what follows is in effect the cultivation (*bhāvanā*) of calm and insight.

Stop here . . . of malice!: the commentary (Sv 632) is explicit here about the metaphor: these thoughts have no place in the house of meditation (*jhānāgāra*).

109 *a mind full of friendliness . . . affliction*: the king thus practises the four meditations known as the 'sublime ways of living' (*brahma-vihāra*) or 'measureless states' (*appamañña*). These are among the most important subjects of meditation. While they can be used as a basis for awakening itself, their practice is traditionally regarded as leading directly to rebirth in the sublime Brahma World, a world free of all ill-feeling. On the benefits of the practice of meditation on friendliness, see the sayings from the Collection of Numbered Sayings (sections on 'ones' and 'elevens').

ebony: literally, simply 'heart-wood' or 'finest wood' (*sāra*).

110 *milking pails*: following *DOP*.

111 *pure and clear . . . skin*: as was the Buddha's skin on the day he died; see above, p. 77.

114 *contentment*: Rhys Davids and Walshe have 'drowsiness', presumably following the commentary's gloss: *bhatta-mucchā*, *bhatta-kilamatha* (Sv 634). While this may be correct in certain contexts, the primary meaning of *sammada* (q.v. MW) in Sanskrit is 'delight', 'exhilaration', and in the present context the emphasis would appear to be on the happiness of King Mahāsudassana's state of mind at death, rather than on his drowsiness.

115 *seventh laying aside of the body*: that is, his death as the Buddha. Both Rhys Davids and Walshe translate as if the seventh time referred to the death of Mahāsudassana, but this cannot be correct since, as there will be no eighth laying aside of the body, it would imply that the Buddha will not die.

117 *Vāseṭṭha*: a singular vocative is used here and throughout the discourse (although some manuscripts witness a variant in the plural), but the pronouns 'you' and the second-person verbs are in the plural: Vāseṭṭha has taken the initiative in approaching the Buddha and so the Buddha addresses him directly, but Bhāradvāja is standing close by listening, so he says 'you' in the plural.

118 *ancestor's feet*: that is, Brahmā's feet.

insulting Brahmā: they are insulting Brahmā for, as the commentary points out (Sv 862), if what they say is true, then Brahmā's mouth must be a brahman woman's vaginal passage.

119 *good practice, not bad practice*: *dhamma* and *adhamma*.

120 *of different birth*: or, as Collins has it, 'from various castes'; the term here is *jāti*, which is literally 'birth', but comes to be used also in the sense of 'caste'.

one whose body is Truth . . . designations of the Tathāgata: Sv 865: 'Why is the Tathāgata "the one whose body is *dhamma*"? Because, having conceived in his heart the words of the Buddha that make up the Tipiṭaka, he gave expression to them through speech. So his body, since it consists of *dhamma*, is *dhamma* . . . and precisely because he is the one whose body is *dhamma* he is the one whose body is *brahma*, for *dhamma* is called *brahma* in the sense of what is highest (*seṭṭha*).' See also Paul Harrison, 'Is the Dharma-kāya the Real "Phantom Body" of the Buddha?', *Journal of the International Association of Buddhist Studies*, 15 (1992), 44–94.

121 *spread out*: Collins (*Journal of Indian Philosophy*, 21 (1993), 357) draws attention to the fact that the narrative here changes from a general one in the present tense to a specific one in the past tense.

milk: Some translators and modern commentators (Rhys Davids, Collins) have referred to 'milk rice' here, but the PTS and other editions read *payaso* (with only the PTS edition giving the variant *pāyāso* from a Burmese printed edition), which is glossed by the ancient commentary with *khīrassa* and means simply 'milk'.

Oh, tasty!: as one might say, 'Bon appetit!'

123 *do not understand its meaning*: the point would seem to be that in the past these substances were thrown out of disgust, but today they are thrown as purifying substances (cf. Collins, 'The Discourse on What is Primary', 366) and in celebration, like rice or confetti.

125 *agreed on by all people*: Mahāsammata (literally 'Agreed-Great') is the name of this first mythic king; this method of unpacking the true, original significance of words (known as *nirutti/nirukti*) often involves a kind of word-play that has nothing to do with the real etymology of words, but is related to Indian theories of the primacy of sounds and spoken words.

the first expression that appeared: that is, to designate the Brahman class.

126 *laid down the pestle*: reading (with commentary and some editions) *panna-musalā*.

keepers of a sacrificial fire . . . meditate: I have followed Collins in taking this as a play on two possible meanings of *jhāyaka* in Pali: 'one who meditates' and 'one who makes a fire'. So when people call brahmans *jhāyakas* they take this as indicating how brahmans keep sacrificial fires. However, the Buddha says, this is a misunderstanding of the original import of the epithet, which was in fact a reference to the brahmans' original taste for meditation. See Collins, 'Discourse on What is Primary', 373.

domestic business: reading (with commentary and some editions) *vissu-kammante*. I follow K. R. Norman (*Collected Papers* (Oxford, 1990–2007), i. 256–58) in deriving *vissu* from Sanskrit *veśman*.

128 *seven qualities that contribute to awakening*: presumably the seven qualities that are elsewhere termed 'constituents of awakening'; see pp. 149–50.

130 *Sigāla*: his name is also sometimes spelt Siṅgala or Si(ṅ)gālaka.

his clothes and hair all wet: suggesting that he had gone down into a pool to make his offerings.

the right way: here translates *dhamma*.

133 *he approves . . . actions*: the PTS edition in fact has *nānujānāti* ('disapproves'), though does record the variant; other editions have *ānujānāti* ('approves'), which seems preferable: the flatterer approves however one acts.

135 *keep his friends together*: I follow the commentary (Sv 951).

136 *they introduce him*: the PTS edition reads *parivedenti* (not cited in *PED*, but MW gives Skt *parivedayate* (*pari-vid*), 'he causes to know thoroughly'); v.l. *paṭivedenti* (followed by the Siamese edition); the Burmese and Ceylonese editions read *paṭiyādenti*; all might in this context be rendered 'introduce'.

disrespectful: reading *anavamānanāya* (cf. *DOP*, s.v. *avamāna*).

being generous . . . equally: these four qualities are elsewhere (e.g. D III 152, 232) referred to as the four bases of kindness (*saṃgaha-vatthu*).

142 *leading directly*: the phrase has sometimes been interpreted as meaning 'this is the one path' or 'the only path', but this seems unlikely. The precise significance of *ekāyana* (literally 'one-way') is uncertain; in describing actual paths it is clearly used in the sense of narrow (a way for only one person), and in the sense of a single path (without forks) going to only one place. What is meant in the present context seems to be that the ways of establishing mindfulness represent a path that is unified, clear, well defined, and single—not confusing and difficult to follow as a result of forks and side-roads. On the expression see Gethin, *Buddhist Path to Awakening*, 59–68.

143 *a monk*: the commentary points out that 'monk' is stated here as the ideal practitioner, but other 'gods and people' also succeed (*sampādenti*) in the practice, and that 'monk' indicates anyone who so succeeds (Ps I 241; Sv 755).

qualities: *dhamma*.

As he breathes in a long breath . . . activity of the body: this description of mindfulness of breathing represents the first of four sets each of four stages that are explained in full in the *Ānāpānasati-sutta* (M III 77–88), not included here.

a skilled turner . . . short stroke: the image is of one using a bow-lathe, turning the wood by drawing the bow back and forth with longer or shorter strokes.

watching the body within . . . within and without as body: the commentary explains that this means watching his own body, the body of others, and both alternately. Significantly, this threefold way of practising mindfulness is also applied to watching feelings, the mind, and qualities; this suggests that 'mindfulness' here is conceived also in terms of a certain awareness and sensitivity to others.

144 *there are head hairs . . . urine*: this is a list of thirty-one parts of the body; later tradition adds the brain, making thirty-two.

rice grains: some terms for different kinds of rice have not been translated.

145 *a body left in a charnel ground*: this and what follows constitute 'the cultivation of ugliness' (*asubha-bhāvanā*), a significant meditation practice. Here imagining (or visualizing) the body as a corpse seems suggested, though the practice of contemplating a corpse directly in a charnel ground (as described later, e.g. Vism XI 27–117) is no doubt assumed as a possible basis.

a hand bone here . . . the skull here: there are a number of discrepancies in the list of different bones in the editions.

146 *connected . . . unconnected with the world*: the commentary explains this as feelings bound up with the household life (*gehasita*) and spiritual life (*nekkhamasita*) respectively (Ps I 279; Sv 774–5).

151 *seven days*: the commentary adds that the decreasing lengths of time needed to realize the fruits of the four ways of establishing mindfulness are stated here with reference to a practitioner of average ability; of a person of keen wisdom, it is said that if he receives instruction in the morning he will be successful in the evening, if he receives instruction in the evening he will be successful the next morning (Ps I 302); cf. *Bodhirājakumāra-sutta*.

152 *Anāthapiṇḍika's park*: according to tradition Anāthapiṇḍika was a wealthy merchant of Sāvatthī and one of the great patrons of the Buddha and his monks; the story of his strewing Jeta's grove with gold coins in order to buy it from Jeta is told at Vin II 158 ff. The park and buildings that he erected there and donated to the community of monks became one of the Buddha's favourite residences.

157 *former vulture killer*: the expression *gaddha-bādhi-pubba* is obscure. The Buddhist tradition interprets it as 'the former vulture killer', meaning that he had been born into a family of vulture killers (Ps II 102), but what 'vulture killers' were is not clear; it might just be possible to interpret it as meaning 'he who had previously been one to check his desires' or possibly 'one whose obstacle was formerly desire'; these at least fit the logic of the discourse.

practices: *dhamma*.

like a skeleton . . . the danger in them: most of these similes are found elaborated in the *Potaliyā-sutta* (M I 359–68), not included here.

158 *who are you . . .* : taking *kassa* as *ko ssa*; cf. *DOP*, s.v. ka[3].

161 *let alone bad practices*: the first part of this sutta plays on different meanings of the word *dhamma*. The sutta opens with Ariṭṭha using *dhamma* in the sense of practices (that may or may not be obstacles). In the simile of the snake *dhamma* clearly refers to the teachings in the sense of oral texts. In the simile of the raft we seem to return to the sense of 'practices'; here what seems to be at issue is attachment to 'bad practices' (*adhamma*) and even 'good practices' (*dhamma*); the commentary suggests (Ps II 109) that what is meant is that one must give up attachment (*chandarāga*) to calm and insight. For a different view, see R. Gombrich, *How Buddhism Began* (London, 1996), 22–6.

162 *The world and the self are the same . . . eternity*: this sixth point of view appears to be a direct reference to a view found in the Chāndogya Upaniṣad (3.14. 1, 3–4); cf. K. R. Norman, 'A Note on *attā* in the Alagaddūpama-sutta', *Collected Papers*, ii. 200–9.

166 *one who is like that*: it seems clear that here *tathāgata* is used not as a title of the Buddha, but more generally (as recognized by the commentary) in something like its literal meaning; see K. R. Norman, 'Death and the Tathāgata', *Collected Papers*, iii. 251–63 (at 257–9). My translation of this passage owes something to both Norman and to Ñāṇamoli and Bodhi's *Middle Length Discourses*, 233.

which previously has been fully understood: it has previously been fully understood as not self. What this seems to be saying is that the Buddha's awakening consisted of a full understanding of how 'this', the things the unawakened consider 'self', are not self, so he does not think of these acts as being done to him or his self. The sentence seems to be very deliberately couched in impersonal terms, and we should take *tattha me* as a *sandhi* or elision for *tattha (i)me*, and reject Trenckner's emendation at M I 140 (line 32) where the sentence is repeated and he conjectures (see M I 542) *tattha no* but the Burmese edition retains *tattha me*. This emendation seems to have led some translators to misinterpret the passage and take *me* as the enclitic form of the first-person pronoun, and so take the sense as 'such acts are done to/by *me*' rather than '*these* kinds of acts are done'. Such an interpretation is not supported by the commentary, which explicitly takes *tattha me* as *tattha ime*, and explains that when people honour the Buddha for teaching the four truths, he neither thinks that people do these things to *him*, nor that it is *he* who experiences them, but rather that it is the collection of aggregates (which he fully understood at the time of his awakening) that is experiencing them (Ps II 118–19).

167 *destined for heaven*: we have here a descending sequence of six types of people defined with reference to the point they reach along the Buddhist path; the first five are described as 'monks', while the last are simply those who have a degree of faith (*saddhā*) and affection (*pema*),which is presumably intended to include laypeople; the point is, of course, not that they are precluded from attaining nibbana, but that if they do no more than achieve faith and affection in the Buddha, they are destined for heaven.

171 *the wild or cultivated*: following the commentarial explanations (Ps III 142).

sithilahanu: according to the commentary, 'the bird of this name' (Ps III 142).

whether the man by whom I was struck . . . or an 'oleander leaf': curiously, the man wounded by the arrow has eleven questions rather than ten.

174 *Gotama sir*: in his instructions to the brahman Sañjikāputta, Prince Bodhi refers to the Buddha as 'the Blessed One' (*bhagavat*), but when he talks to the Buddha, Sañjikāputta addresses him in characteristic brahman fashion as 'Gotama sir' (*bho Gotama*), indicating that he does not acknowledge the Buddha as his superior.

175 *Gather up your cloths . . . later generations*: this incident—also found (with slight variation in wording) at Vin II 127–9—is at best obscure. The commentarial tradition relates it to Prince Bodhi's wish for a son: if the Buddha stepped on the cloths his wish would be fulfilled; knowing that

Bodhi was destined to remain without a son, the Buddha thus refused to step on the cloths. The Buddha also saw, the commentary tells us, that while at that time monks could read others' minds and see what would and would not happen, in the future they would not be able to do so and thus in similar situations would not know whether or not to step on a cloth and might get it wrong; this would lead to disillusion among those whose wishes based on honouring monks were not fulfilled; understanding this, Ānanda comments that the Buddha has regard for the generations to come (Ps III 322–3; Dhp-a III 134–9).

176 *intent on awakening*: the term used is *bodhisatta*, later Sanskritized as *bodhisattva*, an 'awakening being', and understood as someone on the path to becoming a 'perfectly and fully awakened one' (*sammāsambuddha/samyaksambuddha*) as opposed to an arahat or 'awakened disciple' (*sāvaka/śrāvaka-buddha*). In the present context the second element of *bodhisatta* is perhaps better interpreted following the Pali commentaries (e.g. Ps I 113) in terms of either Skt *sakta* (past participle from √*sañj*) in the sense of 'intent on' or Skt *śakta* in the sense of 'capable of'; cf. K. R. Norman, *A Philological Approach to Buddhism*, 2nd edn. (Lancaster, 2006), 136.

learnt his teaching: the verb *pariyāpuṇiṃ* specifically implies mastery of the recitation of oral texts; the noun *pariyatti* (used as a designation of what has been mastered) is then used in the commentaries to refer to the collection of Buddhist scriptures.

assurance: this (with the other places in the Majjhima-nikāya where this passage is repeated) is the only occurrence of the term *theravāda* in the Pali canon. Miss Horner (1964, 164) translates: 'I spoke the doctrine of the elders'; while this is clearly possible, the commentary (Ps II 171) glosses with *thirabhāvavādaṃ*, and so seems to understand *thera* in terms of Skt *sthairya* ('firmness'), which seems to make better sense in the present context and is also followed by Ñāṇamoli and Bodhi, *Middle Length Discourses*, 257.

this teaching that you declare . . . direct knowledge: Ñāṇamoli and Bodhi *Middle Length Discourses*, 257 appear to translate the Burmese edition's *kittāvatā . . . upasampajja viharāmī ti pavedesī ti* rather than the PTS's (and other editions') *kittāvatā . . . upasampajja pavedesī ti*. The Burmese edition's reading seems unjustified, given that *viharāmī ti* is not found even in the Burmese edition in the subsequent *ettāvatā . . . upasampajja pavedesī ti*.

sphere of nothingness: this is understood by subsequent Buddhist tradition as the third of four 'formless' meditation attainments achieved on the basis of the fourth absorption (*jhāna*), and is thus incorporated into the scheme of Buddhist meditation; cf. the account of the Buddha's death in the *Mahā-Parinibbāna-sutta*.

178 *Rāma*: Rāma is presumably Uddaka Rāmaputta's teacher.

neither consciousness nor unconsciousness: the fourth formless attainment; see note to p. 176 above on the sphere of nothingness.

183 *this severe, harsh practice*: on the basis of this passage Bronkhorst argues that we should think in terms of two distinct types of early Indian meditation: the severe, painful practices characteristic of, for example, the Jains, and the peaceful, pleasurable practice of the Buddhist absorptions (*jhāna*), which he sees as the Buddha's discovery; see Johannes Bronkhorst, *The Two Traditions of Meditation in Ancient India*, 2nd edn. (New Delhi, 1993).

184 *The ascetic Gotama*: the PTS and Siamese editions read *no samaṇo Gotamo*, 'our ascetic Gotama'; I have followed Ceylonese and Burmese editions, which read *kho samaṇo Gotamo*.

187 *let the Blessed One teach the Truth*: in Thai Buddhist practice, when a layman makes a formal request to a Buddhist monk to teach Dhamma, he consciously repeats Brahmā's original request: 'Then the Brahmā, Lord of the Earth, with joined palms beseeched the unsurpassed one: There are beings here with little dust in their eyes. Please teach Dhamma out of compassion for them.' See Peter Skilling, 'Ārādhanā Tham: "Invitation to Teach the Dhamma"', *Manusya: Journal of Humanities*, 4 (2002), 84–91.

189 *Ājīvika*: see notes to the *Sāmaññaphala-sutta*.

conqueror: the term *jina* is used, like *buddha*, to signify a teacher who has discovered the truth.

some other path: the term *ummagga* has the connotation of 'the wrong road'.

191 *Indeed not, sir*: the group of five monks now suddenly addresses the Buddha with the more respectful *bhante* rather than 'friend' (*āvuso*).

195 *Bamboo Grove*: the first park given to the Buddha by King Bimbisāra (Vin I 39 f.).

203 *further future existences*: reading *upapajja vā apare va pariyāye* (cf. *DOP*, s.v. *apara*) and following O. von Hinüber, 'The "Threefold" Effect of Karma', *Selected Papers* (Oxford, 2005), 39–51 (at 48–9).

216 *oppressed*: reading with the PTS edition *addhabhūto*, but cf. *DOP*, s.v. *addhabhavati*.

220 *shimmering*: reading *phandati* with the Sinhala manuscripts cited in the PTS edition.

222 *thousand monks*: Vin I 35 adds here that they were all former matted-hair ascetics.

All is burning: the third section of T. S. Eliot's *The Waste Land* is named 'The Fire Sermon', and line 308 ('Burning, burning, burning, burning') has a note referring to the present sutta as 'the Buddha's Fire Sermon', though the sutta is hardly a Buddhist equivalent to the Sermon on the Mount, as Eliot suggests.

226 *This is what I have heard . . .*: whenever the location of a sutta is not stated in full, it is understood to be the Jeta grove at Sāvatthī; cf. Gregory Schopen, 'If You Can't Remember It, How To Make It Up: Some

Monastic Rules for Redacting Canonical Texts', in G. Schopen, *Buddhist Monks and Business Matters* (Honolulu, 2004), 395–408.

227 *immersed in the deathless*: the expression *amatogadha* can be taken in two ways: as '*plunging into* the deathless' or as '*having its footing* in the deathless'. The commentaries give both interpretations: 'inside the deathless' (*amatogadhan ti amatabbhantaraṃ* at Spk III 247) and 'established in the deathless' (*amatogadhā ti nibbānogadhā nibbānapatiṭṭhā ti attho* at Mp III 351). *CPD* (s.v. *amatogadha*) acknowledges the former but implies (s.v. *ogadha*) that the latter is the original meaning; Bodhi, *Connected Discourses*, 1093–4, n. 243, argues for the latter, while *DOP* (s.vv. *ogadha*[1] and *ogadha*[2]) accepts the former. In fact, the ambiguity seems ancient and it is probably not possible to be definitive about the meaning of this expression in the Nikāyas.

232 *monkey lime*: the commentary says that they prepare a sticky paste by combining the sap of the banyan tree with other ingredients. In Europe the similar use of bird-lime was once widespread.

233 *to that same piece of wood*: the Pali text reads *kaṭṭhakataṅgāre*, which appears corrupt; following others, I have taken this as equivalent to *kaṭṭhakaḷiṅgara*, found regularly in the Pali commentaries in the sense of 'block of wood'. See *BHSD*, s.v. *kaḍaṅgara*; H. Bechert (ed.), *Sanskrit-Wörterbuch der buddhistischen Texte aus den Turfan-Funden* (Göttingen, 1973–), s.vv. *kāṣṭha-kaḍaṅkara-ka*, *kāṣṭha-kaḍaṅgara*; *DOP*, s.v. *kaliṅgara*; Bodhi, *Connected Discourses*, 1918–19, n. 133.

239 *Moggallāna the Great*: the disciple of the Buddha said to be the great master of meditation and skilled in all its accomplishments; see *DPPN*, s.v. Moggallāna.

shake those monks up: Pali *saṃvejehi*: arouse in them *saṃvega*, a specifically religious sense of danger, fear, and urgency that follows from the feeling that life is short and that if we fail to pay attention to the spiritual life now, soon the opportunity will have passed.

243 *Turning the wheel of Truth*: this sutta presents the Buddha's first teaching, known as 'the turning of the wheel of Dhamma'. It was given to the group of five monks who were originally fellow companions in his quest for awakening but abandoned him when he gave up the practice of severe austerities (see the *Bodhirājakumāra-sutta*, translated above). In it the Buddha sets out the famous noble eightfold path and four noble truths.

244 *this is the noble truth of suffering*: the grammar and syntax of the various statements of the four noble truths in Buddhist sources has become confused at points as a result of the insertion of the expression 'noble truth' (*ariya-sacca*). This means that a strictly grammatical translation is not possible. Existing translations tend to offer statements such as 'the noble truth of the cause of suffering must be abandoned', when clearly what is meant is that the cause of suffering must be abandoned, rather than the truth of the cause of suffering. See K. R. Norman, 'The Four Noble Truths', *Collected Papers*, ii. 210–23.

245 *three stages and twelve aspects*: the threes stages are: (1) understanding suffering, its cause, its cessation, and the practice leading to its cessation; (2) understanding what must be done in respect of each of these (knowing, abandoning, experiencing, cultivating); (3) understanding that it has been done. The twelve aspects are merely the sum of the three stages applied to each truth.

251 *Kālāma town called Kesaputta*: this sutta is often referred to as the *Kālāma-sutta* in modern literature.

253 *How is it for you*: there is some confusion over the correct reading here: *kathaṃ vā ettha hotī ti* ('or how is it in this case') or *kathaṃ vo ettha hotī ti* ('how is it for you in this case'); since the response is consistently *evaṃ no ettha hotī ti* ('it is like this for us in this case'), I have opted for the latter, although the former is the more frequent reading.

256 *doubly purified*: this passage has been variously understood by previous translators. Woodward (*Gradual Sayings*, I 175) suggests that a person is doubly purified because he does no evil act 'whether inadvertently or intentionally', Nyanaponika and Bodhi (*Numerical Discourses*, 67) because no evil is done by him or befalls him. I take *karoto* in the phrase *sace kho pana karoto na karīyati pāpaṃ* as an agent genitive: 'if evil is done *by* one acting'. Thus the third reason to breathe easily rests on the assumption that evil acts are real and matter: then if one intends and does no evil act one can breathe easily. The fourth reason rests on the assumption that evil acts are *not* real and *do not* matter: then one is doubly purified—because one does no evil act and because acts do not matter anyway. The commentary explains: 'in that I do no evil and also in that nothing is done when one acts' (Mp II 306: *yañ ca pāpaṃ na karomi, yañ ca karoto pi na karīyati*), although Nyanaponika and Bodhi (p. 287, n. 51) take the commentary in line with their understanding of the sutta.

257 *refuge from danger*: according to the interpretation given in the Pali commentaries, what is meant is that he has not done any deed that will protect him from the danger and fear that arise at the time of death (Sp 436).

258 *does not think*: the *not* is missing in the PTS edition, but is clearly required.

259 *excited*: taking *palāḷita* as equivalent to **pralodita* (rather than **pralalita*) in the sense of 'strongly agitated' rather than 'led astray'; cf. *PED* s.v. *palaḷita*; *BHSD* s.vv. *praluḍita*, *pralulita*. The word occurs also at S IV 197, juxtaposed with *pamatta*, 'excited', etc.

scythe and carrying-pole: for cutting and carrying grass respectively (Mp III 224).

260 *specialists in the teachings*: the expression *dhamma-yoga* is found only here in the Pali canon, although *BHSD* records the occurrence of *dharma-yoga* (q.v.) in the Sanskrit *Lalitavistara*. In the present context the commentary explains it as *dhamma-kathika*, 'a speaker on or expounder of the *dhamma*'. What the expression seems to signify is someone who is familiar with the

dhamma in the specific sense of 'teachings' or 'texts' as found, for example, at M I 133, which talks of someone who learns the *dhamma* and then lists various categories of text (see above, p. 000). This sutta thus anticipates a certain tension that later arose in Buddhist monasticism in some countries between two vocations: the work of directly realizing insight into the four truths (*vipassanā-dhura*), and the work of studying books (*gantha-dhura*); see Walpola Rahula, *History of Buddhism in Ceylon: The Anurādhapura Period*, 2nd edn. (Colombo, 1966), 158–61.

260 *of the many*: this form of this stock expression, repeating 'of the many', is peculiar to the Aṅguttara-nikāya and *Itivuttaka* of the Khuddaka-nikāya; the more common form found elsewhere (and in the Aṅguttara-nikāya and *Itivuttaka*) has instead 'out of sympathy for the world' (*lokānukampāya*).

261 *brahmans*: the vocative is singular, but a plural seems required in English.

265 *Blessed One*: although a wanderer rather than a Buddhist monk, he refers to the Buddha as 'the Blessed One' (*bhagavat*).

incapable of . . . when he lived in a house: according to a later tradition, if a layman attains the full awakening of an arahat, he will die or become a monk the same day (Mil 264).

267 *sublime wheel*: here *brahma-cakka* rather than *dhamma-cakka* (the wheel of Truth), but nevertheless equated with the latter by the commentary.

emerge from them: the commentary points out that, since emerging from an attainment may involve moving to a higher attainment, it is closely associated with purifying a meditative attainment (Mp V 15).

INDEX

A SELECTION OF **OXFORD WORLD'S CLASSICS**

	Bhagavad Gita
	The Bible Authorized King James Version *With Apocrypha*
	Dhammapada
	Dharmasūtras
	The Koran
	The Pañcatantra
	The Sauptikaparvan (from the Mahabharata)
	The Tale of Sinuhe and Other Ancient Egyptian Poems
	The Qur'an
	Upaniṣads
ANSELM OF CANTERBURY	**The Major Works**
THOMAS AQUINAS	**Selected Philosophical Writings**
AUGUSTINE	**The Confessions** **On Christian Teaching**
BEDE	**The Ecclesiastical History**
HEMACANDRA	**The Lives of the Jain Elders**
KĀLIDĀSA	**The Recognition of Śakuntalā**
MANJHAN	**Madhumalati**
ŚĀNTIDEVA	**The Bodhicaryāvatāra**

A SELECTION OF **OXFORD WORLD'S CLASSICS**

A SELECTION OF OXFORD WORLD'S CLASSICS

Thomas Paine	Rights of Man, Common Sense, and Other Political Writings
Jean-Jacques Rousseau	The Social Contract Discourse on the Origin of Inequality
Adam Smith	An Inquiry into the Nature and Causes of the Wealth of Nations
Mary Wollstonecraft	A Vindication of the Rights of Woman